ANIMALS IN THE BLOOD
The Ken Smith Story

BY RUSSELL TOFTS

Russell Tofts was educated at Sawston Village College, Cambridgeshire, and the former Cambridgeshire College of Agriculture and Horticulture (now the College of West Anglia), at which latter place of further education he studied biological sciences and animal care. He has been a zoo-keeper and pet-shop owner and has worked for both the National Trust and English Heritage. He has written over eighty articles for zoological journals and in 1998 realised a lifelong ambition by seeing animals in their natural habitat in Africa, a trip that provided the material for his first book, *Kenkay and Colobus: A Tourist in Ghana*. He is a member of the Bartlett Society, the Independent Zoo Enthusiasts' Society, Association of British Wild Animal Keepers (ABWAK), the Durrell Wildlife Conservation Trust, and the Avicultural Society. He lists as his interests: the natural world, zoos, history, the theatre, Great Britain, etymology (the study of the origin and derivation of words), and participating each year in the BUPA Great North Run.

*The Bartlett Society is an organisation dedicated to the study of the history of wild animal husbandry in general and that of zoological gardens in particular. Founded by C.H. Keeling on 27 October 1984, it is named in honour of Abraham Dee Bartlett, the great 19th-century Superintendent of the London Zoo. The Society welcomes enquiries about its work. Membership is open to anyone with an interest in the subject. For more information, please visit the Society's website: www.zoohistory.co.uk

Also by Russell Tofts

KENKAY AND COLOBUS: A TOURIST IN GHANA

RUSSELL TOFTS

ANIMALS
IN THE BLOOD

The Ken Smith Story

A Biography of Gerald Durrell's Right-Hand Man

Published by
The Bartlett Society

First published in 2012
by THE BARTLETT SOCIETY
Email: bartlettsociety@zoohistory.co.uk

10 9 8 7 6 5 4 3 2 1

A CIP catalogue record for this book is available from the British Library

ISBN 978-095315-884-3

Printed and bound in Great Britain by
Printondemand-Worldwide, Culley Court, Orton Southgate, Peterborough
Typeset in Garamond

The song line on page 197 is from the musical *Whistle Down the Wind*
(lyrics, Jim Steinman; music, Andrew Lloyd Webber)

I DEDICATE THIS BOOK TO MY MOTHER

AND THE MEMORY OF MY FATHER,

WHOM I MISS SO MUCH

Contents

Illustrations

Whilst every effort has been made to trace and acknowledge all copyright holders, this has not been possible in every case, and the author apologises for any errors or omissions. *(TS = Reproduced courtesy of Mrs Trudy Smith)*

SECTION ONE *(between pages 32 and 33)*

Market Place, Deddington, circa 1911. *(© Images & Voices, Oxfordshire County Council)*

Harriden's Stores, Harpenden.

Hannah Harlock, Ken, his brother Ronald and sister Violet, and Hannah's friend and housekeeper, Annie Carpenter, circa 1924. *(Courtesy of Brian Smith)*

Arthur and Hannah Harlock's drapery shop in Banbury. *(© Images & Voices, Oxfordshire County Council)*. Inset: Arthur Harlock.

The Friends' School, Saffron Walden. *(© The Friends' School, Saffron Walden)*

Herbert Smith outside his general stores in West Mersea, Essex, circa 1926. *(Courtesy of Brian Smith)*

Bliss Tweed Mill. *(© Absolute Touring Oxford)*

His country calls: Ken proudly shows off his RAF uniform, circa 1940. *(TS)*

Ken with a tortoise he found in the desert, 1945. *(TS)*

A postcard Ken brought back from Eritrea in 1945.

Ken shows off a bird of prey at Whipsnade Zoo. *(TS)*

Wearing what is possibly his demob suit, Ken poses with a fox at Whipsnade Zoo. *(TS)*

At Whipsnade, Ken was entrusted with looking after some rare Pere David's deer. *(TS)*

Ken holding a pair of Golden hamsters, Whipsnade Zoo. *(TS)*

Passenger list for the Blue Star Line ship, *Columbia Star*, bound for South America, 1950. *(Courtesy of The National Archives, ref. BT27/1658)*

Ken with African helper, Cameroons expedition, 1949. *(TS)*

Angwantibo from the forests of the Cameroons. *(© Les Owen)*

Ken Smith, Gerald Durrell and Robert Lowes with an eight-foot boa, British Guiana, 1950. *(© Estate of Gerald Durrell)*

Ken with a captured Bat falcon, British Guiana, 1950. *(TS)*

Ken with a tame Spider monkey, British Guiana, 1950. *(TS)*

SECTION TWO *(between pages 82 and 83)*

Ken exhibits two snakes, an Australian Carpet python and an American Pine snake. *(© Sunbeam Photos)*

Roloway monkey, Paignton Zoo, brought back by Ken from Sierra Leone. *(TS)*

With Danny, a tame eland, Paignton Zoo. *(© Western Morning News)*

Ken feeds Percy the Pygmy hippo at Paignton Zoo. (© *Western Morning News*)
Gerald Durrell on board ship bound for England with Sarah Huggersack, a baby Giant anteater destined to be a star attraction at Paignton Zoo, 1954. *(TS)*
An older Sarah Huggersack with Miss Trudy Hills at Paignton Zoo. *(TS)*
Jeff the Geoffroy's marmoset, circa 1955. *(Vernon Murray)*
Trudy with Dibber, a favourite baboon, at Paignton Zoo. *(TS)*
Ken bottle-feeding a baby Two-spotted civet, Paignton Zoo. *(TS)*
In 1956 Ken mounted a second animal-collecting expedition to British Guiana. *(TS)*
Getting to grips with an anaconda, British Guiana, 1956. *(TS)*
A Silky anteater, British Guiana, 1956. (© *Vernon Murray*)
Ken with his Guianese assistant, Bob Veerasawmy, and a Spectacled owl, 1956. *(TS)*
Ken demonstrates the easiest way to move a sloth... *(TS)*
...And a capybara, British Guiana, 1956. *(TS)*
Ken hand-feeding the pair of White-faced Saki monkeys he acquired in British Guiana, 1956. *(TS)*
A beautiful study of one of the young Howler monkeys. (© *Vernon Murray*)
Trudy with the baby Red Howler monkeys at Paignton Zoo. *(TS)*
Ken brought this Tegu lizard back from South America in 1956. (© *Vernon Murray*)
Ken with two Capuchin monkeys outside the Small Mammal House at Paignton Zoo in 1958. *(TS)*
The same scene as above, fifty-one years later. *(The Author)*
Palmer's Pets, Camden Town, 1950s. *(TS)*
Trudy hand-rearing a jackal cub, Paignton Zoo. *(TS)*
Lucy Pendar visiting Ken at Paignton Zoo with her children, circa 1958. *(Courtesy of Lucy Pendar)*

SECTION THREE *(between pages 132 and 133)*

The animals begin to arrive at Jersey Zoo. (© *Jersey Evening Post*)
The venture begins: Jersey Zoo opens to the public, March 1959. (© *Jersey Evening Post*)
The Monkey House, Jersey Zoo, March 1959. (© *Jersey Evening Post*)
A young drill, seen from the other side of the wire, Jersey Zoo, circa 1959. (© *R.W. Dingle*)
Ken struggles to restrain two Woolly monkeys while Trudy cradles a Common boa, Jersey Zoo, 1959. (© *Jersey Evening Post*)
Lee Thomas. *(TS)*
Ken in an unguarded moment in his office at Jersey Zoo, 1959. *(TS)*
Jeremy Mallinson. *(TS)*
Ken and Trudy with daughter Caroline in front of manor house at Jersey Zoo. *(TS)*
The dingoes at Jersey Zoo. (© *Rosemary Gilliat*)
Ken's mother, Gertrude, visiting him in Jersey. *(TS)*
Ken checking stock in Jersey Zoo's souvenir shop. *(TS)*
N'Pongo instinctively reaches out for the familiar figure of Caroline. (© *Rosemary Gilliat*)

Trudy with one of the leverets born in southern England and hand-reared in Jersey. *(TS)*
  Inset: One of the released hares. *(TS)*
Ken holding up the surprising sign 'Dogs are allowed in the Zoo'. *(TS)*
A Sclater's guenon from Africa, Jersey Zoo circa 1961. *(© W. Suschitzky)*
The only way to move a recalcitrant porcupine. *(© Estate of Gerald Durrell)*
Ken sorting through Jersey Zoo's fruit order with Gerald Durrell, November 1961. *(TS)*
The closest of friends: Caroline and the young gorilla N'Pongo, Jersey Zoo. *(TS)*

SECTION FOUR *(between pages 182 and 183)*

Ken saw one of his most important roles as being to infuse people with an interest for
  the natural world. *(© Tiverton Gazette)*
Ken returns to Whipsnade Zoo with daughter Caroline, early 1960s. *(TS)*
Ken with a kinkajou and a White-throated guenon. *(© Western Times)*
This young cassowary originally had the run of Ken's Poole Park Children's Zoo.
  (© Western Times)
Trudy and fox cubs. *(TS)*
Trudy with baby White-nosed coatis. *(© Chris Ware)*
The perfect upbringing: Kelsay confidently handles a Carpet python. *(© Western Times)*
Kate feeding a baby kinkajou. *(TS)*
Kelsay and kinkajou. *(© Robert Chapman)*
Kate and chimpanzee, Exmouth beach. *(© Freddie Collins)*
Kelsay and Kate play Snakes and Ladders, with real snakes. *(© John D. Drysdale)*
Kate with a Blomberg's toad, Exmouth Zoo. *(© John D. Drysdale)*
Kelsay plants a festive kiss on the nose of a tame muntjac called Bambi at Exmouth Zoo.
A frail Ken Smith deals with an anaconda at Exmouth Zoo, 1970s. *(© Edward Lucas)*
The amusement arcade that replaced Exmouth Zoo. *(The Author)*
The Gerald Durrell Memorial Plaque on the Lemur House at ZSL Whipsnade Zoo. *(The
  Author)*
A remarkable bond between bird and man. *(© Les Owen)*

I believe that in the majority of cases people rather than sites or buildings or animals make or mar zoological gardens. No matter how much money might be lavished on such a place, if the person at the top is unimaginative or uninspired or insensitive it is highly unlikely to succeed in the way it would if the one at the helm, in addition to knowing the subject as thoroughly as it's possible to learn it during a lifetime, is a decided personality and skilful at looking after wild things in confinement, as wild animal husbandry is unusual in being both a science and an art. Such a person was Ken Smith.

From *Where the Crane Danced*
by C.H. Keeling (1985)

Although not a great churchman, he [Ken Smith] will receive a great welcome from his Creator who had entrusted him with the care of all his creatures.

Charles H. Trevisick

The perfect top zoo man is a paragon. He must have an all-round knowledge of zoology and a specialist knowledge in certain fields; the knack of getting on well with all kinds of people; the ability to drive his staff, and the humility to be driven by them when they are right; and he must have that almost indefinable quality of tenderness.

From *Zoos of the World*
by James Fisher (1966)

Zoological gardens are very special places: ergo, they should be operated by very special people.

C.H. Keeling in a Letter to the Editor,
International Zoo News (April/May 2000)

Preface

INEVER HAD THE PLEASURE of meeting Ken Smith, something I shall always regret, but I like to think we would have got on well together. When I was growing up, my heroes were not pop stars or footballers but zoo directors. I was, and still am, passionate about zoos. While other boys were hungry to see the latest model of sports car, I wanted to see my first Bald-headed Rock Crow. As a child I could name the owner or director of every major animal collection in Great Britain, and not a few of the minor ones, too. Those days are long gone and today I would be hard-pressed to name, off the top of my head, the directors of more than about a dozen zoos in total. The reason is these days our leading zoos are more likely to recruit somebody from the business world as their director rather than employ someone with practical 'hands-on' experience of wild animal husbandry as was usual in Ken Smith's day. This makes a kind of sense. Innumerable zoos have failed because the person at the top, whilst he may have been a walking *Larousse* animal encyclopedia, did not understand economics. I know that I am not alone in feeling something has been lost along the way. These days it is often accountants and businessmen that hold sway. This new generation of zoo directors might be comfortable with figures, be *au fait* with spreadsheets, and can navigate their way through the Gordian knot of legislation imposed on all animal collections these days, but do they necessarily know, without consulting their animal curators, what a babirusa eats or the optimum temperature requirement for a Spectacled caiman or what is so unusual about the sweat of a hippopotamus? As somebody, not noted for couching his words, recently said to me: 'Where are the *characters* today? These days zoos are more often than not run by academics, worthy people to be sure but...' here he paused, '...dull as ditchwater, some of them.'

One of the most famous zoo directors of the twentieth century was, of course, Gerald Durrell. For all his flaws, nobody could accuse *him* of blandness. He was someone who really had served his apprenticeship by sweeping out monkey cages, serving chopped brain to a finicky African Golden cat, and treating birds with broken wings. At ZSL Whipsnade Zoo there is a plaque on the outside wall of the Lemur House in memory of Durrell, who was a trainee keeper at the zoo from July 1945 to May 1946. It is quite appropriate that he should be commemorated in this way because after his brief stint at Whipsnade he went on to revolutionise the whole concept of keeping animals in captivity by showing that zoos could have a much loftier purpose beyond that of mere public entertainment. The zoo he founded on the Channel Island of Jersey is often cited as a model for zoos everywhere and has been seen as such since at least the mid 1970s. Nobody was surprised when, in 1983, his achievements finally earned him a well deserved – and long overdue – Officer of the Order of the British Empire medal, the only surprise being that it wasn't a higher honour like a knighthood that had been bestowed upon his fellow naturalists, Peter Scott or David Attenborough.

Many years after their deaths, Gerald Durrell and Sir Peter Scott continue to harvest all the accolades, but there are other estimable zoologists, contemporaneous of Durrell and Scott, who in their lifetime never got the recognition they deserved. They never wrote best-selling books, presented popular wildlife TV documentaries or graced the sofa on television chat shows. They were not garnered with OBEs or knighthoods. Universities did not fall over themselves to bestow honorary degrees upon them. And when they died, there were no headlines in the national papers alerting everyone to their passing, no tribute programmes shown on nationwide television, no strategically sited bronze plaques commemorating their achievements. Not for them a lavish memorial service with hundreds of complete strangers belting out *All Things Bright and Beautiful*. They are not commemorated in the scientific names of animals. They slip away almost unnoticed. In short, they are in danger of fading into obscurity.

Some of them had careers that, for a time, were interwoven with Durrell's own career before their respective paths diverged. However, Durrell's own light burnt so brightly it tended to eclipse theirs.

One such person was Kenneth Smith.

Like Durrell, Ken Smith was one of the old-school. Largely self-taught, he did not have university degrees or trail half the alphabet after his name (though he did occasionally permit the letters F.Z.S. – Fellow of the Zoological Society – after his name). What he did have in spades was practical experience of a huge diversity of creatures, everything from elephants to emus, wolves to wallabies, camels to cranes. There cannot be many people around today who can boast of attending to a more eclectic mix. He was, in other words, a versatile all-rounder, and there were no kinds of animals, as far as anyone could tell, he didn't like. 'Incomparable' – that's how zoologist and founder of the Bartlett Society, Clinton Keeling, described Kenneth Smith, and Clinton did not use words lightly. In the Bartlett Society newsletter for May 1997, he wrote that in the mid 1950s there were probably no more than about seven 'real zoological garden enthusiasts' in the whole country, and he singled out Ken Smith as prominent among this clique. Although I feel that Clinton grossly underestimated the true number of zoo enthusiasts there were at that time, the fact that Kenneth Smith is mentioned by name is indicative of the high esteem in which he was held. And yet Ken appears to have been a relative latecomer. He lived to be sixty-eight, but, aside from a brief spell before the war when he worked at a short-lived zoo, now almost completely forgotten, in Oxfordshire, he did not become a professional animal-man until he was thirty-four, when exactly half his life had gone.

For many years the careers of Ken Smith and Gerald Durrell were irretrievably intertwined. Like Gerald Durrell, Ken found himself at Whipsnade Zoo just after the war. But unlike Durrell there is no memorial to him there. No plaque, no inscription, nothing to show he was there at all. And the same is true at what is now known formally as Paignton Zoo Environmental Park, where he was once employed as its very able Superintendent; or at the former Jersey Zoo (now the Durrell Wildlife Conservation Trust), which he helped build, stock, and set on its path to future glory, of which he was its *de facto* first director. Seven or eight animal species, from a Sri Lankan freshwater crab to a Madagascan carnivore, bear Durrell's name, but the memory of his erstwhile partner is not invoked in the name of a single animal species.

I first became aware of Ken Smith when I was still at school in the mid 1970s. I had just discovered the writings of Gerald Durrell and in two of his very early books, *Three Singles to Adventure* and *The Bafut Beagles*, a minor character crops up whom Durrell refers to simply as 'Smith', but in neither book did this 'Smith' have much more than the most perfunctory, walk-on, part. Then, in about 1977, I was whiling away my lunch hour in the school library at Sawston Village College, where I was then a student, when I found an old, long out-of-date, reference guide to British zoos containing short but glowing descriptions of Exmouth Zoo, Poole Park Children's Zoo and Teignmouth Children's Zoo, three small animal collections on the south coast of England that were owned, at least when the book was written, by somebody called Kenneth Smith. I was quick to make the connexion. So the peripheral character from two of Gerald Durrell's books about animal-collecting in the wilds of Africa and South America had gone on to become a zoo-owner, just like Durrell himself! As my interest in zoo history deepened, I found his name cropping up elsewhere, and slowly I began to join up the dots as I pieced together the story of his life. And what a life it was, and what a tragedy he never set it down in print for future generations to read, because I'm sure it would have made engrossing reading. It seems he was quite a private individual, devoid of egotism, who never actively espoused the limelight. Perhaps it was this humility, even more than lack of time, that caused him to shun autobiography (indeed, he didn't publish any books at all). He evinced very little interest in speaking about himself, and no interest whatsoever in writing about himself. He did occasionally produce short articles for specialist publications such as *International Zoo News* and *The Avicultural Magazine*, but in these his intention was never to draw attention to himself but to disseminate information, based on personal experience, that he thought other animal keepers might find useful. One person I spoke to, who worked alongside him at Belle Vue Zoo (Manchester) in the early 1950s, described him as being like a shadow: one was dimly aware of his presence as he flitted, quietly and efficiently, about his duties, but always in the background. He never imposed himself. A quiet, private person, he was not one to indulge in self-aggrandizement.

My thoughts returned to him at odd moments over the years and I began to wonder what had happened to him. In 1996 I met Jeremy Mallinson, then Executive Director of the Jersey Wildlife Preservation Trust, for the first time. I knew that Ken had helped Gerald Durrell set up Jersey Zoo and so I asked Jeremy whether Ken Smith was still alive. No, he was not, he said. So that was that. I never would get to meet him.

Since fate had denied me the chance of meeting him, I was keen to make the acquaintance of his widow, Trudy. There was, however, one small snag: I didn't know where she lived or how I might get in touch with her. Then I had the most remarkable piece of luck. Attending a Bartlett Society meeting in Surrey, I planned to ask the assembled company if anyone had heard of Trudy Smith, widow of Kenneth Smith, and knew of her whereabouts. However, with everything else going on at the meeting, it completely slipped my mind to ask and it was only some hours later, as I drove home along the motorway, that I suddenly remembered.

Arriving home, I noticed there was a letter waiting for me. It was from someone in Devon enquiring about my Rodent Appreciation Group, an organisation I had launched some years earlier as a contact centre for people who keep rodents. The author of the letter explained that she had picked up a leaflet about it (goodness knows how, as I didn't think I had sent any leaflets that far afield) and wished to know, since the leaflet was obviously quite an old one, if the organisation was still active. The letter went on:

I have always been interested in Rodents and Small Mammals. I have been involved with zoos and collections most of my life. I'm now a widow and pensioner. Do have some connections still! I keep small hamsters, quite unusual ones I think, and Arabian Spiny mice and chinchillas and would be interested in joining the Group.

The letter was signed…Trudy Smith (Mrs).

I stared at it. It was too incredible for words and at first I refused to believe it. It was the coincidence to end all coincidences. But the facts – the lifetime involvement with zoos, the interest in small mammals in particular, the writer's widowed status – all seemed to fit. The address was in Exmouth, the same West Country resort where Ken Smith did once have a small zoo. It had to be her! I wrote back immediately. Was she, I asked, *the* Trudy Smith (putting an accent on 'the'), once married to zoologist, animal collector and zoo superintendent Kenneth Smith? Within a few days I had her reply:

Dear Russell Tofts,

Thank you very much for your very amazing letter! What a coincidence. I hope we can meet one day. We can have a good 'catching up'. It's lovely that you are interested in Ken. He was a lovely husband and father, and lover of wildlife.

I would love to show you photos and things that may interest you. I have got three very old booklets with articles written by Ken. I don't know how they have survived so long! If you would be interested I could send them, if you would be able to return?

All good wishes.
Yours sincerely,
The Trudy Smith

That last bit was a nice touch, putting the definite article before her signature like that. We agreed to meet up as soon as possible.

As soon as I could, I visited her at her home in Exmouth. It was a home which met with my instant approval. Many framed photographs testifying to a lifetime's professional involvement with animals lined the walls. One of the photos showed Trudy with Sarah Huggersack, the Giant anteater that Gerald Durrell brought back from the Paraguayan Chaco in 1956 and had immortalised in one of his books. She proudly showed me Durrell's book *Island Zoo*, published in 1961 and dedicated to her first daughter, Caroline. There were other mementos, too, of a time that was long gone. She also showed me an original Durrell sketch of an anteater, which she very generously gave to me. Squatting on the carpet was a walnut-brown tortoise. It was immobile, its head and neck partially extended, and at first I couldn't be sure whether it was a carved wooden model of a tortoise or the real thing. I did consider gently nudging it with my foot to see if it retracted its head, but then Trudy laid any doubts I had to rest. 'That's Trevor,' she said. 'His mate, Mrs Trevor, is also around here somewhere.' I love alliteration and there was something about the name Trevor the Tortoise that appealed.

At this first meeting I caught myself repeatedly referring to Trudy's late husband as 'Ken' rather than the more formal 'Kenneth', as if I had not only known him personally but been one of his best mates. Fortunately she didn't seem to mind my rather inappropriate over-familiarity, or, if she did, she was too gracious to say anything.

For a long time I had felt that *somebody* ought to write an account of Ken Smith's life's story for posterity, but I never thought it might be something I would tackle myself, but when I met Trudy, she showed me some of her extensive collection of photographs of Ken and his animals and, as I looked through them, I felt a growing sense they were deserving of a wider audience. Tentatively I broached the idea of publishing a selection, suitably outfitted with captions, in some kind of booklet. I was delighted when she acceded to my suggestion. That was it. Nothing more. At that stage it had not occurred to me to attempt a full biography. Early on I made the decision to include some biographical notes to compliment the photos, but even then all I envisaged was a slim booklet of photographs. Realising my knowledge of Ken's life and career were fragmentary at best, I started in earnest to research his life. As I uncovered more and more, I wove these new discoveries into my story. I honestly cannot remember the exact moment when I realised I was no longer working on a simple booklet of old photographs but unconsciously had embarked on producing something considerably more ambitious and substantial. My simple booklet had expanded to book size. So from then on I knew that if I continued with the project I had to treat it as a full-blown biography with everything that entailed, and that is what I have tried to do. Tackling a task of this magnitude was daunting, to say the least, and I didn't know if I had the ability to pull it off, but having already set off along that path I decided to give it a go. However, I did not approach the enterprise without some diffidence. What Ken Smith himself would have made of a book tracing the story of his life is open to conjecture, but I like to think he would have approved. Being the self-effacing man he was, totally devoid of hubris, he probably would have found it bewildering or bemusing that anyone should be interested in him so many years after his death. I like to imagine his spirit looking down from some paradisiacal *terra incognita* and grinning approvingly: 'Well, it's about bloody time someone paid some attention to me!'

Researching the facts of his life has been a fascinating and rewarding journey for me, but it has also been, at other times, quite frustrating. It has required patience, a certain amount of intuition, and often a great dollop of that most valuable and elusive of commodities – luck. Tracing his footprints – sometimes clearly delineated, in other places along the route barely perceptible with the passage of time – has taken me to many places. I spent several delightful hours wandering round Deddington in rural Oxfordshire, Ken Smith's birth place – not because I expected to find any vestige of him

Animals in the Blood

there, but to absorb what some authors rather pompously call 'atmosphere' and which I prefer to call, perhaps no less pompously, the 'spirit of place'. The trail took me from there to Banbury and Harpenden (where I stood in the shop – now a florist's – once owned by Ken's father), to Saffron Walden (where I was honoured to be given a tour of his old school), West Mersea off the Essex coast, Charlbury, and Great Rollright, and to Bedfordshire, Devon, Dorset, Cornwall and Jersey. I have been to every extant zoo in which Ken Smith worked or managed, and to the sites of some of the defunct ones. I have researched his parents' background and been privileged to interview a number of his friends, family and colleagues. I discovered a school group photograph, showing his entire school, pupils and teachers, taken in 1926. To my regret, lack of time prevented me identifying him from amongst so many near-identical faces, but there can be no doubt he was on that photo somewhere. I have pored over his RAF service record and held the very passport he used to hand to immigration officials during his animal-collecting expeditions.

Anyone who writes about actual events has an awesome responsibility for factual fidelity because any errors or misconceptions that do contrive to slip through the net are likely to be accepted as true. History is awash with these 'urban myths', more so since the advent of the World Wide Web. Whilst it has sometimes proved impossible to verify all details, I have striven to provide as truthful an account of Ken Smith's life as possible. The number of people who remember Ken is diminishing all the time, and trying to track down his acquaintances has been a challenge. Unearthing the facts of his life has been like chipping away at a rock. Slowly the information came my way, a nugget here, a snippet there, and gradually the strands of his life began to draw together. Everyone I've spoken to agrees that Ken knew the animal business intimately; he was hard working but also that he didn't tolerate incompetence or laziness in others (his staff soon realised that the penalty for sloppy work was a severe dressing down from Mr Smith and he was not averse to summarily dismissing someone if he felt their work was not up to an acceptable standard). But he also engendered loyalty, so much so that when he moved from Paignton Zoo, where he had been its Superintendent, to run Jersey Zoo, a number of Paignton's staff upped sticks and moved with him. According to one person I interviewed, part of the reason for his popularity was that he never expected his staff to do anything he wasn't prepared to do himself.

The internet, normally a fount of information on all subjects from the most commonplace to the most bizarre and esoteric, has been of no help whatsoever in researching this book. Both 'Kenneth' and, more especially, 'Smith' are very common names and it is astonishing just how many times the two names crop up in conjunction. Typing in the key words 'Ken Smith' on a well-known search engine gave me a choice of no fewer than 12,100,000 results; whilst typing in 'Kenneth Smith' produced a rather more modest 8,470,000 results. None of the random websites I checked out had anything to do with the late zoologist of that name, but before giving up the search in despair I had found a Kenneth Smith the artist and designer, a Kenneth Smith the flautist, Kenneth Smith the barrister and solicitor, Kenneth Smith the chemical engineer, Kenneth Smith the architect, Kenneth Smith the landscape designer, Kenneth Smith the signalman, Kenneth Smith the wildlife artist, Kenneth Smith the visual effects artist,

Kenneth Smith the actor, Kenneth Smith the advertising executive, and Kenneth Smith the ski mountaineer. There is a Pennsylvanian politician by the name of Ken Smith, and a fictional character in the Australian soap opera *Home and Away* was called Ken Smith. I also found a Reverend Kenneth Smith, a Professor Kenneth Smith (specialising in neuroinflammation and multiple sclerosis) and a Kenneth Smith MD (whose particular line of interest was breast augmentation and plastic surgery).

The internet may have let me down, but a number of people *were* very helpful to me. I should like to thank all those who talked to me at great length and answered all questions patiently and frankly. I am particularly indebted to the following: Judy Banford; Laura Beal; William Beal; Gerry Breeze; Mike Curzon MBE; Robert Golding; John Hartley; Harry Lever; John 'Shep' Mallet; Jeremy Mallinson OBE; Lucy Pendar; Caroline Robbins (*née* Smith); the late Raymond Sawyer; Brian Smith; Tony Soper; Kelsay Williams (*née* Smith); Nigel Wilkinson; and the late Frank Woolham, all of whom had known Ken Smith personally.

I should also like to thank John Adams, for notes he made during visits to Exmouth, Poole and Teignmouth Zoos; Tony Blackler; Paul Boulden; Robert Bradshaw, for his notes on Exmouth Zoo; Tim Brown; Geoffrey Budworth (author of *Poole Park: The People's Park*); Jim Clubb, for his reminiscences of childhood visits to Exmouth Zoo and Poole Park Zoo; Harold 'Topper' Davis (Deddington resident); Dr Lee Durrell MBE (Honorary Director of the Durrell Wildlife Conservation Trust), for putting me in touch with alumni of Jersey Zoo who worked for Ken Smith; Malcolm Ellis (Avicultural Society); Christine Grant; Ronald Green (Mersea local historian); Brian Jay (Mersea local historian); Dr. Andrew Kitchener (Principal Curator of Vertebrates, National Museums Scotland); Tim May; Paula Meyer; Stewart Muir; Peter Murton (Research & Information Officer, Imperial War Museum, Duxford); Ronald Prew (Curator, Charlbury Museum); Donald Rainbird (Mersea Museum); David Round; Claire Soles; Tim Soles; James Straight; Andrew Stevens; Neil Thomas-Childs; Simon Tonge (Executive Director, Whitley Wildlife Conservation Trust); and Rob Vaughan.

I should also like to thank for their invaluable help the staffs of the Bedfordshire & Luton Archives; the Essex Record Office in Chelmsford; Exmouth Library, especially Eve Bollen; Harpenden Library; Mersea Library; Oxford Archives; Oxfordshire Studies at the Westgate Library, Oxford; Royal Air Force Disclosures Section at RAF Cranwell, Sleaford; Society of Friends at Friends House, London; and the library of the Zoological Society of London, in particular assistant librarian Ruth Jones.

I am indebted to the Friends' School, Saffron Walden, especially the Head, Graham Wigley, and two former members of staff, Margaret Brinkworth and Martin Hugall, and a sixth form student, Roland Fischer-Vousden. The latter, who graduated only a few weeks after our meeting, escorted me round the school and I could not have wished for a better guide.

The extract from *Memoirs of a Coarse Zoo Keeper* by George Jacobs, published by Frederick Muller Ltd., is reproduced by permission of The Random House Group Ltd.

Extracts from Clinton Keeling's *Where the Crane Danced* are reproduced by permission of Mrs Pamela Keeling.

I am grateful, too, for being able to quote from several newspapers and magazines, most notably *The Times* and the *Exmouth Journal*.

A special mention must be made of Jill Adams, who possesses an infallible instinct on where to go to find information and who put in many hours on my behalf researching Ken Smith's family history.

I should like to say a special thank-you to Alan Ashby and Phil Chamberlain for their invaluable technical assistance, without whom this book would still be languishing on the hard drive of my computer.

Most of all I wish to express my profound gratitude to Mrs Trudy Smith, without whose hospitality, kindness, support and patience this book would not have been possible.

AUTHOR'S NOTE

Throughout the text I have referred to countries and organisations by the name they were known by at the time. A number of them have changed their name (in some cases more than once) in the intervening years. Those that occur most frequently in the text are listed below, with the modern name in parenthesis.

Abyssinia (Ethiopia)
British Cameroons (Cameroon/Nigeria)
The former territory of the British Cameroons no longer exists. In the early 1960s the map was redrawn. The southern part of what was once the British Cameroons, together with the neighbouring French Cameroons (Cameroun), formed a republic (called Cameroon) in 1961; while the northern part of the former British Cameroons has become part of Nigeria.
British Guiana (Guyana)
I have, however, chosen to use the modern 'Guyanese' as the adjectival form rather than the archaic 'Guianese'. *Guiana* was the original name for the region that now includes Guyana, Suriname, French Guiana, and parts of Venezuela and Brazil.
Jersey Zoo (Durrell Wildlife)
London Zoo (ZSL London Zoo)
Paignton Zoological and Botanical Gardens (Paignton Zoo Environmental Park)
Teignmouth Children's Zoo (Shaldon Zoo/Shaldon Wildlife Trust)
Whipsnade Zoo (ZSL Whipsnade Zoo)

It is a traditional practice in books of this nature to provide an exhaustive list of source notes at the end. I have decided against doing this because, wherever possible, I have made it clear in the text where my information has come from, rendering pages of detailed and repetitive end notes, carefully delineated by chapter, unnecessary.

Chapter One

Delivery in Deddington *(1911–1926)*

KENNETH JOHN SMITH was born in Market Place, Deddington in north Oxfordshire, on 20 July 1911, the second eldest of five children, to Herbert Smith, a thirty-eight-year-old master grocer born in Charlbury, Oxfordshire, and Gertrude Emmeline Smith (*née* Jolly), aged thirty-one, originally from Faringdon.

Today Deddington is a very pleasant little town, in scale more like a big village – in 1911 the population numbered less than 1,500 – but with a clearly defined town centre. The debate as to whether it qualifies as a town or a village has never really been resolved. Officially it is classed as a town, inasmuch as a market is held there once a month and there is a Town Hall. There is also a Deddington Town Football Club. Of the Deddingtonians I've spoken to, however, many are resolute in calling it a big village. Many of the houses are built of the local honey-coloured ironstone, technically known as Marlstone Rock. There was once a castle on the eastern outskirts, still indicated on all the maps, but anyone expecting to find it, or its ruins, is doomed to disappointment. Already in a state of decay by the end of the thirteenth century, nothing remains of it but a grassy mound, a favourite haunt of dog-walkers and courting couples. Deddington's main claim to fame is that it was the place where, in 1312, Piers Gaveston, the ostentatious favourite of King Edward II, was brought following his surrender to the Earl of Pembroke at Scarborough. Lodged in the rectory while his captor (who had previously assured him his life would be spared) was away, he was seized by his enemy, the Earl of Warwick, and carried off to his death on Blacklow Hill near Kenilworth.

The basic layout of the town has probably changed little since those days. The main thoroughfare is New Street, though it's hardly *that* because it has been known by this name since at least the early thirteenth century. At around the time of Ken Smith's birth, Deddington, for all its manifold charm, had an unfortunate reputation for rowdy behaviour and one could generally rely on there being at least three or four street brawls at 'turning out time'. The locals even had a saying: 'If yer wan' a black eye go to Dedd'nton on a Sa'adi ni.'. There was more than a ring of truth about it.

Such obstreperousness contrasted markedly with the staid respectability of the Smith family. Ken came from a comfortable lower middle-class Quaker background. His family had been Quakers (members of the Society of Friends) for generations. His great-great-grandfather, Thomas Smith (born c.1760), was received into the Society of Friends in about 1785. Throughout the nineteenth century and into the twentieth, the Smith family remained steadfast Quakers and were regular attendants at meetings of worship. Such was their unwavering fervour that in the 1890s Ken's paternal grandfather, Thackwell Smith, presided as the clerk at the monthly meetings.

Thackwell, who died in 1905, was a man of not inconsiderable means. He had been a bank manager, a self-employed family grocer, provision merchant, druggist and draper; he commanded a 240-acre farm, employing up to a dozen people to work on the farm and in his grocery, and his household chores were performed by domestic servants. He was, in short, the paradigm of a Victorian gentleman and the model to which all his sons, including Ken Smith's father, would aspire, not always successfully. At this time the family lived in Charlbury. As well as being a successful businessman in his own right, Thackwell had married into a prosperous family. His wife was Marianna Gillett of the famous banking family, who, like his own antecedents, were firm Quakers. In 1823 one branch of her family had created Gilletts Bank, latterly known as Gillett & Co. – 'Bankers at Banbury and Oxford'. By the turn of the century the Gilletts had established branches in several Oxfordshire locations including one (open on Fridays) in Market Place, Deddington, only a few hundred yards from the house where Ken Smith would be born. In 1919, Gillett & Co. would merge with Barclays Bank – or rather, more correctly, be absorbed *by* Barclays Bank. (The Gilletts finally chose Barclays, after rejecting approaches by other banks, mainly because Barclays was itself based on a merging of many Quaker banking families.)

Further evidence of Thackwell's affluent status is provided by the 1881 national census, in which his eldest daughter, Hannah, is listed as being a scholar at the unusually late age of seventeen – this at a time when most boys, let alone girls, left school at the tender age of twelve (in fact the mandatory school leaving age had been raised to twelve only a year earlier, in 1880). The census also provides proof that his house was quite a substantial one, because in that year of 1881 he and his wife were sharing their home with no fewer than eight of their children, with ages ranging from three to eighteen years old, in addition to four lodgers or servants: a total of fourteen people.

The male members of the family were fiercely competitive chess players, regularly excelling in matches at county level. According to the *Oxford Times* for March 1900, Thackwell and his sons had long been in the front rank of Oxfordshire chess. Thackwell himself had played for the county on several occasions and his four surviving sons were no less enthusiastic. The eldest, Thackwell Gillett Smith (not to be confused with his father), was the Charlbury secretary and a reserve to the county team, Frank Scuse Smith (described in the *Oxford Times* as being 'a very strong player') was the Oxfordshire secretary, Herbert was a member of the Oxford City Chess Club, and Arthur John Smith was 'playing good chess in Scarborough'. The Oxfordshire contingent of the family got together regularly, sometimes as frequently as twice a week, for matches against rival teams. With Thackwell's death on 24 January 1905, Herbert and his brothers lost not just their father but one of their keenest, most competitive players. The chess matches continued, however, and Hannah's husband, Arthur John Harlock, whom she married in 1891, was competing in chess tournaments almost until his death in 1937, as a photo I came across quite by chance, taken in Charlbury in 1936 of Arthur and five of his chess-playing buddies proudly showing off a cup they had just won, proves.

*

By 1901, according to the national census, Herbert was no longer living with his father Thackwell in Charlbury, but with his uncle and aunt, Edward and Eliza Walter, in Reading. We have no way of knowing whether this was a permanent or short-term arrangement. If he was lodging there permanently, as seems quite likely, the Walters would certainly have been grateful for his rent money (though the amount Herbert paid could not have been much for he was only a humble grocer's despatch clerk by then) because it seems that Edward Walter was down on his luck: a draper by profession, in the census Edward describes himself as being 'Out of Business'.

Sometime between 1903 and 1906, Herbert left Reading and moved to Deddington, where he took over a grocery shop in Chapel Square from a Mr Fred Bolton. It was presumably not long after this that he met his future wife Gertrude. She and her family had lived in the parish for about ten years. In the early 1900s she was still living at home with her parents, younger sister Nellie and elder brother Frederick. The circumstances of the couple's first meeting are lost in the mists of time, but it is easy to imagine her being one of his regular customers, perhaps sent there daily by her mother to collect provisions.

Gertrude was born in London Street, Faringdon, in 1879, one of eight children. In those days, Faringdon was in Berkshire but since 1974 it has been placed over the county border in Oxfordshire. Her father, John Jolly, was a foreman tailor (the family name, Jolly, is sometimes – apparently arbitrarily – spelt 'Jolley' in the records). The family had moved to Deddington in the 1880s. They did seem to have something of the peripatetic about them, moving, in very quick succession, from one address to another in the parish: New Street (by 1895), Earl's Lane (by 1901), Horse Fair (by 1903), and finally Hudson Street (by 1907). Four addresses in just over ten years, all within the same locale and sometimes hardly any distance at all from the previous home, does seem rather eccentric and one must wonder what lay behind so many moves. It can't be that John Jolly and his wife Mary were downsizing as their children grew up and departed the familial home because in Hudson Street they settled, according to the national census, into The Priory, a grandiose building erected by Charles Duffel Faulkner, an inveterate collector of curios of all kinds, as a private museum to house his extensive collections. However, the present occupant, who has lived there since 1939, believes the family lived not at The Priory but in the adjoining house, now called Priory Dene.

Herbert and Gertrude were married in Deddington parish church, the Church of St Peter & St Paul, on 3 November 1908 when Herbert was thirty-six years old and Gertrude was twenty-nine. In the 1900s it was quite unusual for a woman to wait until she was almost thirty before marrying, but it was not the only irregular thing about this marriage. Herbert, like his father, was a proud Quaker. In choosing Gertrude (a non-Quaker) as his bride and electing to marry her in a church, he showed he was not afraid to stray from rigid conventionality. At one time, Quakers were expected to marry only other Quakers. Half a century earlier, the law had not even recognised marriages between Quakers and non-Quakers, but in 1859, with membership of the Society of Friends in serious decline, the marriage rules – and the law – were amended in an attempt to arrest the decline, and by the 1900s a more liberal attitude was emerging, and 'marrying out', as it was called, was not seen as being quite so scandalous. All the same, it is rather surprising that Herbert should embrace a traditional *Ecclesia Anglicana* church wedding with its usual accent on sacraments, ritual and formal ministry, all customs normally rejected by devout Quakers. Today it is not uncommon for Quakers to marry non-Quakers in church, but back then Herbert's decision to opt for a church ceremony would almost certainly have caused eyebrows to raise and tongues to wag among the more conservative practitioners of the faith. The Society of Friends was one of the few Nonconformist factions to be granted the privilege of being free to marry in a meetinghouse instead of a consecrated building. It was a privilege the Society guarded jealously and officially took a dim view of anyone going against the grain. (In Victorian times there was markedly less tolerance, with those Quakers who were accused of ignoring the principles on which the denomination was built being at severe risk of ostracism.) Herbert was not excluded from the fold as a result of this momentary transgression, and the ceremony was very well attended, attesting to the popularity of the couple, as this paragraph from the *Deddington Deanery* magazine, dated December 1908, makes clear:

> A marriage which attracted a good deal of attention was that of Mr. Herbert Smith and Miss Gertrude E. Jolly, which took place at the Parish Church on November 3rd. The bells rang out merry peals both before and after the ceremony, and a large number of people besides guests were present at the Service. The bride was given away by her father and attended by four bridesmaids and other friends.

As a grocer, Herbert was a linchpin of the community. This was the golden age of shopping. At a time when it was not easy to keep food fresh, most housewives visited the grocer's almost daily, but running a grocer's shop was extremely hard work, and no doubt Gertrude helped her husband in the shop, serving customers, packing goods, sorting out the orders and helping to organise deliveries. By the time George V came to the throne in 1910, pre-packed goods were starting to appear on grocers' shelves, easing the burden of work to some extent, but such things as sugar, flour, dried fruit, soda, and many more items had still to be weighed and packed by the grocer. Providing customers with a personal level of service was key, as was a sound knowledge of the merchandise, and customers would have expected Herbert to know all about the latest blends of tea, coffee and other goods.

Business was good and in 1910 he and Gertrude moved to larger premises a short distance away in Market Place, a move perhaps necessitated by the fact that Gertrude was by now pregnant with their first child. The future could not have looked rosier for the couple. Everything indicates they were prosperous, confident, and more than a little well-off. Not only was Herbert building up a good business selling groceries, wines and spirits, most probably from a shop beneath their living accommodation, but he also owned the freehold on cottages in Chapel Square. Nothing, it seemed, could go wrong, and now, with a baby on the way, the couple's happiness was about to be complete.

The new premises were quite substantial by the standards of the day and, according to the national census for 1911, boasted no fewer than nine rooms. Almost certainly this house still stands, but identifying it has proved difficult. A book, *Tangled Tapes*, compiled by the late Dorothy E. Clarke that recorded for posterity the memories of one Fred Deely, a lifelong resident of Deddington born in 1903, seemed at first to cast a shaft of light on the matter. In a chapter devoted to some of Fred's earliest memories of Deddington, there is the following intriguing paragraph:

> There was a house on the Bullring called 'Whichway House' because it had two doorways. It's made into flats now, but painted on the side in big white letters were the words 'Cheapest House for Blankets and Flannels' but they sold everything, even groceries…The name was Smith, but they went broke.

Fred Deely recalled that the business had two horses and carts, and that the horses were stabled round by the doctor's surgery. On Saturday mornings, one heavily laden cart would deliver provisions to the villages to the south, the other would take deliveries to the west and north.

Could this have been the house where Herbert and Gertrude lived and where Ken and his elder brother would be born? However, if Herbert Smith, master grocer, did trade from this address, wouldn't groceries have been the mainstay of his business? Yet Fred Deely had marginalised the grocery side of the business ('*even* groceries'). Furthermore, Fred emphatically stated that Whichway House (sometimes spelt Wychway House) was on the street known as the Bullring, but both Ken and his elder brother's birth certificates, as well as the 1911 national census, tell us the family lived in a house in *Market Place*. However, the Bullring does articulate with Market Place and, moreover, the building faces *onto* Market Place, so we can't completely rule out the possibility that this was the house.

The trade directories for the period succeed only in muddying some already very turgid waters, because Herbert was not the only Smith trading in Deddington at that time. There were several other, unrelated, traders by the name of Smith, including at least one, a Miss Mary Ann Smith, dressmaker, operating in Market Place. Herbert wasn't even the only grocer in the parish. In the trade directories we find an all too laconic reference to a firm known as the 'Smith Brothers – grocers'. As Herbert and the 'Smith Brothers' are listed separately, it is quite reasonable to assume the two businesses were unconnected. So the mention of 'Smith' in *Tangled Tapes* is ambiguous. When Fred Deely said to Dorothy Clarke, 'The name was Smith, but they went broke' was he referring to Herbert Smith or to the 'Smith Brothers' (whoever *they* were)? Unfortunately old Fred isn't around to clarify matters as he died in 1998 at the grand old age of 94.

Bennett's Business Directory was slightly more helpful. Like the others, it was frustratingly vague about the exact whereabouts of Herbert Smith's business, merely reiterating that he was based in Market Place without giving any clue as to the precise location of his shop, but it did resolve one matter: Bennett's clearly states that it was the 'Smith Brothers' who occupied Whichway House. This was not what I hoped to find – I rather hoped it would say that Herbert Smith was the occupant of Whichway House; nonetheless, the possibility that Herbert was also present cannot be completely discounted. Who *were* the 'Smith Brothers' and was there a link between these two apparently separate businesses? It does seem a coincidence that Herbert Smith and the 'Smith Brothers' of Whichway House should have been in the same line of business. Were they even Herbert's own kin? If there was a fraternal connection, it is entirely plausible that Herbert traded from the same premises. Despite being listed separately in the trade directories, did he and the 'Smith Brothers' operate together? However, there is no evidence that any of his brothers were active in Deddington. His eldest brother, Thackwell Gillett, was certainly running a grocery business at that time, but in nearby Charlbury. Arthur was a master grocer who now lived at the Red House, Adderbury, about three miles from Banbury – although it is possible his *business* may have been based in Deddington – and brother Frank was a café proprietor in Oxford, where he plied his trade at the Creamery in Cornmarket Street. (In 1918 Herbert's brother, Thackwell Gillett Smith – who described himself at the top of his invoice docket, one of which I managed to obtain, as a family grocer, provision merchant, and tea and coffee specialist – would be declared bankrupt, which carried more of a stigma in those days than it does now, and it is not hard to understand why the business ultimately failed, for some of his customers were allowed to run up bills of up to fifty or sixty pounds – enormous sums in those days – and he also operated a barter system for two or three local farmers with butter and eggs, which didn't help his cash flow.)

So, on the face of it then, it begins to look far less likely that Herbert Smith and the traders listed in the directories as the 'Smith Brothers' were related, but there are a couple of reasons why I believe one cannot completely discount the possibility of some connection between them. In the early 1900s, Whichway House was owned by W. Churchill & Co. Ltd., a company that, according to Fred Deely, went broke. Churchill's relinquished Whichway House in about 1910 – around the same time that Herbert moved from Chapel Square to Market Place.

This could be nothing more than coincidence, of course, were it not for something else I uncovered while searching through the various trade directories for the period. In 1910 Herbert was registered not only as a grocer but also as a dealer of wines and spirits. The 'Smith Brothers', on the other hand, were originally listed in Bennett's and other trade directories simply as grocers. When, a few years later, Herbert's name abruptly disappeared from all the directories, the entry for the 'Smith Brothers' changed and suddenly they were listed as grocers *and* wine and spirit dealers, suggesting either that they absorbed Herbert's business or that the two businesses had been run in conjunction. Later trade directories would list the 'Smith Brothers' as 'grocers, provision merchants, drapers, ironmongers, furniture dealers and spirit merchants', confirming Fred Deely's assertion that 'they sold everything' (but notice that groceries are listed first), until they too disappeared from the listing before the decade was out.

*

On 5 June 1910, Gertrude gave birth to the couple's first child, a son whom they called Ronald. The boy was given the middle name Thackwell in memory of Herbert's father. It wasn't long before Gertrude found herself pregnant again, and thirteen-and-a-half months after Ronald had made his appearance in the world, Kenneth was born.

But already the family's days in Deddington were drawing to a close.

Herbert and Gertrude, along with Ronald and Kenneth, left Deddington in about 1914 or 1915. The most likely explanation for the sudden move is that Herbert, businessman and property-owner, had gone bust just as his brother, Thackwell Gillett, was to do three years later. Whatever went wrong must have happened suddenly because up to that point Herbert's business appeared to be progressing well. The timing might be a clue. Like all shopkeepers, he would have struggled during the Great War. Now in his forties, he was too old to be called up for active service, but almost without a doubt he would have bade a sad farewell to younger male employees. With so many men at the Front, there was a serious labour shortage, and he may not have found it easy to fill those vacancies. With German U-boats laying siege to the country, imports of goods were severely curtailed and there can be no doubt he would have found it increasingly difficult to replenish his shelves – shelves that before the war had been groaning under the weight of the merchandise stacked upon them. With supplies dwindling, the prices he was paying to his wholesalers rose sharply. Herbert was just one of countless grocers forced to shut up shop during this period.

We now come to a bizarre period in Herbert and Gertrude's lives as Ken's father struggled to get his career back on track following the family's precipitous exodus from Deddington. For five or six years the Smiths bumped around the Home Counties, drifting like flotsam from one place to the next in quick succession, seldom settling anywhere for more than a few weeks or months at a time. Not surprisingly, Herbert's name rarely figures on the electoral rolls at this time and tracking their movements has proved difficult. Ronald's son, Brian Smith, believes that during her long life his grandmother Gertrude moved house at least eighteen times, but this, of course, includes the frequent moves she made with her parents before she married Herbert and probably includes the several moves she made after he had died. What *is* clear is that from about 1915 to 1920, Herbert and Gertrude were always on the move. Why? Brian thinks he may know the answer. 'You see, Herbert did not flourish in business,' he told me.

> Nothing seemed to work for him, not for long anyway – the family had to help him out more than once – and he moved around a lot as a result. Things sometimes started off quite promisingly, as they had in Deddington, but sooner or later they always seemed to go wrong for him. I think he probably made some bad decisions. The multiple house moves might indicate he couldn't settle or, more likely, each new business venture of his kept failing.'

Whatever his motives, Herbert drifted round the Home Counties like an itinerant player, which was hardly conducive to his aim of re-establishing himself in business. One of his and Gertrude's first stops was in Wallingford, midway between Pangbourne and Oxford. Here, Gertrude had a job working in a shop. 'I don't know when this was – just another of the eighteen house moves, I suppose,' said Brian, adding:

> I remember her telling me she used to recite the most indispensable goods to her customers like a litany to ensure they didn't forget anything important, that

went: 'Butter, sugar, tea, lard, flour, eggs, bacon, soap, soda, starch, blue.' She would run through this list with all her regular customers so they didn't forget anything. She told me this more than forty years ago, but I can remember her saying it to me as if it were yesterday. The list gives an indication of the sort of things that were stocked.

('Blue' were soluble crystals that acted as a mild bleach when added to the 'whites' wash of a laundry session, in use in England until at least the 1950s.)

Brian remembers his grandmother showing him the little push-down bell customers had used to summon her to the counter. The fact that she was able to retain the bell as a keepsake of her time there suggests she was probably the manageress of the shop rather than an ordinary employee, an opinion also held by Brian. 'I believe Herbert and Gertrude ran the shop in Wallingford,' he told me. 'I still have that bell. She gave to me when she realised I was interested in all that. It's a fairly plain, copper, cone-shaped bell about four or five inches high with a plunger on top and makes a "ding" sound.'

Even at his lowest ebb, Herbert continued to make a special effort to attend meetings of worship. It is fortunate for us that Herbert and – when they were old enough – his children were regular attendees at Quaker meetings, because the Society of Friends has always been assiduous in recording the details of its meetings, and it is mainly with the help of these records that I have been able to trace the family's movements. Another way of tracking their movements is by examining the birth dates and places of their children. By the autumn of 1915, Herbert and Gertrude had taken up temporary residence in Swindon. We know this because on 20 October 1915, at 139 Victoria Road, Swindon, Gertrude gave birth to the couple's third child. The baby boy was given the name Herbert Gillett Smith (the middle name was in honour of his paternal grandmother, Marianna, whose maiden name had been Gillett), but to avoid any confusion with his father, he was usually known to his family as Gil (with a hard 'G') and the name stuck throughout his entire life.

Gil's birth certificate reveals something very surprising. On it, Herbert is described under Occupation as a 'grocer's assistant'. Not 'master grocer', nor even 'grocer', but 'grocer's assistant', the same label he had had twenty-five years earlier when he was apprentice to his father, Thackwell. Clearly Herbert's career had stalled in a cataclysmic way and he had been forced to take a regressive, even humiliating, step. No longer the proud master grocer in charge of his own business, he was now, at forty-three, a humble grocers' assistant once more: a considerable climb-down in a very short space of time but entirely consistent with Brian's conviction that Herbert was not successful in business.

Only about three weeks after Gil was born, the family moved to Oxford, possibly at the invitation of Herbert's Oxonian brother, Frank Scuse Smith. By 1917 the family had moved yet again, this time to London Street, Faringdon, the very street in which Gertrude herself had been born thirty-eight years earlier. Did Gertrude still have relatives living in Faringdon who gave them board and lodgings? Being the same street, could it have been the same house? On 22 April 1918 she gave birth again, for the first time to a daughter, Violet Kathleen Smith. Confusingly, Violet's first and middle names are sometimes transposed and I have seen her name written in several documents, including the marriage index (though not, of course, her birth certificate), as 'Kathleen Violet Smith', so it appears, as she grew up, she preferred to be known as Kathleen.

During the time that he was living in Faringdon, according to Violet's birth certificate, Herbert was still ingloriously eking out a living for his growing family as a grocers' assistant. By the end of 1919, the family had moved again, this time to 46 Divinity Road, Cowley St. John, Oxford. It was while they were living in Oxford that Herbert and Gertrude's last child, Frank Eric Smith (named after Herbert's brother Frank), was born on 1 November 1919. Gertrude had taken a chance by allowing herself to become pregnant again. She was now forty years old, and certainly in those days, and to some extent still, this would have been considered quite old to give birth, and riskier for both mother and child. But in so many ways, Herbert and Gertrude's marriage was unconventional; this was just one more manifestation of that. With four sons and one daughter, all born within nine years, their family was complete.

Once again Herbert's name does not appear on the electoral roll (strangely enough, there doesn't appear to be a number 46 in Divinity Road). Whilst living in Oxford, Herbert was forced to sign on the dole, though it is not known exactly when this was, because, as already mentioned, he had found himself in Oxford at least twice and it is impossible to say on which of these occasions he was unemployed. On Frank's birth certificate Herbert's occupation is given as 'grocer', which, if true, is a distinct move in the right direction from the humble 'assistant grocer' he had been when his children Gil and Violet were born, but is this description completely accurate? A birth certificate does not necessarily record a father's current employment status, merely his *usual* occupation. Perhaps all that was missing was the addition of one word. Would 'grocer (unemployed)' have been more appropriate? To someone like Herbert Smith – who was the product of a middleclass Victorian upbringing and who had absorbed, osmosis-fashion, proud Victorian and Edwardian values – unemployment and the stigma of collecting dole money would have been on a par with bankruptcy as the ultimate humiliation; but he could not have been on the dole for very long because in those days claims were payable only up to twelve months, by which time a claimant needed to have regained work. In a way, Herbert was quite lucky. Had he found himself on his uppers even just a few years earlier, his predicament would have been even graver, because unemployment benefit was unknown before 1911 (and then only to job-seekers who were completely up to date with their National Insurance contributions – the so-called 'stamp'.)

The effect such constant upheaval had on both Ronald and Kenneth can only be imagined. Herbert and Gertrude did all they could to minimise the disruption to their children's lives caused by their erratic, nomadic existence but still it must have seared a deep and lasting impression on the two boys at a very critical age of their development. Both Ken and Ronald shared a lifelong reticence about speaking of this period of their lives. Brian Smith told me his father Ronald had once rebuked him quite severely when he tried to bring up the subject: 'He made it quite clear to me it was a no-go area. My father never seemed to talk about his past and I vividly remember him biting my head off about wasting time when I should be studying for exams when I came home from the library with a book about ancestor-tracing.'

Despite his straitened circumstances, Herbert wanted the best for his young family. It is probable that Ronald and Kenneth, being the two eldest and therefore the ones whose education might suffer as a result, did not accompany their parents on all their many house moves, but stayed with relatives, most likely with the Harlocks. In the 1930s, all the Smith children, with the possible exception of Violet, were to stay, at various times, with their aunt, Hannah Harlock, in Charlbury, but before moving to Charlbury she and her husband Arthur were living in Banbury where they ran a drapery shop – or perhaps emporium would be a better word for it because this was no small corner shop (although it was on a corner) but something altogether grander and more majestic. Did Ronald and Ken stay with the Harlocks at this early juncture, too? There was certainly plenty of room for the boys above the drapery shop. What is beyond doubt is that all the Smith children were very fond of the Harlocks, whom they looked upon almost as surrogate parents. With Herbert and Gertrude flitting like butterflies from one address to the next, never alighting too long in any one place, aunt Hannah and 'uncle' Arthur (as Ken and his siblings would no doubt have called Hannah's husband) would have provided a measure of stability for the two boys.

Hardly anything is known about what Ken did during his formative years. How did he spend his days? What animals, if any, did he keep as a child? Did he, like so many other young aspiring naturalists, begin by collecting fossils and frogspawn, butterflies and beetles, perhaps even birds' eggs? Growing up in rural Oxfordshire, he must have prowled round the countryside armed with a butterfly net and a knapsack and a battery of jars and matchboxes in which to transport some of the insects and other small creatures he captured. We must also speculate on whether he was a studious, attentive pupil at school or, like so many of his ilk who enjoyed the company of animals, was he bored by the routine of school-life, impatient for the bell to ring signalling the end of lessons for another day, so that he could get out into the countryside again?

Which schools did the young Kenneth attend? Despite making exhaustive searches I have drawn a blank, the one person who could have told me, Ken's youngest brother Frank, sadly having died in 2009 before I could speak to him. One very slender possibility is the Deddington C. of E. Primary School, a fine Victorian building on the corner of Earl's Lane and Banbury Road. However, the family left Deddington when Ken was still very young and probably too early for him to have started school in the parish. Another reason why it is unlikely that Ken attended the school is because its doctrine, as enshrined in its name, was Church of England, and Herbert was naturally keen for his children to be brought up in the Quaker faith. More likely, Ken attended school in Charlbury or Chipping Norton, possibly Harpenden or Oxford. The museum at Chipping Norton does keep some school registers from the period, but there is no record of Ken or indeed any of his siblings, and the primary school at Charlbury has no registers or photographs going back that far. Frank went to Chipping Norton Grammar School, but we can discount Ken having attended the same school because it didn't open until 1928, by which time he had left school. The only school where I can definitely place him is the Friends' School at Saffron Walden in Essex, but he didn't start *there* until 1926 when he was fourteen. In the entry register for the Friends' School, it does refer to new boy Kenneth as having previously received an elementary education, but makes no allusion to a particular school.

*

After almost five years of drifting like a ship without a rudder, Herbert was at last showing signs of putting down roots. In late 1919 or early 1920 he entered into a partnership with one Arthur J. Harriden to take over a well-established grocery shop – Clarke's Stores – in Harpenden in rural Hertfordshire. In the 1920s, Harpenden was a large, pretty, even sleepy, village. Since then it has expanded to the size of a small town. Clarke's Stores, at 5 The High Street, was not a big shop. The shop had been in existence since 1895 and had been run all that time by one Thomas John Clarke. The first thing Herbert and Arthur did after they took over the shop was to change the name of it to 'Smith & Harriden'. Herbert and Gertrude lived above the shop and Arthur Harriden a short distance away at 5 Manland Avenue. Groceries were the mainstay of the business, but the place was also to become popular as a coffee shop. A coffee grinding machine was given pride of place in the window display, surmounted by a notice in big, bold capital letters that read FROM THE BEAN TO YOUR CUP. In time this grinder became quite a well-known feature of Harpenden, even something of a local landmark, with people unfamiliar with the area being told to look out for it: 'You want to go where? Ah yes, follow the road down there, past the shop with the coffee machine in the window, you can't miss it…'

Previously, Herbert had been a regular attendee at the Witney Monthly Meeting of the Society of Friends, but now that he was living in Harpenden he fell within the compass of the Luton and Leighton Monthly Meeting and on 10 June 1920 he made a formal application to transfer his membership. Acceptance into a Monthly Meeting was by no means certain, even if one was already a member of a neighbouring group. Each Monthly Meeting had a screening process. A longstanding member whose judgement could be respected would be appointed to interview the applicant, usually in the applicant's own home, in a friendly discussion that could go on for up to two hours or more. Based on this meeting, a recommendation would be made to approve or reject the application. For Herbert, the outcome was favourable, for in the minutes for the Luton and Leighton Monthly Meeting, held on 11 September 1920, it states that the Friend appointed to visit Herbert Smith 'reports having attended to the duty. The Clerk is directed to sign and forward the usual form of acceptance to the Clerk of Witney Monthly Meeting.'

With their father's side of the family being such devoted Quakers, it was only natural that Ken, his brothers and sister should be raised in the faith, as was their birthright, and soon enough they too would be regularly attending Meetings, even before they had become fully fledged members themselves. (Today things are rather different, and children born into a Quaker family do not automatically become Friends themselves; since 1940, full membership has depended on personal acceptance after the age of sixteen.)

Herbert had often relied on his Quaker contacts in the past and in 1925 he wrote a carefully worded letter to the Society to enlist its help to secure a placement for Kenneth at the Friends' School, Saffron Walden. The school, with its excellent reputation, was often over-subscribed and it wasn't always easy to get a place there, but a glowing testimonial from the Clerk, Herbert reasoned, might just swing things his way. At a Meeting of the Luton and Leighton Society of Friends, held in London on 9 December 1925, his request was discussed. In the minutes it states, 'An application has been received and read at this time from Herbert Smith of Harpenden, asking this Meeting to recommend his son Kenneth John (not in membership) as suitable to receive education at Saffron Walden School.'

Two people were duly nominated to visit Herbert at his home (standard procedure with requests of this kind) and report to the next Meeting to be held at Luton on 8 January 1926. This they dutifully did, as the minutes for the meeting show:

> Henry and Marion L... [surname indecipherable] report having had a satisfactory interview with Herbert Smith of Harpenden on the subject of his letter regarding his son Kenneth John. They are satisfied that the parents intend to bring their son up in accordance with the principles of the Society of Friends and that they see no reason why the Monthly Meeting should not recommend Kenneth John Smith as a boy suitable to be admitted to Saffron Walden School.'

Not only was the Friends' School widely praised for its teaching methods but was generally seen as a trailblazer. None of Ken's siblings were ever enrolled there, and such evidence as there is – which isn't much – suggests Herbert's resolve to send Ken there – as a *boarder* – caused some friction within the family who saw it as favouritism. It would have done nothing to assuage their jealousy when they realised that Ken was, to use the modern parlance, 'fast-tracked'. With less than a week between the Luton and Leighton Monthly Meeting in the second week of January and Ken taking up his placement at the school, there was insufficient time for the Clerk to write to the Head of the Friends' School and for the school to reply with a formal letter of acceptance. Clearly the Clerk must have written to the Friends' School with his recommendation *before* the January Meeting took place without waiting for Henry and Marion to present their official report. In other words, it was generally expected that the report would be favourable and presenting it at the January Meeting was merely a formality. In the minutes it declares, 'This Meeting hereby confirms the action of the Clerk in signing and forwarding the recommendation.' So he *had* already written to the school. Just as well the report was positive, then.

There was good reason the Clerk hadn't waited for the report before making his recommendation. Ken had already missed one term and, with the commencement of the next term looming, it was crucial his application was processed without delay if he was not to find it even harder to catch up with the work.

The reason that only one of Herbert and Gertrude's children received an education at the prestigious Saffron Walden school must have had a lot to do with the expense.

The average school fees per annum for boarders from Quaker families was £81 and from non-Quaker families, £99 – a not inconsiderable sum in 1926. In addition to this basic cost, from time to time supplementary expenses were incurred, all of which had to be budgeted for, such as clothing supplied by the school, the cost of sheet music for those pupils learning an instrument (which did not include Ken), workshop fees and other sundries. It all added up to quite a sizeable bill. One did not pay a whole year's fees all at once but term by term, payment being due at the beginning of each term. About half a dozen pupils were lucky enough to have won scholarships, and although Ken was not among them he may have been awarded a grant based on parental income. The total cost varied, depending on personal circumstances. Interestingly, the Fees Book for 1926–27 reveals that Ken's basic school fees were just £21 per term (or, put another way, £63 per annum).

£63 per year was not £81 but to the average family in 1926 it represented a considerable financial outlay. How could Herbert, who had had a rather chequered career in business up to that point, afford to send his son to a fee-paying school and, moreover, as a boarder? The record, sadly, is silent, but the most credible explanation is that Herbert did not foot the bill, or at least not all of it – somebody else did. Did Ken have a wealthy benefactor? While researching this period of his life, I came across a first-hand account of one boy's experiences at the Friends' School in the mid 1920s written by a contemporary of Ken Smith by the name of Charles Kohler. Like Ken, Kohler was a boarder at the school. Although his account doesn't mention Ken, the two boys almost certainly knew each other very well and they could even have been classmates. They were the same age and their time at the school overlapped (Charles Kohler started almost two years earlier and left seven months later than Ken). Kohler was a German émigré. Following the breakup of his parents' marriage, he was brought to Britain by his mother in 1917. Unsurprisingly, with Britain still at war with Germany, he and his mother were viewed by most people with suspicion, even contempt. But not everybody had treated them with disdain. They were befriended by a Quaker couple, Henry and Lucy Gillett. Dr. Henry Tregelles Gillett (1871–1955), born in Banbury, was a medical doctor practising at 15 King Edward Street, Oxford. Later on he would serve on the Oxford City Council, becoming mayor of the city from 1938 to 1939 and helping to deal with refugees from Nazi Germany who came to Oxford. Chairman of several humanitarian groups, he travelled widely in England and Europe, as well as the U.S.A., visiting Meetings of the Society of Friends, where he was always very well received. If anyone could be said to be the personification of Christian charity, it was Dr. Henry Gillett. A wealthy philanthropist, responsible for the establishment of several trusts and a founder member of OXFAM, it was Henry Gillett and his American wife Lucy who paid Charles Kohler's school fees in full.

Ken was, in fact, distantly related to Henry Gillett (Ken Smith's great grandfather and Henry Gillett's grandfather had been brothers). Henry and Lucy had regularly attended the Witney Monthly Meeting of the Society of Friends at the same time as Herbert. No doubt Herbert knew them well and probably mentioned to them that he hoped to send Ken to the Friends' School at Saffron Walden. Did Henry and Lucy contribute towards, or even underwrite, Ken's school fees? It is a distinct possibility.

They had money. They were well known for their charitable deeds. They were driven by an altruistic desire to help others. Since they were prepared to fund Charles Kohler – a friend but not a relative – isn't it more than likely they paid Ken Smith's fees, too?

Ken started at the Friends' School, Saffron Walden, on 14 January 1926. Having already missed the first term (the school having reopened after the summer recess on 17 September), he would have had a fair bit of catching up to do, but it was not unknown for pupils to start at odd times of the school year. Three other students, all girls, were enrolled at the school on the same day as Ken. One of them, Brenda Smalley, was to leave on the same day as Ken two years later. Someone who has studied the history of the school and knows it better than most is Margaret Brinkworth, who told me:

> Children did, and still do, join the school during the course of the school year – sometimes because parents have moved, sometimes because they are not satisfied with the child's previous school. Sometimes they cannot afford the fees for the whole of the secondary school period, and choose to send their child for the couple of pre-exam years.

At fourteen, Ken was at an age when most of his contemporaries would be leaving school and stepping out into the cold, hard world of work. He, however, still had another two years of fulltime education in front of him. It wasn't all algebra and logarithms, though. The Friends' School ran several clubs and societies, one of which was of great interest to Ken for this was the Senior Natural History Society. He was not able to join immediately – there was a waiting list and numbers were strictly limited – but join it he did. He already had a burgeoning interest in natural history, but what the Natural History Society did was to nurture that emergent enthusiasm, helping to set him on a course – igniting an initial flare, if you like – that would define his life's work.

Chapter Two

Essays and Excursions *(1926–1927)*

NOTHING DEMONSTRATES Herbert's desire for Kenneth to be raised in the Quaker faith more than his determination to get his son accepted into the famed Saffron Walden school, about which he had heard so many good reports. In the 1920s, the governors were all Quakers, the staff were nearly all Quakers, and getting on for forty-four per cent of the pupils were Quakers. A Bible was on every student's list of *Requirements*. For boys (boarding), other requirements were:

3 Day shirts, without collar	3 Pairs of loose linings or
3 Night shirts or sleeping suits	summer and winter pants
3 Vests (if worn)	2 School caps
4 Pairs of socks, run in the heel	2 Pairs of strong boots or shoes
8 Collars (soft)	1 Pair of football boots
12 Pocket handkerchiefs	1 Pair of leather slippers
1 Dark suit for best wear	1 Pair of rubber shoes
– preferably dark grey	1 Overcoat
2 Strong suits for general wear	

The list was slightly different for girls. Another *sine qua non* was white flannels 'marked and provided with hanging tapes' for drilling and games. School caps, as well as 'Football shirts, knickers, and stockings in School colours' were provided by the school and added to the bill. One can imagine the scene in the Smith family household in the days leading up to Ken's departure for Saffron Walden as he, assisted probably by his mother, frantically assembled everything stipulated on the list, checking and rechecking to make sure nothing had been overlooked.

Like most boarders, Ken probably made his way to Saffron Walden via Liverpool Street railway station, from where he would have caught a packed train (the so-called *London Squash*) to Audley End, a journey of a little over an hour. At Audley End – a tiny settlement consisting of no more than a few higgledy-piggledy farm buildings – he would have changed trains for the very short onward journey to Saffron Walden. The railway station in Saffron Walden was demolished many years ago. However, the street is called Station Road to this day, and one of the signs, very rusty now, looks original. The only other reminder to survive to the present day is a pub, still bearing the name 'The Railway', that at one time stood across from the station entrance. Once Ken and the other children had disembarked, it was an easy five minute walk up the hill to the school, drawn by the sight of the water tower that stood next to the school and provided a useful landmark – as it continues to do to this day. There were no formal lessons on the first day, this being spent unpacking and getting to know the layout of the school and the other students with whom one would be sharing a dorm. Ken was very lucky to have been accepted at the Friends' School. In March 1926, barely two months after he was enrolled there, it was announced that the school was almost at capacity. Altogether there were ninety boys and eighty-two girls – a grand total of 172 scholars – prompting the school's in-house magazine, *The Avenue*, to comment, 'Next term the School will be full, and a "waiting list" is once again in existence.' Children who were, themselves, Quakers, or who came from Quaker families, were, of course, given priority, the remainder of the students being made up of non-Quakers. The Annual Report gives slightly different figures than those published in *The Avenue*. According to the 1926 Annual Report, the school had 171 pupils, eighty-seven boys and eighty-four girls, of which forty-six boys and twenty-nine girls were Quakers.

Ken's first sight of the school must have infused him with a mixture of awe and nervous anticipation in equal measure. Built in 1879 of red brick in a grand mock Tudor style and renowned for its warm, friendly atmosphere, the school, set in thirty-five acres of grounds, had originally been commissioned as a replacement for the Friends' School in Croydon, which was permanently closed due to the high incidence of typhoid fever among the students. Saffron Walden was chosen as the site for the replacement school. 'The locality is a very healthy one, the air bracing, and the water supply good,' chimed the school's official Prospectus for 1926, omitting to mention that the school was perched on an open – and very breezy – hill above the town. These days the school, which is still going strong, is no longer exposed to the elements as once it was, the town having grown around it, enveloping it like a gall on an oak tree. Whereas once it overlooked the town, it now finds itself in the leafy suburbs. In Ken Smith's day, the principal was one Charles Brightwen Rowntree B.A., a short, dignified figure, who always wore the same incongruously formal attire. Known affectionately to all the children as Chas, his small stature belied his superior position. In his characteristic black jacket, high stiff collar and striped trousers, his face set off by a pair of pince-nez glasses through which his merry blue eyes blinked rapidly, as if trying to expel some grit, he looked more like a bank manager or a solicitor than a headmaster, but was highly regarded and well-liked by children and teaching staff alike. He was assisted in his duties by the headmistress, Miss Florence D. Priestman.

There were three categories of pupils: full-time boarders like Ken who stayed there all the time, returning home at the end of each term; part-time boarders, who went home for the weekend; and day pupils. The boys' dormitories were monastic in their simplicity. Each contained about ten iron bedsteads with starched cold white spreads stretched over them – and precious little else. There were no chairs or curtains and no heating. Beneath each bed lurked that most functional of accoutrements: a chamber pot.

Dorms were strictly for sleeping in. Since there were, at that time, no dedicated common rooms for relaxation or recreation, the form-room was where the children went to read, write, play board games or indulge in simple, private hobbies such as philately. Solitude within the school was impossible. Food was nutritious but plain, varying little from day to day or even from meal to meal. But these were austere times and nobody complained, because the simple but wholesome fare was comparable to, or even exceeded, what some pupils could expect to receive at home. Ken, who was below average height for his age, did put on a bit of weight while he was at the school, but not much. In the Summer Term of 1926 his weight was precisely recorded as 7 stone, 7 pounds and 1 ounce. A year later it was 8 stone, 1 pound and 4 ounces.

The average day began between 6.30 and 6.45. The children would be roused from their beds by the clanking of a heavy brass hand-bell (almost everything they did, from the moment they got up to the moment they went to bed, was ordained by the bell). Yawning and stretching, they made their way in long, snakelike processions to one of the washrooms where their olfactory senses were assailed by the overwhelming stench of carbolic soap. The importance of cleanliness was installed in everyone. All boys were required to strip to the waist and sluice themselves with water, as cold as a mountain stream, both mornings and evenings. Ablutions were followed by private Bible reading at 7.15 and breakfast at 7.30. At eight o'clock, pupils were free to play, and lessons commenced at 8.50. The rest of the daily timetable went like this:

8.50am to 12.50pm. – Morning School, with short recesses between lessons,
and thirty minutes at eleven o'clock.
1.00 – Lunch.
1.40 to 3.30 – Play.
3.30 to 5.30 – Afternoon School.
6.00 – Evening tea.
6.30 – Prep. ('Homework'). 1 to 1½ hours, according to age.
8.00 to 9.00 – according to age – Bed.

The Friends' School, with its motto of *Per Ardua ad Alta* ('Through Hard Work, Great Heights are Achieved'), was seen as something of a maverick amongst educational establishments of the time and known for its very progressive, enlightened attitudes. Since as early as 1910 the school had been co-educational, a radical development that was fiercely opposed by some of the more conservative male members of staff at the time. At first, girls had not been able to enjoy all the activities available to the boys (to begin with, for example, girls were not allowed to go on field trips, although by the time Ken started at the school, that rule had been relaxed) but gradually concessions were granted until eventually girls enjoyed most of the same rights and privileges as the boys. Far from being segregated as was the norm in most schools, boys and girls were encouraged to interact, to socialise, and to work, eat and play together, as a wonderfully innocent promotional piece in the *Time and County News* for 8 May 1931 makes clear, even if, to our twenty-first century way of thinking, it could have been worded rather better: 'The provision of such opportunities for intercourse between boys and girls at school makes their life happier, as there is then no need for suppression of instincts.'

Boys and girls sat next to each other at breakfast and at midday lunch (though not, for some inexplicable reason, at teatime, when they sat on opposite sides of the dining-hall), and it was not unusual to see a boy and girl strolling together up and down 'The Avenue' (a promenade of Lime trees) or around the playing fields as a 'couple'. They might even hold hands, but that was the accepted limit. Girls, as well as boys, were taught carpentry. There was even a girls' cricket team (although it did find it quite hard sometimes to arrange matches owing to the paucity of female cricket teams elsewhere).

There wasn't complete integration of the sexes. In gym classes the sexes were separated, and until as comparatively recently as the mid 1970s boys and girls had separate playrooms at opposite ends of the main building. Classes were mixed, but the form meeting each day, when the register was taken and notices given out, was split into two, the boys of each form in one room and the girls in another. The school ran several clubs and societies, which were open to all, but it was only in the Boys' and Girls' Reading Clubs that the old idea of sexual apartheid persisted, but this was probably because some literature appealed more to boys and other literature had more of a feminine appeal.

Each term, boarders like Ken were allowed to take ten to sixteen shillings pocket money for small incidental expenses, and this was given out every Saturday morning. They presented their account book and could withdraw up to 6d (2.5p in modern money) which was spent mostly on sweets, chocolates and fruit from the tuck shop (called 'Tintacks') at the bottom of the hill, run by Mr and Mrs Fitch. The stout figure of Mr Fitch, in his shop-coat, was often in evidence, hovering in the background, but it was usually Mrs Fitch or her pretty dark-eyed niece who served the customers. Unlike the boys, however, the girls were not free to stroll into town alone. The only time they could go outside the school gates was when accompanied by a teacher and as part of a group. The pull this little shop exerted on the students was only partially due to the gob-stoppers, jelly babies and the thick, sickly bars of marzipan that they procured there. For the pubescent boys from the Friends' School there was also the exciting prospect of being served by Mrs Fitch's attractive niece. Pupils were allowed to spend only a small weekly sum on confectionery (just four years later, in 1930, 'tuck' would be prohibited at the school in an effort to improve the health of students), nor were they allowed to bring to school, or have sent to them, any extra eatables other than eggs, jam and fresh or dried fruits. 'Experience has shewn that the general health of the Scholars has sometimes suffered when they have been too liberally supplied with sweets, cakes, etc.,' a note in the Regulations read. Pocket money also paid for subscriptions to school societies, such as the Senior and Junior Natural History Societies, the Senior, Middle and Junior Literary Societies, or the Wireless Society, and for pens, pencils, nibs and other essential scholastic equipment – but not exercise books: these were provided, free of charge, by the school. The importance of budgeting was emphasised, and boarders had to make sure they saved at least two shillings so that at the end of term they could pay for their luggage to get home.

Fire drills were a regular inconvenience and could take place at any hour of the day or night. Pupils were warned when there was going to be a drill, and if the alarm sounded at night they simply slipped on their dressing-gowns and shoes and were led down the worn stone stairs to the gravelled playground where their names were called. It is not recorded whether nocturnal fire drills were reserved for summer or could take place on cold winter nights, too.

Pupils were expected to follow strict rules of etiquette at mealtimes, and to pass food to their neighbours at table, never to grab any for themselves. Despite certain strictures such as this, it was a fairly easy regime. The children had many hours of leisure time on Saturdays and Sundays (there were lessons on Saturday mornings). They also had Wednesday afternoons off, which compensated in some measure for the fact that the school's strict Quaker moral code forbade the playing of games on the Sabbath, with the result that children often found Sundays relaxing if rather dull. Every Sunday morning, after rising later than normal, the whole school would troop down to the local Friends' meetinghouse in the town for a Meeting of Worship, which lasted about an hour. (When the school was built, this meetinghouse had had to be enlarged to cope with the high volume of additional attendees.) They had hymn-singing on Sunday afternoons and an extra Meeting (this time held in the school) in the evening. There was no general half-term holiday, but children were allowed to spend one day in the term with relatives and, if all the children had worked hard and there had been no serious lapses of discipline, the whole school could win an occasional extra half-day holiday 'on merit' to be taken at the discretion of Mr Rowntree.

The Friends' School was decidedly unconventional in other ways, too. It even made some concession for vegetarians (not that Ken was a vegetarian – he wasn't), which was highly unusual at the time. At mealtimes, vegetarians – of which there were not many – sat together at a designated table. Another area where the school was ahead of its time was its discipline policy. In most other educational establishments of the period, obedience to the rules was generally enforced by the severest of chastisements. That was not the Quaker way. Corporal punishment was forbidden, so at a time when the cane and the belt were held in awe in many schools, and grammar school boys in particular dreaded receiving a summons to report to the headmaster's office, Ken was fortunate to find himself at a school where such punishments were considered draconian and anachronistic. Pupils were accorded a level of respect well in advance of their tender years. They were treated not as children who needed to be beaten and bullied into submission for the slightest transgression, but as young people with a capacity for original thought. Everyone was worthy of dignity and respect. *This* was the Quaker way. Teachers believed that by giving their charges a high degree of independence and the same level of respect normally afforded to adults, they hoped the children would reciprocate by respecting the rules of the school, and in general this deceptively simple approach – a policy based on self-discipline – did seem to work. Miscreants were made to feel they had let down both themselves and the school. Minor offences were dealt with by a simple reprimand, and generally this was sufficient. Mr Rowntree himself rarely meted out punishment. 'Words' – between thirty to sixty depending on the severity of the misdemeanour – were his favoured method of chastisement. If the offence warranted sixty-five or more words, the miscreant could expect to be 'Gated' – which was not as horrific as it sounds. It simply meant that the student was forbidden to leave the school premises for a fixed amount of time. Generally this punishment was set for a Saturday afternoon for maximum effect. Persistent offenders, or those who had committed a more serious offence, were given detention after classes or barred from games or treats like attendance at a fete. If they still refused to conform, a terse letter might be dispatched to their parents. Usually just the threat of a letter was enough to cause them to amend their ways. In extreme cases, boarders in breach of the rules could be sent home, but in reality this hardly ever happened because scholars realised how fortunate they were to be there. 'We were encouraged to respect everyone and the environment,' wrote Charles Kohler many years later. 'It was therefore understood that we were in honour to obey rules.' But in one surprising area at least, the school was peculiarly strait-laced and puritanical: 'Woe betide any boy who locked himself in the lavatory.'

Children revelled in the sense of freedom they had at the Friends' School. There were late night swims in the pool, immensely popular Saturday evening lantern lectures during the winter term, and visits to the opera in Cambridge where they saw such stellar performances as Rossini's *The Barber of Seville*. There was rivalry in sport, with the school's football and cricket teams competing against other local schools from Saffron Walden, Newport, Harlow and Cambridge. The various societies organised frequent, well-attended excursions to local areas of interest (inevitably scheduled for Saturday or Wednesday afternoons to avoid disrupting lessons) and there were even educational holidays to places further afield, such as the New Forest. The school's unofficial credo was 'A child who is busily occupied is likely to be a content child. A content child has little cause to misbehave.' The School Regulations for 1926 gave a fair idea of what new pupils could expect: 'Special efforts are made to encourage and help the scholars in the pursuit during leisure hours of such hobbies as Carpentry, Woodcarving, Photography, and Natural History. Such spontaneous effort is found to have a valuable influence on the character in drawing out individual taste and in forming habits of industry.' That last sentence would prove especially true for Ken Smith, though nobody at the time could have predicted quite how much influence one of the school's societies, the Natural History Society, would have on Ken's life and future career.

On Saturdays, a boy could, if he wanted, cycle – either by himself or with friends – to Cambridge, a round trip of just over thirty miles, returning after dark. Nothing provides a more evocative picture of that long cycle ride to Cambridge than this description by Charles Kohler:

A Saturday afternoon in October was ideal for such a jaunt, with the weather sunny, though not too hot. Cycling was easy as soon after leaving Walden the land flattened, clouds billowing above the wide horizon. We passed through sleepy villages like Littlebury and Great Chesterford: the whole afternoon was before us so we could stop, if we wished, to watch a horse-drawn plough turning up a stubble field. An hour later those twin humps – the Gog Magog hills – came into view and then the spires and towers of Cambridge.

Once in Cambridge we could stroll through the archways of colleges or sit on the banks of the river. We enjoyed browsing in the second-hand book shops and then finding a restaurant and spending a shilling on a cream tea. It was dark on the ride back to school, not much traffic on the quiet roads. We kept our eyes on the beam of light cast by our lamps, aware only of the humming of the bicycle wheels.

There is a simple timeless quality to the prose and one can easily imagine the young Kenneth Smith, carefree, full of youthful vigour, undertaking the same jaunt; cycling past the stunning seventeenth century mansion at Audley End on a leisurely ride to Cambridge in the company of one or two of his friends in that cosy bygone era that exists now only as flickering images on shaky old sepia film shot on handheld cameras. A bicycle offered freedom, and the children spent many hours on their bikes exploring the local area. In so many ways, students at the Friends' School enjoyed a rather privileged existence, leading Charles Kohler to remark wistfully in old age, 'When I'm ill and feverish I often have the same dream. In that dream I'm a boy again at Walden. Sometimes I'm sitting in the lecture room, at other times in the dining hall, but there are always boys and girls by my side. Maybe this is a regression, a return to childhood. But for me it expresses a longing for a lost family, for the community of friends.' With its relaxed, familial atmosphere and so many extra-mural activities to choose from, it is no wonder that children had been known to weep when the time came for them to leave the cosy, safe environment of the Friends' School.

But not everybody was convinced, as the 1920s gently rolled by and one season morphed imperceptibly into the next, that the Friends' School was continuing to uphold its reputation for excellence. A few dissenting voices pointed to what they perceived as a lamentable slip in standards. In July 1926 the school received a strongly worded missive from a disgruntled former pupil (who signed himself 'Mournfully Yours'), appalled by what he saw as an unacceptable *laissez faire* attitude among some of the new generation of scholars. It concerned, of all unlikely subjects, the colour and pattern of their neckties:

I have returned home from Walden a sad and disappointed man.

I thought Walden was 'it'. In our days it was *the* School. To-day I find present scholars deliberately wearing in the School, and on holidays, the ties of other schools to which they are not entitled. Alas! I never thought the time would come when scholars would let their School down thus. I hear of one member of the cricket team who went to Cambridge wearing a Perse School tie!

It's sad. The world looks black. Where's the Walden spirit?

The school was quite a closed community and this didn't suit everybody. 'Children keen on games or hobbies, or very sociable,' wrote Charles Kohler, 'found plenty to occupy them, but those without close friends or special interests often felt isolated and homesick.' There was an emphasis on organised sport, and for those pupils with little sporting aptitude it could seem that the emphasis was disproportionate. Boys had compulsory games twice a week: football in the winter, cricket and tennis in the summer. There was also swimming, gym, athletics, paper chases and – most exhausting of all – cross-country running. Ken had never been a very sporty person, so one would think the school's concentration on physical exercise would have been an ordeal for him and whenever possible he would have found ingenious ways to wangle out of it – but it seems even he found himself swept up in the euphoria of it all. Surprisingly, on Sports Day, 26 March 1927, he succeeded in coming second in the Senior Mile Race, run at five-thirty in the afternoon. Students were not press-ganged into competing in important events like this, but volunteered themselves, so Ken must have been sufficiently enthusiastic and competitive enough to put himself forward or to be selected by his games master. Never again would he show much interest in sport. The school published an in-house magazine each term called *The Avenue* in which most of the features were contributed by the students themselves. Naturally, Sports Day and in particular the Senior Mile Race received good coverage. 'It was a good race,' *The Avenue* reported, 'K. Smith keeping well up to the winner until the last lap, but was forced to run on the outside all the way.' The event is also mentioned in the Diary of the Senior Literary Society. As with *The Avenue*, the writer commented on how closely-run the race had been. Originally the anonymous diarist had written, 'K. Smith coming in second', but then had obviously thought about it some more and felt this statement was in need of elaboration, because he or she had inserted three extra words in the space above so that the sentence now read 'K. Smith coming in *a very good* second'. Ken's achievement was all the more remarkable because the winner, Ivor Parley, was a superb all-round athlete who was soon to break the school's high jump record, set many years earlier, and to set a new record for swimming. For Ken to have almost outrun him over a distance of one mile was an achievement of some substance. But Ken's moment of sporting glory was a momentary aberration. In general, he was an academic pupil, not normally given to sporting prowess. I have found his examination results for July 1926. Frustratingly, as with all the other students, he does not appear to have been accorded a grade or a percentage, but against each subject there is either a tick or a cross or, oddly, a question mark as if the invigilator was undecided whether the student had passed or not. His twelve exam results show five passes (arithmetic, English literature, geography, nature study, drawing), five failures (algebra, geometry, elocution, history, and music), and two with question marks (composition and carpentry). But at one subject he excelled. One subject, and one subject only, against which there is a different symbol. It is an 'X' but with a dot in each quarter. It took me some time to figure out what this mysterious icon symbolised, but I have found out it is a little-known (these days) and little-used symbol meaning 'very good' or 'passed with distinction'.

Unsurprisingly that lone subject was…Nature Study.

*

Some of the teachers lived on site, either in small bedsitting rooms or, in the case of more senior members of staff, in the relative comfort of two-bedroom flats. As there was no staff common room, just as there was no common room for the children, teachers tended to fraternise with the pupils quite a lot, even after school and at weekends. In this way, the children got to know them very well, learned their personalities and background, their interests and pastimes. They were not seen as remote authority figures, but became like substitute parents, and they were a varied bunch, each known to the children by an affectionate sobriquet.

There was the sardonic David Pearson, known simply as D.P., a bachelor in his early fifties who believed that only things accomplished through perseverance could be truly appreciated and whose favourite leitmotif was 'Always take the harder path, *boy*!' with a clear emphasis on 'boy'. There was the long-haired Mr Beer, or Booze, the gracious and charming history master and a talented pianist. More than sixty years before the film *Dead Poets Society*, he brought humour into his lessons by the use of unorthodox teaching methods and unusual props (once he even wheeled in a motorbike with a defective sparking plug as a metaphor for the human body), stimulating his pupils' imagination in a way that dry textbooks could not. During the 1914-18 war he had been imprisoned in Dartmoor Prison as a conscientious objector. Mr Beer was an extrovert and delighted in entertaining his wards – unlike the more reserved Mr Smiley, otherwise known as Jock, a former World War I pilot from Scotland, who took the boys for carpentry and gym. Although Jock, too, was genuinely liked by all the children, he was far less outgoing and, it was widely speculated, a loner.

Another confirmed bachelor was Mr Whitlow (Fishy or JPW to the children), who taught mainly English literature. A voracious reader, he impressed everyone with the depth of his knowledge. He excelled at producing and appearing in school plays, read to his students the books he had personally enjoyed, not restricting himself to classic or prescribed texts but ranging much more omnivorously, and was an excellent slow, right-arm bowler. Not having children himself, he had an avuncular attitude towards his charges borne out of real affection. Nobody had a bad word to say about Mr Whitlow.

But by far and away the most important teacher as far as Ken was concerned was the volatile but enthusiastic George Morris (or Moke as he was dubbed by the children for some long-forgotten reason) because it was he who taught natural history, he who ran the school's Natural History Society (in fact there were two separate Natural History Societies: one for the junior pupils and one for the seniors), and he who led the Society's various field excursions. Charles Kohler remembered George Morris well. 'I recall his shaggy, leonine head, his shambling walk and his untidy, unbuttoned clothes,' Kohler wrote sixty years later.

> Erratic, fiery-tempered, enthusiastic, his voice would rise with his emotions. I remember, during my first term, that he once struck a boy on the head. It was only a cuff and no doubt deserved. But a few minutes later Moke went back to that boy, saying: 'I'm sorry. I should not have hit you.' Moke wasn't an outstanding class teacher and because of his temper he had to put up with a lot of ragging. But we all recognised his sincerity and respected him. He opened up Natural History and Geology to many boys and girls. I think that he was most effective as a teacher on excursions into the country with a small group of attentive children. Fossils in the chalk railway-cutting or ancient burial mounds roused his enthusiasm and brought out his stores of learning. He was one of those who could read and interpret the landscape.

Moke was exceptionally knowledgeable about all aspects of natural history. He could identify birds by their calls and recognise which nests belonged to which bird species. At one fortnightly meeting of the Natural History Society, which threatened to end much earlier than normal due to a lack of things to discuss, he stepped into the breach and, with hardly any preparation or recourse to notes, proceeded to give a talk on snails of the British Isles – though he did complain afterwards that he would have liked a *little* more time to prepare.

The full title of the Natural History Society was the 'Natural History and Archaeology Society', because its agenda went beyond natural history to archaeology, embracing geology, meteorology and other natural sciences, and even extended as far as the study of church architecture, but hardly anyone bothered to use the full name. Excursions were organised to such places as Hadstock Church and Ickleton Church, and while on a bird-watching trip to Debden Park, the party could not resist taking a break from ornithology to inspect Debden Church. On 5 October 1927 the majority of Natural History Society members (which must have included Ken unless he was otherwise engaged on that Wednesday afternoon) set off on their bicycles to visit all the buildings of archaeological interest in Little Chesterford and Littlebury. For a time the Society was divided into three sections – zoology, botany and archaeology – but although that seemed like quite a logical, even sensible, approach at the time (would somebody interested in pond-dipping be as passionate about Gothic arches?), at the first meeting of the Society in the autumn term in 1925 (only about three months before Ken started at the school) it was decided to abolish this system – which had had more than a year's trial and was not considered a great success – in favour of amalgamating the three sections.

Ken did not become a member of Moke's Senior Natural History Society immediately because membership was originally strictly limited to a maximum of twenty boys and sixteen girls. Anyone wishing to join had to wait for a vacancy to become available when an existing Society member of the appropriate sex resigned or graduated from the school. It made perfect sense for places to be limited to no more than thirty-six members: too many members and it would have been difficult to fit everyone comfortably into one room for meetings, and even more difficult to organise transport (usually a charabanc or a fleet of smaller vehicles) for field excursions. With spaces being so limited, it was essential that only dedicated candidates were offered a permanent place. To this end there was a vetting procedure. Applicants were elected by the other members, becoming, at first, probationary members until such time as they had proved their commitment to the Society.

In the summer term of 1927 the rule governing the maximum number of members was changed. It was decided – not without some opposition – that in future the composition of the membership by gender would be immaterial, and the number of boys should no longer be limited to twenty or the maximum number of girls to sixteen. Now, whenever a place became vacant, it could be filled by someone of either sex as long as the total number of members still did not exceed thirty-six. It was probably this tweak to the rules that enabled Ken to join the Society at last.

Meetings were held on alternate Thursdays and members were encouraged to submit – and read – essays they had written on any aspect of natural history, geology or archaeology. Essays from new members were obligatory. A list of current members was always published at the beginning of the autumn term. Ken's name does not appear on the list from September 1926, but he must have joined not long afterwards because from the Minutes of a meeting held on December 9, we learn that he read an essay he had written on the subject of elephants. Moke was clearly impressed and one feels that even he, knowledgeable as he was, learned something about elephants because he commented afterwards:

> Kenneth Smith read an essay entitled 'Elephants'. The Indian and African kinds were clearly differentiated. The teeth were described and some specimens shown, and many other points of interest about the elephant were included. It was also mentioned that the African elephant had been in danger of extinction, but that now large tracts of land were set apart for its protection. This paper also was well written and was much enjoyed by all.

This was praise indeed coming from someone like George 'Moke' Morris, a man notoriously hard to please, and what a pity this essay has not survived. Meetings were very enjoyable affairs. After an essay had been read, it would be appraised, Moke famously not tempering his words. If he felt that an essay failed to deliver what it promised, was sketchily researched or poorly written, or – his most frequent complaint – inadequately illustrated, he would say so in no uncertain terms. He lambasted some members for suffusing their essays with unintelligible jargon, and others for not tackling their chosen subject in sufficient detail. But his criticisms were always *con*structive, never *de*structive, for he would point out exactly where, in his opinion, the writer had gone wrong and what action could have been taken to salvage the piece. However, it seems even he couldn't fault the essays Ken turned in, for each one elicited an encomiastic response from him.

Meetings always included a report on the most recent excursion, details of planned future trips, a meteorological report and the Current Events Report. Each meeting opened in the same way with the Diary. A detailed natural history diary was kept, in which were entered observations of animals and plants around the school grounds or surrounding countryside. Members would take it in turns to be responsible for the diary (as they did with the Current Events Report), but tiredness at the end of a full day of lessons was apt to take its toll and occasionally mistakes crept in which were not always rectified when the latest entries were read out at the next meeting, as the extract below, for June 1927, shows. Two crucial letters had been carelessly omitted, altering entirely the meaning the writer intended to convey.

> The Tawny owl disappeared a week ago; and three young larks in a nest below the new tennis court we killed the night after, and it is thought that the owl was the murderer.

It should, of course, read '*were* killed the night after.' The diarist's emotive use of language is interesting, and quite surprising for a member of a natural history society. Owls aren't murderers; they kill to live, even if it is, to our misplaced sentimentalities, regrettable that the baby larks were the victims.

At a meeting of the Natural History Society, held on 16 June 1927, Ken read an essay he had composed entitled *Rare Zoo Inmates*. His use of the term 'inmates' would be frowned upon by zoo enthusiasts today. Because of its negative associations, 'inmates' is now hardly ever used, but back then it was perfectly acceptable practice to refer to zoo animals in this way. Once again Moke gave Ken's essay a panegyrical report:

> Owing to his intimate knowledge of the Zoological Gardens at London, Smith was able to give us a paper of unique interest dealing in various degrees of detail with a large number of rare creatures, many practically extinct and of which most members knew, at the most, only the names.
>
> The paper, besides being extremely interesting on account of the descriptions of so many rare creatures, was also entertaining, containing many amusing stories of incidents in the Zoo together with accounts of various houses in it. Altogether, Smith is to be congratulated on producing so interesting and well illustrated a paper.

On Saturday June 18, just two days after the meeting, a hotly anticipated excursion to Wicken Fen nature reserve in Cambridgeshire took place under the tutelage of George Morris. Three contemporary accounts exist, which between them paint a vivid picture of what went on that day. Two of the students wrote reports for the school's excursions book, and Moke himself penned an account for *The Avenue*. Almost the entire Natural History Society, with only one or two exceptions, assembled at half past eleven for an early lunch before setting off for the Fen. This was the Society's biggest excursion of the year and everyone had been looking forward to it for weeks. The only thing that threatened to cast a damper over the occasion, quite literally, was the 'adverse' weather conditions as the party prepared to set off, but presumably it brightened up later in the day because large numbers of butterflies were seen during the afternoon. The school had made three previous excursions to Wicken Fen, one of Britain's oldest nature reserves. The first of these had been in 1908, followed by another visit the following year and a third in 1914, but for thirteen years the high cost of transport had placed it outside the radius of the Natural History Society.

The children's enjoyment of the occasion was heightened by the fact they would be travelling by car – quite a novelty for them. The fleet of five motors left the school slightly before midday, reaching Wicken Fen via Newmarket, Fordham and Soham by half past one. (In 2002 the hitherto peaceful town of Soham attracted nationwide notoriety as the scene of the murder of two schoolgirls.) Owing to the fact that the hoods of the cars were up, it was not possible for the children to make observations of a faunal or floral kind for most of the journey, but by the time they were nearing their destination the party had noticed a change in the nature of the countryside – the dark flat fields, planted mainly with potatoes and beans, and the frequent appearance of windmills. The broad beans were in flower, their strong, sweet scent very apparent.

Almost the first discovery they made on arrival was a Pygmy shrew. Unfortunately it was a dead one lying in the middle of the pathway, but still it was of interest to the party as most of the children had never seen a shrew in the flesh before. Apart from birds, insects and frogs, the shrew was the only other wild animal they saw. George Morris talked about the process of peat-cutting for fuel 'which is not so extensive now as before the war', and the party was fortunate to witness a sackful of peat being delivered outside a cottage.

There was a footpath of sorts, a narrow, earth trail, but this often descended to the level of an open pond, making it important for the children to watch where they were treading. 'The Fen itself is very treacherous,' observed student Bessie McGowan in her account of the trip for the school's excursions book. 'One step in the wrong direction and you were deep in black filth. It is not surprising that Hereward the Wake was able to keep the Normans at bay for so long.'

The marshy conditions were all the more annoying for the young naturalists because the white and yellow water lilies (in full bloom) and other fenland plants grew tantalisingly out of reach. About seventy species of terrestrial and aquatic plant life and twenty-one species of birds were recorded by the party, and the nests of Reed bunting, Reed warbler and Sedge warbler were examined for the presence of eggs or chicks. Other things of interest were the many dragonflies, the empty husk-like cocoon of a Drinker moth pupa, an ants' nest found beneath an old bucket, and a sizeable cluster of spiders, some carrying egg-cases.

The major entomological attraction of Wicken Fen was (and I use the past tense advisedly) the presence there of Swallowtail butterflies. It was one of the very few areas in Britain where this large and impressive butterfly (the UK's largest breeding butterfly and a distinct subspecies from Swallowtails occurring on the Continent) could be found. On the journey to the Fen, the eager young naturalists had barely been able to contain their excitement at the thought of seeing this most beautiful of British butterflies. It was, therefore, something of a letdown that the first example of the species they saw was one floating, lifeless, on the water. But then the party moved onto another portion of the Fen which seemed a more promising location to observe Swallowtails and other butterflies. 'It was here that the butterfly hunters searched assiduously for Swallowtail butterflies,' wrote Bessie McGowan. Five Swallowtails were eventually seen on the wing, but none was caught. Many other kinds of butterfly were also seen, and the larvae of Peacock, Tortoiseshell and Orange-tip butterflies and Drinker, Oak Eggar and Tiger moths were collected.

From Wicken Fen, the party walked along a dyke, past a wooden windmill pumping water from the ditches surrounding the fens, to the little settlement of Upware, where a small quarry pit was found to be of great interest, both botanically and from a paleontological point of view. During the Jurassic period 150 million years ago the area had been part of a tropical coral reef and was rich in fossils. A pleasant half-hour was spent collecting and examining the fossils of corals, univalve and bivalve molluscs, worm-tubes and sea-urchins, and exploring the swampy bed of the quarry for marsh and water plants. Leaving Upware, the party returned to Wicken where a sumptuous picnic tea was waiting for them, prepared by George Morris's wife and a Miss Waites, both of whom had stayed behind to get this welcome largesse ready. By now everyone was ravenously hungry, and the marvellous spread of doughnuts, bread and butter, jam and cakes, according to Bessie McGowan, 'disappeared like magic'. The party left Wicken at six o'clock to return to the school, tired but contented.

I have gone into some detail about the Wicken Fen trip, not just because Ken was almost certainly present, but because it is *un exemple parfait* of the type of excursion enjoyed by the school's Natural History Society during Ken Smith's time there, an era in education which has now passed into history. Surviving records clearly show the boys' and girls' enthusiasm and sense of wonder, not just for wildlife but for all things relating to the countryside, and their appetite for knowledge. To them, the distinction between a Sedge warbler and a Reed warbler was important. On these jaunts they collected artefacts and even – occasionally – living things for the classroom, to be gloated over and studied later: caterpillars, fossils, a desiccated pupal case; perhaps even that dead shrew was tenderly placed into a matchbox and brought back to the school in triumph to be pickled in formalin. In this context, Ken's animal-collecting expeditions over twenty years later to the remoter parts of Africa and South America can be seen as just a bigger and more ambitious version of the excursions he had once enjoyed as a member of his school's Natural History Society when he was fifteen.

Birds' eggs, too, were sometimes collected on these excursions. The collecting of wild birds' eggs by amateurs, or 'egging' as it was called, was once considered a respectable part of ornithology, and before this unethical practice was finally made illegal in the Wild Birds Protection Act (1954) there were few amateur naturalists who did not, at one time or another, succumb to the temptation. Pupils at the Friends' School not infrequently indulged in 'egging', as a remark in the school's diary, dated May 1925, shows. This entry, written with great restraint by one of the female scholars almost eight months before Ken started at the school, is pertinent to the story because it reveals that members of the Natural History Society were not discouraged from taking birds' eggs if such collecting fulfilled a 'useful purpose', although what constituted a useful purpose had not been clearly defined:

> Some boys evidently misunderstood some remarks made in the Natural History Society meeting to the effect that collecting birds' eggs would be permissible if for a useful purpose. Their purpose certainly was useful but Mr Rowntree had to remind them at dinnertime that our neighbour Mr Housden was also a keen collector particularly of Turkeys' eggs and that he would no doubt wish that our boys should not specialise in that species.

During the course of researching this chapter, I made a special pilgrimage to Wicken Fen to see how much had changed since Ken Smith and his friends were there. I fully expected to find it would now be a much more commercialised place with wildness replaced by comfortable hides, sturdy boardwalks, picnic tables and interpretation graphics everywhere, a solidly built visitor centre, and all the other trappings of civilisation. There is indeed a comfortable reception building and shop where you can buy a tea towel or a pair of oven gloves as a memento of your visit. There is also a pay and display car park, a café, an admission fee to enter the reserve, a dragonfly centre, and brown and white tourism signs on the approach roads. The place is also much more popular now. I visited in midweek in early March and yet I counted thirty-three cars, one minibus and one coach in the car park. There were, however, not nearly as many boardwalks as I expected, no educational display boards at regular intervals, and the picnic tables were confined to the vicinity of the car park. Things are a lot more regulated now, with a strict code of conduct for visitors. You can still see school parties indulging in the traditional pursuit of pond-dipping, though these days it is from small ponds expressly maintained for this purpose, but generally collecting is firmly discouraged. Even in the case of the tiny creatures scooped out of the dipping ponds, children are taught to observe them, admire them – and then release them. Collecting of Lepidoptera (butterflies, moths, and their caterpillars) is allowable now only by obtaining a written permit in advance of a planned visit and, needless to say, examining birds' nests is (quite rightly) completely prohibited. The wooden windmills, such a prominent feature on Ken Smith's visit, are now all gone, save for one preserved as a relic of a bygone era. But perhaps the most profound change, and certainly the saddest, is that the Swallowtail butterflies, which so excited the party from the Friends' School all those years ago, are long gone. Tragically, the species became extinct at Wicken Fen in the early 1950s. Several reasons have been put forward for this, the most likely one being a drop in the water table resulting in a decline in the Milk Parsley, the caterpillars' food plant. Since then, numerous attempts have been made to reintroduce it from its last remaining British population in the Norfolk Fens but, alas, all attempts have failed.

*

Not long after the excursion to Wicken Fen, the annual school exams took place. But this year something went wrong for Ken because against his name in the column beneath each subject on the results sheet is the single word 'Absent'. Why? One possibility is that he may have gone home suddenly to see his father, whose health, as the decade wore on, was beginning to fail. The problem with this hypothesis is that Herbert's illness seems to have been of a chronic, not an acute, nature, unless of course he suffered a sudden deterioration in his health about now, prompting Ken to forsake, or at any rate delay, his exams.

Or was Ken himself unwell, perhaps confined to the school's sanatorium, too ill to take his exams? Certainly his time at the school coincided with outbreaks of whooping cough, conjunctivitis, measles, jaundice, rubella, influenza, and there had even been a few cases of scarlet fever and diphtheria. In the spring term there had been a serious rubella epidemic within the school, to which eight boys, thirty girls, three mistresses and a maid had succumbed, but since then there had been few maladies and all the children affected had made good recoveries. In a statement dated 11 October, the medical officer proudly declared that since his last report in June the health of the school had been excellent. Twelve pupils – all girls – had gone down with tonsillitis, he reported, the cause of which was a mystery, and three boys had been laid low with fever. Was Ken one of them? If so, this would explain why he missed his exams. But why put 'Absent' below each subject? Why not 'Sick'? If his failure to sit his exams was through no fault of his own, surely he would have been offered the opportunity to take them at a later date. Since he was to leave school at the end of the year, these would have been his final and most important exams, which makes it even odder that I can find no record of his having sat exams of any kind in 1927.

*

If Ken *was* ill, he was well enough by the autumn to present his final essay for the Natural History Society at a meeting held on 13 October 1927. By any standards, the essay was an eclectic and extremely ambitious one, combining several ostensibly unrelated topics. In a single piece of prose he embraced the breeding of animals in zoos, animal behaviour, characteristics of certain baby animals and even, almost unbelievably, a subjective view of evolution. Each theme was really a subject for an essay in its own right, but Ken somehow successfully welded all the disparate parts into an apparently coherent and seamless whole, imbuing it wherever possible with humour, and he must have pulled it off successfully because Moke did not censure him for attempting to shoehorn so many big subjects into a single essay. Once again, Moke was unstinting in his praise of Ken's literary efforts:

> Kenneth Smith read us an essay entitled 'Some Zoo Youngsters & Views on Evolution'. Commencing with apes, chimpanzees and etcetera, the writer went on to tell us about young baboons and monkeys and from thence to elephants. He informed us that some animals were rarely born in the Zoo and others not at all. To the former class belong hippopotami and to the latter the rhinoceros. Of most of the animals he described, he gave the habits, such as the habit the llama has of spitting.
>
> Then young animals were described including the zebra, lion, the wild cat, the flying fox, the sea lion and kangaroo. The laughable incidents in the lives of these animals as described by Smith made the essay more enjoyable for everyone. The writer ended up by giving some of the views on evolution as put forward by scientists today and some views of his own on the same subject.
>
> Kenneth Smith is to be congratulated on the large collection of illustrations he had obtained for his paper.

Conscious that he was about to lose his star pupil, Moke charged Ken with the responsibility of compiling the next Current Events Report and presenting it at the November meeting (one of the last he attended). For this, Ken was expected to produce a report of approximately one thousand words encapsulating some of the most interesting archaeological and natural history events of the day culled from various newspapers.

Unlike his previous essays, this one has survived. Signed at the bottom 'Kenneth Smith', it is an incredibly neat piece of work, meticulously written and with hardly any mistakes. Only two words are crossed out (he had changed his mind over the best choice of word) and there are just three minor misspellings. His punctuation and grammar are almost flawless, even punctilious. He rigidly obeyed conventions of English composition, many of which are no longer followed today. To give just one example, he was careful to add an apostrophe after *photo* to make it clear it was an abbreviation of a longer word: perfectly sound etiquette, but there can't be many people today who would bother. Surprisingly, one of the few words he misspelled (and he obviously never noticed his error because it was not corrected) was 'scientific'. It is strange that he should get the spelling of this word wrong in view of his strong interest in zoology. As wide-ranging as his report was, he didn't waste words. Indeed, one could accuse him of being *too* sparing in some details, but of course he wasn't writing for the benefit of future generations. The news stories he referred to in his report are long forgotten now, but at the time everyone in the Natural History Society would have read about them, known about them, talked about them, and so there was no need for him to go into great detail. In what was a fairly short essay, he covered a lot of ground. He wrote about the wildlife and people of northern Australian swamps, and he ruminated upon a recent archaeological expedition to Palestine and excavations in Egypt, Persia and France. He discussed the sexual morality of animals and the eagerly anticipated arrival at the London Zoo of a pair of koalas. He wrote about the lifecycle of midges and about a very rare albino elephant that was on temporary exhibition at London Zoo. 'It arrived yesterday,' he wrote, 'but was greyish black in colour, having been painted with glycerine and charcoal to keep out the cold and to make it less noticeable in the streets.' One can't help feeling that an elephant being paraded through the streets of London on its way to the zoo (it was probably walked there from the London Docks) is pretty noticeable *whatever* its colour. In fact, there was something of an elephant theme to Ken's essay. He hadn't planned it that way, but obviously elephants were much in the news at that time, whether it was an elephant hunt in Mysore, the difficulty that staff at London's Natural History Museum had when they tried to re-install a mounted specimen of an elephant that was found to be too big to fit through the main entrance, or the news that the same museum had just taken receipt of some rare film footage of wild elephants in Siam (now Thailand):

A copy of that wonderful film of Siamese jungle life – 'Chang' – has been deposited at the Natural History Museum, where it is to be kept sealed for fifty years. 'Chang' is the native name for elephant, and the film – which is one of the most remarkable ever taken – deals with a family's struggle for existence against the beasts of the jungle.

Apparently Ken didn't think it was important to explain *why* the film was to be kept in a sealed canister for fifty years – or perhaps the original newspaper article hadn't given the reason either. In fact, the answer can be found in a letter dated 8 September 1927 from one W. Peet Leslie of Paramount Pictures to Arundell Esdaile, Secretary of the British Museum. In the letter, Leslie wrote that 'As I explained to you this thought occurred to my Directors after hearing from Mr J.E. Saunders, the eminent authority on mammals, that in his opinion some of the species shown in this picture would be extinct within forty years and it is their thought that if the copy of this picture was placed in an air-tight case and deposited at the Museum not to be opened until 1977, it would prove of great interest to Scientists, Anthropologists, Wireless and Cinematograph experts of that period.'

Another story Ken alighted upon was sobering for a different reason and involved a shot gorilla:

> The *Sphere* of November 19th gives a splendid full page photo' of a huge male gorilla shot in the Belgian Congo by two English big-game hunters for Lord Rothschild's private museum at Tring. The great ape put up a running fight for three hours before it was slain by the English hunters and their pygmy guides. The dead gorilla has a barrel 62" in circumference and a biceps measurement of 18". The natives and pygmies of the Congo relish the flesh of the gorilla.

One cannot imagine a picture like that, glorifying the achievement of the shameless trophy hunter, appearing in a newspaper today except perhaps to highlight the evil of the bushmeat trade or the immorality of poachers who think nothing of killing gorillas for body-parts to be flogged as souvenirs to unsuspecting tourists. The cool, detached tone Ken chose to adopt in telling the story is very surprising. Rather than condemning the action of the hunters, he seemed content to report the story in a dispassionate way. And yet a little further on, he describes the annual slaughter of migrating wild birds as 'pitiless', obviously feeling that the regular massacre of migrating birds to be unwarranted and unjustified. Was the youthful Kenneth Smith making a distinction between killing for sport and killing in the name of science? Did he feel that because the gorilla was destined to be displayed in a museum – a scientific establishment – where it could be studied by zoologists and anthropologists and perhaps add to our sum of knowledge of these magnificent and misunderstood beasts, this went some way towards justifying the killing? If so, it was not a stance he would hold in later life. When he wrote that piece in the late autumn of 1927, he was doubtless well aware that no adult gorilla had ever been seen alive in any zoo. Possibly he shared the gloomy prediction of William T. Hornaday, first director of New York's Bronx Zoo (now the Wildlife Conservation Park), who as late as 1915 had written, 'There is not the slightest reason to hope that an adult gorilla, either male or female, ever will be seen living in a zoological park or garden…It is unfortunate that the ape that, in some respects, stands nearest to man, never can be seen in adult state in zoological gardens; but we may as well accept that fact – because we cannot do otherwise.' Capturing an adult gorilla was virtually impossible, and the few young ones that had made it to the zoos of Europe and America had seldom survived longer than a few months. Usually they succumbed to enteritis as a result of being fed an unsuitable diet or else they contracted human infections to which they had no immunity. Sometimes it was the trauma of capture and a long sea journey that did for them. It would take a very long time for the problems of maintaining gorillas in captivity to be cracked, and the species would not be successfully bred in a zoo until 1956 (nowadays births are commonplace). Ken may well have believed that the only way scientists were ever going to be able to study the anatomy of a mature gorilla, or the only opportunity most people would have to marvel at one, was by having mounted specimens in museums such as the one at Tring.

*

Market Place, Deddington in Oxfordshire, around the time of Ken Smith's birth there in 1911.
© *Images & Voices, Oxfordshire County Council.*

Harriden's Stores, Harpenden. In the early 1920s Herbert Smith, Ken Smith's father, ran this shop in partnership with Arthur Harriden. At that time the shop was called SMITH & HARRIDEN. This photo was taken around 1930, about five years after Herbert had departed to run another shop in West Mersea, leaving his erstwhile partner in sole charge.

Ken (the smaller of the two boys at the back), his older brother Ronald, sister Violet and their aunt, Hannah Harlock (seated on left, in her dark Quaker clothes), circa 1924. The little lady seated on the right is believed to be Hannah's friend and housekeeper, Miss Annie Carpenter. *(Photo courtesy of Brian Smith).*

Arthur and Hannah Harlock's drapery shop in Banbury. © *Images & Voices, Oxfordshire County Council.* Inset: Arthur Hanlock.

The Friends' School, Saffron Walden, where KS was a pupil from 1926 to the end of 1927. The school was to play an important part in his development as a naturalist. This photo shows the finish of the junior cross-country run. © *The Friends' School, Saffron Walden.*

Herbert Smith (on left in long shop coat) outside his general stores in West Mersea, Essex, circa 1926. The other, younger, man and a clear subordinate is Ron Thursby. *(Photo courtesy of Brian Smith).*

Bliss Tweed Mill, where Dorothy Soles worked. © *Absolute Touring Oxford*.

Left: His country calls: KS proudly shows off his RAF uniform, circa 1940. Right: Being posted to the desert had its compensations. This footstool-sized tortoise was among the many animals KS found there in 1945.

COLONIA ERITREA - Carro indigeno

A postcard KS brought back from Eritrea in 1945.

Left: Rather bravely forgoing the use of gloves to protect his hands from the bird's sharp talons, KS shows off a bird of prey at Whipsnade Zoo, where he had bagged a job after the war. Right: Wearing what is possibly his demob suit, KS poses with a fox at Whipsnade Zoo.

All Creatures Great… Whipsnade Zoo had been entrusted with some very rare (at the time) Pere David's deer, and KS had been entrusted with looking after them.

…and Small. To show Whipsnade Zoo was not concerned solely with big animals, KS is shown holding a pair of Golden hamsters. 'Would you mind holding that one closer to your face?' the photographer asked, with the unfortunate result that it looks like KS is sniffing the hamster, which wears a wonderfully surprised expression on its face. These Golden hamsters were very precious. In the 1940s the Golden hamster was almost unknown and still very rare in captivity. Today it is one of the most popular children's pets, numbering literally millions all over the world.

Left: KS with African helper, Cameroons expedition, 1949. Note the sticking plaster over tropical ulcer on Ken's leg. Right: Angwantibo from the forests of the Cameroons. © *Les Owen*.

P.M. 21

Name of Ship "COLUMBIA STAR". Date of Departure JANUARY 19ᵈ 50 Where Bound ~~BUENOS AIRES~~ TRINIDAD

Port of Departure **LONDON**   Steamship Line **BLUE STAR LINE**

NAMES AND DESCRIPTIONS OF **BRITISH** PASSENGERS EMBARKED AT THE PORT OF **LONDON**

(1) Contract Ticket Number	(2) NAMES OF PASSENGERS	(3) LAST ADDRESS IN THE UNITED KINGDOM	(4) CLASS	(5) Port at which Passenger have contracted to land	(6) Profession, Occupation or Calling of Passengers	(7) AGES OF PASSENGERS — Adults of 12 years and upwards — Accompanied by Husband or Wife — Males	Females	Not accompanied by Husband or Wife — Males	Females	Children between 1 and 12 — Males	Females	Infants — Males	Females	(8) Country of Last Permanent Residence — England	Wales	Scotland	Ireland	British Possessions	Foreign Countries	(9) Country of Intended Future Permanent Residence
242	1 AITKEN, William. K.	Hatching Vicarage, Barlow, Sussex.	First	TRINIDAD	AGENCY MANAGER	41									1						BRITISH GUIANA
249	2 CAMPBELL, Isabel. E.	c/o Mrs. James Palmer, 23, Richmond Rd, Horsham, Sussex	"	TRINIDAD	HOUSEWIFE		59												1	TRINIDAD
250	3 CRIGHTON, Barbara. M.	13, York Road, Woking, Surrey.	"	TRINIDAD	HOUSEWIFE		30								1					ENGLAND
250	4 CRIGHTON, Timothy. D.A.	-do- -do-	"	TRINIDAD	NONE					1					1					ENGLAND
246	5 DURRELL, Gerald. M.	52, St. Albans Avenue, Bournemouth. Hants.	"	TRINIDAD	ZOOLOGIST	24									1					ENGLAND
244	6 FRASER, William.	2, Knockles Biggar, Lanarkshire, Scotland.	"	TRINIDAD	ENGINEER	26											1			BRITISH GUIANA
243	7 GRANT, Ian.	30, Poole Hill, Bournemouth. Hants.	"	TRINIDAD	ENGINEER	47											1			BRITISH GUIANA
261	8 LYON, James. G.	"Maybank". RALIMO, Scotland.	"	TRINIDAD	OVERSEER	22									1					BRITISH GUIANA
253	9 McAULEY, Arthur.	35, Sunningdale Road, Portchester, Hants.	"	TRINIDAD	MARINE R/OFFICER	43														WEST INDIES
259	10 McGILL, Alexander.	Torregles Town Farm, Dumfries, Scotland.	"	TRINIDAD	MECHANIC	30											1			BRITISH GUIANA
248	11 McELHATTON, George.A.R.	North Woodlands, Welsh Road, Ledsham, Cheshire	"	TRINIDAD	SURVEYOR	27											1			BRITISH GUIANA
255	12 MONTGOMERY, Pembroke.J.	St. Christopher's College, Blackheath, S.E.3.	"	TRINIDAD	STUDENT	25														BARBADOS
254	13 POTTER, Frederick.S.	Ringles Cross Hotel, Uckfield, Sussex.	"	TRINIDAD	MANAGER	50											1			ST. LUCIA
254	14 POTTER, Daisy. M.	-do- -do-	"	TRINIDAD	HOUSEWIFE		49										1			ST. LUCIA
256	15 QUINN, Ambrose. A.	Kiltimagh, Co-Mayo, Ireland.	"	TRINIDAD	ENGINEER	27											1			TRINIDAD
247	16 SMITH, Kenneth. J.	52, St Albans Avenue, Bournemouth, Hants	"	TRINIDAD	ZOOLOGIST	38									1					ENGLAND
241	17 THENEN, Freda.	61, Elgin Crescent, W.11.	"	TRINIDAD	HAIRDRESSER		21								1					BRITISH GUIANA

Passenger list for the Blue Star Line ship, *Columbia Star*, bound for South America, January 1950, on which the names of Ken Smith and Gerald Durrell can be clearly seen. *(Courtesy of The National Archives, ref. BT27/1658)*

KS (on left) and Gerald Durrell (far right) with an eight-foot boa, British Guiana, 1950. The man in the middle is Robert Lowes, an inveterate artist who had gone to Guiana with the intention of painting the Amerindians but was cajoled into assisting Messrs Smith and Durrell with their animal-collecting aspirations. © *Estate of Gerald Durrell.*

Left: KS with a captured Bat falcon, British Guiana, 1950. Right: Ken was particularly interested in primates. A Spider monkey, British Guiana, 1950.

In the December issue of *The Avenue*, Ken and another boy were praised for the consistently high quality of their essays: 'A distinct improvement has been noted in the standard of the essays, those of G. Tawell and K. Smith being exceptionally good. K. Smith has interested us with his animal essays, introducing us to many of the inmates of the Zoological Gardens [of London].'

Ken was well-read, he was bright. Someone as intelligent and articulate as him could have been expected to become a prefect like Charles Kohler and Bessie McGowan, but I have seen a list of prefects dating from that time, and his name is not among them. It could be that he was never elevated to prefect status because he was not thought extrovert enough, or possibly he just didn't *want* the position.

He was lucky to have been a scholar at a school where individuality was embraced, seen as something to be nurtured, not smothered. His time at the school had made him a more confident, more independent, person, capable of almost anything, ready to make his mark on the world. Without this background it is quite possible he would never have done all the things that he eventually went on to accomplish.

Ken left the Friends' School on 22 December 1927, aged sixteen. He had been a student there for exactly two years, but now he had a living to earn. Rather curiously, he does not appear to have sought a career with animals immediately, but, apart from a brief diversion when he worked at a zoo in Oxfordshire, toiled away in unrelated spheres until he finally found his true metier after the war.

Chapter Three

Oxford Zoo and the Man from the Pru' *(1928–1939)*

AT FIRST IT MIGHT SEEM STRANGE that Ken should have left school so late, since the mandatory school-leaving age was not raised to sixteen until 1960, but once again the Friends' School was ahead of its time and as long ago as 1906 the School's Committee agreed that the school should cater for children up to the age of sixteen or seventeen to give them courses in preparation for higher examinations. 'It is generally desirable that they should remain until seventeen to take full advantage of the School Course,' trumpeted the school's official Prospectus. Some scholars did stay on to take the school Leaving Certificate exam and the London Matriculation exam. In 1927 eight students from the school passed Matriculation (three with honours) and three the School Certificate. However, Ken's name does not appear among them.

As 1928 dawned, Ken was contemplating his options. Opportunities for zoo work were severely limited, there being only a fraction of the animal collections around then that there are today. Since so many of the Smith family were, or had been, grocers, it would have surprised no-one if he had followed in what was clearly the family business, but, if he did, he did not do so for long. What is incontrovertible, however, is that his first course of action on leaving school would have been to go to see his parents Herbert and Gertrude, no longer resident in Harpenden but living near Colchester.

Approximately eighteen months earlier, in the second half of 1926, Herbert had given up the shop in Harpenden after only about six years to embark on yet another business venture, leaving his erstwhile partner, Arthur Harriden, in sole charge of the Harpenden store. Had he and Harriden had a falling out? Whatever the circumstances, Herbert and Gertrude transplanted to Mersea Island (pronounced 'Mer-zee') in the low-lying south-eastern corner of Essex, approximately nine miles south of Colchester. This remote island in the briny estuary at the confluence of the rivers Colne and Blackwater is divided into East and West Mersea. In West Mersea, Herbert took over the running of a general store from one W. Mynott. Only two of their children, Gil and Violet, accompanied their parents to Mersea Island. Ken was, in any case, in his first year at the Friends' School by then over on the other side of the county, and Ronald and Frank were staying with the ever-accommodating Hannah and Arthur Harlock in Charlbury.

Herbert's new shop, opposite the entrance to the school in Barfield Road, West Mersea, was provided for him by the family, an extravagant gift indeed for someone with a profound lack of success in business. Mersea was a strange and remote choice of destination even for the nomadic Smiths, being on the very edge of England, and one is led to wonder why, after floating round Oxfordshire and Hertfordshire for so long, they should suddenly strike eastwards. As a location for a shop, it could hardly be said to be strategically placed. Only four-and-a-half miles long by two miles wide, this tiny island – the most easterly inhabited island of Britain – is connected to the mainland, like an umbilical cord, by a single half-mile-long Anglo-Saxon causeway called The Strood (pronounced 'Strode'). In times of high tides, the fabled Strood is covered with seawater and becomes impassable for about an hour. It is said that occasionally you can still hear the cries of drowning sailors as you cross the causeway – but it could be the howl of the wind. When Herbert, Gertrude and two of their children moved here, it must have been like moving to the end of the world. The island was still almost completely unknown to outsiders, had few amenities and a resident population of only 2,200. (Things *were* soon to change, however, and from about this period onwards it started to be marketed as a handy seaside destination to the people of Colchester, and suddenly beach huts and other traditional seaside accoutrements began to pop up, but the main industries remained fishing and boat-building.)

Why did the Smiths choose West Mersea, of all unlikely places? Their motives for leaving Harpenden and moving eighty miles away to the extreme east of England seem baffling. If Herbert was so keen to leave Harpenden and set up business on his own, why did he not simply find a shop nearer his home patch, where trade wouldn't be dependent on the ebb and flow of the tides? The obvious inference is that he was running away from creditors, but this theory does not stand up to scrutiny because on 11 September, soon after moving to Mersea, he formally applied for a Certificate of Removal from the Society of Friends' Luton and Leighton Monthly Meeting, of which he had been an active member for six years, in order to join the Colchester Monthly Meeting now that he was resident in Essex. This is not the action of a man seeking to disappear without a trace. Just over a month later it was announced he had been accepted into the Colchester Friends. His grandson, Brian Smith, is equally perplexed as to his grandfather's motives for choosing West Mersea, as he explained to me:

> I had thought that West Mersea was a bit of a jump, but I had looked at it through modern eyes and never realised how much more isolated it would have been in the early 1900s. Either Herbert wanted to restart his life after his previous business failures – an overwhelming need to get away from it all – or maybe there was a positive reason for moving there. Most likely there was already a family member there, though not as far as I am aware, or a fellow Quaker or simply a good friend. I know that Frank was subject to asthma when he was young, and sea-air is – and was – reputed to be beneficial, but I think Frank stayed in Charlbury and didn't move with his parents to Mersea.

Another reason why it is fairly unlikely the move was prompted by a need to escape from creditors is that his former shop in Harpenden continued to operate – very successfully – with his former partner, Arthur Harriden, at the helm. If Herbert *had* run up big bills on the shop that he was unable to pay, wouldn't Harriden have been jointly responsible for their repayment? Any creditors would simply have gone round to see *him*. But the shop did not founder, or even stall, but forged on ahead through boom times and economic depression. After Herbert decamped from the scene in 1926, his former shop in Harpenden went on to enjoy a long and prosperous life. The lettering above the shop window was immediately changed from 'Smith & Harriden' to 'A.J. Harriden, groceries and provisions'. Despite competition in the form of another grocer's shop only two doors away at number 9, the little shop flourished. Arthur Harriden ran it successfully for many years, after which it continued under the auspices of a succession of proprietors, but always it remained a general grocery and delicatessen under the name 'Harriden's Stores'. It survived the Great Depression of the 1930s, a world war, and post-war austerity. It finally closed down on 21 July 1975, fifty-five years after Herbert Smith and Arthur Harriden had taken it on. It is now Perry's, the florists. The coffee grinding machine that was once such a notable feature in the window is, of course, long gone and the frontispiece is now bedecked with flowers but, as I discovered when I visited the shop, in all other respects the façade has changed remarkably little in the interim. As I stepped through the door, I could almost imagine Herbert Smith standing behind the counter, looking up from his ledger and asking how he might be of assistance.

It is a cruel irony that the shop which Herbert had walked away from turned out to be the most successful and longest lived of all his business ventures. Another business, another wrong decision. Perhaps he didn't see it that way, because in his new shop in West Mersea he was his own man once more and free to run the business exactly as he wanted. If he did have any regret about leaving the shop in Harpenden, he didn't show it. Outwardly at least, he presented a confident figure. I have seen a photo of Herbert taken just after he moved into his new shop in West Mersea. It shows a proud man, dressed in a long white shop-coat, standing outside the shop, the characters 'H. SMITH' in big prominent lettering above the door (more prominent, in fact, than the name of the shop – 'Central Stores').

For Herbert, the move represented a final throw of the dice, though he probably didn't know it at the time. This was to prove to be the last of his many moves. As the 1920s drew to their close, his health was giving cause for concern. Not long after moving to Mersea, Herbert became chronically ill and by 1929 had been admitted to a Colchester hospital, where he remained for the rest of his life, and Gertrude took over the running of the shop. Herbert's illness leads me to wonder whether Ken, in fact, was forced to leave the Friends' School slightly earlier than expected to assist in the Mersea shop following his father's incapacitation. Usually a full term's notice, or the equivalent in weeks, was required before a child could be withdrawn early from the school, but, of course, Gertrude may have given the statutory amount of notice. If true, this would explain why I can find no record of Ken having sat any exams in 1927, the year he left school, and why he never went on to do higher exams like the School Leaving Certificate or the London Matriculation exam.

In any case, by 1929 it was Gertrude, not Herbert, who was named in trade directories as the proprietor of Central Stores. That year she placed an advertisement in the Official Guide to West Mersea, an advert which re-appeared in the guide every year up to about 1933. Once again, there was no mention of Herbert. He was languishing in a hospital ward and the strain on Gertrude, trying to run the shop and maintaining an upbeat attitude towards her customers whilst worrying about her husband, must have been considerable.

For QUALITY and PRICE go to—

THE CENTRAL STORES
(*Opposite Schools*)
WEST MERSEA

Danish Bacon	Noted for the
a	BEST
Speciality	Aylesbury Butter

All Orders receive Prompt Attention from
MRS. G. E. SMITH

Gertrude never did like her birth name, and yet she made no attempt to change it. She could, of course, have chosen to reverse her first and second names, as her daughter Violet Kathleen and her mother Mary Elizabeth (both of whom preferred to be known by their middle name) tended to do, but Gertrude elected not to do so. (Gil's wife, Melissa, whom he married in 1939, addressed her as Janet – a name she was much happier with – and possibly some other family members did, too.) Meanwhile, at some point, Ken had moved in with Hannah and Arthur Harlock at their cottage at The Lawn, Market Street, Charlbury. It is impossible to say exactly when this was, but he was certainly there by 1931 and possibly moved there shortly after leaving Saffron Walden. Hannah was a kindly old lady and a staunch Quaker, with whom all the Smith children clearly got on very well. Not only did Ken take up residence there, but so too – at various times – did his three brothers, though not all at the same moment. According to Quaker registers, Ronald and Ken were living there in 1933, Ronald and Frank in 1935 (Ken having moved to Burford by then), and Frank and Gil in 1937. The only one of Herbert and Gertrude's children for whom I can find no evidence of having lived with aunt Hannah in Charlbury is Violet. This is not to say she didn't, of course, but when she returned from West Mersea, according to Quaker registers, she took up residence in Lee Place on the outskirts of Charlbury.

So far, animals do not seem to have figured large in Ken Smith's life. Living in Oxfordshire, his nearest zoo was at Kidlington, five miles north of Oxford. The Oxford Zoological Gardens was a brand new zoo, so new in fact that the paint on the animal houses was barely dry. Opened in July 1931 (the same year as the zoos at Chester, Chessington and Whipsnade), this short-lived (it lasted less than six years) and now almost completely forgotten menagerie was situated at Gosford Hill along the Banbury Road where the Thames Valley Police headquarters are now to be found. In an editorial on 4 July, the day after the zoo was declared open, *The Times* predicted great things for it: 'All good lovers of animals will be glad for the lucky inmates of a modern zoological garden, and glad also for the human beings who will be able to study them more or less in their natural condition.'

Oxford Zoo was no hastily pitched menagerie, but a major animal collection owned by the recently inaugurated Oxford Zoological and Horticultural Association Ltd. In charge of it were no fewer than seven directors, a superfluity that is so often a recipe for dissent and disaster. In an advertisement in August 1932 the *Oxford Monthly* enjoined its readers to 'Visit Oxford's Zoo!' (Admission 6d, Children 3d). Ken must have been thrilled when a major zoo like this set up shop, so to speak, just a few miles from where he lived, and he probably paid his first visit there not long after it opened. Getting there presented no problem. For a shilling, he could have bought a combined bus and admission ticket from Castle Street, Oxford.

Ken now took his first tentative steps towards his future career. He applied for – and got – a job working at the zoo, though when or for how long he worked there is unclear, but the fact remains that Oxford Zoo seems to have been his first professional involvement with animals. For a very long time, I had thought it peculiar, given his enthusiasm for animals and the proximity of Oxford Zoo, that he had not worked there, so it came as no surprise – something of a relief, in fact – when I discovered he *had* worked there. The first clue I had was when I found an Oxford Zoo postcard (depicting an Arabian camel and its keeper) in amongst a collection of Ken's photos. Postcards from this zoo are quite rare. By itself a lone postcard didn't prove anything: he could have bought it as a souvenir of a day spent at the zoo. But why keep it for so long? Further investigation showed that he had indeed worked there as a young man, but not for very long. But when was this? I believe he must have started work at Oxford Zoo in either 1931 or 1932. It is very unlikely it was any later than that because, by 1933, he was working for an electrical company and only a few short years after that the zoo closed down. In his book, *Where the Leopard Lazed*, Clinton Keeling reproduces a grainy black-and-white photo of a very rare Iberian wolf by the name of Bobby, which he purports to have been taken by Ken Smith at the Oxford Zoological Gardens in 1936 shortly before the zoo was disbanded, though he does not say whether Ken took the photo while he was working at the zoo (indeed, Clinton might not even have known that Ken was once employed there) or during a visit to the zoo. Unless the date is wrong, it is hard to see how Ken could have been a keeper there at the time he took the photo. Most likely he took it while on a day out at the zoo. In January 1937, Oxford Zoo hit the headlines when three wolves contrived to escape. Two of them were shot dead almost immediately by a rapidly formed posse of sharp-shooters, as was an innocent German Shepherd dog, mistaken for an absconding wolf by one of the hunters.

Open six and a half days a week (on Sundays it didn't open until half past two in the afternoon), Oxford Zoo was a traditional mixed collection with many of the most popular animal groups represented: animals such as the wolves and camels already mentioned, bison, deer (including the white variety of Red deer and the now-almost-extinct Persian Fallow deer), bears, big cats, a wonderful collection of Old World monkeys, and an elephant called Rosie, but no apes of any kind, not even gibbons. An apologetic note in the zoo's guide book explained that gorillas, orang-utans, chimpanzees and gibbons were 'difficult to maintain in the English climate and are at present unrepresented in the Gardens.' Another animal domiciled at the zoo was a formidable Alligator Snapping turtle. This impressive reptile was destined to be sent to the Manchester Zoo (Belle Vue) when the Oxford Zoo closed down. Many years later, Ken was to renew his acquaintance with it when he worked at Belle Vue in the early 1950s.

Oxford Zoo closed its gates for the last time in 1937 and its animal collection was dispersed. The bulk of the collection formed the nucleus of the new zoo at Dudley, which opened that year, so in a sense Oxford Zoo didn't disappear; it just relocated. Thirty-three years were to pass before another zoo (apart from the occasional small and insignificant bird garden) would open in the county.

Today the Oxford Zoo has disappeared into obscurity and few people are aware that a zoo ever existed at Gosford Hill, but this long-forgotten place should be commemorated for giving Ken Smith his first taste, as far as anyone can tell, of what eventually would be his life's work.

For some reason, Ken did not remain there long and by the hot, cloudless summer of 1933 he was working as an electrical wireman for a branch of the Wessex Electricity Supply Company located in Sheep Street, Charlbury, run by a Mr L.A. Pitt. We can't know the reasons why Ken left Oxford Zoo so soon. Perhaps that perennial bugbear – low wages – was a factor. A job as an electrician may not have been his preferred choice of career, but it *paid* rather better and had the added advantage that the company was only a few minutes' walk from his home at that time, being quite literally in the next street from Arthur and Hannah Harlock's cottage. It might seem extraordinary that for someone destined to become a prominent zoologist, as a young man Ken Smith should have gravitated towards a career as an electrician, but one must remember this was the Great Depression, when jobs of any description were harder to come by and he could not afford to be choosy.

1933 was a calamitous year. In Germany, Hitler's National Socialist Party was swept to power on a wave of nationalistic support, the first Nazi concentration camp opened, and Japan seceded from the League of Nations, quickly followed by Germany. For the Smith family, the year brought great personal sadness as well. On Tuesday 18 July, Herbert Smith died in hospital of a cerebral thrombosis (a type of stroke) and cardiovascular degeneration. According to his death certificate, he was just sixty-two. There is a slight inconsistency here because if his date of birth – 8 August 1872 – is correct, that would make him sixty-one, not sixty-two, at the time of his death. But he was *almost* sixty-two, all but three weeks, and doubtless the registrar felt justified in rounding up. Ken's brother Ronald (who now worked for a builder in Great Tew) was the informant. According to Herbert's death certificate, Ronald was living in Banbury at that time, which is inconsistent with Quaker records that appear to show that he, like Ken, was staying with the Harlocks in Charlbury.

Just two days after his father died, Ken had his twenty-second birthday, which must have been a muted affair in the circumstances. Not very long after Herbert's death, the grieving Gertrude, now embarking on forty years of widowhood, had given up the shop in West Mersea and returned to Oxfordshire where she moved in with Ronald in Banbury. The shop she left behind, Central Stores, went on to enjoy a long life under new ownership. It was run for many years by the Whiting family who eventually sold it to the Co-op to extend the supermarket. Looking at West Mersea Co-op today, it is hard to tell whether any of the building is original, but frankly I doubt it; it was probably all demolished when the supermarket was enlarged.

Herbert had tried so hard and for so long to be a success, but time and again his efforts had been dogged by bad luck, or bad judgement, or poor business acumen, and sometimes all three. But there is another, less overt, explanation that, if true, absolves him. It propounds that Herbert's lack of success in business could have been inherited from his maternal grandfather, John Gillett, and therefore he was always doomed to fail no matter what he did. The Gilletts were, as mentioned earlier, a wealthy banking family. But there is a black sheep in every family, and the prodigal in the Gillett family was Marianna Gillett's father, John Gillett (1801–1868), a manufacturer of 'agricultural implements and engines'. To describe him as a 'black sheep' is perhaps rather unfair because he had been essentially well-intentioned, but luckless. John Gillett was an inventor who had cost the Gilletts a fortune filing patents for, among other things, an improved plough, a hayrick ventilator, two types of 'Guillotine Chaff-cutting Machines' (one horse-powered, the other hand-powered) and a self-acting Alarum Gun – the latter advertised as an 'Improved Apparatus for Protecting Property'. John Gillett had been the eternal optimist, perpetually confident that his next invention would be the one that finally struck the jackpot, but his confidence had turned out to be misplaced every time, and each new gadget he devised had served only to push him further into debt. If a faculty for making ill-judged business decisions *can* be found in the genes, Herbert had inherited them from John Gillett.

*

In about 1935 Ken moved to the High Street, Burford, some fifteen miles from Charlbury. He now took a job as an insurance agent for the Prudential, and in this halcyon pre-war time he zipped round the Cotswolds on his bicycle, collecting customers' premiums. Trudy Smith told me she thought that Ken (together with his mother) possibly lived for a while in either Upper or Lower Slaughter around this time. Although it is hard to see exactly when this might have been, a quick look at the map shows it is entirely credible. The twin Slaughters lie next to each other just over the county border in Gloucestershire, only about twelve miles from Burford and eighteen miles from Charlbury, but, if he did live in either of the Slaughters, he did not live there long.

Ken was still registered as an insurance agent as late as 1939. There is an anomaly here, though, because when he enlisted in the RAF in 1940 he gave, as his civil occupation, 'electrical wireman'. So he was still an electrician! It is, of course, quite possible that Ken, recognising the RAF would have no use for an insurance salesman whereas an experienced electrician was a different matter entirely, simply gave his former occupation rather than his current one, but a much more likely explanation for the apparent contradiction is that he performed the two jobs simultaneously, weaving the insurance work (which was probably part-time) around his main occupation as an electrician. His nephew, Brian Smith, agrees that the insurance job sounded like it was just a sideline to earn some extra money.

'I wouldn't be at all surprised if Ken was doing two jobs at the same time,' Brian told me. 'Thinking back, my father [Ronald] was also an agent for an insurance company, though that was a lot later. I think *that* was the Prudential. It was all very casual. As far as I know, it didn't involve any work if Dad didn't want to – just ten per cent commission if he sold a policy, and it was probably no different for Ken.'

That decade saw Ken becoming increasingly involved with the Society of Friends and he regularly attended the Witney Monthly Meeting. But that is not to say he didn't occasionally allow his membership to lapse. The Quaker registers, whilst not complete, show he was a full member of the Society in 1933, 1940 and 1944, but only an attendant (non-member) at meetings in 1931, 1939 and 1941. As the 1930s marched on, he became ever more active within the Society as a note in the minutes for the Charlbury Preparative Meeting of 6 February 1938 (when Ken was still only twenty-six) proves: 'We appoint Kenneth J. Smith to audit the Treasurer's accounts for 1937,' it read. He clearly did a good job because in the minutes of the next Meeting, exactly a month later, it was reported that 'Kenneth J. Smith has audited and found correct the Treasurer's accounts for 1937.'

In later life, Ken was quite taciturn about his early years, rarely talking about this obscure period of his life even to his family, but he clearly enjoyed being an insurance agent because this was one thing he did occasionally venture to talk about – at least to his close family if not to his wider circle of friends and relatives. It was an undemanding job, unlike his more tightly scheduled work as an electrician. When out on his rounds in the glorious Cotswold countryside he had no authority figure scrutinising his work, no disapproving boss leering over his shoulder. He revelled in the sense of freedom, freewheeling on the downhill bits. He was at one with nature in all its boundless glory. But those halcyon days were not to last. Like everyone else, increasingly his thinking was focused on the approaching thunder. Being Quakers, the Smiths did not believe in direct confrontation and followed the sabre-rattling developments in Germany and the Far East with rising consternation. In the mid 1930s he and Ronald were clearly pacifists. Ronald was appointed Peace Correspondent for his local Quaker Meeting and his first suggestion was for some disarmament posters to be obtained from the Friends' Peace Committee, which he and Ken, with all the idealism of youth undimmed by time or cynicism, volunteered to display at strategic locations. At the next Meeting, Ronald reported that he and his brother had put up some disarmament posters and were hoping to place more.

While Ken and Ronald were doing what they could, the Society of Friends discussed the worsening political situation. With Germany embarking on a massive rearmament programme in blatant violation of the Treaty of Versailles, it was obvious to most people where things were heading. The executive committee sent letters to both Britain's Prime Minister, Ramsay MacDonald, and the President of the United States, Herbert Hoover, calling on them to demilitarize and not be provoked into embarking on an arms race that could propel the world into the abyss. The Society argued that rearmament had been a significant cause of the Great War; therefore it followed that the simplest way to avert a repeat of that monumental folly was to disarm. In 1936 the Society of Friends sent letters to all members of Parliament, protesting against proposals for an increase of armaments. Such action, it insisted, would be regarded by other nations as an example to be followed and would serve no purpose other than to intensify the stockpiling of armaments already in progress in other countries.

That same year Nazi Germany reoccupied the Rhineland.

The descent into war was gathering momentum and it would take more than a few disarmament posters to stop this runaway cart now. In September 1939, German troops invaded Poland in an unprovoked assault, and Britain found itself at war again. Fathers who had fought in the last conflagration now faced the harrowing prospect of seeing their own sons whisked off to battle.

For Quakers like Ken, it presented an awful dilemma.

Chapter Four

To Aden with the RAF *(1940–1946)*

BY THE SUMMER OF 1940, Ken was living back in Charlbury again with his aunt Hannah (Arthur Harlock having died in 1937). As a young able-bodied man, he could have expected to be conscripted into the armed forces, but Ken didn't wait for his call-up papers to arrive. A year after war was declared, he volunteered – *volunteered*, mark you – for service in the Royal Air Force. It was not a decision he would have taken lightly. His astonishing volte-face did not go down well with his family who judged his decision to be tantamount to a betrayal of Quakerism, for one of the pillars of the faith was its advocacy of passivism. The Society of Friends was very clear on this point. In an official proclamation it declared, 'We utterly deny all outward wars and strifes [*sic*].' A letter in the Minutes of the Luton and Leighton Monthly Meeting went even further, leaving one in no doubt that the Society as a whole took a very dim view of any of its members supporting aggressive action on either side: 'We believe that our peace testimony is not only one of our most ancient testimonies but that it is also a vital thing in the life of the Society and that any weakening of it is a weakening of the structure on which the Society stands.' Strongly-worded stuff indeed – although the Society did reluctantly accept that, faced with the threat of totalitarianism, 'There are a number of *individual* Friends who have found it difficult to act on the absolute pacifist position.'

Ken was just one Quaker among many who were wrestling with their conscience as the war began. Unlike the First World War, this time around it looked like innocent civilians on both sides would bear the brunt of the suffering. Apart from the fact he must have agonised long and hard before finally volunteering for service in the RAF, one must ask why he waited a full year after war had been declared before enlisting. Perhaps his delay had something to do with the so-called 'Phoney War', a strange calm of eight months' duration following the declaration of war in September 1939 during which neither side committed to launching a significant attack and there was relatively little fighting on the ground. As the days and weeks slipped into months and still the expected invasion failed to materialise, people began to be drawn into a false sense of security. The hope that maybe things were not going to be as bad as everybody had feared was suddenly blown away on May 10 when German troops marched into Belgium, France, Luxembourg and Holland, and the Phoney War was over.

Only a few years earlier, Ken, with his brother Ronald, had been putting up disarmament posters; now he was signing on the dotted line to join one of His Majesty's armed forces. What had happened to cause him to make such a radical change of direction and compromise his earlier pacifist principles, much to his family's disapproval? The answer may be nothing more than the passing of time. One needs only to look at the Flower Power generation of the 1960s to realise how quickly people can abandon principles they once held dear in the first flush of youth. The hippies who got high on drugs at Woodstock, championed free love and campaigned to Ban the Bomb, eventually embraced conventionality, settled down, married, saddled themselves with mortgages, had 2point4 children, and not infrequently ended up as stockbrokers and accountants.

It was not completely different for Ken. He was showing signs that he had lost some of his original idealism (though in every other respect he seems to have remained a committed Quaker). Outwardly his passivism was waning. But there was another reason why he was prepared to forsake his original ideals at the risk of provoking his family's ire. When, in about 1933, he had offered to help put up those disarmament posters, war was still avoidable. Now it was a brutal reality and in 1940 the stakes could not have been higher. England was fighting for its very survival. In June, its nearest neighbour, France, capitulated and in the same month the Nazis overran the Channel Islands, condemning their inhabitants to five years of harsh subjugation. With France and the Channel Islands having fallen, the enemy was kicking at the door. Throughout that long hot summer of 1940, everyone waited anxiously, convinced that a German invasion of mainland Britain was imminent. But before he was prepared to launch an invasion force, Hitler demanded that his Luftwaffe should have supremacy of the air, and so began the Battle of Britain with hundreds of separate aerial engagements taking place over the counties and cornfields of southern England. The Luftwaffe's failure to beat the Royal Air Force resulted in Hitler postponing the invasion indefinitely, but it had been a near thing and one can understand how Ken Smith, listening with rapt attention to the news reports on the wireless or watching Pathe News film reels at the cinema, might have been stirred by a sense of nationalism, despite his earlier passivism, to want to do something to ensure his country did not suffer the same fate as all the others that now trembled beneath the Swastika.

Or perhaps his motive was an altogether more personal one. By the middle of the war, Gertrude was living in Parkstone, a rather exclusive borough of Poole. Was she already there by 1940? If so, being on the south coast of England, and, moreover, very close to such obvious naval targets for Hitler's bombers as Portsmouth and Southampton, she would have found herself in a very vulnerable part of the country indeed. It is easy to understand Ken wanting to get back at the German war machine for the nightly blitzkrieg that was placing his beloved mother in such grave peril, in apparent contradiction of his earlier passivist ideals, and perhaps it was *this* that finally galvanised him into doing something.

The RAF normally refuses to allow anyone to see the records of Second World War service men – the records still being classified as private – the only exceptions being the person to whom the record relates, if he or she is still living, or their next of kin if deceased. I was very fortunate, therefore, to obtain a copy of Ken's service record, from which I learnt that Kenneth John Smith enlisted with the Royal Air Force as AC2 Smith – a second class aircraftman (a rank that author Graham Lord called 'the lowest form of human life in the Royal Air Force'), Serial No. 1189128 – on 8 September 1940, at RAF Cardington.

The huge sprawling RAF station at Cardington, about three miles southeast of Bedford, became famous as the place where the early airships including the R-100 and the R-101 were built, and the enormous twin pair of airship hangers, each 157-foot-high, dominated the landscape, as they continue to do to this day. During the war, the base at Cardington was a station for training balloon operators, as well as the place, within those vast, cavern-like airship hangers, where barrage balloons were made, tested and repaired, but it also operated as a major enrolment and demob centre for the air force. It was here that new recruits were marshalled for processing. I have found a national serviceman's description of what RAF Cardington looked like in the mid 1950s and there is no reason to believe it was any different in Ken Smith's day: sleeping accommodation consisted of long green wooden huts with polished brown linoleum flooring, each containing about twenty or more iron beds, separated by narrow wardrobes and lockers, arranged along the walls.

For Ken and the other new recruits, the first few days at Cardington were a maelstrom of dehumanising activity. There were forms to be filled in, interviews to attend, aptitude tests to pass, physical examinations to be endured, hair to be shorn, and uniforms and equipment to be collected. Ken was to be denied the chance to get to grips with the enemy, which probably came as a great relief to him. On his service record, in big letters, are the words: 'Not Recommended for Training as Aircrew'. Why? Possibly it took into account the fact that, when asked about his religion, he answered Quaker. The RAF respected people's religious beliefs. It realised that certain principles of Quakerism conflicted with those of the air force – although plenty of Quakers did see action in World War II. The British military was by now much more tolerant and understanding of pacifists (unlike in the First World War when 279 Quakers in Britain had been imprisoned for refusing military service). One was still required to serve one's king and country, but often it could be done in some ancillary capacity that didn't involve direct combat. The RAF was so short of aircraft, and had many more volunteers than it could ever send into the air, that it could afford to be choosy. His RAF inquisitors would no doubt have been very interested to learn that his civil occupation was an electrician; they could certainly find work for a skilled tradesman. Someone with skills like that was too valuable to risk putting in the cockpit of an aeroplane, probably to get shot down. He was much more useful to them in a non-active, support role. A rather more prosaic explanation is that he may have been just too short to be considered for aircrew. His service record shows that he was just 5 feet 6½ inches in height, distinctly on the small side for a man. Strangely, the passport issued to him in 1948 gives his height as 5 feet 8 inches, a full inch and a half taller, but I'm inclined to believe the RAF record is the more accurate because of course his height would have been precisely measured at his medical, whereas for a passport one supplies the details oneself and with such details as height there is always a tendency to approximate.

So which of these conjectures is correct? I put my assumptions to the Imperial War Museum (Duxford). Was his low stature a factor barring him from consideration, or was it due to his being a Quaker that excused him from being selected, or the fact that, as an electrician, he possessed a useful skill?

'Two of your theories as to why Smith was not recommended for training as aircrew when he joined the RAF are eminently sensible,' Peter Murton, the Museum's Research and Information Officer, told me.

You can discount the matter of his short height, which was actually quite common during the 1940s. It would in fact have been an advantage if he had been selected to train, for example as an Air Gunner, when he would have been required to occupy the restricted space of a gun turret while wearing full, bulky, flying fatigues.

The fact that he was a Quaker is a definite factor. I am rather surprised that he did not, apparently, register as a conscientious objector. If you hadn't told me he had volunteered for the service, I would have presumed he must have been conscripted. I guess he made clear at his Selection Board that he could not – given his religious beliefs and passivism – morally serve as an active combatant, but would be willing to serve in a support role.

The fact that he was already a qualified electrician is, however, the most telling point. The RAF was very keen to recruit qualified and experienced engineers, mechanics, electricians and other types of technicians. This was because they required comparatively short training courses on particular aircraft, aero-engines, instruments and weapons, and so on, so could quickly be posted to the squadrons and stations where they were much needed.

There were, as a point of interest, thousands of cases during the Second World War when such peacetime trained and skilled recruits – both officers and airmen – were denied their first choice of pilot or other aircrew training, simply because they were much more useful to the RAF in their appropriate ground support technical trades.

The timing of Ken's entry into the air force could not have been more infelicitous. At the time he was courting a young woman by the name of Dorothy Eileen Soles (occasionally 'Sole' – the spelling of the surname varies) who worked in the local cloth mill, and on 5 October, less than a month after he joined the RAF, he must have been given some compassionate leave because he and Dorothy were married at the Chipping Norton Registry Office. They must have been hoping he wouldn't receive notification of his enrolment into the air force until after their marriage, but things did not turn out as intended. It seems odd that he and Dorothy didn't just move the date of their wedding forward. One look at the marriage certificate provides a possible answer. Dorothy's age at the time of their wedding is given as eighteen. Ken, at twenty-nine, was a fair bit older. Possibly the reason they did not move the date of their wedding forward by a few weeks was because they were waiting for Dorothy to turn eighteen, as it probably looked more respectable for him to be marrying an 18-year-old rather than a 17-year-old (in fact Dorothy was born on 18 October 1922, making her thirteen days shy of her eighteenth birthday when they married, but, with Ken stationed in Bedfordshire and due to be posted onto another camp at any moment, probably with little or no warning, the couple couldn't afford to delay any longer).

Dorothy was tall, elegant and extrovert, and lived in the small Oxfordshire village of Great Rollright with her mother, Winifred Lily Soles (her father, boot-repairer Thomas Soles, being deceased). Dorothy worked at Bliss & Sons, a tweed mill just outside Chipping Norton. The Bliss Tweed Mill – an imposing structure which was decommissioned as comparatively recently as the early 1980s after more than a century producing cloth coats that were so sturdy they were said to last a lifetime – was a major employer in the area, and Dorothy was one of several girls from Great Rollright who caught the early train to Chipping Norton every day to work in the mill. Designed to give the appearance of a magnificent country house but with an incongruous Tuscan factory chimney towering above it that has been likened, not inaccurately, to a gigantic toilet plunger, the mill survives as a distinctive landmark to this day, now converted into a residential block of thirty-four apartments. Dorothy was employed as a 'specker', and a more tedious job is hard to imagine. A 'specker' was a term given to a person using a very fine needle to remove odd bits of fibre and other imperfections from the finished cloth. She and her fellow speckers must have heaved a huge sigh of relief when the bell sounded to mark the end of the working day.

Dorothy and her mother lived at Ivy Cottage, and this became Ken's home too after he and Dorothy were married, not that he would have been able to spend much time there, except occasionally when he was due some leave from the air force. They planned to live there until such time as they could afford a home of their own. In fact, Ivy Cottage was one of a short row of identical dwellings that all went by the rather twee name of Ivy Cottages. It is hard to say whether the outward appearance of these cottages matched the cosy, biscuit-tin-lid, image invoked by the name because these extremely small, some might even say pokey, cottages were demolished many years ago and all that is left of them today is a barn that once stood at the end of the row. With Ken in the air force for the next five years, the couple could not have seen a great deal of each other and his visits home could only have been fleeting at best. However, both of them attended meetings of the Society of Friends whenever they could. Dorothy was never a full member, but she does appear in the Quaker registers as an attendee, probably having been encouraged to go by her husband.

With most airstrikes being directed against London, the South Coast and the industrial heartlands of the Midlands and the North East, Ken might have thought that Dorothy, at home in sleepy, harmless Great Rollright, was relatively safe from the German bombers, but he was soon to be disabused of that notion, for on the night of 24 October 1940, just nineteen days after their marriage, three bombs fell on the village, jettisoned by a bomber returning from a raid on a town in the Midlands. By a stroke of good fortune, the bombs fell in fields, causing no damage and there were no casualties.

*

Gradually adjusting to life in the RAF, Ken found himself engaged as an electrical engineer, Grade II. The wiring on an aircraft being rather different from the domestic wiring he was used to, he was placed on several training courses and sat a number of exams, his results ranging from a more than respectable 82.4 per cent to a disappointing

29 per cent. Ken left RAF Cardington in May 1941 and for most of the rest of the war he was stationed at Weston Zoyland, an airfield four miles southeast of Bridgwater in Somerset. The airfield (which closed in 1969) became a permanent RAF base as late as September 1940 (before then, it was in use only during the summer months). When Ken arrived there for the first time in the late Spring of 1941, it was still little more than pastureland with only the most rudimentary grass runways (concrete runways were finally laid there in 1943) and a few buildings, mostly Nissen huts of various sizes, randomly situated around the site as if scattered from a giant salt shaker. At its peak it provided accommodation for 1,530 personnel from both the Royal Air Force and the United States Army Air Forces. Although based at Weston Zoyland, Ken was occasionally sent elsewhere for short periods, possibly for more training, possibly in response to calls for assistance. From 18 January 1942 he spent a week at a firm known as Rotax Ltd., which I have been told was 'something' to do with aircraft, returning to Weston Zoyland on the 25th. It has not been possible to find out more about Rotax, as there were several companies trading under that name. It is unclear whether he was sent there for further training or, as a qualified electrician, to fix a specific problem the company was having with its electrics. In September he was dispatched to Bristol for a few days.

Ken was a conscientious serviceman and in November 1943 his punctiliousness was rewarded with a good conduct badge. Only once, not long after he joined the RAF, was he guilty of misconduct, but, whatever his offence was, it must have been quite a minor infringement because his punishment was quite mild, consisting of the forfeiture of 'one day' (the loss of a day off, presumably). Having started his RAF career as a humble AC2, he was promoted in October 1941 to AC1 status and, in January 1942, to Leading Aircraftman (LAC), entitled to wear the badge of a horizontal two-bladed propeller.

Whenever he could, Ken took the opportunity to explore the county and take in the sights. The postcard he sent to Dorothy from the historic Somerset town of Glastonbury on 23 April or 23 August 1943 (half the postmark is missing so I can't be sure of the month, except the initial letter was an 'A') shows that, at this stage, his feelings towards his first wife hadn't dimmed:

> Darling,
>   Having a look at Glastonbury, but it is raining a good deal so I will probably go to the pictures.
>   Love
>   Ken
>   x x x x x x

What film might he have gone to see? Despite the war, or possibly because of it, 1943 was a good year for the cinema with the release of a clutch of films that have since assumed cult status. Perhaps he was attracted by the wartime classic *For Whom the Bell Tolls*, starring Gary Cooper and Ingrid Bergman. Or did he succumb to the lure and rousing patriotism of *Victory Through Air Power* or *We Dive at Dawn*, with John Mills in the lead role. Maybe he favoured thrills of an entirely different kind courtesy of *Son of Dracula*, or *Phantom of the Opera* starring Claude Rains. *The Ape Man* would have appealed to his interest in natural history more than *Lassie Come Home*, also doing the rounds in cinemas that year. If he was looking for something more cerebral, the Alfred Hitchcock thriller, *Shadow of a Doubt,* would have fitted the bill. Or perhaps he preferred something light-weight to take his mind off all the doom and gloom in the news, such as the Abbott and Costello comedy *It Ain't Hay*, or Will Hay larking about in *My Learned Friend*.

This apparently insignificant postcard, containing, as it does, just one terse sentence, is an important find because of what it tells us about Dorothy's movements. It was addressed not, as one might expect, to Ivy Cottage in Great Rollright, but to Dorothy Smith at 'Wychwood', Harbour View Close, Parkstone in Dorset. Named after a forest in Oxfordshire, this was Ronald's house and also the place where Gertrude was living by now. It shows that by the middle of the war Dorothy was no longer living in Great Rollright but had taken up temporary residence on the south coast with her mother-in-law. The lively, outgoing Dorothy would have found the relative isolation of her sleepy home village quite stifling. Parkstone, on the other hand, offered rather more stimulation for the gregarious Dorothy. But even more important than that, however, was the fact that Ken, at Weston Zoyland, was stationed little more than sixty miles away, and they could now see each other more frequently than would have been possible had she chosen to remain in Oxfordshire. Without any doubt, this was the main reason for the move. But there is another reason. The Luftwaffe was still bombarding the south coast of England, and Gertrude was doubtless very grateful for Dorothy's reassuring presence at this worrying time.

*

Towards the end of November 1944, with the war in Europe drawing to its protracted, chaotic and bloody conclusion, Ken might have expected a swift return to civvy street, but the RAF was not finished with him yet. He was sent to a Personnel Despatch Centre, an interim camp for onward mobilization. So far he had had a relatively easy war, but now, with the allies pushing towards Berlin, he must have considered the distinct possibility that his services might be required in the final assault on Nazi Germany, but then, on 13 December, his service record was stamped 'M. EAST'. So the Middle East – not mainland Europe – was to be his destination.

In fact he wasn't moved out until 1 May 1945, only a week before Victory in Europe. In the Middle East (more correctly, the Near East, but the two terms seem to be interchangeable now) he was attached to 621 Squadron, a reconnaissance unit stationed at RAF Khormaksar in Aden, South Yemen. During the war, 621 Squadron had been very active but, by the beginning of 1945, activities had dropped so low that the squadron was being reduced from sixteen to eight aircraft. Ken's reaction to being posted overseas (and, moreover, to a *desert*) at the very moment that many other servicemen were preparing to return to 'Blighty' and the welcoming arms of their relieved families, can only be imagined, but it would be a mistake to presume his reaction must have been one of antipathy. As far as anyone can tell, he had never been abroad before, so while it is easy to think he may have been dreading the moment of departure, it is equally possible he was quietly excited and looking forward to the posting and the chance it gave him of seeing a different part of the world and experiencing a different culture and, more importantly, observing some of the wildlife of the region.

In 1945 the British were spreading their influence deeper into the Arabian Peninsula and as part of this process the air force station at Khormaksar (later to become Aden International Airport) was being enlarged. As an electrician serving with the RAF in the middle of the desert – and attached to only a small squadron at that – Ken had to contend with long periods of enforced inactivity. To relieve the tedium, he combined his service with the RAF in Aden with a survey of the fauna of the desert and salt marshes, and even captured various small animals for the London Zoo and possibly other zoos. Earlier that year, the Zoological Society of London had issued an appeal to returning servicemen to bring back live animals for the depleted zoo, either such creatures as they were able to catch themselves or else could procure from local markets. The report in the *Sunday Dispatch* on 11 February was typical:

Zoo asks troops for lizards
The London Zoo has appealed to servicemen abroad to bring back livestock when they come on leave because they are 'desperately short of exhibits'.
Said an official: 'Snakes, lizards, small rodents or birds would be most welcome, with the possible exception of certain classes of monkeys'.

Almost certainly, while waiting to be posted to the Middle East, Ken had read with great interest of London Zoo's plea for specimens and resolved to bring back whatever animals he could find and was able to capture. It was a defining moment of his life. He now had a definite goal. It may not be hyperbolic to suggest that that appeal changed the whole course of his life.

Ken did much of his collecting around Aden, where he was primarily based, but during later reconnaissance sorties with his squadron to other regions he found himself in Eritrea (and probably also neighbouring Abyssinia), a short hop across the Red Sea, and here, too, he whiled away his spare time capturing a variety of the smaller animals of the region, mainly reptiles but possibly also invertebrates and even rodents. But Ken wasn't only interested in capturing animals. Wherever he went, he delighted in watching wild animals. Around the town of Keren in north-western Eritrea, he saw trees loaded with nesting Abdim's storks. Many nests overhung people's huts, and some could almost be reached from the ground, but the native Africans did not molest the birds because they believed their dead relatives entered the bodies of the storks. Later he descended to the hot Eritrean plain and on a small rock mid-stream of the Setit River saw his first hammerkop, a bird closely affiliated to the storks. It was unforgettable experiences like that that would give him his lifelong interest in storks.

On 16 June, Ken was admitted to an RAF hospital in Aden, though for what reason does not appear to have been recorded, but it must have been serious because he was hospitalised for quite some time. His service record is rather ambiguous, but it seems he was in hospital for over a month, and possibly much longer. After serving in the Maintenance Unit following his discharge from hospital, he was transferred to a Release Embarkation Centre on 4 November, pending his return to the U.K., and at the end of

November he found himself back in Britain at a Personnel Dispatch Centre, a staging post prior to his discharge from the air force.

Many years later, in a quick throwaway reference in the Exmouth Zoo guide book, he was to give the inaccurate impression that the time he had spent in Aden and the Horn of Africa had been part of a full-blown animal-collecting expedition, an assertion some way wide of the mark because, as we have seen, collecting had been only a pleasant diversion from his RAF responsibilities. But this does suggest he brought back a sizeable collection of animals, not just a few. So what kind of animals did he collect? Without doubt, his captures were all fairly small fry – nothing too big – and probably mostly reptiles. This is confirmed by Jeremy Mallinson, who knew him quite well in the early 1960s when Jeremy worked for him at Jersey Zoo: 'I remember Ken once mentioning he had served with the RAF in the Middle East, during which time he put together a small collection of reptiles he had caught.' Certainly, both Aden and Eritrea were good places for finding tortoises, lizards and snakes of various kinds. In addition to reptiles, he simply must have collected some of the plentiful desert insects such as Thistle and Dung beetles, locusts and mantises, or arachnids like scorpions. Nor is it completely unreasonable to assume he also pursued, and caught, some of the small desert rodents like jirds and jerboas, although that is slightly less likely because they are rather more demanding, requiring fairly bulky cages. If he was collecting animals with the intention of depositing them with the London Zoo, the obvious place to look for more information on what animals he brought back is London Zoo's Daily Occurrences Book. Strangely, however, I can find only one record. On 27 November 1945, Ken Smith presented the London Zoo with a type of gecko he had caught in the Hiswa Scrub Desert near Aden, described in the Daily Occurrences Book as an Elegant Scrub gecko. The scientific name *Pristurus crucifer* reveals it to have been the species known today as the Cross-marked Sand or Valenciennes Rock gecko (the strange name in honour of the man who first described it). The arrival of this specimen delighted the Reptile House staff as it was the first of its kind to be represented at the zoo. But what happened to all the other animals he brought back? In the case of any invertebrates he may have collected, there is no mystery. Invertebrates hardly ever figure in these venerable, leather-bound books. But the arrival at the zoo of reptiles, birds and mammals *was* usually recorded along with the name of the seller or donor – but not always; and I am not the first person to remark on the inexplicable omissions and inconsistencies in these elegant tomes. Or perhaps, after its appeal for animals to replenish its depleted collection, the London Zoo suddenly found itself overwhelmed by donations of animals from returning servicemen and was forced, albeit reluctantly, to refuse many of the commoner species that Ken brought back, which then went to other zoos or enthusiasts like Sir Garrard Tyrwhitt-Drake, proprietor of a small private zoo (but one that was open to the general public) near Maidstone. Sir Garrard once memorably quipped, 'Give me a chimpanzee, a python and a bear and I have a zoo.' Towards the end of 1945, Sir Garrard's collection included an Ornate Dabb lizard and a Short-fingered gecko, two species common in Arabia and North Africa. Had these lizards originally come from Ken Smith? Ken may even have kept some of the reptiles and other animals himself. Another possibility is that some of his collection at least might have been sold to a famous pet emporium in Birmingham called Tyseley Pet

Stores, and the clue for this can be found in a letter Ken wrote to the editor of *The Times* on 29 December and published on 1 January, concerning the unforgivable killing of two eagles. It was one of his first published pieces of writing, perhaps the very first.

> Sir, – The killing of the Sussex white-tailed eagle has been followed by an unfortunate occurrence in the Midlands. According to the Birmingham Press a golden eagle was shot near Kidderminster on Christmas Day; it had been in the neighbourhood for about three weeks. It is indeed sad that such rare wanderers should meet an untimely end.
>   Yours faithfully,
>   KENNETH J. SMITH

How did Ken hear of a story that had been reported in the Birmingham Press? Had he, perhaps, gone to Birmingham on a short excursion in order to visit Tyseley Pet Stores, hoping to sell some of his reptiles and, whilst in the city, picked up a copy of a newspaper, where he read with dismay of the sad demise of the Golden eagle?

The address he gave in the letter was 'Wychwood', Harbour View Close, Parkstone, Dorset, the same address he gave when he presented the Scrub gecko to London Zoo. So even before he was officially discharged from the RAF (on 6 February 1946) he had taken up residence at the home of his brother Ronald. This is the first inkling we have that already his marriage to Dorothy was in serious trouble and that he no longer considered Ivy Cottage in Great Rollright as his home.

Ken intended to stay at 'Wychwood' only for as long as he needed to take stock. As he prepared to put one part of his life behind him, the question uppermost in his mind was what to do next. Carry on as an electrician, or try his hand at something else?

He thought he would try something else.

Chapter Five

Whipsnade Zoo (1946–1947)

WITH A NATIONAL SHORTAGE of skilled tradesmen in the immediate aftermath of the war, Ken should have had no trouble re-entering his old profession of electrician had he chosen to do so. Instead, he veered off onto a radically different path. In February 1946, within days of leaving the air force, he took a job at Whipsnade Zoo in Bedfordshire. It is possibly because of his contacts at the London Zoo, whose parent body, the Zoological Society of London, owned Whipsnade Zoo, that he was hired. His nephew, Brian Smith, agrees it was an abrupt switching of tracks from being an electrician to zookeeper, but the end of the war was as good a time as any for a career change. 'I would guess he was bored with the electrician job. I think he must have seen the magic of something completely different. Perhaps he was subject to impulses, such as when he volunteered for the RAF without thinking what the family reaction would be.' According to Lucy Pendar, who lived at the zoo and got to know Ken quite well, his position was Head of Section. It may seem surprising that Ken was appointed to such a responsible position when he had only just arrived, but it was not as unusual as it might appear. Most of his colleagues had been farm labourers or contractors originally engaged to erect the perimeter fence who were, much to their surprise, subsequently retained as animal keepers and section heads when the zoo opened to the public. Ken, on the other hand, because of his previous work at Oxford Zoo and then collecting animals in the desert during his RAF service, had a great deal more experience of wild animal keeping than many of his fellow Heads of Section had had when *they* started. There is not universal agreement that Ken was a Section Head. Unfortunately, many of Whipsnade Zoo's files, including records of personnel, were lost in a fire that totally destroyed the office block in July 1962 (a terrible conflagration that claimed the lives of the caretaker, who lived in the flat above the offices, and his dog). But I think it's highly likely that he *was* employed at Whipsnade as a section head. He was certainly able to delegate work, which alone suggests he was in a position of some authority, but the most convincing evidence is a set of photos taken at Whipsnade Zoo in 1946 or 1947 for a national daily newspaper in which a lean Ken Smith, wearing what appears to be his demob suit, is pictured with various animals. It is very unlikely Whipsnade Zoo's management would have chosen an ordinary keeper to appear in such a prestigious photo shoot; much more credible is that a more senior member of staff, such as a section head, would have been chosen to represent the zoo.

Ken soon struck up a friendship with Phil Bates, the cheerful, perpetually whistling head keeper; so much so that he was able to ease some of his responsibilities from him. As a result, Ken was put in charge, along with two or three other trusted individuals, of some newly arrived and very precious Pere David's deer calves. Pere David's deer, a native of China, is one of the great success stories of conservation and the example most likely to be cited whenever proof is required of the efficacy of captive breeding as a means of preventing extinction. The story of how this species was saved from extinction by the timely intervention of just one man, the 11th Duke of Bedford, is well-known, having been told and re-told in countless books. It is a classic example of what one conservationist called 'the fire brigade' approach to captive breeding. Around the turn of the twentieth century the far-sighted Duke, knowing the species to be extinct in the wild and aware, too, that the few animals, numbering less than twenty, that survived in European zoos were non-viable, set about gathering together the remaining animals, mostly singletons or non-breeding pairs, and in this way established the nucleus of a breeding herd in the grounds of his ancestral home at Woburn Abbey. By the mid 1940s, with the Woburn herd now numbering several hundred animals, his son and successor, the 12th Duke, knowing how risky it was to have all his deer in one basket, so to speak, decided the time had come to send surplus animals to other places to form new herds as an insurance in case some disaster (such as an outbreak of foot-and-mouth disease) should strike down his own animals. Whipsnade Zoo was chosen as the first place to receive them, and two male calves duly arrived at Whipsnade in 1944. They were no more than a day old and were hand-reared. Then the Duke announced he was going to let several other zoos have pairs, including more for Whipsnade. An agreement was reached whereby keepers from Whipsnade would collect the Pere David's deer calves as soon as they were born at Woburn and would hand-rear them at Whipsnade until they were old enough to be sent to other zoos. This method, heartless as it might seem to routinely remove them from their mothers at such a young age, ensured they were tame and less likely to panic, perhaps injuring themselves in the process, when as sub-adults they were crated up to be moved onto their final destination. Nowadays, of course, most zoos prefer their animals to be reared naturally, but in the days before tranquillising darts revolutionised the business of catching large mammals things were very different. The calves were the rarest animals at Whipsnade (in stark contrast to today when Pere David's deer are quite common in zoos all over the world and even farmed for venison in New Zealand) and Ken felt immensely honoured to be given the job of hand-rearing them. He called the calves his 'good little naughty ones' and he was very proud of them. He was assisted in his hand-rearing duties by William Beal, the son of Whipsnade Zoo's first Superintendent, the booming, portly and jovial Captain W.P.B. Beal. He remembers Ken with affection. 'I can see him now,' he said to me recently; 'brown receding hair with a quiff, a widow's peak, in the front. A tanned complexion. A tremendous character and very passionate about his animal charges. I mean he really did know his stuff. I liked him.'

Another keeper, new to Whipsnade, who helped hand-rear the Pere David's deer calves was a lanky, fair-haired, and somewhat idealistic young man who became so inspired by their story that he resolved that the zoo he had dreamed of establishing since the age of six would be dedicated to the breeding and preservation of rare and endangered species just like the Pere David's deer. His name was Gerry Durrell.

Gerald Durrell had started work at Whipsnade in July 1945, about six or seven months before Ken. His unofficial title was Odd Beast Boy, because he was not tied to any one section but was put anywhere that required an extra pair of hands. This arrangement suited him very well because it gave him experience with a much wider range of animals than if he had been permanently assigned to just one section. It wasn't long before he found himself working with, and for, Ken Smith.

'Ken had his own section, whereas Gerry was the lowest of the low, a floating keeper, drifting from section to section,' Lucy Pendar told me. 'Oh yes, Ken was Gerry's boss on those days when Gerry found himself assigned to Ken's section.' Lucy was the teenage daughter of Whipsnade Zoo's resident engineer. She remembers that Ken and 21-year-old Durrell got on very well from the start. 'It was obvious from the outset they would develop a rapport,' she said. Many years later, after a rift had split the two friends apart, Gerald Durrell would imply it was Phil Bates who had hand-picked him to assist in the task of hand-rearing the Pere David's deer. More likely it was Ken Smith.

Lucy remembers Ken as a kind, gentle man, totally devoted to his charges. The Pere David's deer calves were given goats' milk and sometimes he let her assist with bottle-feeding duties. It was a tricky job because great care had to be exercised to prevent the calves, in their enthusiasm to get at the milk, from swallowing the rubber teats. Other times he would send her to milk the goats. Ken came to rely on Lucy's help with some of the other animals, too. Another animal on his section was Alec, the solitary sealion who swam in the moat surrounding the former chimpanzee island, the apes having been removed, and he would often send her off with a pungent bucketful of fish to feed Alec. Once Ken handed her an eighteen-inch baby alligator suffering from hypothermia, with instructions to try to resuscitate it by bathing it in a bowl of warm water. She sat with the comatose reptile for what seemed like hours in a little shed in the Works Yard diligently doing as she was asked. Ken probably realised the alligator was a hopeless case, but Lucy persevered anyway until eventually, with no response from the reptile, she was forced to admit defeat. 'Only as I wandered off, disconsolately, through the wood,' she reminisced, 'did I suddenly wonder just what would have happened if it had revived.'

The problem with reptiles like the alligator was that they did not really conform to the Whipsnade theme. The zoo was famous for its herds of deer and antelope displayed in wide open paddocks, and for its lions, tigers and bears which were kept in large, heavily vegetated dells. The few reptiles that *were* kept seemed out of place. Alligators were summer visitors to Whipsnade. Two or three crocodiles or alligators would be sent up from London Zoo most summers and returned to London in the autumn. There was no dedicated reptile house at Whipsnade and they were usually deposited in a pond in a corner of the huge paddock known as Spicer's Field where they could benefit from natural sunlight. The pond had a muddy bottom, and on chilly days (and perched on top of the Dunstable Downs, it could be very chilly indeed at times) and at night the alligators would sink into the insulating mud. Had one succumbed to hypothermia during a late (or early) frost? Maybe it wasn't located for several days, by which time it was too late to save it. William Beal also remembers that an alligator sickened and died at around this time. I tried to find an exact date when it died, without success. I have searched the surviving records for both 1946 and 1947 but inexplicably there is no mention of the alligator found in an icebound condition. I can only conclude that, for some reason, the reptile's demise was not logged. From Whipsnade Zoo's Daily Occurrence Book for 1947, I discovered that two Mississippi alligators were received from London Zoo on 31 July, but both reptiles were duly returned to London on 25 September. It is, I suppose, just possible that originally three alligators had been despatched to Whipsnade but, on being unpacked, one was found to be in a moribund condition and died very soon thereafter and, since technically it had never been part of the Whipsnade collection, its arrival and death were not recorded. However, by the end of July, Ken may already have left Whipsnade, which means the episode of the sick alligator must have taken place some time before this. An alligator did die on 24 March 1946 – but, according to London Zoo's Daily Occurrence Book, at London Zoo, not Whipsnade. So the mystery remains. But there is no doubt that, at some point, an alligator did perish because not only does Lucy Pendar remember the incident, but William Beal is certain of it, too.

Another animal that didn't quite fit into the overall Whipsnade design was also one of the smallest species kept there at that time and an animal that we now tend to be rather complacent about simply because we are so familiar with it: the Golden hamster. On 24 August 1946, Whipsnade received four Golden hamsters from the London Zoo. Ken was inordinately proud of them – which may seem an odd thing to say when today there are literally millions of Golden hamsters kept as children's pets all over the world, but, in their own way, Golden hamsters were every bit as special as those Pere David's deer. The world's most popular species of small pet was virtually unknown to science until 1930 when it was 'rediscovered' (having previously thought to be extinct) in northern Syria in April of that year. When Ken started at Whipsnade, the species was still extremely rare in captivity and of great interest to zoologists, and it is little wonder that he was thrilled to make the acquaintance of such a noteworthy creature.

While working at Whipsnade, Ken lived in the Bothy, the less than salubrious residence for bachelor keepers (although he was probably still married at that time) and nicknamed by them 'the Brothel', that lay not within the precincts of the zoo itself but in Whipsnade village. It was a great echoing, barn-like building containing none of the trappings of warmth and hospitality. Up to five keepers normally lived in the Bothy at any one time. Each had his own bedroom but they shared the other facilities, such as they were. Gerald Durrell, who also lived in the Bothy, later described it as 'stark' and 'reformatory-like'. Working and also living together, it was inevitable that he and Ken would be drawn together. However, when they first met, Ken was rather better off, for whereas Durrell rode a pushbike, Ken whizzed around in a red, open-topped, Singer sports car.

William Beal remembers that red sports car quite clearly. A pelican had escaped and as many vehicles as could be mustered, including Ken's sports car, were mobilised to scour the park for the escapee. Ken, William, Phil Bates and one or two others piled into the car and roared off in search of the truant. On reaching the sharp incline known (after its most famous inhabitants) as Bison Hill, Ken found he was unable to coerce the car into a low gear to go up the steep slope. Eventually, after much cursing and ineffectual grating of gears, he was forced to swing the car round and drive up the hill in reverse gear.

William's sister Laura also remembers Ken, and in particular she recalls that even at that early stage Smith and Durrell were already a 'double act' and it was obvious to everyone they got on very well together despite the disparity in their ages and personalities. They may have been drawn together by their mutual fascination for wildlife, but this was one of the few things they did have in common. In some ways it was a case of opposites attract – the 34-year-old Kenneth, a quiet, retiring figure who tended, by choice, to shrink into the wings, and Gerry Durrell, the brash, opinionated young man, ready to take on the world. Ken was a realist, with a practical mind; Durrell, on the other hand, was an idealist, an ideas-man even if he was not always clear on how to put those ideas into practice. It was a double act that was to last for many years. They spent a lot of time together. So it might seem strange that when, over a quarter of a century later, Durrell came to write *Beasts in My Belfry*, the light-hearted account of his year at Whipsnade Zoo, Ken is not mentioned once, but by then their friendship had long since broken down amid recrimination and accusation.

*

Staff were entitled to one day off a week, but Ken often seems to have worked longer than this without a break, and sometimes up to a fortnight would pass before he took a day off. According to Whipsnade Zoo's Daily Occurrences Book for 1946, he appears to have had only one day off in May and only two days off in June. A year later and a similar thing happened: in May and June 1947 he was off duty just once in each month, which rather begs the question: did something happen in May and June every year which meant he was less inclined, or found it harder, to take time off?

His health during the time he worked at Whipsnade was good, in contrast to the frequent bouts of ill health he suffered after he came back from his later animal-collecting expeditions. In the eighteen months or so that he was at Whipsnade Zoo, he does not appear to have taken a single day off work as a result of illness or injury – unlike Gerald Durrell, who frequently suffered bouts of ill health. In the early part of 1946, Durrell had several spells of absence. In January, in addition to the seven days when he was on officially sanctioned leave of absence, there were two days when he was off sick and – more intriguingly – six successive days when he was reported as simply 'Absent'. Was this period of absence perhaps unauthorised? He was off sick again on 10 February, and again from the 1–9 March, and also on the 21 and 22 March. The exact nature of Durrell's frequent maladies must remain a mystery as the Daily Occurrences Books are woefully short on detail. The major deficiency with these books as a reference source is that they were never compiled with an eye to posterity. These handsome, handwritten tomes tantalisingly offer just a few laconic notes on what was happening at the zoo each day. Generally the responsibility of noting down each day's events fell to the zoo's Superintendent, Captain Beal, but like successive superintendents after him he would never use two words when one would do, with the result that the information beneath each heading was usually no more than a perfunctory list concealing more than it revealed. For example, each day any animals observed by their keepers to be unwell would be recorded, but not what was wrong with them, their symptoms or, indeed, what treatment had been prescribed. The books are full of interesting information, but you are left wanting to know so much more. On the night of 17 March 1947 a 'terrific gale' ripped through the park, threatening to devastate the hundred-year-old pine wood in which the wolves lived. About twenty trees were blown down or broken off. With trees and heavy boughs crashing down, four keepers were stationed all night by Wolf Wood, ready to act immediately if the perimeter fence of the enclosure was breached by a falling tree. But, annoyingly, the entry doesn't tell us *which* keepers drew the short straw. Was Ken Smith one of them? (This entry is fascinating in showing us how much things have changed. Nowadays, of course, with health and safety dominating every aspect of modern life, keepers would not be permitted to camp overnight in a wood during a gale of such magnitude.)

Towards the end of 1946, despite having been at Whipsnade for less than a year, Ken somehow managed to bag, as his annual leave, that most highly prized of holiday periods: the two weeks surrounding Christmas and the New Year, and it is not unreasonable to suppose he probably drove, or caught the train, down to Poole to visit Gertrude or Ronald, or back to Oxfordshire to celebrate the festivities with other members of the family. One person it is probably fair to say he *didn't* go to see was Dorothy.

Chapter Six

A Short Sojourn North of the Border *(1947–1948)*

THE FACT THAT KEN LIVED IN THE BOTHY while he was working at Whipsnade says much about the state of his first marriage. If he were happily married, wouldn't his wife Dorothy have moved with him to Bedfordshire? The truth is that the marriage was already in very serious trouble. It is particularly telling that by the time he left the RAF, his service record had been amended. It was now his mother, not his wife, who was named as Next of Kin and the person to be notified in event of casualty. There it is: Gertrude E. Smith (Mother), followed by her address. The implication is clear: by the end of 1945 Ken and Dorothy's marriage was effectively over.

It is not altogether surprising the marriage failed. Broadsided before it had even got underway by the double whammy of Ken's absence in the RAF and the eleven-year age gap between them, the marriage probably never really stood much of a chance. On its own, the age difference wouldn't have mattered all that much. (There was a nineteen-year age difference between Ken and his second wife, but *that* marriage succeeded.) Much more important was the fact that Dorothy herself was very young – just eighteen – when she married Ken. They were married less than a month after Ken had enrolled in the air force and for the next five years he barely saw his wife, except at brief, irregular intervals. A much stronger marriage could have endured long periods of separation, but Ken and Dorothy's could not.

Dorothy returned from Parkstone to her home village of Great Rollright, although we can't know exactly when this was (electoral rolls – one of the best sources of reference – were not compiled during the war), but she was certainly living back in Ivy Cottage with her mother Winifred, in 1944. At that time the marriage still seemed strong because, in the Quaker register of attendees of the Witney Monthly and Charlbury Preparative Meetings, Dorothy Smith's name appears just below Ken's, not that Ken was in a position to get to many of the meetings. According to the register, Ken was a full member of the Society of Friends, but Dorothy was never an official member, only an attendant at meetings.

However, by the summer of 1944, chinks had begun to appear in the marriage. Facts are quite hazy but her niece thinks she met an American G.I. during the war. It certainly sounds plausible. The number of American servicemen stationed in Britain swelled dramatically to one-and-a-half million in the weeks and months leading up to D-Day. Ivy Cottage stood only a few hundred yards from a pub called the Unicorn Inn. The Unicorn closed down in the mid 1990s and, at the time of writing, lies derelict and boarded up (it has been on the market for a long time but the current owner is thwarted in his efforts to sell by the council's dogged refusal to de-licence the premises), but during the war it was

– to use a kitsch expression – 'jumping', a favourite watering hole for American servicemen stationed at nearby Over Norton Park in readiness for the Allied invasion of the Normandy beaches. Oozing suavity, the Americans would breeze into the pub in their smooth, well-cut uniforms. They spoke in a drawling, Hollywood accent; they wore smarter clothes than their British counterparts and their pay-packets were fuller. They had charm; they had confidence; they had charisma. They had brought comics with them, which were passed around from hand to hand until they were ragged. Many even carried their own prophylactics. They had access to a range of goods that were in short supply, or even unattainable, to everyone else, including cigarettes and – that most highly prized of commodities in war-ravaged Britain – real chocolate.

Charm, confidence, charisma, comics, condoms, cigarettes, and chocolates. The 7 C's. An irresistible combination. It is easy to see how a young woman, chafing from wartime privations, bored, lonely, and craving personable companionship, might be smitten. Many, of course, did succumb to temptation. Did Dorothy allow herself to be led astray by one of these uniformed, smooth-talking, debonair, chocolate-dispensing matinee idols while Ken was absent in the air force and powerless to do anything about it?

Whatever the exact circumstances behind the parting, Ken and Dorothy's marriage was soon to be formally dissolved. She was quite a private person and rarely talked about the past – in this respect, she and Ken were very similar – but I have been able to find out a fair bit about what became of her. She and her mother continued to live in Ivy Cottage until at least the latter half of 1947, but by October 1948 both she and Winifred had gone and from then onwards there was no more mention in the electoral roll of Ivy Cottage. Possibly it was around this time that it was demolished. Winifred left for the U.S.A. in about 1948 to visit a sibling. Dorothy did not go with her. Whilst there, Winifred became ill, forcing her to extend her stay. (Eventually she returned from America and went to stay with a sister-in-law. She died in 1956 in the Chipping Norton area, aged 67.) Dorothy may already have gone away with her American G.I. friend, according to her niece, but if she did it was a short-lived infatuation, possibly no more than a momentary fling, because he seems to have dropped out of her life as suddenly as he entered it. Following the dissolution of her marriage to Ken, Dorothy remarried (in Fulham, London, in 1959) to a man who worked for Taylor Woodrow, then one of the largest British housebuilding and general construction companies. Her second marriage ended when he died. It was while on a cruise that she met her third husband, a Purser on board the cruise liner. They were married for twenty years, spending time in Scotland and Spain and travelling a great deal. Following her third husband's death, Dorothy returned to Chipping Norton, where she died in 2009.

*

Ken was never one to talk about his personal life, and so it comes as no surprise that nobody who remembers him from Whipsnade Zoo can recall his even once speaking of Dorothy. If he was stressed by the deterioration of his marriage, he didn't let it show, and, besides, there was little time during the course of the normal hectic working day for introspection, and now he had found an ally, someone with whom, before long, he would be entering into a partnership of a different kind that would have profound repercussions for the rest of his life. For Ken, Whipsnade turned out to be a springboard to greater things, much of it accomplished in the company of a certain Gerry Durrell.

It was a happy coincidence that Ken Smith and Gerald Durrell were at Whipsnade Zoo at exactly the same moment. How different things might have been for both men, but particularly for Durrell, had the pair never met. In Ken Smith, Durrell found a kindred spirit, someone as passionate about animals as he was, and someone he was to turn to for help several times in the years – and the struggle – that lay ahead. It had not escaped Durrell's notice that Ken was highly unusual among his other colleagues at Whipsnade. He combined skill with motivation and a sound knowledge of the creatures in his care. He was also intelligent; that much was obvious. The other Whipsnade keepers were personable fellows, and Durrell got on well enough with them, but with one or two exceptions they lacked Ken's obvious enthusiasm for wildlife and for zoos. This was not their fault. Most were former farm labourers with no desire to be animal experts. To the majority of keepers employed there at that time, it was just a job of work, nothing more, a job they did to the best of their ability, but they had no interest in finding out more about their animal charges. Most gave the impression they would have been equally content in a different line of work. Durrell, on the other hand, couldn't imagine working in any job that didn't involve animals. To him it wasn't just a means of earning a living, it was a vocation. No wonder the other keepers were suspicious of him, with his endless questions and his notebooks in which he hoped to record his observations and any pearls of wisdom that might drip from the lips of his fellow workers. And as for Durrell's avowal that he had come to Whipsnade to *learn* about the techniques of keeping animals, that was totally beyond their comprehension. What was there to learn about anyway? How to fork hay from a trailer or clear a blocked drain in the tiger dell? Rather than being pleased to share their knowledge with him, as Durrell had expected, they became rather taciturn whenever he whipped out his notebook, or else, in response to his earnest questioning, they just shrugged their shoulders and murmured, 'Dunno, boy.'

Durrell was bitterly disappointed by the *laissez faire* attitude of his workmates. 'Here I was surrounded by a thousand questions,' he later wrote, 'and I was also surrounded by people who could not answer them.'

Ken Smith was different. It was obvious to Durrell that here was someone tuned in to his own wavelength. Ken *liked* zoos. He liked *visiting* zoos whenever he got the opportunity. Even by that stage, Ken was probably dreaming of one day having a zoo of his own. That is not to say the two men thought completely alike; inevitably there were differences of opinion, and one of the ways they differed in their thinking was on the role of zoos. At Whipsnade, Durrell had started to think about the plight of endangered species and how, for certain species, captive breeding could be their only salvation – although these ideas would take a long time to crystallise – and he had even gone so far as to compile his own 'Red List' of threatened species, pre-empting the famous Red Data Books published many years later by the IUCN (International Union for the Conservation of Nature and Natural Resources, now the World Conservation Union).

Durrell's thoughts on the matter were still in embryonic form and it was to be the late 1950s before he felt confident enough to risk ridicule by going public with them, but it was at Whipsnade that the germ was sown in his mind, and the Pere David's deer were without doubt a major influence on his thinking, as were certain other rare species that he got to work with at Whipsnade, such as the White-tailed gnu, nearly exterminated in Africa by hunting in the nineteenth century.

Ken, on the other hand, zoo enthusiast though he clearly was, would never become as passionate or outspoken as his younger companion about the importance of captive breeding. Ken was more conservative in his thinking, less willing to make bold strides. He recognised that zoos were important cultural institutions, but as for transforming them into centres for the captive breeding of endangered species, that was an entirely different matter. You can breed most animals in captivity once you have found the right techniques, but can you ever breed them in sufficient quantity to make a difference? Ken wasn't sure. Later in his career, he was to write several articles for various zoological publications, but I have come across only one article he wrote (for *International Zoo News*) and one letter to *The Times* where he makes the case for captive breeding. As far as he was concerned, the Pere David's deer may have been saved from extinction by being bred in captivity, but, to use a well-worn adage, one swallow does not make a summer. And what about the problems of in-breeding, inherent with too limited a gene pool? How do you surmount *that* hurdle?

But Gerald Durrell was too preoccupied with the big question of how to get a zoo of his own to wrestle with the finer details such as these. Disillusioned, Durrell left Whipsnade in May 1946 after only one year to embark on what he hoped would be a lucrative career as an animal-collector *for* zoos, apparently failing to see the paradox of what he was doing. But the young zoologist and ex-Whipsnade trainee keeper was not yet a conservationist. 'There was a time,' wrote Clinton Keeling, who first met Gerald Durrell in the pre-Jersey Zoo days, 'when no animal was safe in any patch of forest, grassland or scrub that he entered – anything, yes, anything he or in his minions could catch, trap, snare or net was bundled into a box with scant ceremony.'

Although Clinton had no time for Durrell, he had a lot of respect for Ken Smith, even though Ken also went on several Bring-'Em-Back-Alive expeditions – two of them with Durrell – but rather inexplicably Ken is absolved from the charges of over-collection that Clinton levelled against Gerald Durrell.

*

The harsh winter of 1947 was one of the worst on record. For two months, beginning on 21 January, Britain lay buried beneath a deep blanket of snow as a result of a static anti-cyclone over Scandinavia. In February, in some parts of the country, it snowed for twenty-six out of the twenty-eight days. Bedfordshire was one of the counties most severely hit, and on 25 February a temperature of minus 21° C was recorded at Woburn, only a few miles from Whipsnade. Attending to animals high up on the exposed Dunstable Downs in conditions like these was a test of endurance and it was a considerable relief to everyone when finally, in March, milder air caused the snow to thaw.

Ken left Whipsnade Zoo abruptly. So sudden was his departure that he didn't have time to say goodbye to his friend and part-time helper, Lucy Pendar. In the summer of 1947, about eighteen months after he started work at Whipsnade, a vacancy came up at the new Calderpark Zoo near Glasgow. Ken did mention to her that he was considering it. In the last conversation he had with her at Whipsnade he said he was having second thoughts about moving to Glasgow and would probably remain where he was. Not long after this, however, Lucy was away from Whipsnade for a short while and when she returned she found him gone. She assumed, correctly as it turned out, that he must have taken the Calderpark job after all. Exactly when he left Whipsnade is unclear, but it was probably in July or early August. The last time his name appears in the zoo's Daily Occurrences Book is on 8 July, when it was noted that he was absent from work, it being his day off. After that, there is no further mention of him. Almost ten years were to pass before Lucy saw him again. The next (and last) time she met him was at Paignton Zoo in about 1958. She was holidaying in Weymouth with her family when she suddenly remembered that she had heard that her old friend Ken Smith was now Superintendent of Paignton Zoo. On an impulse she suggested to her children that they go to see him. She was in luck; he was on site at the time, and delighted to see her again after so long an interval.

*

Calderpark Zoo, about five miles south-east of Glasgow, opened to the public on 9 July 1947, the first British zoo to be opened after the end of the war, and Ken was one of its first employees. The zoo (which closed down in 2003) was a typical mainstream zoo with a general animal collection, but it was never to make the great strides everyone hoped for and development was always fitful at best. Conventional building materials being unobtainable, many of the early animal cages were, from necessity, constructed from stocks of redundant war material and whatever could be salvaged from naval scrap yards. Bars for some of the cages were improvised from old railway lines and wooden sleepers, and other cages were crudely built from the netting used for tank exercises over soft ground during the war. The lion cage was cobbled together from the floors of railway wagons.

Glasgow city was in a terrible mess when Ken Smith arrived there in 1947. Bomb craters were everywhere. Buildings lay derelict and crumbling. Ken was appalled by the post-war degradation, the poverty and the squalor he found in Glasgow. His new life north of the border was certainly a startling contrast to the one he had left behind in comfortable Bedfordshire, which, despite the ongoing rationing and the unavailability of so many commodities, was still a relatively affluent place to live. Glasgow could not have been more different. He felt he had stepped back in time to Dickensian slums. He was even more appalled by the callous attitude of the average Glaswegian zoo-visitor who saw nothing wrong in harrying the zoo animals. Bare-footed children would derive a great deal of amusement from lobbing stones at the seals, sealions and penguins. Yelling at them had no effect whatsoever because he realised the moment he walked away they would be back, and being powerless to stop them depressed him. He did not remain there for long. He had stayed in touch with his old Whipsnade colleague, Gerald Durrell, and in 1948 Durrell invited him to join him on his forthcoming animal-collecting expedition to the (then) British Cameroons. It was with a sense of relief that Ken handed in his notice of resignation.

Chapter Seven

Two in the Bush *(1949–1950)*

IN 1949 THERE WERE LESS THAN TWENTY ZOOS in the whole of Great Britain. Despite the dearth of animal collections open to the public, it was a propitious time to be an animal-collector *for* zoos. The zoos of Europe were anxious to replenish their depleted collections after the war and there was comparatively little bureaucracy to hinder the import of most animals. Almost all were generalist collections. With very few exceptions (of which Peter Scott's Wildfowl Trust at Slimbridge was the most famous), most animal collections made no attempt to specialise, so in theory whatever animals Ken and Durrell succeeded in bringing back were likely to appeal to the majority of them. Of course it wasn't all plain sailing. Planning an expedition on this scale was an organisational nightmare. In the aftermath of the war, large swathes of the globe remained off limits and, with rationing still in force in Britain, equipping an expedition with up to six months' worth of supplies could be somewhat problematical, to say the least. But there is no doubt this era represented the last hurrah for the traditional animal-collecting expedition. The days of the great animal-collectors were numbered, and Durrell and Smith would be among the last of them. Before too long, discordant voices would start questioning the ethics of removing animals from the wild to display in zoos. In 1949, however, that was not yet a serious issue. This was to be Durrell's second expedition, and his first with Ken Smith. The destination, as with Durrell's previous trip a year earlier, was the little known territory of the British Cameroons in Central Africa.

Gerald Durrell had been accompanied on that occasion by an associate of Peter (later Sir Peter) Scott by the name of John Yealland. The affable Yealland, an aviculturist, had concentrated on birds, and Durrell on mammals and reptiles. One of the main objectives of that expedition had been the acquisition of an obscure nocturnal, lemur-like, primate called an angwantibo, which Dr Geoffrey Vevers, then Superintendent of the London Zoo, was anxious to show in the Small Mammal House. In May 1948, Ken received a letter written by Durrell from Kumba giving the exciting news that he had been successful in his quest and had not one but three angwantibos at his base camp. They were doing well, Durrell reported with pride, and he was praying 'to all the Gods of Natural History' that he would get them back to England alive. He succeeded, and at last the London Zoo was able to study living and healthy angwantibo and exhibit this elusive and little-known species to zoo visitors. This was possibly the first time ever that London Zoo had possessed angwantibo (there is a vague, unauthenticated, reference to what was believed to be an angwantibo having been kept at the zoo in about 1905, but it cannot be verified – it could have been a closely related species – and in any case this treasured rarity lived only a very short time).

John Yealland was unavailable to join Durrell on his second expedition, and so he turned instead to his former Whipsnade ally. Ken was not sorry to leave Calderpark Zoo. Relieved to escape the degradation and post-war depression of Glasgow, and its callous zoo-visitors, he migrated south and, as before, moved into 'Wychwood', his brother Ronald's house in Harbour View Close, Parkstone. By a stroke of good fortune, Gerald Durrell was a near neighbour in the contiguous resort of Bournemouth and so they were able to meet up frequently during their preparations for the African trip.

At Whipsnade, Ken had been superior in rank to Gerald Durrell but now the positions were reversed and it is Durrell who assumes the prominent role. Although senior in age, Ken Smith seems to have been content to adopt the role of junior partner. This made good sense: Durrell had organised a major expedition to the Cameroons before, knew the country and what to expect, and generally had more experience to draw on. In January 1949, preparations complete, the two friends climbed aboard the cargo boat, M.V. *Reventazon*, at Liverpool docks at the start of their first collecting trip together.

We now come to a major mystery. Where did Ken get the money to go gallivanting off to Africa and, a year later, South America? Even allowing for the fact that at Whipsnade he used to sail around in a sports car while Durrell slogged about on a bicycle, it was still a considerable amount of money to find, possibly as much as one-and-a-half thousand pounds. We know where Gerald Durrell got his money: when he turned twenty-one he had inherited £3,000 left to him in trust by his father. That is well documented in numerous accounts. What is not recorded anywhere is the source of Ken Smith's money, but at the time he was obviously quite well-off because he was able to continue going abroad in search of animals when Durrell was forced to suspend his own animal-collecting career after *his* money ran out. So how *did* Ken finance his expeditions? The obvious explanation is that he was bequeathed the money, but from whom? My first thought was an inheritance from his father, Herbert. The problem with that hypothesis was that Herbert Smith, as we have seen, was less than successful in business and probably did not have much to show for all his years of endeavour. If he made out a will at all, it has not surfaced, and I am forced to the conclusion he died intestate, with his estate, such as it was, passing to his widow, Gertrude.

Ken's paternal grandfather, Thackwell Smith, had enjoyed much more success in business, but he died as long ago as 1905 and once again I have been unable to locate a will. If not Ken's father or grandfather, did he receive a legacy from another family member? At first, one very promising candidate in the frame was his aunt, Hannah Harlock. Ken had clearly got on very well with his aunt. As I have said, she and her husband, Arthur, once had a very successful drapery business in a grandiose three-storey building in Banbury. The shop, on the corner of Parson's Street and Market Place, wouldn't have looked out of place transplanted to Knightsbridge or Oxford Street. Perched atop the roof in huge standalone letters, testament to the prosperity of the owners, was the single word 'HARLOCK'. The expansive shop windows displayed a selection of the wares and, on the glass, in big white lettering guaranteed to attract the salacious attention of teenage boys, was the legend, 'Celebrated Corsets'. (The shop is still there to this day. Although much altered, it remains instantly recognisable from old photographs. At the time of writing the shop lies empty and available to let. The current

rent – presumably for just the ground floor – of £35,000 per annum (exclusive) is a reflection of its prime town centre location but would be totally incomprehensible to the ingenuous Harlocks.)

Arthur and Hannah did not have any children of their own. When she died, Hannah (who outlived her husband by fourteen years) left the princely sum in her will of £6,800 (excluding the sale of her cottage, which she bequeathed to her housekeeper for life), a fortune in those days, divided unequally amongst nineteen named beneficiaries. Kenneth and his brothers, Ronald, Gil and Frank, each received £500, a tidy sum to be sure but not enough to finance an animal-collecting expedition, even allowing for the fact that Gerald Durrell put in at least half the money. (Illuminatingly, when the will was drafted, Frank's place of residence was given as Parkstone. Was Frank also living at 'Wychwood'?) However, the amount Ken inherited from his aunt is academic because the timing is all wrong. Hannah didn't die until 1951 (29 October), with probate being granted on 26 January 1952. All of Ken's privately funded collecting trips took place before this. After 1952 he was to go on only one more animal-collecting expedition, and *that* was financed by Paignton Zoo. So the source of his money for his early collecting trips remains a mystery.

In so many ways, Hannah Harlock's last will and testament, which she signed on 26 April 1951, six months before she died, is a paradoxical document, remarkable for the anomalies and inconsistencies it contains. For example, it refers to 'the said' Sophia Smith (another aunt) and Walter Ernest Harlock without their names having previously been mentioned, which implies clauses or pages have been lost. But even more astonishingly, the residences of at least three of the beneficiaries are old addresses. Ken was said to be a resident of Charlbury, whereas in fact he hadn't lived there since 1940, while his sister Violet's address was given as West Mersea, same as their brother Gil, but as far as anyone knows, both of them left Mersea in about 1933, or very soon thereafter, following the death of their father. For several years, Violet (called Kathleen Violet Smith in the document, because it seems she preferred to be known by her middle name) had been living at 7 Milestone Road, Poole, with her husband, Harold Kelland, a departmental manager of a concrete manufacturing firm, whom she married in 1946. This brings me to another puzzle. In Hannah's will, Violet was referred to by her maiden name, even though she had married Harold five years earlier. But the most glaring anomaly of all is the fact that she was named as a beneficiary (£300 being the sum due to her) at all, because she had died five days before the will was signed. All of this points to it being an old will that had not been updated, and yet it is clearly dated April 1951.

*

Gerald Durrell's account of his and Ken's first trip together, *The Bafut Beagles*, published in 1954, is dedicated to Kenneth Smith 'In Memory of Fons, False Teeth and Flying Mice'. Durrell loved cryptic dedications of this sort in his books; dedications that only the addressee could understand. The reason why dentures, of all unlikely things, should crop up is because of an incident involving Ken that does not feature anywhere else in the book, as I'll explain presently. The 'flying mice' was a reference to *Idiurus*, a genus of

Pygmy Scaly-tailed Flying squirrels (not *mice*, although even in some field guides, whose authors should know better, they are sometimes called flying mice – erroneously – on account of their small size and mouse-like appearance) that caused Durrell and Smith considerable anguish due to the refusal of these animals to accept any of the traditional rodent foods that were offered to them.

The Bafut Beagles introduced readers to the rumbustious character of the Fon of Bafut. In later years Ken would point to Durrell's description of the Fon – Achirimbi II – as an example of the way he sometimes distorted the truth in his books for comic effect. The unflattering portrait Durrell paints of this African suzerain is of a swaggering, clownish man who speaks comical pidgin English, has a penchant for neat whisky, and collects wives in the same way other people do stamps or coins. 'Perhaps Gerald never thought the Fon, entrenched in far-off Cameroons, would find out about the book, much less read it,' Ken once told a friend, 'but he *did* find out, and he was pretty livid about the way he was lampooned in the book, made a figure of fun in fact. You'd never guess it from reading the book, but the Fon was a highly cultured, intelligent and urbane man – he was educated at Oxford – but none of that comes across in Gerald's book.'

The Fon (whom Ken probably never met but knew all about him from conversations with Gerald Durrell) is a leading character in the book, but the same cannot be said for Durrell's unassuming partner. Although *The Bafut Beagles* was dedicated *to* Ken Smith, surprisingly there is hardly any mention of him in the book. He pops up, suddenly and without introduction, in the prologue, and then disappears again for almost the whole of the rest of the book. It is extraordinary how little Durrell wrote in his books about his colleague. They were, after all, supposed to be equal partners. The only story involving Ken that Durrell chose to relate in *The Bafut Beagles* is towards the end of the book when, as they prepare for the long voyage home, they discover to their horror that the captain of the ship is not only unsympathetic towards them personally but also staunchly anti-animal – which was unfortunate in view of the fact that most of their luggage consisted of five hundred assorted mammals, birds, reptiles and other creatures: a total of seventy species ranging from Red River hogs and monkeys to Land crabs. The animal cages – more than a hundred and thirty of them – are piled up on the forward deck of the ship under the disapproving gaze of the captain. 'A hunched and terrifying figure,' Durrell wrote. Ken, having cleaned out the monkey cages, sternly lectures Durrell that they must be on their best behaviour and on no account must they do anything calculated to incur the captain's wrath – and then trots to the side of the ship and casually hurls a basketful of dirty sawdust over the rail into the sea without taking the precaution of checking the wind direction. Needless to say, the sawdust, in a vast swirling, choking fog, envelops both the captain and his precious and hitherto spotless bridge. 'Trust you to know the right way to a captain's heart,' reproaches Durrell, bitterly. In the book, Durrell makes it all sound good fun, a bit of a wheeze, but in reality he was probably furious with his companion.

It is quite an achievement to go on an animal-collecting expedition with someone and then afterwards to write a best-selling book about it which hardly mentions that person. But there is no mystery why Ken does not feature more prominently in the book. Durrell was writing from his own point of view and it was only natural he should be more interested in relating his own experiences, rather than those of his companion. For another thing, the two collectors split up in the Cameroons, each operating in a different area to maximise the variety of animals they might catch. Ken mostly stayed behind at base camp in Mamfe, whilst Durrell roamed further afield including making a prolonged, month-long foray up-country to the highland fiefdom of Bafut, about a hundred miles to the north-east. The area around Mamfe, where the Cross River cuts steep gorges through the basin of the great rainforest, was certainly rich in wildlife but it was not a comfortable place for an Englishman to live and work. Being set in a river valley, humidity could be over 90 per cent and regularly reached 100 per cent and for much of the year the temperature exceeded 120°F. Only in the latter part of the expedition did Durrell rejoin his partner in sweaty Mamfe (when Ken was at last able to set off with unbridled enthusiasm, like a schoolboy let out of detention, on an excursion of his own – to the mountainous Endop Plain – eventually returning with many more animals), so was not witness to any adventures Ken had had up to that point. They were to reprise their respective roles on their next trip together the following year, with Ken once more keeping the base camp going, freeing Durrell to explore further afield, and so once again we find that in Durrell's book of that expedition, *Three Singles to Adventure* (which was actually written before the African book), Ken appears only fleetingly – in the prologue and the epilogue.

In *The Bafut Beagles*, Durrell does not refer to his partner by his first name even once – on the rare occasions when Ken pops up in the narrative at all it is always as 'Smith' – and in *Three Singles to Adventure* his first name appears only once (in the prologue), whereas all the other characters are routinely called by their first names. In Durrell's unpublished diaries, too, more often than not he is known only as 'Smith'. Why Gerald Durrell should choose to address his partner and companion in such an irreverent and impersonal way is, at first, puzzling. Unless you happen to be a sports star, in which case it is customary to be known by your last name, generally the only people likely to habitually address you by your surname are those whose status makes them superior to you such as your teacher, your boss at work, or your commanding officer if you're in the armed forces. Less commonly it can also be a term of endearment (one of my mother's closest friends was never known to call her by her first name, only by her surname) and we must accept this is why Ken was always known to his younger companion simply as 'Smith'.

This was Ken's first experience of a tropical rainforest, the first time he had set foot in the most species-rich ecosystem on earth, and he was overwhelmed by it all. After the drabness and austerity of post-war Britain, everything was an assault to all the senses, and for the first few days he wandered around as if in a daze, imbuing the vibrant colours, the profusion of plant, bird and insect life, the polychromatic hues of the birdlife, the unfamiliar sounds, the rich intoxicating scents, the whole unreal atmosphere. Everywhere he turned, he found some new wonder to mesmerise him. Every bush he investigated yielded some new and mysterious insect he had never seen before that defied identification. Mammals were harder to find but smaller creatures abounded. Flitting amongst the flower corollas were the sunbirds, the males distinguished by their vivid, metallic colours. Not for nothing were these living jewels bestowed such vernacular names as Splendid sunbird, Superb sunbird and Beautiful Long-tailed sunbird. Along the coast lay the mangrove swamps. Here, at low tide, mile upon mile of dark grey mud, eighteen inches deep in most places, was exposed, over which the mangroves grew thickly on their reticulate roots. This was the haunt of the mudskippers, hundreds being in sight at once, skating effortlessly over the mud or, when they felt threatened, gazing out suspiciously with bulbous eyes from the relative safety of the twisted mangrove roots. Durrell, of course, had been to this part of the world before and knew exactly how Ken must be feeling. Shortly after the ship had docked in Victoria (renamed Limbe in 1982) in February 1949, Durrell wrote in one of his infrequent letters home to his mother that his partner was walking around 'with his mouth so wide open that I am afraid his teeth will drop out.'

In fact, later on in the trip, his teeth *did* fall out. Ken was bathing in a river when he sneezed, suddenly and explosively, jettisoning his dentures some distance across the water, much to the amusement of the watching Africans.

Taking a dip in a waterway in that part of Africa was not a wise activity unless one could be sure of the purity of the water. Bilharziasis, a water-borne illness caused by blood flukes, is rampant in rivers and lakes in many parts of sub-Saharan Africa, and indeed it seems as if Ken may have contracted the disease, along with a whole litany of other debilitating tropical complaints, and for years afterwards he was in and out of the Hospital for Tropical Diseases in London. In Africa he was quite phlegmatic about his ailments. Living as they were in primitive conditions in a very unhealthy environment that sapped both men's strength, disease was a constant threat. It didn't help that the most potent weapon in Ken's first-aid arsenal was a bottle of Dettol. Photos taken in Africa show him looking thin and gaunt and with sticking plasters covering the tropical ulcers on his legs. Rather than seek professional medical attention, he preferred to investigate the contents of the first-aid kit and stoically treat his internal complaints with nothing more efficacious than aspirin, and his external complaints with Savlon and band-aids.

It took Ken some time to get used to the fact that the Africans referred to some of the denizens of the forest by the wrong names, in some instances calling them by the names of animals not even native to Africa. In pidgin English, a leopard became a 'tiger' and a python was known as a 'boa', terminology which Ken found very disconcerting at first.

Ken and Durrell slept in the animal tents with the birds, reptiles and mammals assembled around them as a precaution against invasion by marauding Army ants. A single column can contain well over a million individuals. Such huge, incalculable numbers could rapidly overwhelm and devour any animal incapable of getting out of the way in time and caged animals, being unable to flee, were utterly vulnerable to attack. It was imperative that the scouting party of an Army ant column was detected and headed off in time. As before, Durrell was fired by a desire to obtain angwantibos. It turned out the animal was not quite as rare as previously thought, and angwantibos once again turned up, native hunters bringing them in from the surrounding forest. At night Ken and Durrell often watched, entranced, as the angwantibos went about their business, feeding, grooming and exercising themselves in their cages. In the daytime the angwantibos rested propped in the fork of a branch, looking rather like curled-up teddy bears, but at night they unrolled, and by the dim light of their kerosene lamps the two collectors would be treated to remarkable gymnastic performances from the angwantibos as they climbed and ran along the branches. Ken was quite amazed by this, as previously he had always understood the angwantibo to be quite a sluggish animal. In reality it was a surprisingly nimble and agile creature after dark, in marked contrast to its slothful lemuroid relative, the potto. In an article he wrote many years later he described them as moving around 'like wide-eyed teddy bears on stilts'.

To Gerald Durrell, Ken was a source of much derisive amusement. In a diary entry early on, Durrell wrote: 'I am going to make a packet on this trip. I feel it in my bones, and Smith feels it in his varicose veins.' One gets the impression he saw Ken as a slightly comical middle-aged uncle. Durrell ribbed him over the episode of the false teeth. Following the acquisition of some particularly rare and unusual species targeted by the expedition, Ken would sometimes become almost delirious with excitement, on one occasion prompting his younger companion to note in his diary that he had been vastly amused by the rather incongruous sight of the balding, thirty-seven year old Smith 'fluttering round the tent like an elderly will-o'-the-wisp.'

At thirty-seven, Ken was hardly 'elderly' but obviously seemed that way to the much younger Gerald Durrell.

Then there were the dreams. Ken was prone to dreams in which he imagined himself intrepidly pursuing gorilla or buffalo with only the most rudimentary catching equipment, or sidestepping a charging elephant. These dreams were so vivid that while he slept he sometimes became alarmingly animated, fighting with his bedclothes and kicking and yelling out, the sweat pouring off him, as he closed in on the imaginary wild beasts.

In his dreams Ken may have been gung ho, but in reality he had a healthy respect for wild animals and was frequently alarmed by his partner's naivety and recklessness. Being older, he felt an avuncular responsibility towards the twenty-four year old Durrell, who tended to be too impetuous for Ken's liking. He thought the headstrong Gerald was inclined to take unnecessary risks and he constantly impressed upon him the need to be careful when in close proximity to potentially lethal animals. He even felt compelled to write to Durrell's mother, back in sleepy Bournemouth, reassuring her, not altogether sincerely, that he was sure her son had heeded his advice.

Durrell was a talented caricaturist and in idle moments throughout his life produced lightening sketches of animals and people. Some of these have since been auctioned to raise money for conservation. With all his sketches of friends and family, his sharp eyes homed in on certain distinguishing features, accentuating or exaggerating them. It might be the size or shape of someone's nose, for example, or some other distinguishing characteristic, but it was never cruel. If you were fortunate enough to be the subject of a Gerald Durrell sketch, you could be certain you were looked on with genuine affection. If imitation is the sincerest form of flattery, so too was appearing as a Durrell caricature. It was difficult for the subject to take offence because they knew there was no malicious intent. In Ken's case, his balding pate and, in particular, the little quiff of hair at the front made him ripe material for the Durrellian treatment, and Gerald affectionately sent him up in a number of swiftly executed sketches in which Ken bore more than a passing resemblance to *Tintin*, the eponymous hero of a comic strip created by the Belgian artist Hergé which was popular at that time.

Despite all the dangers and discomfort, Ken and Gerald arrived safely back in England on 25 August 1949 after spending six months in the British Cameroons without having been eaten by leopards or trampled to death by hippos to find a media circus awaiting them when they disembarked at Garston Docks, Liverpool. Although they had hoped to bag the really big 'box-office' creatures commanding the highest market value, like buffalo, gorilla or hippopotamus, most of the animals they returned with were rather less glamorous. Awaiting them on the dock were the directors of the major British zoos, anxious to beat their rivals in closing the deal on the choicest specimens. Identically dressed in long mackintoshes tightly secured around the waist with a wide belt, to Ken they bore a sinister resemblance to what he imagined members of the Mafia to look like. As the ship, the Elder Fyffe liner *Tetela*, tied up and the two collectors watched with a mixture of pride tempered with more than a tinge of apprehension, as the animal crates were slowly swung ashore by crane (at which point the zoo directors moved in predatorily), they had every reason to feel pleased with themselves. They had amassed a formidable haul including a number of species rarely seen before in British zoos. In some cases the animals were 'first-timers'. The most popular animal was Charlie, a young incorrigible chimpanzee with a penchant for causing mischief, destined for Paignton Zoo. There is a picture of Charlie in the Paignton Zoo guide book for 1957, smoking a cigarette (just imagine the horror such an image would provoke today!). This highly intelligent ape was later bought by the Chipperfield organisation and, I was told, died as comparatively recently as the early 1980s.

At the docks the two collectors obligingly posed for photos with some of the animals they had brought back. The results of their endeavour 'occupied 500 cases of varying size, many of them no bigger than a portmanteau,' reported *The Times* the next day.

> Many of the animals were of types with which zoos are familiar, but there were some rarities, such as the Golden Cat, Moustached Monkey, Water Chevrotain, and Hairy Frogs, the last-named being the first of their kind to be brought to this country.
>
> The consignment consisted of 139 crates, among them 42 for reptiles, 27 for mongoose, one for civets, one for the Red River Hog, two for chevrotain, and one for birds.

The number of crates for mongooses seems excessively high and may possibly have been a misprint. Not every animal was captured alive. A few had been shot either to provide meat for the carnivores in the collection or as museum specimens but, as *The Times* was quick to emphasise, a gun played a comparatively small part in the operations, stressing that Mr Durrell and Mr Smith were out for live animals, in which they had considerable success:

One of the methods adopted was the smoking of hollow trees in which animals were lurking. Some of these trees were 200 ft high, and at the top there was a native waiting for the animal to emerge.

The collection is being distributed. Some of it, including the Hairy Frogs, is going to the London Zoo; Belle Vue, Manchester, will have rare monkeys and other animals; the Edinburgh Zoo will have part of the collection and Dublin may also have some of it.

From a purely scientific perspective, the Hairy frogs were arguably the most interesting animals of the whole collection. The two proud animal-collectors probably did genuinely believe that the Hairy frogs they had brought back were the first of their kind to be exhibited alive in this country, as reported in *The Times*, but unfortunately it wasn't true, a group of four Hairy frogs having been presented to the London Zoo in 1938.

The Hairy frog gets its name from the presence of hair-like filaments (in fact, fine filaments of skin, richly supplied with blood vessels, believed to be an aid to respiration) along the sides of the body and legs of the adult breeding male. Three Hairy frogs were landed, two males and a female, and they, along with other creatures of most scientific merit, were destined for the London Zoo. The single female, however, was not strong and succumbed before reaching London, leaving just two males, one semi-adult and one fully grown. The Hairy frogs were so unusual that their arrival at London Zoo eclipsed the fact that in the same consignment were several other kinds of frog that had never before been seen at the zoo, but because these other amphibians were rather nondescript they failed to make much of an impact.

In September, *The Times* published a further article: 'The collection recently brought to the London Zoo from the British Cameroons by Mr. Durrell and Mr. Smith included a number of types never before seen alive in the country. Many of them are not, perhaps, of great exhibition value,' it conceded, 'but they are of considerable interest to scientific visitors.' As well as the Hairy frogs, other animals that found a home at London Zoo included about a dozen other kinds of frogs, some of them arboreal forms, and several unidentified bush vipers of the genus *Atheris*. At least five of the frogs and two of the viper species were thought to be completely new to the collection, as were two species of chameleon and one species of skink. In all, about nine or ten kinds of reptiles and amphibians were new to the collection. The invertebrate house at the zoo was enriched by the addition of some sinewy giant millipedes of four different species, the biggest being about eight inches long and dull black in colour, some giant snails, and three types of Land crab, of which at least one kind, a small, rather pretty red and grey crustacean, was new to the collection. In the end, most of the larger animals went to other zoos, but London did receive two of the eastern form of Bosman's potto, along with an angwantibo, a Red-flanked duiker, a trio of Giant Booming squirrels, and a quantity of Fruit bats. In addition, two Water chevrotains, a cusimanse (a forest mongoose) and a few other animals were placed at the zoo on deposit.

The only birds to go to the London Zoo were all birds of prey, namely Chestnut-flanked goshawk, African Barn owl (similar to, but rather larger than, the British kind),

White-faced Scops owl, and Sjostedt's owlet. Of the birds, only the Scops owls had been previously exhibited at the London Zoo.

As the animals were being distributed to zoos around the country, already the thoughts of Ken Smith and Gerald Durrell were turning towards their next trip. They let it be known that their next animal-collecting expedition would be to South America, specifically the little-known territory of British Guiana in the fauna-rich north-east corner, a hot humid land of creeks and pristine forest and wide, open savannah, a variety of habitats that would ensure an abundant diversity of wildlife. The New Year saw them climbing aboard the Trinidad-bound, Blue Star Line ship, *Columbia Star*, at the port of London on the first leg of their South American journey, travelling first-class. And why shouldn't they have travelled first-class? Resigned to the fact that for the next few months they would have to rough it, they were determined to enjoy some luxury on the passage out. The passenger list reveals something very interesting: Ken's address was given as 52 St. Alban's Avenue, Bournemouth – the same address as Gerald Durrell. So it seems that, for a while at least, Ken had moved in with the Durrell clan, Gerald, his mother and sister Margaret. In 1948, Ronald Smith had married his girlfriend, Doreen Crook, so obviously Ken thought this was a good time to move out of 'Wychwood'. Ronald, a builder by trade, worked for a local construction firm called John Jagger (Parkstone) Ltd. Following the death of John Jagger, he sold 'Wychwood' to raise the capital to buy the company and moved to Holly Tree Cottage, Sandbank's Road, Poole. Their mother, Gertrude, settled into number 255, Sandbank's Road.

*

On 27 January 1950, the two collectors disembarked at Demarara, British Guiana, at the start of their second animal-collecting expedition together. Eighty per cent of British Guiana was covered by tropical rainforest stretching north over the Orinoco River into Venezuela and southwards continuing unbroken into the Amazon Basin and the Mato Grosso. In the southwest of the country the forest became more fragmented, thinning out to be temporarily replaced by flat grassland, the Rupununi savannah, and in the east, as it neared the Atlantic coast, the forest had been cleared for rice and sugar plantations. When Ken Smith and Gerald Durrell were there in 1950, a great deal of the country was still unexplored by Europeans, and it is easy to understand why. Travelling in the interior of the country was difficult. Roads were almost non-existent, and the easiest, and often the only, method of transport was by river. As on their previous trip, Ken seems to have drawn the short straw because while Gerald Durrell travelled far and wide around the country, much of Ken's time was spent at the base camp at Kissy, on the outskirts of the capital, Georgetown, but he did manage to make several short journeys to the interior after Durrell returned to England in April. In *Three Singles to Adventure*, Gerald Durrell gives the definite impression he was in British Guiana for the full six months. In fact this was not true. He was forced to return after less than three months in the country when the money ran out, taking the entire collection of nearly five hundred animals with him (save for some of the reptiles which had already been despatched back to Britain in March in the care of a helper named Robert Lowes). Ken stayed on. A plan was hatched whereby the animals collected so far would be sold to zoological gardens in Britain and, with the money raised, Durrell would remit funds back to the waiting Ken Smith in Georgetown to enable him to start a fresh collection, settle any outstanding debts, and to pay for his ticket home. There was another reason why Durrell returned home earlier than anticipated. He had met and fallen in love with a young woman in Manchester by the name of Jacqueline Sonia Wolfenden and was impatient to see her again. After Durrell left, Ken visited a region along the Berbice River, and in May spent two weeks collecting in the Pakaraima Mountains and in the largely unpopulated Ireng River valley on the Brazilian border to the southwest of that mountain range. He also strayed over the border into Brazil where he collected more animals.

Along the Ireng River he saw Maguari Stocks, handsome birds looking not unlike a bigger version of the more familiar European White stork. They would not allow close approach and so he took his binoculars and studied them from a hillside overlooking the valley. He later wrote, 'Their posture suggested contemplativeness, like the herons standing by English willows on the banks of the Evenlode I watched years before.' He hoped he might see wild Jabiru storks, but this was one species that eluded him and he had to content himself with an encounter with a single tame specimen in a small zoo, opened only three years earlier, attached to the old Georgetown Museum. He took some photos, realising sadly that this might be the closest he would get to a Jabiru stork. A photo he took of this stately bird appears on the back cover of this book.

*

Before they had even ventured onto South American soil for the first time, both Ken and Gerald Durrell had heard that in general the animals from that continent were more demanding and often fared less well in captivity than the ones they were used to from Africa. This was a gross generalisation but it did contain more than a grain of truth. Many animals *were* difficult, some almost impossible. But in spite of a few setbacks, the expedition was a big success. In an article Ken wrote for *Oryx* magazine, he records that among the many animals obtained were Giant anteater ('Specimens brought to my camp from the North-West, Demerara area, and Rupununi'); tamandua (Lesser anteater); the arboreal, prehensile-tailed, Silky, Pygmy or Two-toed anteater (it's all the same animal and is sometimes known in that part of the world as the 'Tank 'e God' because of the praying attitude it adopts when raising its hooked front claws in defence); anacondas ('Often find their way into the irrigation channels between the sugar plantations'); and Emerald Tree boa ('A most handsome snake, I received three specimens'). The tiny Silky anteaters, several of which were brought in, Ken released back into the forest after examining and photographing them as he realised he could not provide the conditions they needed. He found Guiana to be a paradise for frogs and toads, a particular interest of Ken's and he was well read on the subject. Two of his favourites, examples of which he sent to the London Zoo, were the Pied or Yellow-banded Poison-dart frog and a species he called the Reticulated frog, both from the Pakaraima Mountains. My first thought was that the Reticulated frog must be Reticulated Poison-dart frog (*Dendrobates reticulates*), but the scientific name he gives, *Atelopus flavescens*, is that of the Cayenne

Stubfoot toad.

Nowhere on earth is richer in birdlife than this north-east corner of South America, and among the many birds Ken and Durrell obtained were cowbirds and marshbirds, tanagers, tyrants, guans, saltators, birds of prey, egrets, herons, Sun bitterns, the primitive hoatzin, and a Boat-billed heron captured on the Mahaica flats in the north of the country. This provides a striking contrast with their previous expedition to the Cameroons when surprisingly few birds were caught.

An animal that made an indelible impression on Ken was the Red Howler monkey. He was captivated by his first sight of wild-living howlers. Later he wrote, in almost poetic prose, 'As the animals feed they move through the trees with peculiar deliberation. At times they look like giant hairy spiders, as with limbs extended they reach to pluck leaves. The spectacle of a party of Red howlers, clad in fiery auburn and coppery-tinted coats, feeding amidst sun-flecked jungle greenery is not easily forgotten.' At that moment he vowed to add the species to the collection if he could, even though, as he was well aware, they were renowned for being 'difficult' in captivity, often showing little inclination to feed or exercise and becoming quite morose. (At that time, the longevity record for the Red howler, set by the New York Zoo in 1928, was only three years and four months.)

It was a red-letter day for Ken when he managed to obtain two baby Red howlers. 'Charming mites with mournful expressions, looking very like tiny old men,' he wrote. But they were slow to settle to a life in captivity and it was a long time before they consented to accept any petting or devotion. As they were obviously very nervy and distrustful of any attention, he gave them two guinea-pigs for companionship, and the monkeys began to take more interest in life and fed quite well. Everything that the guinea-pigs ate was sampled by the howlers, often probably out of curiosity, and a quaint and rather touching friendship developed between them. At night Ken would often find each baby howler asleep with an arm clutching a guinea-pig across the back. The youngsters were ultimately bought by Chester Zoo but, upholding the howler's reputation for being difficult, sadly they did not survive long in their new home. Ken was upset to hear of the early death of the two monkeys that he had invested so much time, energy and love into raising.

Six years later Ken Smith was to try again with Red Howler monkeys.

Chapter Eight

Interlude in Manchester and Margate *(1950–1952)*

KEN RETURNED FROM BRITISH GUIANA with a fresh collection in July 1950. The animals he and Durrell had brought back were temporarily deposited at Belle Vue Zoo (Manchester) until they could be dispersed to other zoos around the U.K. While they were in Manchester, both men stayed in a hotel owned by Jacquie's father. For Gerald, living under the same roof as the young woman he was by now courting was a perfect arrangement, even if her father wasn't of the same opinion. What is not well known, and has never to the best of my knowledge been recorded before, is that Ken Smith had a room at the same hotel.

Although he and Durrell were partners, they were free to act unilaterally if they wished, so while Durrell presented the London Zoo with a Soldier rat, a species not seen in Britain for many years, Ken, for his part, donated two Red-breasted marshbirds. Many other animals went to London Zoo. George Cansdale, the Superintendent, particularly welcomed the arrival of the Sun bitterns, which he described as the 'most ornamental and interesting' of that group of birds, and Tricolored herons, the latter new to the zoo. Inevitably some of the new arrivals failed to thrive, in some cases because their requirements in captivity were not fully understood. Amphibians in particular need conditions to be just right, and so it is no surprise to find that many of the fatalities were frogs and toads. On one day alone, 19 September, no fewer than eight amphibians brought back as part of Ken Smith and Gerald Durrell's expedition to British Guiana and sold to London Zoo – an Emerald-eyed Tree frog, another tree frog and six Granular frogs – died after only a few months at the zoo. It is easy for us, at this distance, to criticise the actions of animal-collectors like Ken Smith and Gerald Durrell in bringing back creatures which they knew would be difficult, but it is worth remembering that many species commonly seen in zoos today were once considered very difficult, if not impossible, to maintain in captivity. It was only because animal-collectors and zoo directors were prepared to persevere that eventually the problems of keeping the more difficult species were cracked.

There was a certain amount of resentment amongst the management and staff at Belle Vue that priority often tended to be given to London and Chester and Paignton Zoos, with the cream of the Durrell-Smith collections usually destined for these zoos. The rarest animals were generally reserved for London Zoo because of its impeccable scientific credentials, with Paignton Zoo often taking the lion's share of the rest due to Ken Smith and Gerald Durrell's rapport with its founder and director, Herbert Whitley. It is true that plenty of animals from the expeditions did find themselves permanently domiciled at Belle Vue, but there was certainly a feeling amongst some of the people who worked there that other, more scientifically-inclined zoos were given first refusal on the animals and that Belle Vue often ended up with those animals that none of the other zoos wanted. But not always. Harry Lever, who worked on the bird section, recalls a Pygmy kingfisher that Ken and Gerald had brought back from the Cameroons. It was, he said, a lovely bird, its back and wings an iridescent violet-blue, its belly a pale rufous colour like autumn leaves. Pygmy kingfishers feed on insects. This one, though, was finicky about its food and refused anything larger than a mealworm. The public never got to appreciate this beautiful bird, however, because for some inexplicable reason the zoo's director, Gerald Iles, took the decision to give it a small cage behind the scenes.

'Gerald Durrell and Ken Smith were an inseparable team when I met them at Belle Vue,' Harry Lever told me. 'They had already carved out a name for themselves as animal-collectors, but in those days it was Durrell *and* Smith; the two names were always expressed in conjunction. Then Durrell got famous, and dear old Ken Smith – we all knew him as "Ken": I don't think we ever called him "Kenneth" – he sort of shrunk into the background.'

The kingfisher was not the only creature that Ken and Gerald Durrell sold to Belle Vue Zoo not to be put on view to the general public. In fact, several animals they brought back were unceremoniously stashed away out of sight of the zoo's visitors. In a private service area at the back of the Reptile House was a potto and Black-eared squirrels from the Cameroons expedition and a pair of Squirrel monkeys from British Guiana, but nobody, apart from the people who looked after them, was aware they were even there.

Several species of reptiles and amphibians from the recent expedition to British Guiana found a permanent home at Belle Vue, though due to lack of space most of them were also housed off-view. Clive Bennett and David Barnaby's book *The Reptiles of Belle Vue 1950-1977* mentions two venomous South American Coral snakes, two eight-foot Green anacondas, some Common iguanas, four Cooke's Tree boas, four Giant toads, and four Pipa toads. Of these, only the Pipa toads – on view in the zoo's Aquarium – were placed on display to the general public. Other animals from the same expedition were accommodated in a variety of unusual locations around the zoo, most commonly in the large service room at the rear of the tropical bird house. One such was a Brazilian Tree porcupine that rejoiced in the name of Esmeralda. She, too, was not put on view to the general public, possibly because her nocturnal proclivities made her a poor exhibit, but remained in this service area all the time that she was at the zoo. It was usual practice to house new arrivals – mammals as well as birds – here until such time as more suitable, permanent accommodation could be found elsewhere around the zoo. That, at least, was the intention, but in more than a few cases animals remained in a kind of limbo in this service area, well cared for but admired only by their keepers and occasionally by specially invited guests, until they died or were sent to another zoo. Such was the fate of Esmeralda. 'I had a very soft spot in my heart for her in spite of the fact that she was hardly a pet to stroke or play with,' wrote Gerald Iles in 1960. 'I well remember head keeper Kelly picking her up on one occasion. He found it most painful as we pulled the barbed quills out of his hands.' Over seven years later Esmeralda was sent to Chester Zoo as a mate for a lonesome male being held there.

They may have been at the top of their game, but Ken Smith and Gerald Durrell had learned the hard way that collecting was not a way to get rich quick. An animal-collector might, if he was lucky, recoup his losses, perhaps even make a modest profit, but the profit was never enough to live on for long. Sooner or later the money always ran out, and both the African and South American trips had been financial disasters. By now Gerald Durrell was on his uppers, his collecting career on hold for the simple reason that having invested – and lost – his inheritance on three very costly trips to the tropics, he was now almost penniless. Only after becoming a successful author was he able to resume his collecting trips, but for the moment his prospects seemed dire. For Durrell, the need to find a job that paid a reliable weekly wage was paramount. Despairing of finding a more senior position in a zoo, trading on his contacts he cadged a low-key position at Belle Vue, where he was put to work as a temporary keeper in the Aquarium, occasionally helping out in the Reptile House, part of the same building.

At the same time, Ken also found employment at the zoo. According to Harry Lever, Ken did not seem bound by fixed working hours but appeared to come and go as he pleased. 'The other keepers arrived early for work,' Harry recalled. 'We often turned up much earlier than we were required to because this quiet early morning period before too many people got about was the best part of the day in which to observe our animal charges and spot anything out of the ordinary that might indicate a specimen was off-colour, for instance. Time spent quietly standing and watching was *never* time wasted. But Ken rarely seemed to put in an appearance much before ten o'clock.'

To all the employees, Belle Vue Zoo Park was known, for convenience, simply as B.V., and it wasn't long before Ken, too, was automatically referring to the zoo by its abbreviation. Every keeper has his or her favourite group of animals and with Ken it was the primates (among certain others) – the zoo was renowned for its excellent primate collection comprising about thirty species, ranging from anthropoid apes to lemurs and galagos – and so it comes as no surprise to find that for much of his time at Belle Vue he worked in the Monkey House.

'Ken was a genuinely nice bloke, and smart, too,' Harry Lever told me. 'He had brains, that much was obvious. But if he had any other interests, that is apart from animals, he never spoke of them.'

I enquired whether he had ever talked about his early life or his family.

'No, never, he didn't talk about himself at all.'

Would he describe him as introverted, I asked, perhaps even shy?

Harry mulled the question over for a bit. 'Yes, that is the impression I got. He was on very friendly terms with some of the other keepers and in particular he soon developed a rapport with young Jimmy Beechy, who worked alongside him in the Monkey House, but generally Ken kept himself to himself. He was the opposite of Durrell, who enjoyed company, particularly female company, whereas I don't recall seeing Ken with a woman when he was at Belle Vue. Ken was quite reserved, even taciturn. His interest was focused entirely on the livestock. He would never initiate a conversation. But I don't want to suggest he was aloof. Far from it. He was very polite but he enjoyed talking about the things that interested *him*. He had the ability to turn any conversation round to whatever *he* wanted to talk about, which usually centred around animals and zoos, and then he could hold sway for ages. The transformation could be quite dramatic. I think he found social situations quite awkward, but as soon as the conversation turned to animals, he was a different person; his diffidence dropped away and he became a less inhibited, more confident person. But, when I knew him, he hated confrontation, and he would never be drawn into an argument.'

Someone else who worked at Belle Vue and remembered Ken Smith was its one-time Head Keeper of birds, the renowned aviculturist, Frank Woolham. He recalled Ken as being 'very nice and knowledgeable', but then added that in some ways he was a 'strange man', 'stiff and prickly', 'didn't suffer fools gladly', and 'was a stickler for the work ethic'. Quite possibly, Ken's natural reserve was misinterpreted by Frank as stiffness. Unfortunately, Mr Woolham was not well enough to speak with me directly (he died soon afterwards), but chose to communicate with me via Malcolm Ellis of the Avicultural Society, so we are left to ponder on what he meant by 'strange'.

As for being a stickler for the work ethic, several people I've spoken to agree that Ken was a hard, conscientious worker who expected nothing less in others. For instance, during the expedition to the British Cameroons he had taken Gerald Durrell to task, accusing him of not pulling his weight, and Durrell, indignant at this slur, had demanded an apology (which he received).

Ken's trips abroad in pursuit of rare and unusual animals had filled him with wanderlust. At Belle Vue he was restless and hankered for the vibrancy and hibiscus-scented air of the tropics and he had no intention of hanging around in grey, austere Manchester for any longer than was necessary. Once the animals that he and Durrell had brought back from South America had been found homes in zoos around the country, he was ready to move on.

Frank Woolham remembered things rather differently. He told me that Ken worked at Belle Vue for quite a long time – up to three to four years – but Frank must have been mistaken about the duration because towards the end of 1950, only a few months after starting at Belle Vue, Ken went off on another animal-collecting expedition, although it is of course quite possible he took leave of absence. Frank accepted that his memory might have been at fault. As hard as he had tried to remember more precisely, he couldn't, he told me.

Ken's destination this time was the then British colony of Sierra Leone in West Africa. For financial reasons, Gerald Durrell was unable to accompany him and for the first time Ken was in sole charge. Leaving his impecunious former partner back at home, Ken flew to Lungi airport, Sierra Leone (via Dakar in Senegal) in November 1950. Although only a small country, Sierra Leone is endued with a diverse range of habitats. There are coastal swamps rising to a heavily forested, albeit extensively cultivated, undulating plateau in the east; there are rainforests and mountains and savannahs. Ken established his camp in a native village called Koribundu in the heart of the forest and before long he had obtained Colobus and Diana monkeys (the latter destined for Paignton Zoo), sixteen chimpanzees, and the small forest-dwelling antelope known as duikers, as well as storks, herons, pythons, and many other animals.

Unlike many other naturalists who naturally gravitate towards one particular group of animals, Ken was profoundly interested in the full panoply of animal life. The great

Dutch ethologist, the late Niko Tinbergen, opined there were two breeds of naturalist: the 'diggers', who concentrate on only a few species, or even just a single species, until they have learnt all that they can, often never diversifying; and the 'spreaders', who surround themselves with hundreds of different animals. Ken Smith was, by inclination, a 'spreader'. Although not known primarily as an ornithologist (his interest in wildlife was much too catholic for that), Ken delighted in birds as much as he did in mammals (unlike Gerald Durrell who admitted he was more mammal- than bird-orientated) and as early on in his career as 1947, when he was still at Whipsnade Zoo, he had joined the Avicultural Society, an international organisation dedicated to the study of birds in the wild and in captivity. He found Sierra Leone to be a particularly good place for birds, with no fewer than 626 recorded species. Among the birds he brought back were several Hooded vultures (including at least one exceedingly tame specimen) and a number of Cattle egrets. Many of the birds were destined for Paignton Zoo, and over a year later he was to be reunited with them when he was appointed Superintendent of that zoo. At Paignton, he was fascinated to see that in summer the egrets strutted through the long grass in their aviary, arching and stretching their necks as they searched for insects, just as they had done back in Africa.

Of all the birds he collected, it was the storks, cranes and herons that held a particular fascination for him. 'All birds add charm and interest to the natural scene, but none excels these long-legged species in lending elegance to panoramic beauty,' he wrote in 1955. He bemoaned the fact that few zoos, with the exception of San Diego Zoo, and even fewer, if any, private aviculturists concentrated on storks to any extent. 'I have often thought,' he wrote, 'that a place for storks (and perhaps cranes and herons too!) conducted on the Slimbridge style, would be delightful.'

In Sierra Leone he saw several kinds of storks. On Lake Mabesi, in the south of the country, flocks of Open-bill storks flew from the topmost branches of partially submerged trees as his canoe pushed through the tall reeds towards them. Elsewhere he came across Woolly-necked or Bishop storks. Four of these engaging birds were brought to his camp, looking, as he put it, 'very pious and important'. The appearance of piety was even more marked at feeding times when they bowed repeatedly over the fish and meat offering, as if giving thanks in prayer. Three of the four Woolly-necked storks went to San Diego Zoo, where they were the first of the African race to be shown there.

A bird that Ken had no success with at all was the genus known scientifically as *Picathartes*. For both Ken Smith and Gerald Durrell, *Picathartes* had assumed an almost mystical quality. This rare bird, also known as the Bald-headed rock-crow or rockfowl, of which there are two species found in the rainforests of tropical West and Central Africa, has never been a common subject in aviculture. It is a strange-looking, but not unattractive, lanky bird with a bill shaped rather like a crow's, a long neck and tail, and long legs and stout feet. Its most distinctive feature, as its common name suggests, is its naked brightly coloured head, which, in the species occurring in Sierra Leone, is patterned yellow and black. *Picathartes* was Smith and Durrell's Holy Grail, and both men were more than a little piqued by their failure to bring back a live *Picathartes* from the Cameroons in 1949. On that earlier trip, four young birds had been collected but had not survived. It was particularly galling for them that their Cameroons rival, the veteran animal-collector C.S. Webb, working for the London Zoo, had succeeded in bringing back a live specimen (the first known *Picathartes* to be seen in a zoo) in September 1948, only a few months before Smith and Durrell had sallied forth on their own expedition to the Cameroons.

So when Ken was planning his expedition to Sierra Leone, the acquisition of the western form of the bird was a priority and top of his hypothetical 'Most Wanted' list. Personal pride also played a not insignificant part. Had he succeeded in his goal, he would have had the satisfaction of achieving something on his own that had defeated Gerald Durrell. Ken hoped to find some nestling *Picathartes* and hand-rear them. Nestlings would be easier to capture than the adult birds, even though he realised that even locating a nesting site would be a challenge. He was ecstatic when he succeeded in his ambition and obtained some *Picathartes* at a nest site not far from the capital, Freetown, but his jubilation was short-lived and, despite his best endeavours, he did not manage to keep any of them alive.

*

While Ken was in Sierra Leone, his sister Violet fell seriously ill. She was admitted to Poole General Hospital where she died on 19 April of leukaemia, three days short of her thirty-third birthday. An emigration stamp in Ken's passport is testament to the fact that he left Sierra Leone for Britain on the very day that his sister died. Coincidence? Or had he received the devastating news that she was gravely ill and decided to cut short the expedition? If he did, he was too late, for by the time he got home, Violet was gone. Ken was greatly downcast by the news. He had been very close to his sister and was badly shaken up by her death.

Unlike his two previous expeditions, when he had docked in Liverpool, this time the animals were unloaded at the London docks. While dealing with the grief of losing his sister, Ken teamed up with Robert Jackson, a well-known animal-dealer based in Park Avenue, Timperley near Manchester, to organise the distribution of the Sierra Leonean animals to various zoos in Great Britain and abroad. (Jackson would go on to establish a zoo in North Wales in 1963. He died when a tree fell on him while he was fishing in 1969.)

Ken was kept very busy and for this he was grateful, for it gave his mind something to do rather than dwell on his sad loss. To his relief, the London Zoo agreed to temporarily hold many of the animals allocated to other zoos, either while arrangements could be made for their onward journey or in a quarantine capacity.

On 5 May, the London Zoo purchased a number of the animals, including a female Temminck's Western Red colobus, a Red River hog sow as a mate for one that the zoo's own Jack Lester had brought back from Sierra Leone the previous year, a Bay duiker and a Maxwell's duiker, both males, a fine young male Harnessed antelope, a cusimanse, and an Ayre's hawk-eagle.

The colobus deserves a special mention. It was only the second time in the zoo's history that this rare subspecies, the most westerly form of the Red colobus, had been represented (the first time was only two years earlier, in 1949). These leaf-eating monkeys

KS exhibits two snakes, an Australian Carpet python and a North American Pine snake. © *Sunbeam Photos*.
Right: A Roloway monkey, Paignton Zoo, brought back by KS from Sierra Leone.

With Danny, a tame eland, Paignton Zoo. At nearly six feet in height, Danny was a particularly fine example
of his species. © *Western Morning News*.

Ken feeds Percy the Pygmy hippo at Paignton Zoo. © *Western Morning News*.

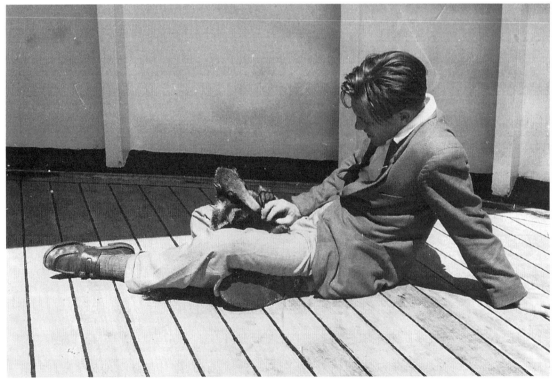

Gerald Durrell on board ship bound for England with Sarah Huggersack, a baby Giant anteater he had obtained in the Chaco region of Paraguay and destined to be a star attraction at Paignton Zoo, 1954.

GREAT
ANTEATER
MYRMECOPHAGA TRIDACTYLA
PARAGUAY

An older Sarah Huggersack with Miss Trudy Hills (soon to be Mrs Kenneth Smith) at Paignton Zoo. Note the misleading sign. In those days Paignton Zoo had an odd habit of putting the individual animal's country of origin on the cage label, rather than where the species as a whole could be found. The label on Sarah Huggersack's pen suggests that Giant anteaters were to be found in Paraguay and apparently nowhere else. In fact, Giant anteaters have a wide area of distribution within South America.

Left: Jeff the Geoffroy's marmoset, which took up residence at Paignton in 1955. © *Vernon Murray*.
Right: Trudy with Dibber, a Guinea baboon at Paignton Zoo that Ken took to many of his lectures.

KS bottle-feeding a baby Two-spotted civet, Paignton Zoo. Never a heavy smoker, Ken gave up the habit after his children were born.

In 1956 Ken mounted a second animal-collecting expedition to British Guiana. This time the objective was to procure animals for Paignton Zoo. In this he was successful and returned with arguably the biggest single consignment of creatures ever to be brought back to the U.K. from that country.

Left: Getting to grips with an anaconda, British Guiana, 1956. Right: This odd-looking animal adopting a defensive 'praying' posture (hence the local name 'Tank 'e God') is a Silky anteater. A number of these were brought into Ken's camp but he released them back into the forest as the species was a 'poor doer' and rarely survived for long under captive conditions. British Guiana, 1956. © *Vernon Murray.*

KS with his Guianese assistant, Bob Veerasawmy, and a Spectacled owl, 1956.

KS demonstrates the easiest way to move a sloth…

…And a capybara, British Guiana, 1956.

KS hand-feeding the pair of White-faced Saki monkeys obtained in British Guiana, 1956.

Above: A beautiful study of one of the young Howler monkeys. © *Vernon Murray.*

Right: Trudy with the baby Red Howler monkeys at Paignton Zoo.

Left: KS brought this Tegu lizard back from South America in 1956. Tegus have a formidable bite and he has taken the wise precaution of wearing gauntlets. © *Vernon Murray*. Right: KS with two Capuchin monkeys named Jonny and Bimbo outside the entrance to the Small Mammal House at Paignton Zoo in 1958. This building housed an eclectic mix of small and medium-sized mammal species.

Scroll on more than fifty years. The same scene in 2009, the peacock helpfully showing the exact spot where KS had stood in the other photograph above (right) more than half a century earlier. The building is still in use as a Small Mammal House, albeit given over mostly to tamarins these days, but visitors are no longer able to stroll inside, the animals being on view in outdoor enclosures.

Above: Palmer's, Camden Town, 1950s. Here, in those pre-legislation days, could be purchased many animals that could not, by even the broadest definition of the word, be labelled by that debasing word 'pet'.

Left: Lucy Pendar visiting KS at Paignton Zoo with her first two children, Rebecca and Paul, circa 1958, shortly before Ken moved to Jersey Zoo. *(Photo courtesy of Lucy Pendar).*

were by no means easy to cater for back then, and even today, although the problems of keeping Black-and-white colobus have been largely overcome, Red colobus are still difficult and hardly ever seen in zoos. At the time of Ken Smith's birth in 1911, no colobus of any kind had survived at the London Zoo for more than thirteen months. By the time Ken went to Sierra Leone, things had not improved much. He did exceptionally well to land Red colobus in the U.K. However, there is a tragic postscript. On 7 May, a Red colobus at London Zoo, presumably the same animal, was observed to be unwell. What *is* known for certain is that on 28 May, after little more than three weeks at London Zoo, the female Red colobus that Ken Smith had succeeded in bringing back against all odds and in defiance of perceived zoological wisdom, died.

Also bought by the London Zoo were two White-faced Tree ducks, a Piping hornbill (Ken must have been delighted when he added this specimen to his collection for he was very fond of hornbills), a Great White heron, a Woolly-necked stork, a Grey-breasted Helmeted Guinea fowl, two African Rock pythons, a Royal python, a Smyth's Water snake, and three African Bullfrogs. In addition, Ken presented London Zoo, *gratis*, with one West African Little sparrowhawk, a Long-tailed cormorant, African Cattle egret (not, as was thought by the zoo at the time, a Little egret), and two West African goshawks, the latter originally misidentified as Black-&-White sparrowhawks which is how they are described in *Zoo Life* magazine. The goshawks were put in part of the old Tropical House where they performed a useful service ridding the house of an infestation of mice. According to *Zoo Life*, Ken also *presented* London Zoo with a Black heron, but the zoo's own Daily Occurrences Book for 1951 states that this bird was *purchased* from Kenneth Smith. Two monkeys (a King colobus and another Red colobus), both from Sierra Leone, arrived at London Zoo in early May 'in transit to Kenneth Smith'. Dublin Zoo took two Yellow-bellied Senegal parrots, eight Red-faced lovebirds, two Rock pythons and three African Bullfrogs, and Belle Vue Zoo bought two Spotted Eagle owls (these would have been the northerly Vermiculated race, considered by some modern authorities to be a distinct species in its own right), a trio of Green-headed sunbirds, and a serval.

*

After returning from Sierra Leone, Ken seems to slip under the radar (in his passport, there are three more stamps, which appear to date from later on in 1951, but these are smudged, indistinct, and it is not clear what they relate to) and when he resurfaces a year later in 1952 he is managing a tiny menagerie in Margate. Somehow a whole year of his life appears to have gone missing. Did he resume work at Belle Vue Zoo? This would be consistent with Frank Woolham's contention that Ken was at Belle Vue for quite some time. But there is another, more convincing explanation. A clue to his whereabouts during that 'missing year' is provided by a passionate missive he fired off to *The Times* in July 1952, concerned about the risk posed to the wildlife of the Monte Bello Islands off Australia by a proposal to carry out nuclear testing in the archipelago. Revealingly, in the letter, Ken gave as his address the Hospital for Tropical Diseases, 4 St. Pancras Way, NW1. In the early 1950s, Ken was regularly in and out of hospital while he was treated for tropical maladies contracted in Africa. The fact that in 1952 he was disposed to give the hospital as his contact address strongly suggests that this time his stay was more prolonged. In fact, it seems he was in hospital for several weeks, if not longer, which would certainly explain the 'missing year'. From his hospital bed he wrote to *The Times*:

Sir, – On July 24 the Prime Minister declined to order a new inquiry into the dangers to bird and animal [*sic*] life on the Monte Bello Islands before the atom bomb explosion is carried out there. Must the matter remain like this? Mr A.H. Chisholm, the prominent Australian naturalist, has stated that at least 20 kinds of birds inhabit the islands, including a spinifex bird of a sub-species not found elsewhere. On Barrow Island, 10 miles north of the Monte Bello group, there is a distinctive species of kangaroo which is found nowhere else. While the annihilation of any species of the fauna of the islands is regrettable enough, the destruction of the spinifex bird and the Barrow Island kangaroo will, or may, result in the greater tragedy of total extinction.

The irremediable act of extinction of any species, or even sub-species, is, in the view of many naturalists and others, a denial of our duty to posterity to preserve our wild life heritage. Surely it is possible, even now, for satisfactory arrangements (commensurate with security interests) to be made with Australian conservationists to allow and encourage them to catch up some of the Barrow Island kangaroos for transfer to sanctuaries or zoological parks and gardens. This would save the species, as the marsupials would continue to breed under such new conditions. Some spinifex birds, as well as any other kinds of particular rarity, could also be trapped for release in selected areas. Such action is quite practicable, and would show to the world that even in the dire necessity of atomic research Britain had regard for one of the finer manifestations of civilization.

I am, Sir, yours faithfully,
Kenneth Smith

It is surprising a good naturalist like Ken should write 'bird and animal life' when of course he meant 'bird and mammal life'. His letter to *The Times* is the first tangible piece of evidence we have that Ken was more than a mercenary animal-dealer. Some ten years before the World Wildlife Fund was launched, he was already aware that wild places were not a limitless bounty. He even hints that transferring certain threatened species to zoos may save them from extinction, but stops short at believing this will work in all cases, accepting that some species will always be easier to breed under controlled conditions than others (so in his view the Barrow Island kangaroo, more often called the Barrow Island wallaroo, was a prime candidate for captive breeding, the Spinifex bird – a type of warbler – less suitable in his opinion). Needless to say, the letter didn't sway the politicians and the nuclear tests went ahead regardless. In October, Britain exploded its first atomic bomb off the coast of Western Australia, and by doing so became the world's third atomic power after the U.S.A. and the Soviet Union. The letter, one of Ken's earliest published pieces of writing, shows an articulate, erudite writer capable of presenting a well-constructed argument. He wrote clearly and succinctly. He had a good grasp of language, as his use of 'commensurate', a word hardly in everyday usage, demonstrates, and the fact he was able to cite A.H. Chisholm (this was probably Alexander Hugh Chisholm, a noted Australian journalist, newspaper editor, prolific author and amateur ornithologist) is proof that he was well-read and interested in the conservation problems of parts of the world that he had never visited and in animal species he had never encountered.

*

Meanwhile, Gerald Durrell and Jacquie had eloped, fleeing Manchester owing to Jacquie's father's disapproval of the liaison. With her father conveniently away on business for a few days, they took the train to Bournemouth. Ahead of them lay the Durrell family home in St. Alban's Avenue, where the couple could be assured a warm welcome and where they could take stock of their parlous situation. The elopement was obviously a spur of the moment thing. So suddenly did they bolt from Manchester that it appears that Durrell never even had chance to say goodbye to his work colleagues at Belle Vue Zoo. He and two of the senior keepers frequently enjoyed an after-work drink in the old Palm Court bar inside the zoo. 'See you tomorrow,' said Durrell one evening as he usually did. But he didn't turn up for work the next day. He was already on his way to Bournemouth with his bride-to-be. His money almost exhausted, he realised it was imperative he find a job. From his tiny flat, Durrell wrote to all the major zoos in Britain, Australia, the U.S.A. and Canada, to no avail. Eventually he was offered temporary employment as the relief manager of a small menagerie at Margate. Being only a three week contract, it was far from ideal but it would have to do, and Durrell leapt at the chance of getting back to working with animals again. In her provocatively entitled book *Beasts in My Bed* (Collins, 1967), Jacquie recalled that stopgap job:

> About this time a former associate of Gerry's asked if we would like to look after a seaside menagerie that he was in charge of at Margate. He could not afford to pay us a salary but would cover the cost of our lodging and our food, plus our fares.

That unnamed former associate could only have been Ken Smith. In 1952, Ken had taken over the management of the Margate Aquarium and Mini Zoo at the Cliftonville Lido. It is clear that Ken took pity on Gerald Durrell – still unable to find permanent work in a zoo – and wanted to help his erstwhile partner. What was the reason for Ken's absence? He rarely took holidays and, when he did, they were often just short breaks of no more than a few days. To be away from his work for so long, something else must have happened. No doubt this was when he was admitted to hospital, and he looked to Gerald and Jacquie to tend the animals while he was away.

The Margate Aquarium and Mini Zoo was a typical seaside menagerie. In the 1950s, owners of guesthouses disapproved of their guests returning to their rooms during the day. Guests were expected to leave the guesthouse shortly after breakfast and not return until the evening. 'Once out, you stay out,' seemed to be the rule, to allow the rooms to be cleaned without interruption. Town councils of popular holiday resorts like Margate, realising that holidaymakers needed somewhere to go once the allure of the beach had lost its initial magnetism or when the rain clouds started to gather, were quick to sanction a whole host of leisure attractions, resulting in a proliferation around the coastline of small catchpenny menageries.

So Gerald and Jacquie took over the running of the Margate menagerie from Ken while he was incapacitated. Typical of the kind of small seaside resort menagerie that mushroomed in the 1950s, '60s and early '70s, this disparate animal collection, part of a small entertainment complex on the seafront, was little more than a peepshow, lacking any *raison d'être* beyond the base one of public entertainment. Not surprisingly, it did not appeal to Durrell, with his lofty ideas of how zoos should be run, although he was grateful for the work, short-lived though it was.

For Ken Smith, too, managing the Margate Aquarium and Mini Zoo was no more than a diversion, a pleasant but ultimately inefficacious interlude, and he did not linger there for more than a few months. *His* boat, like Gerald Durrell's, was about to come in, because in the autumn of 1952, with Durrell on the cusp of becoming an international best-selling author, Ken landed the plum job of the new Superintendent at Paignton Zoological and Botanical Gardens.

Chapter Nine

Entrée Torbay! *(1952–1956)*

IT WAS A PRESTIGIOUS CALLING. In terms of the number of species on exhibition, Paignton Zoo was the third largest zoo in the U.K. Only London Zoo and Chester Zoo could boast of having more species.* Think of practically any mammal, bird, reptile, amphibian or fish species, and there was a good chance that either it or a close relative was represented at Paignton Zoo. To be Superintendent of such an important collection was a big honour and an even bigger responsibility. Ken took over from the outgoing superintendent, the Turkistan-born, and one-time celebrated strongman, Alexander Zass, who was retiring after eleven years. A showman like Zass (who died in 1962) had been a rather peculiar choice for animal manager. When he was packing the halls in his strongman days, his act had included such extraordinary feats as lifting a steel girder with his teeth and carrying a live carthorse round his neck – though not at the same time – hardly work which prepared him for running a busy zoo. Ken Smith was a more conventional appointment; with his knowledge and experience he was just what Paignton Zoo needed at a pivotal point in its development as it attempted to remodel itself after the war. Many of the animals from his expeditions had been bought by Paignton Zoo, so he suddenly found himself reunited with old friends, including Charlie and Sue, two chimpanzees he had obtained on his collecting expeditions to the Cameroons and Sierra Leone, respectively. As soon as he took up his post at Paignton, he threw himself into his work. It was a heady but also a very hectic time. The zoo was just beginning to recover from the deprivations and stagnation caused by the war and was looking to replace many of its older, less suitable buildings and enclosures. It was hard, sometimes stressful, work and the hours could be long, but despite the rigours of the job – and living in a bungalow in the grounds, as he did, meant being on call twenty-four hours a day – he still found time to attend Quaker Meetings, and in 1954 he made a formal request to transfer from the Paignton Meeting to the Torquay Preparative Meeting. But Ken kept his religious convictions to himself and few, if any, of his staff were aware of his affiliations for he never discussed them.

As the new Superintendent, Ken was one of only a handful of people to have regular, unlimited access to the zoo's owner and founder, the eccentric – and forthright – millionaire Herbert Whitley.

Whitley was a man who refused to bow to convention. An odd but sometimes brilliant character with a natural affinity for animals of all kinds, he took the rule book… and threw it away. He was prone to obsessions, one of which involved trying to breed blue colour mutations of animals: blue bantams, chickens (the Coronation Sussex was one of his creations), turkeys, ducks, pigeons, even blue Great Danes. Ken's association

By the end of the decade, Paignton Zoo was to have more animal species on display than even Chester Zoo but would rank ninth in terms of the number of individual animals.

with him began in 1949 when, fresh back from the British Cameroons, he had visited Whitley at his home at Primley, next to the zoo. Ken got on very well with him, which was an achievement because not everybody did. Whitley was a shy recluse, the zoo world's Howard Hughes, with a reputation for being 'difficult' and 'prickly'. Stories are legion of the lengths he went to in order to avoid meeting someone if he didn't want to see them, even dashing through the house before escaping in an elevator rather than face them. Anchorite as he was, Whitley was nonetheless highly regarded by his peers for his zoological expertise.

By 1952, when Ken was appointed Superintendent of Paignton Zoo, Whitley was nearing the end of his life. He had always been an introvert, never at ease in social situations, but towards the end he had become a virtual hermit, rarely straying from his house during daylight hours and reliant on Ken for daily news briefs of what was happening at the zoo. There weren't many people whose company he enjoyed or whose advice he would listen to, but Ken was one of this very select band, in some ways becoming a sort of unofficial P.A. to Whitley. As taciturn as he was, Whitley was sometimes able to conquer his shyness for the chance to converse informally with likeminded individuals on a one-to-one basis. When he heard that the renowned aviculturist Raymond Sawyer was exhibiting some of his birds at the Paignton Town Hall, Whitley immediately dispatched Ken into the town to meet Sawyer and invite him back to Primley for a meal. Unfortunately Sawyer, much to his regret, was unable to spare the time and asked Ken to convey his apologies to Whitley.

Ken might have been on friendly terms with Whitley, but that is not to say he didn't find some of his idiosyncrasies infuriating at times. Much to Ken's annoyance, Whitley invariably did his rounds of the zoo after everyone had gone home so there was no chance of running into anybody. The following morning Ken would find gates and doors left open and animals in the wrong pens. 'Bloody Whitley's been round at night again,' he would moan exasperatedly. It wasn't only Ken who found the founder's nocturnal perambulations and constant interference irksome. Whitley was at his most active from about ten o'clock at night to about two o'clock the following morning. This was the time of day he enjoyed the most, when the zoo was empty of staff and public alike and he was free to get on with things without fear of interruption. He busied himself in his greenhouses late into the night, and in the morning the gardeners would find tools and other utensils missing or in the wrong places.

Ken would sometimes repair to Primley at the end of the working day in order to keep Whitley updated on zoo matters, occasionally joining him for a game of billiards. The disparity between the two men was profound. The shabbily dressed Whitley was never known to wear a tie and, living up to his persona as the eccentric millionaire, often had a length of twine wrapped around his waist as a makeshift belt to stop his trousers descending, concertina-like, to his ankles. Since he was almost never sighted around the zoo, or indeed anywhere, he couldn't see any point to dressing smartly – in striking contrast to Ken, who was always immaculately attired and was rarely observed without a necktie even on the most informal of occasions. Herbert Whitley, a chain smoker, the inevitable cigarette hanging damply from his lips, would often stay up most of the night playing billiards if he could find a partner, and Ken was content to oblige if he had nothing else on. Ken wasn't particularly interested in the game, nor could he play particularly well; the prime attraction of those long evenings spent with Whitley as far as he was concerned being the chance afforded him to look round his employer's vast library of natural history books. A zoological problem, more often than not, demanded research, when reference would be made to the many fine books for checking and cross-checking. Ken was well read, as a former keeper at Paignton Zoo, Gerry Breeze, can attest. Gerry Breeze was none other than Gerald Durrell's nephew (his mother was Durrell's sister Margaret – 'Margo' in the famous trilogy of books that Gerald Durrell wrote about his childhood on the Greek island of Corfu) and Ken had been responsible for getting him a temporary job working on the reptile section at Paignton Zoo. 'What impressed me most about Ken was his erudition,' Gerry Breeze told me. 'He knew all the scientific stuff. Just mention to him any species, no matter how obscure, and he was able to tell you something about it, its habits, distribution, diet in the wild and in captivity, anything. He was like a walking *Larousse* encyclopedia. I think that's why he and Herbert Whitley got on so well together. They were both keen to learn.'

No wonder Ken enjoyed studying the books in Whitley's library. Discussions often developed far beyond the immediate matters of zoo business. Ken found his boss gave very readily the 'fruits of his mind' to those he considered genuinely or seriously interested. 'He was,' he wrote, 'a unique and wonderful tutor on these occasions; his knowledge on many subjects was, in my view, unrivalled and based on profound wisdom.'

Conversations with 'H.W.', as he was affectionately known to Ken and the few others in Whitley's intimate circle, often ranged far into the night, even extending into the early hours of the morning. One of the last discussions they had together involved Steamer ducks. Towards the end, Whitley was too ill to rise from his sofa to consult the large lexicon in his book-lined study, and Ken went for him to obtain knowledge of some Greek derivatives.

That conversation about Steamer ducks was probably inspired by Gerald Durrell's latest expedition. Having discovered he had a talent for writing, Durrell had by now become an instant celebrity as a result of his books – much to his amusement, even embarrassment, for he never had a high regard of himself as an author. To his great surprise, his books had caught the mood of their time, that elusive *zeitgeist*, and they sold extremely well. His debut book was chosen as a *Daily Mail* Book of the Month and a Book Society Choice and rapidly sold 27,000 copies. Subsequent books promised to do equally well if not better. With his fortunes revived, towards the end of 1953, together with his wife Jacquie, Gerald Durrell embarked on an animal-collecting trip to Argentina and Paraguay.

Herbert Whitley had bought many fine specimens from Durrell in the past and had followed his career with interest. Ken was still regularly in touch with his former collecting partner and was able to keep Whitley informed. Although Ken would not be accompanying the Durrells to the South American pampas, he knew all about the planned expedition. No doubt at some point Gerald apprised him of the fact that one of the objectives of the expedition was the procurement of Steamer ducks for Peter Scott's Severn Wildfowl Trust. Ken relayed this to his boss, and this ignited Whitley's interest in learning more about Steamer ducks. In the event, Durrell was unsuccessful in his quest and he returned to England *sans* Steamer ducks.

In fact the whole expedition was something of a failure, but among the relatively few creatures Gerald Durrell *did* bring back were some cuckoos and jays for Paignton Zoo. Although Whitley was very ill by this stage, his passion for all animals, but birds in particular, was undiminished, cementing Ken's belief that an interest in nature was a great life-enhancer. Ken was with him when he saw the new birds for the first time and witnessed first-hand his excitement on that occasion.

> Whitley's understanding of birds, both as an aviculturist and as a fancier, was extraordinary. His enthusiasm was great too. I remember, for instance, his pleasure at seeing newly-arrived Guira Cuckoos from Paraguay, his gratification on picking out a Blue-bearded Jay from a group of Pileated Jays.

Another animal brought back from the Paraguayan Chaco by Gerald Durrell as part of the same expedition in 1954 and eagerly snapped up by Paignton Zoo was a tame baby Giant anteater by the name of Sarah Huggersack, where she was immediately adopted by a twenty-four-year old female keeper known as Trudy Hills.

Trudy was in charge of pets' corner, and she and Sarah Huggersack made several television appearances together and even accompanied Gerald Durrell to a lecture he was giving at London's Festival Hall to promote his books, where the pampered anteater was allocated the No. 1 dressing room.

Trudy was soon to make a big crater-sized impact on Ken Smith's life because, before the decade was out, she was to become Mrs Trudy Smith.

Ken Smith found himself powerfully attracted to her. Here was a young woman, a keeper, who was enthusiastic, hard-working, and intuitive (this latter an essential quality when working with animals). He recognised immediately her natural aptitude for that kind of work, but, much as she showed great promise, he could also see that her position in the pets' corner was rather a squandering of her talents. Trudy had started work at Paignton Zoo before Ken arrived there. It was her first job and in future years she would look back with considerable affection on this part of her life, and in particular she relished the variety of animals she saw there on a daily basis. From the start, she showed considerable initiative obtaining new stock for her section. Herbert Whitley was famously reluctant to sign cheques, particularly for things, such as the pets' corner, for which he was unsympathetic because he felt they lacked a serious purpose. His reluctance wasn't just because he was thrifty – although that was certainly part of the reason – but because cheques had to be countersigned by the zoo's co-director, Norman Dixon, a businessman originally from Birmingham. The two men detested each other, and by refusing to sign cheques, Whitley was doing what he could to thwart Dixon in the most infantile way. Such petty arguments hindered progress at the zoo. So Trudy struck up a deal with Palmer's, the famous pet emporium in Camden Town, not far from London Zoo. Also known as the Regent Pet Stores, this famous establishment specialised in animals that could not, by any stretch of the imagination, be termed 'pets'. According to one account, Palmer's was a 'stuffy little shop' with a pervading odour of 'birdseed, catshit and the musk of monkeys.' (John Pearson, *The Gamblers.*) From the front it looked like an ordinary high street pet shop, but that innocent façade was deceptive because in the back it was like descending into the bowels of the Ark. Animals arrived by the crateload, day and night, from all over the world, and only a few pounds could buy you a really rare or endangered creature. John Aspinall was one of Palmer's customers and it was here that the future zoo-owner bought his first Capuchin monkey and a pair of Himalayan bear cubs.

Trudy was on good terms with the owner, John Palmer, and whenever she needed more animals for her section, she would pack a hamper with surplus mice and as many as twenty rabbits and about the same number of guinea-pigs, all of which she had bred in pets' corner, and catch the midnight train to London, exchange them at Palmer's for other, more desirable, animals and be back at work on time the next morning.

She always felt a huge surge of relief by the time she reached Palmer's because during the train journey the animals in her charge would while away the time demolishing their cardboard carrying boxes and there was the constant worry they might escape into the train. But her initiative and entrepreneurial flair had greatly impressed Paignton's new Superintendent. Knowing of her special fascination for small mammals in particular, and having seen something of her affinity with animals, Ken went to Whitley and said, 'Why not give Trudy a chance to work with small mammals other than those in the pets' corner? There's always something needing to be hand-reared and I've seen the way animals respond to her touch.' Whitley listened. Ken was one of the few people whose judgement he trusted, and so, if still a little doubtful, he agreed.

Had it been anybody else but Ken who had done the asking, he probably would have refused the request. Herbert Whitley had a reputation for being a misogynist; in general he didn't trust women. Peter Carroll, author of a short history of Paignton Zoo, sees things differently: 'I believe he was not a misogynist at all; he was simply overcome by his shyness towards the opposite sex which remained with him all his life.' There is, however, no doubt he believed that female keepers should be responsible only for the domestic or baby animals – the usual occupants of a zoo's pets' corner – feeling that all other animals were best left to their (physically stronger) male colleagues. Ken had no truck with such blatant sexual discrimination (although Paignton was certainly not unusual in this and it was fairly standard practice in most zoos of the time). Trudy soon showed she had a winning way with the young of many small mammal species – the zoological equivalent of the horticulturist's green fingers – and to her was often entrusted the tricky job of hand-rearing orphaned animals or ministering to the sick, the finicky and the delicate. She reared baby civets, coatis, foxes and jackals, among other animals, often devising quite novel, even devious, ways to encourage the babies to feed. Almost the only small mammals she could never bring herself to trust wholeheartedly were mongooses: 'No matter how hand-tame they are, sooner or later they bite the hand that feeds them.' She did, however, make an exception for cusimanses, shaggy forest mongooses from West and Central Africa, which she found enchanting. Although birds in general couldn't compete with mammals in her affections, she was always very keen on birds of prey. Conversely, parrots just left her cold, which is rather surprising because most people (myself included) would probably rate them among their favourite birds. 'At

Paignton Zoo I had a very nice Blue-fronted Amazon, which accepted grapes from my hand,' she recalled. 'but most of the parrots I've known since then have been unresponsive, noisy, destructive things.'

*

As well as being responsible for the zoo's permanent residents, Ken soon found himself inundated with injured and orphaned wild creatures brought to the zoo by well-meaning members of the public. With the zoo being so close to the coast, at times there seemed an almost constant procession of marine life casualties, a problem he had not had to face before in the other zoos where he had worked (with the possible exception of Margate). At times the number of ailing seabirds presented to the zoo threatened to overwhelm him, prompting him to write a letter to *The Times* in February 1954 calling for action to be taken to protect maritime species from the constant menace of oil pollution:

> Sir, – Oiled and helpless sea birds, chiefly guillemots, razorbills, and Manx shearwaters, are brought by rescuers to these zoological gardens in pathetic procession. We do what we can for them, but for every bird we receive scores of others linger to die on Torbay beaches. The melancholy spectacle of dying birds has become so commonplace that at times one fears that the tragedy is in danger of being regarded as inevitable – instead of being considered intolerable. It is to be hoped that Her Majesty's Government will lead all international efforts to prevent the pollution of the seas by oil.

The following year Ken had another letter in *The Times*, this time railing against the shooting of eagles by an Australian minister. Once again the understated letter was a study in succinctness:

> I am sure I am not alone in feeling consternation on reading in your columns yesterday that Mr R.G. Casey, Australian Minister for External Affairs, is on holiday shooting wedge-tailed eagles from his private aircraft. The wedge-tailed eagle is a magnificent bird, one that has been sadly reduced in numbers in many parts of Australia. Though it may have a reputation as a lamb killer, many authorities consider that it feeds mainly on rabbits and carrion.
> The shooting of birds from aircraft is, in my opinion, deplorable, and it is my fervent hope that the practice will not become commonplace.

Ken was visited at Paignton by Marvin Lee Jones, an American in his mid-twenties serving with the United States Army stationed in West Germany. The army may have been Marvin's career, but zoos were his passion. Facts and figures were Marvin's thing and during his lifetime he compiled meticulous zoological records. In about 1955, while on leave, he went on a grand tour of twenty European zoos. British zoos on his itinerary were London Zoo (where he spent three days looking round the collection),

Chessington, Whipsnade, Paignton, Bristol, Dudley, Edinburgh, Belle Vue, and Chester Zoo. Of Paignton Zoo he wrote (in *International Zoo News*):

> The next zoo was Paignton, out in Devon, and most pleasant. Mr Kenneth Smith took excellent care of me and we toured the zoo together. Of the collection now in the zoo, all is in excellent condition, with food being the primary thought of this zoo. Rarities seen were Noble Macaw, Formosan Deer, Pygmy Hippo, Canadian Lynx, Roloway Monkeys and some nice mangabeys.

Marvin Jones was clearly impressed, but as comprehensive as the collection at Paignton was, it was planning to increase the variety of animals on show still further by sending its own animal-collecting expedition to South America. An expedition of this magnitude needed an experienced person in charge of it, and they didn't come any more experienced than Ken Smith, and so it came as a surprise to no one that he was chosen to lead it. For the first time he didn't have to worry about the finances, because Paignton Zoo was underwriting the whole operation. It was to be the first full-scale animal-collecting expedition sponsored by a provincial zoo; it was also to be Ken's final collecting trip (though whether he intended it to be so is unclear) and a fitting way to end his animal-collecting career.

As well as bringing back a representative collection of South American animals, Ken was also under instructions from Whitley to return with as many fine botanical specimens as possible. Herbert Whitley was as passionate about the plant kingdom as he was about the animal kingdom, and to prove it he had several greenhouses where he grew and propagated a profusion of tropical species, and Paignton Zoo was promoted as a zoological *and* botanical garden. Ken didn't have a licence to import plants, and pointed out to Whitley the illegality of what he was proposing. 'I'm not allowed to bring back plants,' he protested, reminding his boss that import licences for plants were notoriously difficult to obtain because of concern that fungal spores or other botanic diseases might be inadvertently introduced into Britain, and the effect this could have on the farming and horticultural industries. But the contumacious Whitley, who was unwilling even to license his car and had twice closed his zoo to the public in protest against the entertainment tax he was obliged to pay, had a contemptuous attitude for authority. He resented being told what he could and could not do. He wanted Amazonian plants, and Amazonian plants he had to have. Eventually a scheme was hatched whereby Ken would smuggle the plants into the U.K. concealed in the reptile crates. It was unlikely the port authorities would insist on taking a look into crates containing snakes or caiman.

'But supposing an observant official should notice that a number of the crates appear to be packed with tropical plants, what then?' asked Ken.

'That's easy,' Whitley replied, batting away his concerns with the finesse of a world-class cricketer. 'Just tell him the plants are in there to keep the moisture levels high, and that without a certain amount of foliage to retain the humidity the atmosphere in the boxes would be too dry for the delicate reptiles and amphibians to survive.'

Whitley was delighted to hear that preparations for the forthcoming expedition were in full swing and he was excited and impatient to see what animals and plants Ken would bring back with him from South America. But sadly it was not to be. On 15 September 1955 Whitley died, aged sixty-nine, after a long and painful illness. Ken mourned his death. For all his foibles – and he could be exasperating at times – Whitley had been a kind and sincere man, totally focused on his flora and fauna. His enthusiasm had been infectious. Ken missed that. He missed the evenings spent at Primley, the games of billiards (though Whitley hadn't been able to play for some time) and the long eclectic discussions they had had together. He missed seeing the founder's elation on hearing of the birth of an animal and most of all Ken lamented the fact that 'H.W.' had not lived long enough to rejoice in the successful outcome of the South American expedition. In an obituary to his former boss in *The Avicultural Magazine* he wrote,

> His methods, like his opinions, were forthright. His ideas on the governing of zoos were sound, and if the standards he set are followed today zoo science will progress in the right direction.

Before setting off for the New World, Ken ordered from an animal-dealer a pair of Lesser (Red or Common) pandas from the Himalayas, which had been advertised for £100 for the two animals, and these arrived shortly before he was due to depart. To his anguish, instead of the pair of flossy-coated, fox-red animals he had been expecting, the pandas, when they arrived, were in a terrible mess. Worse, they were dysenteric. In those days it was common practice for unscrupulous dealers to fob zoos off with ailing or even moribund animals. In those cases, no money would change hands immediately. There was an unwritten understanding that if the animal rallied, the dealer got paid; if it died, the zoo had the inconvenience of disposing of the body but had not lost out financially except possibly on vets' bills. The two pandas were very ill and Ken rated their chance of survival as no more than 50:50. With his departure date imminent, he had to make a quick decision on what to do with them. 'Would you look after them for me?' he asked Trudy. 'But don't worry if they don't make it, because the poor little things are so far gone already that it's touch and go whether they'll recover.' Trudy found an effectual medicinal powder and began treating them in earnest and gradually they responded to her patient ministrations, eventually regaining full health, their lovely ginger coats fluffing out.

*

On 17 February 1956, Ken sailed in the S.S. *Arakaka* (first class) from Liverpool on a four-month animal-collecting expedition to his old stamping ground, British Guiana – the scene of his 1950 trip – docking in Georgetown in early March. One of the most important objectives of the expedition was the acquisition of macaws, Amazons, caiques, conures, *Pionus* and other Neotropical parrots to restock Paignton Zoo's newly renovated Parrot House, generally acknowledged to be the finest of its kind in Britain. With the acquisition of parrots being fundamental to the success of the expedition, Ken may well have seen in the name of the ship a favourable portent. The *Arakaka* was actually named after a community on the Barima River at the centre of Guiana's gold-bearing district. Ken probably knew this but it would not have escaped his notice that the first half of the word – 'Ara' – is also the scientific (generic) name of many macaws, whilst, coincidentally, the second half – 'kaka' – is the name of another kind of parrot (albeit one found in New Zealand).

In addition to parrots, Ken hoped to bring back many other birds for the new Tropical Bird House (due to be opened towards the end of 1956) and a collection of South American reptiles for the combined Reptile House and Aquarium, which was being extensively renovated in readiness for an improved collection. Parrots, other tropical birds, and reptiles were his main goals, but he had no intention of restricting himself to these groups and planned to capture many other animals; in particular he hoped to return with such archetypal South American creatures as anteaters, armadillos and sloths.

In this he succeeded magnificently, bringing back what was generally agreed to be the biggest collection of living animals to come from British Guiana – and probably from South America. It contained several species that had never before been seen in the U.K. The haul included two Red Howler monkeys, the prize of the collection and considered to be the only ones in captivity anywhere in the world. Howler monkeys had a reputation for being 'bad doers', but Ken was convinced that with the right diet and level of care they would not only survive but thrive in captivity.

'I had often thought that howlers need not be miserable, and certainly not impossible, as zoo animals,' he wrote.

> Therefore, when I returned to Guiana in 1956 to obtain specimens for Paignton Zoo, I decided that Red howlers should be a 'must'. I collected scores of monkeys as the weeks went by, including even the comparatively rare White-faced saki, but it was not until a month before I sailed for home that I received my first Red howler. It was a young male, caught in the Essequibo forests, and later I was brought a second young male.
>
> The little howlers adjusted themselves slowly to cage life. Their food consisted of tropical fruits cut into small portions, mainly sapadillos, guavas, mangoes, paw-paws, pineapples and bananas. They also took hard-boiled egg, and several times daily they were given a mixture of bread-and-milk with glucose added. This diet was continued throughout the nineteen-day voyage from Georgetown to Liverpool.

Ken received considerable help with the expedition from Vincent Roth, O.B.E., the director of the British Guiana Museum and Zoo in Georgetown. A small corner of the zoo was set aside for the animals Ken collected. The zoo, small as it was, was popular with all races, especially school children; East Indians and Chinese, Portuguese and native Amerindians, as well as the children of expatriate Britons – all were interested visitors. Not only was Vincent Roth an invaluable source of advice and contacts, but he also helped to supply some of the creatures on Ken's wish list. Ken had taken with him to British Guiana a small collection of various British native animals, such as foxes, hedgehogs and badgers, animals which were virtually impossible for Latin American zoos to obtain, and these he had exchanged for a variety of typical South American animals from the zoo in Georgetown, including a Crested curassow, two Brazilian Barn owls, and some Crab-eating raccoons. Best of all was a young Harpy eagle. With a wingspan of nine feet when fully grown, the Harpy eagle, an incredibly powerful bird of prey that would have made short work of those precious Howler monkeys given the opportunity, was presented to Ken by the Georgetown Zoo as a gift from the Guianese government. When it took up its place at Paignton Zoo, it was the only example of its species to be seen in Britain.

Several sloths were brought to his camp, including the notoriously difficult Three-toed kind. Ken knew all about Three-toed sloths. He knew they had so far defied all efforts to maintain them in captivity for more than about eight months at most, due largely to their very specialised diet of *Cecropia* leaves but also because of their requirement for very high humidity. Much as he was pleased for the opportunity to study them at close range and compare their behaviour with that of the more familiar Two-toed sloth (all sloths have the same number of claws on their front legs – two – but the number of their hind legs differs), he realised they could not be expected to survive a long sea voyage or confinement in a British zoo, and chose not to attempt to export them. In comparison, a Two-toed sloth ('Sammy') procured on this expedition was kept with outstanding success on a most unlikely diet of bread-and-milk and bananas. At Paignton Zoo it was exhibited in the Monkey House to gain benefit from the heating system.

Vincent Roth shared Ken's stoical attitude to illness and injury. On one occasion Ken approached him for assistance, having been bitten by an unidentified snake of unknown potentialities. Instead of ordering him to seek medical treatment immediately, Roth invited him to 'Come in and have a rum and we'll wait to see if anything happens'.

After a while, when Ken's condition did not appear to worsen, Roth asked, 'Well, do you feel all right?'

'Fine,' reported Ken.

'Ah well, in that case, it must have been a harmless species, or, if venomous, then only very mildly so, possibly a rear-fanged species. There was no cause for alarm.'

Ken departed British Guiana with the entire collection on the same ship on which he had arrived, S.S. *Arakaka*, in the middle of May, docking in Liverpool on 4 June. Accompanying him on the voyage was one of his Guianese helpers, Bob Veerasawmy, to assist in looking after the collection. He could allow himself more than a smidgen of pride. Among the many mammals he had acquired were two acouchis (a large type of rodent he was sure had not been seen in Britain for over a hundred years; at Paignton they shared a cage with the sloth), two pacas (stocky, burrowing, cavy-like rodents with white-spotted brown fur), a Giant anteater, a tamandua, a douroucouli (Night or Owl monkey), and a pair of White-faced Saki monkeys (known locally as 'Huruwee'). Like the howlers, Saki monkeys were always reckoned to be very hard to acclimatise and maintain, and Ken was very proud to land this pair. But not everybody was enamoured of Paignton Zoo's new arrivals. The well-known primatologist, Dr. Osman Hill, was nonplussed by the Saki monkeys, describing them rather unfairly as 'dismal-looking creatures of not very pleasing appearance though of great scientific interest.'

Reptiles included a Mexican Dwarf python, previously thought to occur only in Mexico and the Central American isthmus but hitherto unrecorded in Guiana, a Green Tree viper, and no fewer than eighteen Green anacondas and the same number of Brazilian tortoises. The ship reverberated with the raucous cries of a hundred parrots, including five specimens of the second largest parrot in the world, the Green-winged or Red-and-Blue macaw. Other notable birds in the collection included the Harpy eagle, some rare Mount Roraima aracaris, two species of tinamou (primitive terrestrial birds superficially resembling quails but so distinct from all other birds as to be placed in their own Order), a Tiger bittern, a flamingo (caught in the Corentyne region to the east of the country), several Red-billed Whistling (Grey-breasted Tree) ducks, a Surinam Jacana or Lily-trotter, Grey-winged trumpeters (related to the cranes), and a number of storks, egrets and herons, including Night herons (called 'Quaaks' in Guiana). It pleased Ken enormously to have obtained the Mount Roraima aracaris, as these were the first examples of their kind ever to leave South America. He originally had half a dozen specimens, three adults and three babies, but only four of them finally arrived at Paignton Zoo, so possibly two did not survive or were deposited with another zoo. There was even an Electric eel, destined for Paignton Zoo's Aquarium where it would prosper on a diet of fish and strips of fresh raw meat. Remembering Herbert Whitley's last wish, Ken also brought back, discreetly lining the reptile crates, a collection of plants including orchids and bromeliads that he knew would delight Paignton Zoo's gardeners.

The great majority of the animals were bound for Paignton Zoo, but some, surplus to requirements, went to the London, Bristol, and Chessington Zoos and the Blackpool Tower Zoo, after a short stay at Paignton. Among the specimens sent to the London Zoo on 29 June were a Two-lined Pit viper, a Cooke's Golden Tree boa, a Magpie tanager, and five rats comprising three different kinds (Savannah, Red Marsh, and Long-tailed Tree, the latter species, which today goes by the name of Venezuelan Climbing Mouse, being new to the collection there, as was the Red Marsh rat).

At Paignton Zoo the two Howler monkeys were housed in what Ken described as a 'medium-sized cage' – at just 5 feet high by 4 feet wide by 3 feet deep, it actually sounds quite a small cage, but of course they *were* only youngsters, and a smaller cage was deliberately chosen in preference to a more commodious one because it was felt it would be easier to monitor their feeding habits and general behaviour. Naturally it fell to Trudy, with her proven track record of caring for delicate animals, to look after the baby howlers. Her natural aptitude for this kind of work, her dedication and resourcefulness, had always impressed Ken. She lavished care upon the young Howler monkeys and her unstinting efforts were rewarded because they became devoted to her, even coming forward to play with her whenever she opened the cage door, leading Ken to conclude that constant individual attention was probably the single most important factor in keeping Howler monkeys. Every effort was made to give them as varied and interesting a diet as possible and they were showered with an astonishing variety of food, some of it quite surprising. Lettuce was eaten in prodigious quantities, as were the leaves of elm in the summer months. Bamboo, too, was fed to them daily. Apples, pears, melons, oranges, bananas, grapes and diced carrots were eaten with relish. A little of the white meat of chicken and cooked pork was given at times, as very occasionally were tiny pieces of choice red meat. The meat was always cooked because they would never take raw meat (oddly enough, a Red howler that Ken kept many years later at Exmouth Zoo *was* very fond of raw meat, which shows that, even within a species, all animals have widely differing tastes). As a special treat, a buttered current bun or sweet biscuits dipped in warm milk were offered; so too were aniseed, liquorice and peppermint sweets. Brown bread and milk, with glucose or honey added, was fed to them three times a day and they were also given rose-hip syrup and multi-vitamin preparations.

The babies were very sensitive creatures and easily upset, any departure from the routine causing them considerable distress. Once, carpenters working in a nearby cage resulted in them going into a nervous decline and refusing all food. They soon perked up though when the work was finished and Ken had high hopes of succeeding where others had failed. In the end, one lived for twenty months at the zoo, a British longevity record for the time but nonetheless disappointing, as it fell considerably short of the animal's natural lifespan, so obviously something still wasn't right.

The two young howlers and the pair of White-faced Saki monkeys lived in the Small Mammal House, a long narrow building that was home to an extremely interesting and heterogeneous assortment of small to medium-sized mammal species. This was one of Ken's favourite parts of the zoo precisely *because* the occupants were so varied. It was a complete miscellany, and it was this aspect that he so adored about the building. Housed in cages alongside one another were such diverse creatures as Lesser pandas, squirrels of various sorts, three or four species of mongoose, the nocturnal douroucouli, kinkajou and Tree porcupine, as well as a fascinating potpourri of genets, civets, chinchillas, Fruit bats, and several kinds of galago from the tiny Demidoff's that would sit comfortably in a teacup to the cat-sized Greater or Thick-tailed galago (making Paignton Zoo's collection of these so-called 'bushbabies' the best in Britain). This was also the house where the two chimpanzees, Charlie and Sue, that Ken had brought back from his earlier expeditions to the Cameroons and Sierra Leone, respectively, could be seen in a cage at the end of the house with an outdoor extension.

It was an exciting time for the zoo, with rare and seldom-seen animals arriving from all over the world and new ground being broken all the time. Ken's work didn't leave much time for holidays, but occasionally he did manage to escape for a few days – usually to Poole to see his family, or to London to visit his very good friend John Yealland, the noted aviculturist, in his home patch as London Zoo's Curator of Birds.

John James Yealland was a fair bit older than Ken, but in personality the two men were very similar. Like Ken, Yealland was reserved and modest, and hated talking about himself, feeling there were many more important things to talk about. He was born on the Isle of Wight on 20 March 1904 and from an early age birds were his passion (by a strange coincidence, John's mother's maiden name had been 'Bird'!) and he really knew his subject. He had, as mentioned before, accompanied Gerald Durrell on his first animal-collecting expedition to the British Cameroons. He had also helped Peter Scott to set up the Wildfowl Trust, before joining the staff of the London Zoo.

Shortly after his return from South America, Ken made a two-day visit to London Zoo. In a letter to a colleague he expressed his delight at seeing so many new specimens that had arrived there while he had been abroad. 'These,' he wrote, 'include a Storm's Water Cobra, some Lake Galam Frogs, 2 Blesbok, 2 Kuhl's Deer, 2 Peter's Dwarf Mongoose, 2 Great Bustards, several Rockhopper Penguins, and some Gough Island Coots and Antarctic Skuas.'

Six Antarctic skuas, a group of twelve Rockhopper penguins and twelve Gough Island coots were presented to the zoo in May by the Gough Island Scientific Survey. The pair of bustards had arrived in the same month (in this case from Iraq) and no doubt it was Ken's good friend John Yealland, as London Zoo's Curator of Birds, who had alerted him to the exciting arrival of all these rare birds. All were something special, but none more so than the Gough Island coots which had never before been kept at the zoo, and almost certainly it was the first time that Ken had seen the species.

Whenever he could get away – which wasn't often – Ken enjoyed having a chat over a meal with his zoological colleagues: people such as his good friend Donald Risdon, General Manager of Dudley Zoo, Robert Jackson (soon to open the Welsh Mountain Zoo), or Reginald Greed, the director of Bristol Zoo (it was during one of these informal conversations over lunch in 1963 that Reg Greed alerted Ken to the imminent arrival at Bristol Zoo of the first pair of white tigers to be seen in the U.K.). Ken continued to see Gerald and Jacquie Durrell quite regularly. Gerald Durrell loved entertaining, and once both Ken and John Yealland, along with their mutual friend Raymond Sawyer, were invited round to the Durrells' flat in Tolworth, South London.

'I remember it was a good, albeit very tiring, evening,' Raymond Sawyer told me. In his narrative he kept referring to Ken as 'Kenny' – the only time I have come across this.

> Gerald's secretary and mother were there, too. Gerald was a true bon viveur; he loved the company of friends, good food and copious drink. Even by that early stage, Gerald was drinking heavily and throughout the evening plied me with more and more. He drank gin out of a lager glass. Although I was living in London, thank goodness I had decided to travel the short distance by train, rather than drive to the flat, because when I left later that night I felt like a hackney horse stepping in the air, so much alcohol had I consumed. Gerald did most of the talking, but I can remember Kenny sitting there, laughing in all the right places, having a good time but in a more measured way. He was the opposite of Durrell. Whereas Gerald was loud and rather haughty, and became louder as the night wore on and the alcohol kicked in, Kenny was very quiet and unassuming, as was dear old John Yealland. In fact he and John were very similar in many ways, not only in personality but stature as well. Both men were quite short, much shorter than Gerald or myself, and Kenny was quite thickset, both in face and body.

It will come as a surprise to no-one that animals dominated the conversation. Nothing pleased Ken more than the chance to discuss what was happening in the world of zoos with likeminded individuals in a friendly and informal atmosphere. On 2 August he wrote to Marvin Jones. Marvin was planning a visit to Paignton Zoo later in the summer and Ken was looking forward to welcoming him again and showing off the new arrivals. 'I am particularly pleased with the Red Howler monkeys and with the Saki monkeys,' he wrote with ill-disguised pride.

> All are doing remarkably well, and I am most anxious to establish a record in respect of the howlers. I checked up on London Zoo records and they have kept neither species very long. The Preuss Guenons are thriving, and since you were here we have added a fine pair of Brazza Monkeys to our Monkey House.
>
> Please do arrive at Paignton at whatever hour you wish, and if you phone me from the station I will come to meet you. My bungalow now has the phone connected.
>
> I am grateful to you for mentioning the matter of collecting to Mr. Shelley. I shall be most pleased to meet him in 1957, unless I can get to Philadelphia before then. I shall be glad of the opportunity to discuss the American angle when you come over here.

Mr Freeman Shelly – without the supererogatory extra 'e' – was the director of Philadelphia Zoo, a post he held for thirty years from 1936 to 1966. Sadly, there is no evidence that Ken fulfilled his wish to visit America's fourth largest city (a city famously founded by the Quakers). So Marvin Jones was a very useful conduit to what was happening Stateside.

*

Ken had now made four major animal-collecting expeditions in eight years, but his latest trip to British Guiana was to be his last foray into the wilds. It does seem rather odd that he should suddenly draw a line under this part of his life when he had so obviously enjoyed the tropics and the animals he had found there. Researching the story of someone's life is a paper trail, but documents as well as interviews with a person's friends, colleagues and relatives, provide a biographer only with the events of the subject's life, not their motivation for doing (or not doing) something. One factor might have been his health. The tropics, for all their obvious allure, were an unhealthy place to be and ever since his expedition to the British Cameroons with Gerald Durrell he had suffered bouts of ill health, sometimes necessitating a stay in hospital. But in any case time was almost up for the traditional animal-collector. The late 1950s and early 1960s marked a watershed in the way we thought about our fellow creatures and it would not be too long before people would start to question the morality of removing animals from the wild to put them in zoos. Suddenly the word 'conservation' was being bandied about. In 1961 a group of concerned people, headed by Peter Scott, got together to launch the World Wildlife Fund (WWF). The following year Rachel Carson published her seminal work, *Silent Spring*, a personal *cri de coeur* for mankind to stop behaving in a profligate way and to start being a custodian for the planet. Suddenly the kind of expeditions that Ken Smith and Gerald Durrell were associated with were out of vogue. But as well as increasing awareness of the urgent need for conservation, there was another reason why the days of the old-fashioned animal-collecting expedition were numbered. Improved husbandry and greater success breeding animals in captivity meant that, before long, zoos would be net producers for many species including a number hitherto labelled as 'poor doers', obviating the need to capture any more from the wild and making the role of the traditional animal-collector redundant. It had always been difficult to make a living as an animal-collector; soon it would be almost impossible.

There were of course exceptions; men who defied the trend. Gerald Durrell continued to organise animal-collecting expeditions, and indeed would do so until he was in his mid sixties (and he was a mere stripling compared with Wilfred Frost, who would still be mounting collecting expeditions at the age of 82), but from the mid 1960s onwards all of Gerald Durrell's trips had a firm conservation agenda, with only a few carefully selected endangered species, needed to set up breeding colonies in progressive zoos, being targeted. Gone were the days of bringing back a big collection of many different species.

Another thing that sounded the death knell for the animal-collecting expedition was the emergence of air travel. Jet aeroplanes were making the world smaller. Now, instead of a collector having to spend up to six months in the tropics assembling a representative collection of the fauna of the region and then bringing the entire collection back by sea, it was now possible for local people to set themselves up as animal-dealers and catch the animals almost to order, dispatching them more or less straightway by air to buyers in Europe and America.

But there may have been a much more personal reason why Ken did not go on any more collecting trips. Before long he would be married for a second time and, soon enough, he would have a young family to bring up; the thought of leaving his family at home while he plunged into the bush for months at a time would then hold no appeal for him. Perhaps, more than any other reason, *this* was his main motive for putting the animal-collecting trips behind him.

Chapter Ten

Room for a Zoo? *(1957–1958)*

AS HE ENTERED MIDDLE AGE Ken had begun to fill out. No longer the lean man he had been when he and Gerald Durrell had first set forth together in search of animals, he now presented a stouter figure to the world. In 1957 he and Paignton Zoo's director Norman Dixon started a mini zoo at Exmouth, about thirty miles distant. Ken had the idea that a sister zoo at Exmouth would be an asset to Paignton Zoo, as well as a holiday amenity for the popular seaside resort. The Exmouth Summer Zoo was started in direct response to the political debacle that was the First Suez Crisis, the rationale behind the nascent zoo being to attract visitors who could not make the longer trek to visit the parent zoo at Paignton, further to the west, owing to the fuel shortage. As its formal name suggested, it was a summer only attraction; the zoo was closed during the off-season and the animals were withdrawn to Paignton until it reopened the following Spring. At first, and for many years afterwards, the zoo was entirely indoors (a small parcel of adjoining land was acquired and a few outdoor cages were added later). The building was formerly used as a golf clubhouse (some sources say a cricket pavilion). Commanding an ideal position in an area called The Maer on Exmouth seafront only about 100 yards from the beach (so a perfect location for when people tired of sea and sand), it was, according to Clinton Keeling who went there on several occasions over the years, 'A large, airy and well-built structure.' The snug compartments, arranged around the inside walls on all four sides, suited the majority of the inhabitants very well. Exmouth Zoo was officially opened on Wednesday 5 June by the popular broadcaster and one-time superintendent of the London Zoo, George Cansdale. The emphasis was on small mammals and reptiles, but not all the animals on display fitted this theme and, for such a small and totally indoor zoo, there were some quite surprising residents. The initial collection included a young chimpanzee, a Giant anteater, baboons and other monkeys, a young Sloth bear, and an assortment of reptiles and fish. Although Ken could not have suspected it at the time, one day it would become his own zoo.

*

In 1958 Ken received an unusual request from his old comrade-in-arms, Gerald Durrell, who was in a predicament, having arrived back from yet another expedition to the British Cameroons (his third to that part of the world) the previous year with literally hundreds of animals – and nowhere to put them.

When Durrell had returned to the Cameroons in 1957 he originally intended the trip to be a simple rerun of his earlier expeditions: the plan, as before, being to capture as wide a range of animals as possible to sell to the zoos of Britain. But soon after arriving in the Cameroons, and with collecting having started in earnest, Durrell suddenly changed his mind. Why, he asked himself, collect animals for other people's zoos when his ambition had always been to have a zoo of my own? In that Damascene moment he decided that all the animals he caught on *this* trip should not be dispersed on his return but would form the nucleus of the zoo he planned to create. At first the majority of the hardier animals he brought back lived in a marquee erected in his sister Margaret's garden in St. Alban's Avenue in Bournemouth, with the more delicate ones (squirrels, galagos, turacos, reptiles, frogs, and so on) in cages set up in the garage, which had been specially insulated for the purpose, while he began his search for a suitable property. Most municipal authorities that Durrell approached were not interested and on the rare occasions when he did stumble across a site that looked as if it would make a good place for a zoo, it was too expensive or required too much work. For a time the neighbouring borough of Poole seemed a possibility, in that the local council there did see some merit in the idea and even offered him a place next to the harbour, but negotiations dragged on interminably until eventually Durrell was forced to abandon any hope of establishing his zoo in Poole.

By this stage he was getting more and more disheartened. Obviously the animals couldn't remain in a back-garden in Bournemouth indefinitely. Not only were the cages little more than travelling boxes, but the neighbours were growing increasingly restless about what they saw as an unofficial zoo suddenly appearing in their midst and already complaints had been made to the council. First to go was a vociferous young chimpanzee named Minnie. She screamed incessantly. Nothing could shut her up, and the neighbours were unanimous in their outrage at this disturbance to their serenity. With Ken Smith's connivance, a home was found for her at Paignton Zoo. Not long afterwards, Minnie was followed by all the reptiles and some of the other more delicate creatures, as Margaret's garage could not provide them with the high temperature they needed with winter approaching. Once again, Ken Smith stepped into the breach by offering to accommodate them at Paignton. But this still left quite a sizeable private menagerie behind the house in St. Alban's Avenue. With the onset of winter, a temporary exhibition for the rest of the Cameroon animals (monkeys, mongooses, birds of prey, etc.) was installed in the basement of J.J. Allen's department store in the town as an attraction for customers over the Christmas and New Year period, but when the festive season was over that exhibition had to be dismantled, so it was only natural that Durrell should turn, once more, to his old friend Ken Smith for help. 'Could I,' he enquired tentatively, 'keep the rest of my animals at Paignton Zoo until something more permanent can be arranged for them?'

In those days it was not unknown for private keepers to place their whole collection in the care of one of the larger zoos. Of course the zoo's directors, Norman Dixon and Philip Michelmore, would have to be consulted (Michelmore had been appointed on Whitley's death), but Ken felt sure there would be no objection. What objection *could* there be? Paignton would be getting a whole load of new animals for minimal effort. All it had to do was find somewhere to put them all.

Just after the New Year of 1958 the rest of the animals, bar two or three of Durrell's personal favourites, were removed to Paignton Zoo and Margaret's neighbours could breathe a huge sigh of relief at last. One condition was imposed: if Durrell did not reclaim his animals by a given date they would become the property of Paignton Zoo. This was really only fair. Ken was there to supervise the transfer of the animals from Durrell's makeshift cages into proper zoo cages (approximately fifty times bigger). 'A collection left on deposit by Mr. Gerald Durrell, including lemurs, louries, vipers and other creatures, mostly from West Africa, has aroused much interest,' declared the annual report of the Herbert Whitley Trust, the governing body set up after the death of Whitley to manage the zoo. The 'lemurs' were probably galagos and pottos, rather than true lemurs which are found only in Madagascar, and 'louries' are the African birds more commonly known as turacos or go-away-birds.

The consignment included Hairy frogs and West African Clawed frogs, Brow-leaf (Eyebrow) toads, Cameroon Green Tree frogs, a Broad-fronted (Dwarf) crocodile, Gaboon and Rhinoceros vipers, sunbirds, mousebirds, an outstanding African Hawk-eagle, two African hobbies, Woodford's owls, White-faced Scops owls, and a beautiful pair of Guinea turacos (not, as originally thought, the very similar-looking Verreaux's turaco, which is how they are referred to in early reports). Notable among the mammals were some Patas and Mona monkeys, galagos and squirrels of several species, and an African civet. Not all the animals had been brought back by Gerald Durrell from the Cameroons. Although he had yet to find a permanent home for his collection, he had already started in earnest to acquire animals from other sources. The non-Cameroon creatures that he now deposited at Paignton Zoo along with the rest included a Slow loris and two East African Bush squirrels.

Other animals went to Paignton's satellite zoo at Exmouth when it reopened at Easter, where a special exhibition was made of some of the animals that Durrell had brought back with him on his last visit to the Cameroons. Rarest were two Black-legged mongooses. The fine collection of primates included Martin's White-nosed monkeys, Tarquin, a Cherry-crowned mangabey, Green monkeys, drills, and two chimpanzees. Some of Durrell's West African Clawed frogs were shown in the aquarium section, the others remaining at Paignton Zoo. Another species from his Cameroons collection put on display at Exmouth were some resplendent Fernand skinks. Generally known as the Fire or Red-flanked skink, this is probably the same lizard species that Durrell, in one of his books, had called the Que-fong-goo.

*

Since moving to Paignton, Ken had lived alone in the bungalow in the grounds of the zoo, but he did sometimes have guests staying over, including, on occasion, Gerald Durrell. When he heard that Durrell was on his way to Paignton, he would dispatch somebody to collect him from Paignton railway station. The young lady normally assigned the task obviously fancied herself as a female Stirling Moss because she drove her MG sports car so fast and so erratically, with her hands only lightly hooked around the bottom of the steering wheel in a rather casual fashion, that the short journey to the zoo terrified Durrell. Chasing an irascible Giant anteater across the Rupununi savannah was as nothing compared with sitting next to a woman with an insouciant attitude to driving. Depressed by his lack of progress to start a zoo in the south of England, he would pour his heart out to Ken and sleep on the sofa.

But Ken was not to be on his own for much longer. In 1958, Kenneth John Smith, aged forty-seven, and Trudy Hills, twenty-eight, were married at the Totnes Registry Office. That evening found them doing the round of night-feeds at the zoo. So began a very successful personal and professional partnership. Despite the age difference it was a meeting of minds. They shared the same interests, held the same views. There were occasional disagreements, as there are in every marriage, but, looking back, Trudy said she could not recall a single row they had in over twenty-one years of marriage (and daughter Kelsay can remember only one).

Meanwhile, Gerald Durrell's protracted search for suitable premises for his long-dreamed-of zoo was at last coming to an end. Having grown increasingly despondent at his failure to find a site in the south of England, he had widened his search. Eventually he found Les Augres Manor (pronounced 'O Grey') in Jersey, the largest of the English Channel Islands, lying nearer to France than to England. It seemed tailor-made for his purpose, but before he signed the lease (which he did on 7 November), he had to make sure he was doing the right thing as he would be mortgaging his future for many years to come, so he sought advice from his circle of zoological doyens – and then ignored it. There was also the small matter of the Cameroon animals ensconced at Paignton Zoo (the ones at Exmouth Zoo having joined them when this zoo closed for the winter). The deadline for reclaiming the animals was almost upon them. Fortunately, Paignton Zoo agreed to go on housing them a while longer. Durrell would be reunited with his African animals soon enough. The pressing problem for now was that he would not be present to oversee the building work, or any of the other jobs that needed to be done before the zoo was ready to be opened to the public, having already made plans to return to Argentina on yet another animal-collecting expedition. It soon became apparent to him that he would need to engage a manager, someone who could be entrusted with the practical day-to-day running of the new zoo. Someone loyal. Someone bright. Someone with plenty of experience of wild animal husbandry. Preferably a pragmatist to confer a much-needed counterbalance to his own idealism. Any manager he hired would have to be that *rara avis*: someone with managerial know-how, organisational flair and the ability to handle staff but who was also familiar with the dietary requirements of a tapir or the optimum cage temperature needed for a Royal python.

Someone, in other words, like Ken Smith.

It was only ever going to be a short list of one.

Chapter Eleven

Landfall in Jersey and the Birth of a Zoo *(1958–1959)*

GERALD DURRELL HAD NEVER BEEN a very practical man. All through his life he came up with bold original ideas, most of them highly innovative and some of them more than a little avant-garde, but he relied upon other people to deal with the practicalities of turning those dreams into reality. Inviting his fellow expeditionary to become Superintendent of Jersey Zoo was a shrewd move on his part. The animal-collecting expeditions aside, Durrell had no experience of organising and administering anything, and certainly nothing as complex as a zoo with all the multifarious tasks which that entailed. The problem was that he was not, at heart, a businessman (the financial failure of his collecting trips was testament to that) and minutiae just bored and irritated him. Ken Smith, on the other hand, was practically-minded in a way that Durrell was not. He already had managerial experience at Paignton Zoo and had proved himself to be an able and conscientious administrator. Jersey Zoo was on a much smaller scale, but the job was essentially the same. Furthermore, he had already helped launch one zoo (Exmouth) and knew the problems involved, having already confronted them at first hand. In future years Durrell was to claim that it was with the utmost reluctance that he took the decision to employ a manager. We have no way of knowing if this was how Gerald Durrell truly felt at the time, but it is hard to imagine anyone better qualified to manage Jersey Zoo than Ken Smith.

Ken was at a T-junction in his career. Which way to go? To carry on indefinitely at Paignton Zoo – or uproot and move to Jersey? In addressing the dilemma, he had much to weigh up. By defecting to Jersey, potentially he had a lot to lose. At Paignton his job was secure; at Jersey it was anything *but* secure. Launching a new zoo, as with embarking on any new venture, is a risky business. Even with the considerable advantage of Durrell's fame, there was no guarantee it would succeed and, being based on a small island only 45 square miles in area, lying a hundred miles from the English mainland, Jersey Zoo – more so than any other zoo – would be utterly dependent on the capricious holiday trade for its survival. A wet summer, or too many people opting to go elsewhere for their holidays, and it would be in very serious trouble. If it didn't attract sufficient visitors, the zoo could fold in a matter of months (as indeed it very nearly did) in which case Ken would find himself out of a job.

It would also mean taking a drop in salary, as there was no way that Jersey Zoo would be able to afford to pay him what he was earning for doing the same job at Paignton. It also crossed his mind that, if the coffers dipped too low, he might even occasionally find himself working for no remuneration at all. Furthermore, his original contract at Jersey was only for three years, at the end of which term it might be renewed or it might not.

Trudy was even more reluctant than her husband to make the move; it was too big a step, too risky an undertaking, but she trusted his judgement and unfailingly supported him whatever he eventually decided. According to Trudy – who was of course privy to Ken's thought processes – he took a long time coming to a decision and when at last he did agree, it was not without some reluctance for he enjoyed his job at Paignton Zoo and was loathe to leave. 'But of course in the end he said "yes" as I knew he would because of his strong sense of loyalty to Gerald Durrell. That was really what clinched it. I had cause to wonder in the years that lay ahead whether he'd made the right choice; we both had misgivings,' said Trudy.

Jacquie Durrell had a different perspective. According to her, Ken had not taken much persuasion. She insisted that he had always relished new challenges and new experiences, and the thought of being intimately involved with the birth of a new zoo from the moment of conception, held irresistible appeal for him. Already he had been largely responsible for Exmouth Zoo, of course, but there he had been very limited in what he could do. In terms of both scope and ambition, Jersey Zoo was on an entirely different canvas – the difference between producing a miniature portrait for a locket and a mural on a wall. So much more was possible. It also had one enormous advantage over Exmouth Zoo, and over every other zoo including that most famous of zoos, London: it would have, as its owner, director and figurehead, a best-selling author and broadcaster to publicise it through his books and T.V. appearances. Durrell told Ken that the scheme already had the backing of the President of the Tourism Committee in Jersey, Wilfred Krichefski. 'The island has pledged its support,' Durrell said excitedly. Ken knew how important it was for a zoo to be supported by the local community, particularly the governing authority.

However, before committing himself, Ken felt it was imperative to see the site and judge its potential for himself. He duly flew to Jersey where he booked into a hotel. Trudy did not accompany him. She was pregnant with her first child and was advised to avoid air travel. Gerald Durrell proudly showed Ken round the thirty-six acre estate and gushingly outlined his plans, pointing out where he intended to build the animal houses, aviaries, paddocks, and visitor amenities. Ken could see at once the huge potential offered by the site. Not only was there a fair amount of space available (about the same in area as London Zoo) but there were many features that could be adapted relatively easily. As well as a magnificent granite farmhouse, parts of which dated back to the fifteenth century, there were numerous outbuildings, also solidly built of granite, ideal for conversion into animal quarters; there was a beautiful walled garden ablaze with rock plants, and there were fields, ancient trees and a lovely valley through which snaked a tiny stream which fed a small tree-ringed lake. As Durrell led Ken round, he allowed his imagination and enthusiasm to get the better of him as he extolled his grandiose vision for the site, pointing out the various features and the potential that each one offered. But unlike Durrell, who was inclined to veer towards idealism, Ken was more of a pragmatist. He could see that Durrell's ideas for the site, brilliant though they were, were much too ambitious. At the end of that first tour of inspection, he asked to go round

again, this time on his own. Afterwards, he informed Durrell that he had come up with a
few ideas of his own on how the project could be made to work. Not for the first time,
Ken found himself tempering Durrell's idealistic nature. Apologising for playing the
devil's advocate, he advised that, with only limited funds in the pot, Durrell should, to
use the well-worn adage, cut his cloth according to his means. (Originally Gerald Durrell
borrowed £10,000 to set up the zoo but soon found this was nowhere near enough and
he was forced to add to his indebtedness by a further £10,000.) Time was also an issue.
It was imperative, Ken said, that the zoo should start recouping some money as quickly
as possible, ideally by Easter to cash in on the bank holiday trade and to give the zoo the
rest of the season to put some money in the depleted kitty before the onset of winter.
This didn't give Ken – or whoever accepted the post of Superintendent if he declined it
– very much time to realise Durrell's grander visions for the site, even if the money could
be found. With this in mind, he advocated a more cautious approach. Rather than
developing the whole estate all at once, which would be prohibitively expensive and take
up too much time, he suggested a preferable stratagem would be to proceed slowly by
initially concentrating on the area immediately surrounding the manor house. His plan
was simple. To begin with, only six to eight acres should be developed, he suggested,
with the manor as the hub – the focal point – of the whole zoo, and everything else
radiating from it. The other fields could be left as rough grazing, pending development in
the future, or sublet to the farming community. 'I suggest that, to begin with, most of the
animal collection is exhibited in just three main locations,' he said. 'In this way, all the
animals will be contained within a very small area, and visitors won't need to walk far to
see everything. These areas are: within that superb walled garden, along the main drive,
and on the bank behind the manor. From an animal management point of view, it also
helps to keep all the exhibits close together.'

Desperate to get Ken on board, Durrell was receptive to any suggestions he made.
'Do whatever you want, old boy,' he said; 'just so long as you get it up and running.'

Even now, more than half a century later, some of the fields have never had animal
enclosures standing on them.

Ken then turned his thoughts to the projected café. This, he suggested, should serve
only light snacks such as sandwiches, strawberries-and-cream, ices, cakes – nothing hot –
to guarantee a quick turnover of customers. Here he displayed quite a mercenary streak.
'Get the punters in, give them something to eat and drink, and get them out again to
make room for the next load,' he said, making the customers sound like a clothes-
washing cycle. As harsh as this sounded, he was being wholly realistic.

But still he hadn't committed himself, though clearly he was very interested. To
ensure the ball was kicked firmly into the back of the net, a desperate Durrell added a
soupçon of emotional blackmail. 'You've just got to say yes or there will be no Jersey Zoo.'
It was a heartfelt plea, even though it was inconceivable that Durrell, who had wanted
his own zoo since the tender age of six, would have suddenly abandoned all his plans if
Ken *had* refused to join him in Jersey.

It is quite possible that Ken was thinking of leaving Paignton Zoo anyway, even
before Durrell offered him the post in Jersey. At a meeting of the Herbert Whitley Trust
held on 16 October at Paignton Zoo (22 days *before* Gerald Durrell signed the lease for

Les Augres Manor) the managing Trustee '…reported that the Zoo Superintendent (Smith) appeared to be very unsettled and there was a possibility of him leaving the district. It was felt that if a vacancy occurred it was important that his duties should be taken over by a qualified man.'

It is impossible to know for sure why Ken was feeling 'very unsettled'. Perhaps he felt aggrieved that he had not been chosen to replace Whitley as joint director alongside Norman Dixon. Instead the post had gone to Philip Michelmore. Possibly the inadequacy of his accommodation at the zoo was a factor. When he had started in the job, he was provided with a bungalow on site in which to live, but the bungalow had its shortcomings. It was quite shabby with only a few cheap bits of furniture in it. At first it did not even have a phone line – quite a major demerit, one would think, for somebody in charge of a zoo, where almost anything could, and often did, happen, and staff might need to contact him urgently – though he did succeed in getting one put in eventually. At a meeting at Paignton Zoo on 16 April 1957 it was acknowledged that there were serious (but unspecified) deficiencies with 'Smith's Cottage'. Ken was buoyed up by the thought that, at last, his living conditions were about to be made more comfortable. But his optimism was premature and no improvements were made to the property for more than a year.

It is hard to believe that Ken's restlessness did not have something to do with the poor state of the bungalow and the length of time it took to get it fixed (though it was not unusual for staff accommodation in zoos to be substandard). Perhaps he thought that, as Superintendent, he deserved better. Finally, at a meeting on May 16, 1958, it was agreed that the cost of upgrading the accommodation (£345 9s 3d) would be borne by the Herbert Whitley Trust. But if the zoo's directors had hoped that Ken would be swayed into staying by the improvements made to the bungalow – which were done in the manner of a wedding present to him and Trudy – they were to be disappointed, because by the end of the year his thoughts would be on the distant Channel Islands.

Ken and Trudy talked it over at length and in the end they agreed to take the plunge. So the die was cast. Gerald Durrell was thrilled to have his old partner back with him. The old team was back in business – but there was a price. Ken was still not totally convinced he was doing the right thing, and Trudy had even greater reservations than her husband, but they agreed to throw their lot in with Durrell on the condition that, as Superintendent, Ken was given carte blanche on running Jersey Zoo. He insisted on having free rein on selecting the animals, hiring and firing staff, the design of the enclosures, advertising, the lot. By acceding to Ken's demand, Durrell was playing his trump card; as a sop calculated to lure Ken and Trudy away from Paignton it worked like a spell. Ken and Trudy's initial contract would run for three years. 'Do we get time off for good behaviour?' Ken enquired, mischievously.

These terms were acceptable – to Gerald at any rate; his wife Jacquie had misgivings, predicting it to be a recipe for disaster. 'And sadly I was proved right.'

As I've already mentioned, the business side of running a zoo just left Durrell cold. He was an inveterate ideas man, not a practical person. The thorny problem of how to make things a *fait accompli* he delegated to others; so it was probably with some relief that he entrusted the job of getting the zoo off the ground, and after that the day-to-day running of it, to somebody else. With his old friend Ken Smith in charge, it also meant he was free to take time off to go on yet more expeditions (which were providing such a rich vein of material for his books).

At the end of November, Ken and Trudy resigned their positions at Paignton Zoo and moved to Jersey to begin the task of building Gerald Durrell's zoo from scratch. The Paignton Zoo authorities were sorry to see them to go and urged Ken to stay, but his mind was made up. However, the sorrow they felt at his decision to leave was not really reflected in the Herbert Whitley Trust's Annual Report for 1958 which paid tribute to him, and the work he had done at the zoo, in just three short sentences:

A sad blow has been suffered in the resignation of the Superintendent, Mr. Kenneth Smith. Mr. Smith has done much during the past six years to improve the condition of the animals and the way in which they are displayed. He collected a fine lot of animals himself in British Guiana in 1956.

The animals were shipped aboard the S.S. *Sambur* at Weymouth on the last day of November. With the Smiths was their first child, a baby daughter named Caroline, born in Paignton District Hospital less than a month earlier on 1 November (by coincidence, the same date – forty years apart – as Ken's brother Frank). On the boat trip over to Jersey she nestled in her cot surrounded by caged birds in the cabin. The 'zoo ship' arrived in St. Helier harbour the next morning, causing great excitement to the islanders, particularly the children, many of whom had never been to a zoo or seen so many unusual and exotic creatures. The animals, although wild-caught, were in good condition and steady, having been at Paignton Zoo for nearly a year, but at Les Augres there was as yet almost nothing by way of accommodation for them, and Ken had no choice but to put them, most still in their travelling cages, into various outbuildings while their permanent cages were under construction. The most important animals were the Hairy frogs, a tame Needle-clawed galago called Bugs (on account of his 'bug-eyes'), and the two Black-legged mongooses, all three species believed to be the only ones of their kind in Europe. Ken, Trudy and their baby daughter took up residence in a flat in Les Augres Manor. Gerald Durrell was not there. Within days of signing the lease in November, he and Jacquie had boarded a ship bound for Argentina at the start of another filming and animal-collecting expedition, but throughout the trip he was kept up to speed with developments at the zoo by telephone. With carpenters in place, work on Jersey Zoo began in early December. Ken realised he stood little chance of getting everything completed in time for the official opening the following spring, but that didn't stop him throwing himself into the task with gusto. Guests whom he led round, pointing out to them where this or that enclosure was to go, recounted how excited he was, even though there was, as yet, precious little to see. 'I'm planning to have a penguin pool in the shade of those trees bordering the main drive, and over here against this wall I thought a range of about five or six aviaries for birds of prey.'

A Monkey House and several aviaries were among the first things to be completed. 'Among other features which will be ready for opening to the public for Easter,' trumpeted the *International Zoo News* in January 1959, 'are a tropical bird house, reptile house, birds of prey aviaries, parrot house, enclosures for wallabies and lesser pandas, and a pets corner.' But time was against him, and not everything would be ready for the official opening. Indeed, some major exhibits, such as the Parrot House, would not be completed for about a year. Possibly the Lesser pandas never arrived for I can find no record of the species ever having been kept at Jersey Zoo. In a rare example of editorial carelessness, the *International Zoo News* reported that Gerald Durrell's zoo was being built in Jersey, U.S.A.!

Ken and Trudy met with the zoo's landlord, Major Fraser, whose ancestral home, Les Augres Manor, was to be at the centre of the zoo. They warmed to him immediately and he, fortunately, liked them. 'Hugh Fraser was a lovely gentleman; we got on very well with him,' said Trudy. Gerald Durrell's book, *Menagerie Manor*, gives the impression that Major Fraser leased the property to Durrell because he was finding it too expensive to run as a private residence and wanted to move to a smaller place in England. This is essentially true, but what is not generally known is that Major Fraser didn't leave the island straightaway (although he would do so eventually) but hung on in Jersey for while. Once he had relinquished the manor house, he simply moved to another part of the island, from where he kept a benevolent eye on the development of the zoo and sometimes popped round for a chat. He always called Ken 'THE SUPER', alluding to his official status as the zoo's Superintendent.

Ken was determined that the zoo must be up-and-running by the Easter weekend to stand any hope of becoming financially viable on an island where it would be dependent for its survival on holidaymakers – a notoriously fickle market – but he conceded that the chances of finishing everything in time were effectively zero. But it wasn't important; what mattered was that the zoo needed to open as soon as practicably possible to stand any chance of lasting more than a season or two. However, there were a thousand and one things to do before the zoo was ready to receive visitors. Cages had to be built, outbuildings converted for animal use or as service rooms, staff hired, a car park to be laid. And so the list went on: dealers' lists to be perused and animals ordered, food supplies sourced (not always an easy task on an island the size of Jersey especially in the case of the more specialised feeders), and publicity organised. The east wing of the manor was to be prepared as a small café where visitors could recuperate and receive sustenance (in fact, because everyone was kept extremely busy building the animal cages, the café wasn't finished in time, leading to the paradoxical situation whereby the zoo, when it first opened, had a catering manager but no café). Ken poached some of the staff from Paignton Zoo, people he knew were hard-working, whom he could trust, among them Tim Carr, Kay Page, Bill Timmis, Lee Thomas, to name just four. About half of Jersey Zoo's original staff were ex-Paignton Zoo, others he recruited locally, mostly young unattached people prepared to work the long unsociable hours that the job demanded for a pittance. One of those former Paignton keepers, Lee Thomas, was doing his national service, but he spent all his leave from his station in Belgium setting up Jersey Zoo's first Reptile House. Dubbed 'Lord Lee of Aquarium' by Gerald Durrell on account of his rather haughty mannerisms – a characteristic which also annoyed Ken – his dark smouldering good looks ensured he had a succession of female admirers. Lee strode around the place as if *he* were lord of the manor. He took to walking unannounced into Ken and Trudy's flat in Les Augres Manor, and when Ken gently admonished him with the words 'Lee, you simply *must* knock!' Lee responded by saying, 'But *you* wouldn't have knocked on your father's door.'

'But Lee, *I'm* not your father,' Ken cried exasperatedly.

In 1962 Lee would spend six months exploring the species-rich forests and creeks of British Guiana on an animal-collecting expedition for Jersey Zoo.

Someone else who had previously done service at Paignton Zoo was Gerry Breeze, Gerald Durrell's nephew. He helped build Jersey Zoo and, when the zoo opened, was put in charge of the Reptile House. Right from the outset, Ken made it clear to him that there would be no nepotism. 'Just because you're Gerald's nephew, don't imagine that gives you a licence to shirk or arrive late for work. I expect you to work as hard as everybody else, if not harder,' he told him firmly.

The persona Ken liked to present to his workforce was of a strict, no-nonsense martinet, but the fact he was able to convince so many members of Paignton's animal staff to deracinate and follow him to Jersey, where they could expect to work longer hours for less pay, is testament to his popularity. People genuinely liked him. According to Trudy, he did not need to invite them to follow him; they requested to come aboard. This sudden collective defection did not go down well with the Paignton Zoo authorities.

It soon became obvious to Ken that many more animals would be needed before the zoo's scheduled opening in March. Few of the Cameroon animals had what one might call 'box-office appeal'. Only the larger primates could be expected to hold people's attention; most of the other animals were small and, from the public's point of view, unimpressive. Quite a few were nocturnal and made poor exhibits anyway. Since the zoo in its early days would not have the luxury of a nocturnal facility where night and day were reversed, all that visitors could expect to see of these animals would be gently heaving bundles of fur. Ken was quick to recognise the importance of bringing in many other species to make the collection more representative of the animal kingdom as a whole – and more attractive to visitors. Eagerly he pored over dealers' lists, keeping an especially vigilant lookout for good 'show' animals which he knew people would return time and again to see. One of his favourite dealers was Tyseley Pet Stores in Warwick Road, Birmingham, and over the years he had received many animals from there. This emporium was more than just a pet-shop. Like Palmer's in Camden Town, Tyseley Pet Stores had a reputation for selling decidedly unusual animals. The shop was known to sell such unexpected creatures as orang-utans, gorilla, chimpanzees, lions, binturongs, Lesser pandas, Bateleur eagles, vultures, hornbills, and many other 'zoo-type' animals. How many other pet stores have had elephants in stock? Tyseley once did – two female wild-caught Asiatic elephants in the late Sixties. Sometimes the staff there would not know what animals had been included in a consignment from some distant part of the globe until they unpacked them in store – if then, because a minority of newly-arrived creatures defied all attempts by shop staff to identify them. Inevitably they would find animals they were ill-equipped to look after or whose requirements in captivity they didn't fully understand. Having endured a long and stressful journey from the other side of the world, some of them would arrive in very poor condition. When Ken was

Superintendent of Paignton Zoo, the owner of Tyseley Pet Stores had occasionally sent him such specimens because he knew that Ken had the expertise to keep them alive. (For instance, Asian Giant Flying squirrels had sometimes turned up unexpectedly in these consignments and, knowing how extremely difficult these beautiful creatures were to maintain in captivity, Tyseley's owner had never had any hesitation despatching them immediately to Ken at Paignton, rather than allow them to perish in the unsuitable, dingy cages of a Birmingham pet store.) The variety of animals that passed through Tyseley's was incredible. In July 1959 (only a few months after Ken had been frantically buying up animals for Jersey Zoo in readiness for its opening day), the London Zoo purchased from this remarkable establishment a Giant armadillo. This, the largest of the armadillos, can attain a length of 150 cm including tail and weigh as much as 60 kg when fully grown. It is almost never exhibited in zoos and was on Gerald Durrell's wish list of animals he hoped to obtain in Argentina. This was the one South American animal he coveted above all others and he would leave no stone unturned in his efforts to find one, but ultimately he would be forced to return home without having secured a specimen. He was galled, therefore, when he learnt that Dr. Desmond Morris, then Curator of Mammals at the London Zoo, had found one for sale in a pet store in *Birmingham*, of all places! This illustrates the astonishing variety – and considerable rarity – of the animals to be found at Tyseley Pet Stores and why Ken gloated hungrily over the Tyseley and other stock lists, murmuring, as he stabbed at the animal names with his finger, 'We've got to have one of *those*, and we really must have a pair of *those*, and *that*.' There were no Giant armadillos advertised, but there were plenty of other treasures. Many animals were beyond his price range, of course, and Jersey Zoo did not have the elaborate facilities required by the larger beasts, but despite these constraints he managed to obtain some really nice, interesting species, including a few unusual ones. But he was careful to avoid hoofed animals. There were to be no deer or antelope, no camels, and no wild cattle at Jersey Zoo. At first, this might seem extremely odd. After all, ungulates are a major feature of most zoos, and many species require only the most rudimentary of housing. Why, then, did Ken Smith eschew hoofed animals? Most likely because the economy of the Channel Islands is dependent to a very large degree on a flourishing dairy industry, and as a result the authorities take a fairly jaundiced view of the importation of hoofed animals, particularly non-domestic species, which potentially carry the risk of introducing such vile bovine diseases as foot-and-mouth and bluetongue to the islands. Whilst it was certainly not impossible to import hoofed stock, it was, and is, quite a taxing exercise. (Hoofed mammals have never made much of an impact on the collection at Jersey Zoo, and the total number of ungulate species maintained there since the zoo opened in 1959, excluding a few farmyard animals in pets' corner, is no more than about five or six.)

Once all the other zoos heard that a new zoo park would shortly be opening, Ken suddenly found himself inundated with offers, mostly of very common or unsuitable species, as the other zoos saw an opportunity to offload stock they didn't want. Many of the animals were acquired by Ken 'in exchange'. Exchange for what, one wonders? The only animals he had that he could have traded as part of exchange deals were Durrell's Cameroon animals, and there would have been little point in getting rid of one lot of animals merely to obtain others. In later years, Jersey Zoo was to become known and respected around the world for concentrating on what colloquially are known as 'little brown jobbies' – unfamiliar species, often very rare, that, owing to their unprepossessing appearance or shy and retiring nature, were often ignored by the larger zoos that tended to favour big, glamorous, 'sexy' animals. In 1959, however, Ken was less interested in obtaining examples of rare and endangered species (which many people may never have seen or heard of before) than in making the zoo a paying concern. He was shrewd enough to realise he needed to obtain a good variety of animals quickly and cheaply. Predicting the zoo's fortunes would ebb and flow in synchrony with an unreliable tourist trade, Ken felt compelled to add animals that were not necessarily rare or endangered but could be relied upon to pull in the visitors. Trudy showed me a photo of some dingoes at Jersey Zoo. As she pointed out, there was no conservation merit to their being there. They were not endangered. On the contrary, they were (and are) a pest in Australia and a major predator of the indigenous marsupials. They were maintained at Jersey Zoo for no other reason than because they made good exhibition animals; they were easy and cheap to obtain, and undemanding in terms of accommodation and diet. Other animals sourced by Ken to make the place more appealing – and more cosmopolitan – included Indian Fruit bats; Frisky the mandrill; Delilah, a West African Crested porcupine; a North American skunk with the ironic name of Flower; Trumpy the Grey-winged trumpeter bird, who enjoyed complete liberty in the zoo grounds; Galapagos doves (lovely little birds that are never seen in zoos now, but were one of the first species to breed at Jersey Zoo); Stump-tailed and Blue-tongued skinks; and an irascible twelve-foot-long Reticulated python christened, for no good reason other than alliteration, Pythagoras. Ken also acquired wallabies, marmosets, various squirrels (making Jersey Zoo probably the finest collection of squirrels in Europe), raccoons, eagles, a trio of Golden pheasants (from Edinburgh Zoo), cranes, cockatoos, hornbills, toucans, and mynahs, among many other creatures. To make the zoo look as full as possible, Ken did the rounds of the local pet shops and in this way acquired instant cage fillers. Grass snakes were wild-caught in Jersey. The rarest animals he managed to obtain were two baby gharials, which took a long time to settle in. These long-snouted crocodilians caused him considerable worry by refusing to eat, necessitating force-feeding. Where did he acquire such rare creatures as these, which are virtually unobtainable today? As unlikely as it sounds, he probably bought them from a high street pet shop: Palmer's, the Regent Pet Stores, in Camden Town. As we have seen, Palmer's was no ordinary pet shop, but famed for stocking some considerably unusual and unexpected animals. In February 1959, according to its Daily Occurrences Book for that year, the London Zoo purchased from Mr John Palmer, two gharials. Although we can't know for certain, Jersey Zoo's pair were probably part of the same consignment.

With the zoo's official opening fast approaching, things were reaching fever pitch. Posters were printed and adverts placed in the *Jersey Evening Post*, a paper that was soon to become one of Jersey Zoo's staunchest allies. Later on, Ken would picket the airport, delaying arriving holidaymakers, and even took himself off to St. Helier wearing a brightly-painted sandwich board to drum up custom. On 14 March 1959, Jersey Zoological Park Limited was officially inaugurated. Less than two weeks later it was unveiled to the general public.

Chapter Twelve

Master of A Very Fragile Vessel *(1959–1962)*

WHILE KEN, NOAH-LIKE, WAS GATHERING the animals together and overseeing the construction of Jersey Zoo for the scheduled official opening on Thursday 26 March, Gerald Durrell was thousands of miles away in Argentina on another collecting expedition. Before departing for the Argentine, he had left Ken written instructions on how he wished the development to proceed, but there are conflicting accounts on how detailed these instructions were. Jacquie Durrell, outspoken in her opposition to Ken being given autocracy, insisted that he had been given a full and detailed blueprint for the development of Jersey Zoo, but Ken maintained that all he had received by way of a blueprint were a few rough sketches on the back of an envelope which he had interpreted to the best of his ability. Trudy Smith concurs. 'There certainly was no blueprint,' she said, 'unless some hastily executed doodles constitute a blueprint.'

It had been a rush and there had not been time to do everything that was required, with the result that the zoo was forced to open in a clearly incomplete state. There was, for example, no proper café (a very small self-service cafeteria was created shortly afterwards in the old dining-room in the east wing of the manor house, just below the Smiths' flat). One person who had good reason to lament the absence of a café was the Catering Manager, Mr Huckstable, who found he had precious little to manage. Here, recollections differ markedly. Jeremy Mallinson, who started work at the zoo in May, told me that Ken had brought Mr Huckstable with him from Paignton Zoo, where he had been the café manager. However, Trudy claimed that Mr Huckstable was one of the few staff members in the early days *not* recruited by her husband. According to her, Mr Huckstable had been working in a club or pub in Bournemouth when Gerald Durrell discovered him and rashly invited him to Jersey to be the zoo's first catering manager, a grandiose title which soon proved to be rather optimistic. He and his wife lived in the manor, but they were not happy and did not stay there more than a few months. One can't help feeling sorry for Mr Huckstable. Not only did the zoo, at first, not possess a café – a fairly basic requirement, one would think, for a catering manager – but he had no interest in animals, which was rather unfortunate since he lived in the middle of a zoo surrounded by them. As if this were not enough, his wife found the island too small and claustrophobic and missed Paignton.

In the dash to stock all the animal houses, paddocks and cages, not all the animals were labelled, such as many of the occupants of the Tropical Bird House, and even the keepers were sometimes at a loss to recognise them all and had to reach for such books as John Yealland's *Cage Birds in Colour* to identify them. Where labels did exist, they were often no more than a piece of card pinned to the front of the cage, conveying only the minimal amount of information. Realising that many visitors would be making the pilgrimage to the zoo after having read Gerald Durrell's books, Ken occasionally included an extra nugget of information in addition to the species' name and distribution, such as 'Collected by Gerald Durrell in the British Cameroons' or 'Believed to be the only one of its kind in Europe'. If anyone complained about the paucity of information about the animals, he argued that the priority had been to get all the animals comfortably housed; there would be time to improve the labelling and other niceties at a later date.

Ken was all too aware of the zoo's shortcomings. Would people be disappointed by the absence of the really big animals such as giraffes and elephants, which were beyond the zoo's means? Would lorises and Clawed frogs leave the average member of the public feeling nonplussed? In short, would such lesser beasts cut the mustard? That was the problem of calling the place a zoo. People had preconceptions of what a zoo should look like, and in the 1950s and 1960s large mammals tended to figure in the popular image of a 'zoo', which explains why he had succumbed to public demand and bought a four-month-old lion cub, the unimaginatively named Leo, from Dublin Zoo, and why he was pleased to accept the offer of a Himalayan bear (called Misha) from a circus that was closing down. Back then, a zoo without lions and bears was simply unthinkable. At first Leo was installed in a cage in the Small Mammal House. When he outgrew that cage, he was moved to one built for the chimpanzees, whose move therefore had to be postponed until eventually a house and outside compound was provided for Leo at one end of the walled garden. Leo matured into an impressive, blond-maned animal – but with one very noticeable personal problem. The late Graham Lucas, a veteran of Whipsnade Zoo, the zoo to which Leo was eventually sent, told me that Leo was the most flatulent example of *Panthera leo* he had ever known.

And still animals continued to pour in, the overworked builders hard-pressed to keep up. The day before the public was due to be admitted, Ken welcomed the arrival of a Crab-eating macaque and a Blotched genet, both from the London Zoo, and there was not even any let-up on opening day itself with the arrival of a Crested porcupine, also from London Zoo, necessitating housing. It is an exaggeration to say that animals were still being released into their enclosures through a hatch at the back just as the first visitors approached the front, but the truth was not very different.

Seven hundred people visited the zoo on the first day. The entrance price was 2/- (10p) for adults, 1/- (5p) for children and 30/- (£1.50) for a season ticket. The following day – Good Friday – no fewer than 1,950 visitors poured through the gates, proving a zoo didn't need elephants, giraffes and sealions to pull in the crowds. (Ken wisely chose not to hold the official opening on Good Friday itself because he accurately predicted that the grounds were bound to be packed out with people on a public holiday, weather permitting, and, with everything new and untested, it would have been a recipe for pandemonium had anything unforeseen happened.) On the fourth day, Easter Sunday, up to six thousand toured the collection. The zoo was truly up-and-running. (During the first eighteen months, approximately 200,000 visitors were to pass through the turnstiles, not bad going for a new and relatively unknown venture.) 'I am extremely gratified at the public's response to our venture,' he was reported as saying. He had every right to feel proud. In less than four months he had built a zoo. It was far from perfect, and it did not exactly reflect Gerald Durrell's original vision for it (something Durrell would be considerably put out about when he saw the place for the first time on his return from South America), but this should not detract from Ken's achievement. Obviously there were minor teething troubles to be sorted out, but, on the whole, everybody seemed to be enjoying themselves. People were jostling round the cages and buying ice-cream, and at last he had something to show for all his hard work. The poster Ken produced to advertise the zoo gives a good intimation of what the first visitors saw. The strapline – 'YOU MUST VISIT BRITAIN'S NEWEST ZOO!' – was not so much an invitation as a directive to take oneself off to the zoo without delay. The poster went on to list some of the star attractions that awaited anyone who did:

MONKEYS
BUSH BABIES
WALLABIES
EAGLES • PARROTS
TROPICAL BIRDS
SNAKES • CROCODILES
FISH ETC.
and Rare Exhibits
FROM
GERALD DURRELL'S
COLLECTIONS

With so many diverse exhibits, how could anyone fail to be fascinated? Ken believed such animals could be just as interesting in their own way as larger animals, and he soon gave short shrift to any ungrateful schoolchild who complained of ennui.

'Cages have been built, outhouses have been converted and rooms have been insulated, but a certain amount of work remains to be done,' reported the *Jersey Weekly Post* in the first week of April, adding, as a portent of things to come, 'A number of births have been recorded among the zoo inmates, and among the most recent is a Fruit bat baby – seen only occasionally since its birth as it remains enfolded in its mother's wings.'

Before the year was out, births or hatchings had also been recorded for the quokkas, otherwise known as Short-tailed Wallabies (a species, then as now, rarely seen in captivity outside Australian collections), pottos (a baby potto was born on 1 March), Chinese hamsters, dingoes, Ring-tailed coatis, and Galapagos doves (and possibly the Common marmosets). The zoo also managed to breed chameleons in its first year, a not insignificant achievement as back then most species of chameleon were difficult enough to keep alive, let alone breed. This event prompted Ken to fire off a letter to *The Times*, which was printed in the paper in October. In the letter, which had more to do with scoring one up on the London Zoo than simply publicising Jersey Zoo, he was scarcely able to conceal his delight that the U.K.'s most historic and venerable zoological institution had been trounced by the new kid on the block:

Sir, – Your photograph on October 19 of a newly arrived East African chameleon at the London Zoo is interesting.

We received six Jackson's horned chameleons as a gift from Kenya on June 20. On October 16 four youngsters were produced, each about three-quarters of an inch long. They are thriving on a diet of fruit flies and tiny insects and are active in climbing about the foliage in their cage.

Oddly enough, apart from this letter to *The Times*, I cannot find any other record of Jersey Zoo having bred Jackson's chameleons, but that is hardly surprising because records dating from the period are patchy at best. I did find a reference to the zoo once having bred the Common chameleon around this time – a species found in southern Europe, North Africa and the Near East – but, in his letter, Ken clearly says that the chameleons came from Kenya, so it can't be a simple case of misidentification. The Jackson's chameleon is, in any case, one of the most instantly recognisable of chameleon species, the male having three long annular horns on the head evocative of the extinct *Triceratops*.

*

Under Ken Smith, Jersey Zoo was very different from the place it was to become as it matured. These days, no dogs – not even guide dogs – are permitted anywhere in the grounds but, in the beginning, Ken not only allowed people to bring in their dogs (on leads) but, in a bid to make the place as visitor-friendly as possible, actively encouraged them to do so. He even had a large sign printed that read:

DOGS ARE ALLOWED IN THE ZOO PROVIDED THEY ARE KEPT UNDER PROPER CONTROL.

A visiting celebrity, the fantasy writer T.H. White, who had a home on Alderney, one of the smaller Channel Islands, was so surprised by such a relaxed attitude to man's best friend that he asked Ken to pose for a photo holding the sign aloft.

Many people would be surprised to learn that public feeding was once permitted. In *The Stationary Ark*, published nearly twenty years later (in 1976), Gerald Durrell wrote, 'Today, in all the more advanced zoos, feeding by the public is forbidden, and quite rightly too.' He made no mention of the fact that the practice was allowed at Jersey Zoo (admittedly with food bought at the pay kiosk) throughout the 1960s. To do so would have seemed pharisaical. Feeding by the public was originally introduced at Jersey Zoo by Ken Smith and continued long after he had left, and it was only as the 1960s gave way to the 1970s that the zoo finally ditched the practice altogether. Ken knew from his experiences in other zoos just how lucrative the time-honoured practice could be. At Jersey, visitors could buy little bags of peanuts to feed to the monkeys, bringing in much needed additional revenue and adding to the visitor experience. An unpleasant side-effect of this was that it turned the animals into beggars. The monkeys would thrust their arms through the wire-mesh in anticipation of food, and if the food wasn't instantly forthcoming they would grab at their admirers. From day one, Ken received complaints about Frisky the mandrill snatching at visitors' clothing. Then, on 17 June, not quite three months after the zoo first opened, tragedy stuck when a young girl, Susan le Sueur, aged two, was rushed to hospital in St. Helier after a monkey bit off part of her left forefinger when she put it through the wire front of the cage.

Ken liked to explore ways to persuade visitors to leave behind more of their cash. Selling bags of peanuts was one method. Levying a separate parking charge was another. It cost an additional 6d to use the zoo's car park. In addition, visitors were required to dig into their pockets to visit the Aquarium or the pets' corner. There was nothing unusual in this; it was common practice in those days for zoos to charge extra for special attractions. Even the homely act of answering the call of nature wasn't free. Anyone wishing to use one of the lavatory cubicles was required to insert a coin in the slot to open the door.

*

In June, Gerald Durrell returned from the Argentine with a large and varied collection of South American mammals, birds, reptiles and amphibians. Ken travelled to London to assist with the onward passage of the specimens to Jersey. He told the *Jersey Evening Post*, 'When Mr Durrell arrives in Jersey he will be seeing his zoo for the first time, as when he was last in the Island building had not commenced.' The next day the Zoo Ship docked in St. Helier. Ken had been looking forward to showing Durrell round the zoo, but things didn't turn out as well as expected. Durrell had been forewarned by Jacquie, who had returned from Argentina early, having been injured in a car crash, that there were aspects of the zoo that might fall short of his expectations. As he looked round his zoo for the first time, he was perturbed to find that many of his instructions had not been followed. Ken argued that, owing to a lack of time and money, he had had no choice but to adapt the plans to fit the site, and he had done the best he could in the time available. If he had deviated from his instructions, he said, it was only because in their original form they were impractical or too expensive to implement. But Durrell refused to be mollified. A few months later he wrote, 'My zoo in Jersey has now been open to the public for nearly a year. We are probably the newest zoo in Europe,' adding disingenuously, 'and, I like to think, one of the nicest.' His carefully crafted words concealed the dismay he felt that the reality did not match the dream. The zoo had been constructed in a hurry – and it showed. In the haste to get the place up and ready to admit the public, Ken's team had often been forced to use recycled building materials salvaged from scrap yards. Aesthetics had had to go out of the window; improvisation was the order of the day. The zoo was, quite literally, a packing crate zoo, in that some of the cages were constructed out of discarded, untreated aircraft packing crates, a praxis dictated by financial necessity and lack of time. Chicken-wire was used quite extensively. Many of the cages were of less than generous proportions and some might even be considered quite cramped by modern zoo standards. Even when the zoo was up-and-running and time was less of an issue, Ken continued to rely very heavily for his building materials on reclaimed items acquisitioned at the cost of only a few pence from an old quarry located conveniently nearby (among other flotsam and jetsam, discarded park railings, in ten or twelve foot lengths, could be picked up there for the expenditure of a single pound note and made simple but adequate animal pens if one wasn't bothered too much about the appearance). I have examined photographs from the period and there were other enclosures that, whilst not exactly spacious or attractive, were quite adequate. The fact that Ken was able to have the zoo built, stocked, staffed, and ready to admit the public in such a short timescale was a remarkable achievement. But Durrell hated compromise, and was quite distressed that Ken had taken it upon himself to deviate from his 'blueprint', such as it was, with the result that the zoo – from the choice of animals to the design and appearance of the enclosures – was not as Durrell imagined it would be.

Ken's official title may have been 'superintendent' or 'manager', but in reality he was the zoo's director in all but name, and indeed he was even once described unequivocally as Jersey Zoo's director in a newspaper article of the time, much to Gerald Durrell's chagrin. Perhaps the best way to think of Ken is as Gerald Durrell's adjutant. More often than not it was Ken who chose the animals, occasionally even paying for some of them out of his own pocket, and Ken who decided on what new enclosures to build. It wasn't just the outward appearance of many of the enclosures that offended Durrell's sensibilities; some of the cages, planned and built in a hurry, had serious design flaws. The abode of Pythagoras, the big Reticulated python, in the very small Reptile House (a converted garage) was a case in point. Owing to the fact that the two large sheets of plate glass comprising the front of the cage slid over each other on runners, it made it extremely difficult for the reptile keepers to clean out his pond. With a small harmless snake, this would not have mattered too much, but with a powerful, short-tempered snake like Pythagoras it turned what should have been a simple routine procedure into a major undertaking because the only way it could be accomplished was to bundle him unceremoniously into an old wicker laundry basket – a process to which Pythagoras took grave exception – while his cage was serviced. Manhandling him was a tricky, even dangerous, job requiring at least two people, and Durrell blamed Ken for the cage's shortcomings.

Another thing that distressed him was Ken's choice of animals. Whilst some of them fitted in quite well with the conservation aim, others definitely did not. He believed his manager had let him down by filling the zoo up with what he considered to be the wrong type of animal – animals certain to appeal to the public, but which were, by and large, in no immediate danger of extinction. This accusation was unfair. It must be remembered that Ken had less than four months to source the animals. Being reliant on what was available at the time on dealers' lists or on surplus lists from other zoos, it is perfectly understandable that he was prepared to accept so many common species. If he had concentrated mainly on rare or endangered animals, as Gerald Durrell had hoped, it would have been a rather impoverished collection that awaited the first anticipative visitors. In a magazine interview many years later, Durrell remarked bitterly about the uphill struggle he had in the early days to convince people that the special mission of the zoo was to breed endangered species when all his guests could see when they looked out of the windows of his flat above the zoo's offices was a common African lion lolling indolently in the sunshine. (Since those days, the wild population has crashed, with the result, unimaginable fifty years ago, that the African lion, once so common, is now an extremely rare sight outside game reserves.)

*

In between all his other responsibilities, Ken somehow found time to write the first edition of Jersey Zoo's guide book. The front cover, identical to Philadelphia Zoo's guide book – featured an artist's impression of a mandrill. In the introduction he wrote:

> Jersey Zoological Park was established as the result of Mr. Gerald Durrell's wish to find a suitable place in which to accommodate and maintain the collections of animals obtained on his expeditions to the tropics…In choosing Jersey for his Zoo Mr. Durrell has founded the first zoo in the Channel Islands. The climatic conditions of Jersey are ideal for keeping many kinds of animals, also for the Zoo's special aim – the breeding of rare creatures, especially those threatened with extinction in the wild state.

Did Ken really believe it – that this insignificant little zoo, tucked away in one corner of a remote island in the English Channel, could (and in time *would*) save species from extinction? True, he was a zoo man to the core; animals were in his blood, but although he appreciated the need for preservation (his spontaneous letters to *The Times* were proof of that) he was never completely won over by the argument in favour of captive breeding endangered species. Zoos were a means – a very effective means – of getting people interested in nature. Only by seeing animals up close, could they really begin to understand how beautiful were animals or how complex was the web of life. Although the animals at Jersey *were* breeding, it was in a fairly haphazard way; there was no impetus to the whole thing, and keepers were often surprised, on morning inspection, to find that some animal had given birth during the night, but none of the animals bred so far were threatened species.

In the introduction he went on to say that 'particular attention is being paid to the educational aspects of the Zoological Park' – but there as yet was little sign of that, either. At the same time, he took the opportunity to reassure any dissatisfied visitors, who had arrived with unreasonably high expectations and were disenchanted by the reality, that improvements were already in train. 'The Zoo is in its infancy,' he wrote in that first guide book, 'and the present range of exhibits will be increased substantially.' One of the first new attractions to be built was a pets' corner. The area chosen for this was the walled garden. The centrepiece was a model of Noah's Ark inhabited by rabbits and guinea-pigs (a design clearly inspired by the Mouse Village in Paignton Zoo's pets' corner). There is no record of Durrell's opinion of this disparate collection of pet and farm animals, added in 1960 to make the zoo more appealing to children, but it surely must have contributed to his dawning realisation that Ken was intent on creating a conventional zoo, a far cry from the conservation centre that Durrell had envisaged.

This was not the first pets' corner the zoo had had. There was an even earlier one on the upper floor of the long, two-storey Mammal House. Ken defended that first pets' corner and his decision to build a larger one by pointing out it was a hugely popular attraction that generated extra income. Durrell was unconvinced. He wanted his zoo to be known and respected for the rarity of its animal collection and, whilst it did have a spattering of unusual creatures that were the envy of other zoos, it also had rabbits, guinea-pigs, sheep, goats, budgerigars, a piglet and a Jersey calf. Its objective may have been the captive breeding of endangered species but there was, as yet, little to distinguish Jersey Zoo from any other zoo. The first major breeding success with a threatened species – the White Eared pheasant – did not come until 1969, a full ten years after the zoo was launched. In the early 1960s it was still a conventional zoo with lions and penguins and bears, the kind of charismatic animals that people expected to see in any zoo worthy of the name, and every year saw an incredible variety of new species taking up residence in the grounds and buildings of Les Augres Manor as Ken strove hard to give his visitors value for money, even if relatively few of his choices were of any conservation importance.

However, several species *were* decidedly unexpected and there were some that are hardly ever seen in zoos even now. Mention has been made before of the gharials and quokkas. Other rare, threatened or seldom-seen animals sourced by Ken included a pair of Gough Island coots from the London Zoo, offspring of the birds he had so admired during his two-day visit there in 1956. The unusual Crested rat was another quirky animal that was kept – and bred – at Jersey Zoo in its early days.

Ken was quite prepared to buy from dealers – he had, after all, been one himself – and among the animals obtained in this way were two rare Goliath frogs from West Africa, the world's longest frog (fully grown specimens can reach a maximum length of more than 14 in.), a species hardly ever seen in zoos. Gifts of animals were commonplace, and it was rare for him to decline an offer once he was satisfied that adequate facilities were available. The Governor of Gibraltar donated a Barbary macaque, whilst the Government of Northern Ireland, Ministry of Agriculture, presented a group of Hooded crows.

Ken did not pass up an opportunity for free publicity. When, in the autumn of 1960, a report appeared in *The Times* announcing that No. 66 Fighter Squadron RAF was to be disbanded at the end of September and that consequently its mascots – three live rattlesnakes – would soon be homeless, Ken was quick to contact RAF Acklington in Northumberland, where the squadron was based, offering a home in the zoo's Reptile House for the three snakes, knowing full well that this happy outcome was sure to be reported in a follow-up article in *The Times*, as indeed it was. The rattlesnakes duly arrived in Jersey on 12 October in an ad hoc transport in one of the squadron's own aeroplanes, securely locked in a packing case marked *'Mean Creepy-crawlies'* and *'Danger – Poisonous Reptiles'* (strictly speaking the correct term is 'Venomous'). Rattlesnakes might seem like an odd choice of mascot for an aircraft fighter squadron. The squadron badge was a rattlesnake because, in the view of the RAF, it typified 'aggressive spirit and striking power'. The squadron was briefly reformed in June 1962 (until 1969). It is not known whether it asked to have the rattlesnakes back.

As at Paignton Zoo, Ken soon found that in addition to his responsibility for the zoo's permanent residents, he was much in demand to provide assistance for orphaned and injured wild animals, not all of which were local casualties. Orphaned leverets were flown in from southern England. They were hand-reared at the zoo by Trudy, some of them becoming quite tame in the process and refusing to be released. One hare lived in the office. 'I think we just called it Hare,' said Betty Renouf, who joined the zoo as office junior in 1962. Since the Brown hare is not native to the Channel Islands, releasing them in the zoo grounds – or anywhere else on the island – would not be permitted nowadays. The hares did not establish themselves in the countryside. But by far the commonest casualties presented to the zoo were birds. Wild birds brought to the zoo for attention during the first four years included several Barn owls (the commonest owl in the Channel Islands), a single Tawny owl (extremely rare on Jersey), four Water rails, two corncrakes, a Golden plover, a snipe, four kingfishers, several kestrels, two sparrowhawks, and a Grey phalarope.

Towards the end of the first year, Jersey Zoo acquired from a dealer in Birmingham a young female Western Lowland gorilla called N'Pongo. At a cost of £1,200, N'Pongo was the most valuable animal in the zoo (in 1959, £1,200 could buy you a decent-sized house). Gerald Durrell personally flew to London to collect her from the RSPCA animal shelter at Heathrow Airport. According to Trudy, Durrell flew back to Jersey with the baby gorilla sitting on his lap (something that would never be allowed now) but in *Menagerie Manor* Durrell claimed that N'Pongo made the flight from London to Jersey in a crate. Perhaps Gerald Durrell's memory was at fault or maybe he deliberately altered the facts for fear his readers might think that having an unrestrained gorilla, albeit a baby one, in an aircraft cabin was a touch irresponsible. At Jersey airport, Ken and Trudy were waiting with the zoo van to collect them. 'I think Gerry must have regretted his decision to have N'Pongo sitting on his lap for the whole journey because it was with considerable relief that he finally handed her over to us when the plane touched down in Jersey,' Trudy told me.

To begin with, N'Pongo lived in the guest room in the manor until she was big enough to go into a cage in the Mammal House. The young gorilla – for a long time erroneously believed to be a male and described as such in *Menagerie Manor* – quickly became a playmate for Ken and Trudy's daughter, Caroline. 'N'Pongo was incredibly gentle with her,' said Trudy, 'in contrast to the boisterous behaviour she showed to her keepers. It was very touching to watch them. The two of them would roll around together, tickling each other and both squirming with obvious enjoyment.'

They would often sit back to back on the floor, like an incongruous pair of bookends, sharing sweets from a bag. Caroline was quick to emulate her simian playmate, including the gorilla's less appealing habits. N'Pongo, chomping noisily away on jelly babies, would occasionally spit out a semi-masticated jelly baby into her leathery palm, examine it with a fat forefinger, and re-ingest the gelatinous mess, prompting Caroline, under the impression this was correct etiquette, to do the same, much to the revulsion of onlookers.

Everyone was also rather shocked by another habit Caroline had effortlessly picked up. This time, however, the malefactor was not N'Pongo but a human. Jacquie Durrell, seizing on the little girl's propensity to learn quickly, taught her to flick the V-sign. I was unable to interview Jacquie, which is a pity, but the usual perception one gets of Jacquie – who adored Caroline as much as Gerald did – is of a very forthright, no-nonsense Mancunian woman. When her hackles were up, Jacquie took no prisoners, and was not above using four-letter words to get her point across, but in her relationship with Caroline, she showed a softer side to her character. By teaching the child rude gestures, Jacquie revealed an unexpected, endearingly childish, sense of mischief.

A photographer from the *Jersey Evening Post* was dispatched to the zoo to take pictures of N'Pongo, as its most celebrated and valuable attraction. The photographer was one of the first people to get an inkling that Gerald Durrell was not as intimately involved in zoo matters as he liked his readers to think. The baby gorilla was ceremoniously planted in Durrell's lap on the front lawn, with Caroline sitting beside them. But Gerald Durrell was a relatively unfamiliar figure to N'Pongo, and the resultant photos show the baby gorilla, obviously uneasy about this atypical arrangement, staring towards – and instinctively reaching out for – her regular playmate Caroline, in whose company she felt much more relaxed and where she knew she could find solace.

Visitors to Jersey Zoo were amazed by Caroline's lack of fear, and the fact that many of the animals, including some potentially quite dangerous creatures such as some of the monkeys, came in for a petting from her every day as she toddled round the cages, saying 'Hello' to all her favourite animals – like Amos the Giant anteater brought back from the Argentine by Gerald Durrell on his latest trip. Even lions didn't faze her. In May 1962 the then three-and-a-half-year-old Caroline flew with her father to Heathrow Airport to greet Jeremy Mallinson on his return from an animal-collecting expedition of his own to Southern Rhodesia (now Zimbabwe) and the Okavango swamp region of Ngamiland in the Bechuanaland Protectorate (now the Republic of Botswana). With Jeremy was a large consignment of animals he had obtained in Africa bound for Jersey Zoo. Caroline fearlessly inspected the animals in their travelling containers in the cargo hold of the aeroplane before the onward flight to Jersey, including a tame but nonetheless potentially lethal lioness called Chinky, brought back from the Okavango as a possible mate for Leo.

Ken doted on Caroline, whose nickname was Moonbeam (or, less frequently, 'Cuckoo'), cradling her, playing with her every day no matter how tired he felt, treating her to sweets whenever she asked and generally indulging her, which is a father's prerogative. Gerald Durrell, too, was immensely fond of her. Les Augrès Manor is shaped like a capital E without the central bar, and Ken and Trudy's flat was in the east wing above the whimsically named Green Parrot Café. The Durrells' flat was in the central part, and between their flat and the Smiths' living quarters was a connecting door. In the evenings, when Gerald was relaxing in front of the television, a cardboard box of wine (the kind with a little tap on the side) at his elbow as was his wont, he would shout out, 'Send Moonbeam through'. Then she would run through and sit on his lap and the two of them would watch TV together. Not surprisingly, natural history programmes were a must-see. (Ken and Trudy did not have a TV set in their own flat, and so Caroline, whenever she wanted to watch TV, would go next door.) Both Gerald and Jacquie treated Caroline as if she were their own, buying her toys and clothing wherever they went including, on one occasion, a rather fetching pair of 'gaucho' trousers, mini versions of the real thing. One of her favourite toys, which she hauled around everywhere with her, was a cuddly giraffe – another impulsive gift from the Durrells. Everybody agrees that Gerald Durrell probably would have made an excellent father, but he was never to have children of his own. In a way, she became like a surrogate daughter to him. As well as bestowing presents on her, in 1961 he dedicated his new lavishly illustrated children's book *Island Zoo* to her with a characteristically cryptic inscription:

> This book is for Caroline Smith
> who has introduced me to such
> rare animals as the Moo-ha-ha,
> the Dab-dab, and the Mouse-chew.

This book – which looked at some of the earliest animal characters at Jersey Zoo including N'Pongo and Henrietta the Hairy armadillo – may have been dedicated to Caroline Smith, but of her father there was no mention and no indication that the zoo was run by anybody other than Gerald Durrell himself. It suited Durrell that people believed he was in sole command. The truth was that Gerald Durrell was rarely glimpsed outside in the zoo, even by the people who worked there, still less by the general public, remaining holed up in the manor house for most of the day, a remote and unapproachable figure.

This was not so different from the situation that existed when Ken was Superintendent of Paignton Zoo. At Paignton, the zoo's founder, Herbert Whitley, had rarely been sighted by the people in his employ, and Ken had been one of only a handful of people to have access to the top man. It was the same now in Jersey, but with one major difference: Whitley had not been a celebrity like Durrell. None of Paignton Zoo's visitors had arrived hoping they might catch a precious glimpse of Whitley, whereas everybody who walked through Jersey Zoo's entranceway nurtured the hope, slim though it was, that Gerald Durrell would suddenly pop up, in the same way that everyone who goes to the Himalayas is secretly hoping to steal a glimpse of the Abominable Snowman. Few were rewarded with a sighting.

In *Menagerie Manor*, Durrell gives the impression he was very proactive around the zoo in those early days. The reality was very different. He was surprisingly uninvolved with the running of the zoo, preferring to leave everything to his Superintendent. To the staff, Durrell seemed strangely distant, detached, not at all the impression one gets from reading *Menagerie Manor*. Jersey Zoo's staff, most of whom had read Gerald Durrell's books and been looking forward to meeting this paragon in person, were disappointed that they saw so little of him. They weren't the only ones baffled by the founder's odd reclusive trait; so too were the students who came to help out at the zoo during their summer break from college. At night the students bedded down in the long, echoing, entrance hall of the manor house. They had been drawn to the zoo, like moths to a lantern, precisely *because* of Gerald Durrell. They were doomed to disappointment. Like a party of cryptozoologists on the trail of a mythical beast, they detected little sign of their quarry, but Ken did his best to assure them they would meet their hero eventually.

'But Mr Smith…*when*?'

'Er, soon…well…probably…maybe.'

They stood little chance. To what extent Ken actively discouraged Gerald Durrell from involving himself in the zoo's day-to-day affairs is unclear. Certainly, just before Durrell was due back from another expedition, Ken firmly instructed the keepers and other staff, some of whom had only just joined the zoo and hadn't yet met the founder, to refrain from bothering him. Mr Durrell, he told them sternly, was bound to be exhausted after his recent trip and in no mood for idle chitchat. As a famous author, he wanted nothing more than to get on with writing his next best-seller without interruption from them, and most definitely would not want to be bombarded by a lot of zoo business.

Trudy has a slightly different take on it. According to her, it was not Ken who dissuaded him from adopting a more hands-on approach, but rather Durrell who withdrew *himself* from the routine activities of running the zoo. 'Far from being sidelined, Gerald Durrell was more than content to take a backseat and let Ken run things.'

There is a photo showing Durrell and Ken picking through the week's fruit consignment. In fact, this scene is a total fiction for the purpose of the photograph because Durrell was never known to help out with mundane chores of this kind. What *is* known is that Ken resented his authority being undermined by anybody, even if that someone was the director's wife. On one occasion, after Jacquie Durrell had reprimanded an incompetent member of staff for some misdemeanour, Ken stormed into the Durrells' flat and in no uncertain terms threatened to quit if Durrell didn't keep his wife's 'bloody nose out of it', haranguing Durrell that since Jacquie had no official position in the zoo, she had no right to interfere in zoo affairs. Much to Jacquie's annoyance, Gerald Durrell took Ken's side in the argument.

Ken may have been chafing from Jacquie's obvious antipathy towards him, but this didn't stop him throwing himself wholeheartedly into making the zoo a success. He would be sat quietly at his desk, concentrating on the mountain of paperwork, when suddenly his eyes would wander to his watch. Suddenly realising that time was marching on, he would leap to his feet and dash out into the zoo. Grabbing the first member of staff he encountered, he would instruct the hapless individual to stop whatever they were doing and take the zoo's van (bright yellow and luridly painted with stylised images of various zoo animals, as well as details of opening times, etc.) and drive it up and down King's Street (which has since been pedestrianised) in St. Helier to leave shoppers in no doubt about the existence, only about four miles distant, of the zoo.

The only day of the year when Jersey Zoo closed to the public was Christmas Day, but on most days in winter there were so few visitors that it ceased to be economical to employ anybody to sit all day in the ticket-box, and there was nothing to stop the few hardy Jersey folk who did decide to brave the elements, from slipping past the empty pay-box into the zoo. On these days, Ken assumed personal responsibility for collecting the money, and could be seen periodically stalking round the grounds clasping a simple wooden cashbox, selling tickets to any hardened souls he encountered on his perambulations.

According to Gerald Durrell's biographer, Douglas Botting, it was Ken who would personally ring a bell as a signal for work to begin and finish. This was a common working practice in those days. The bell in question was about a foot high suspended in a tower behind the manor house. In times past, the lord of the manor had used it to summon his farmhands from the distant fields. However, everybody I've spoken to about it disputes that it was ever rung as a time signal for zoo staff. Jeremy Mallinson, who probably knows the history of the zoo better than anyone, has no recollection of Ken ringing the bell to mark the start and finish of the working day. 'As far as I remember, the bell was rung only to warn of an animal on the loose, which was the only way to raise the alarm before the invention of two-way radios. It's very unlikely Ken would have rung the bell as early as eight a.m., which was the time we all started work, because he was an habitually late riser.'

Ken, it seems, was usually sighted around the zoo from about nine o'clock, well after the keepers had arrived for work and too late to ring the bell. As for the eventide bell, that is even less likely than the matutinal one, as Jeremy explained to me: 'Nobody that I was aware of in the early days of the zoo *dared* to knock off on time! You certainly didn't down tools according to the clock, but carried on until the work was finished.'

*

Trudy was in charge of the mammal section but, like all the animal staff, she helped out in other areas, too. If a coach party turned up unexpectedly, the clarion call would go out, and she and other staff members who had thought of themselves as zoo-keepers would down tools immediately to attend to the culinary needs of the coach party. One minute they could be re-branching the monkey cages, the next minute they could be preparing sandwiches and washing crockery. At first, keepers were expected to work a basic 6½ day week with one afternoon off a week (by 1962 the staff were getting two afternoons off, but it was not until the mid 1960s that they were getting a full day off, aside from annual leave). The pay, even by the standards of other zoos of the day, was exceptionally low, and nor were staff paid extra for night duty. And some of the work was potentially quite dangerous. For instance, none of the thirty-two cages in the Mammal House was equipped with a shut-off area to contain the animal while its cage was being serviced. This was fine for tame specimens, but not so good if the animal in question was less than trustworthy. To clean out the Palm civet, for example, its keeper had to resort to lobbing in eggs (to which it was very partial), one after the other, to distract the irascible creature for long enough to get the job done, but when the egg supply ran out, he had to exit the cage pretty sharpish. The staff turnover, as might be expected, was high, but there were those who did stay the course.

Among the employees Ken took on were three exceptional people – Jeremy Mallinson, John Hartley and John ('Shep') Mallet – each of whom, fired by an almost apostolic belief in what they were doing, were to clock up around forty years apiece at the zoo. If it hadn't been for these unwavering, selfless stalwarts, it is quite likely the place would not have survived its periodic cash crises, so dedicated were they to the cause. In later years, Ken was to derive considerable satisfaction from the fact that it was he, and not Gerald Durrell, who had discovered this outstanding trio.

In 1959 Jeremy Mallinson was at a crossroads in his life. His plan to start a canine boarding kennel on the island had fallen through and he was undecided which career path to follow. He went round Jersey Zoo as an ordinary visitor on the Sunday after it first opened, liked what he saw, and afterwards, at the instigation of his brother, wrote on spec to 'The Superintendent, Jersey Zoo Park', enquiring if there was, by some remote chance, a vacancy at the zoo. His luck was in. A temporary vacancy had just arisen on the bird staff. Ken had some difficulty deciphering the signature at the bottom of the letter. Under the impression the applicant's name must be either Jennifer or Jemima but in any case female, he began his letter offering Jeremy the job by writing: 'Dear Miss Mallinson…' Jeremy got back in touch immediately and put him straight. 'I'm actually a *boy*, but do I still get the job?'

Jeremy started work at the zoo on May 1, 1959, on the bird section. The vacancy had cropped up only because another keeper, Michael Armstrong, was on sick leave after injuring himself whilst in pursuit of an escaping Goliath heron (or possibly a crane). From the start, Ken made it clear to Jeremy that he was in locum and there was next to no prospect of taking him on permanently. 'Remember, the position is only short-term,' Ken reiterated, lest Jeremy was labouring under any misapprehension. 'At the end of the summer I'll have to let you go.'

'I realise that, sir,' said Jeremy, just grateful to have been offered the job, even if it didn't ultimately lead onto anything. In any case, he didn't plan on staying at Jersey Zoo for long because at that stage he wasn't sure *what* he wanted to do for a living except that it had to involve animals in one way or another. However, Jeremy soon became so absorbed in his work, first with the birds and then with mammals, that he knew that, at the age of twenty-two, he had found his vocation. Ken liked him, and, as the summer slipped by, realised it would be a mistake to let go of such a conscientious, hard-working member of the team. So Jeremy stayed, but the prospect of imminent dismissal never eased up completely but continued to hang over him, and every so often over the next couple of years, whenever Ken thought that Jeremy was becoming too complacent or showing too much independence of thought, he would gently remind him that his contract was only temporary and could be terminated at any time, just to keep him on his toes. That 'temporary' job eventually lasted more than forty years.

In time, Jeremy was to become one of Gerald Durrell's most devoted disciples, in time succeeding him as director of the zoo. Three days before Durrell died in Jersey in 1995, he asked Jeremy from his hospital bed, 'Just how long have you been working for me, Jeremy?' to which Mallinson answered, 'For just over half of your seventy years, Gerry.'

'I'm so pleased that I only took you on on a temporary basis!' said Durrell, showing his legendary wit to the last.

Except, of course, it wasn't Gerald Durrell who had originally employed Mallinson all those years ago; it was Ken Smith.

John Hartley and Shep Mallet both joined the zoo two years after Mallinson, in 1961. Hartley joined in March and Mallet in June. The first time Hartley applied to work at the zoo, he was told by Ken that there were no vacancies but that he could, if he wished, come to Jersey for a few days and shadow the keepers as they went about their work 'on condition you don't get in the way.' Hartley leapt at the chance. His enthusiasm was noted by Ken and when, some time later, a vacancy on the animal staff did crop up, he was a natural choice to fill it. Aged eighteen, he left school on the Friday and started work at the zoo on the following Monday. He did his apprenticeship on the bird and reptile sections before graduating to Trust Secretary in the mid 1960s; later he became P.A. to Gerald Durrell and, ultimately, International Programme Director. For John Hartley, it was his first job after leaving school and the first time he had been away from home for any length of time. A Yorkshire boy originally, he came to Jersey from Exmouth, where he lived with his parents. At the zoo he soon found himself plunged in at the deep end. Being part of a very small team, he was required to lend a hand to almost anything. One moment he could be painting cages or chopping fruit, the next on his way to a farm to collect a carthorse that had just died. The work was varied and rarely dull, but it could also be hard, dirty, unglamorous and unremitting. From the moment the visitors came pouring through the turnstiles, it was a case, in the nautical parlance, of all hands on deck. Getting time off was usually out of the question. Hartley had been working at the zoo for about two or three weeks when he needed to go into town to open a bank account as he had some money to deposit. He duly presented himself in front of Ken with a request to have the afternoon off.

'Oh, I don't know about that,' said Ken; 'terribly busy here at the moment. Loads of things to be done. Never a quiet moment. I'm not sure I can spare you. Is your business in town essential? Can't it wait? Oh I see, well, tell you what, come back and see me at two o'clock. I'll give you my answer then.'

Hartley told me: 'I was asking for the afternoon off but he wasn't prepared to give me his assent until the afternoon was half over. So right up to that moment I didn't know whether I could have the afternoon off or not. Then, when he did finally give me the OK, he added, "But you *will* be popping back later on, won't you." It was said more in the way of a statement than a question. That might seem rather unfair, and it certainly seemed *very* unfair to me at the time, but you can see it from his point of view. Things were very hectic. There were only about ten of us responsible for about seven hundred animals and often it wasn't possible to have even a couple of hours off.'

John Mallet came to Jersey Zoo from the Leckford Estate. To avoid any confusion with Hartley, he was nicknamed 'Shep' after Shepton Mallet, the Somerset market town, and the appellation stuck. He eventually went on to become Jersey Zoo's much respected curator of birds (even though, as he admitted, he was not as conservation-minded as some of his colleagues) and remained at the zoo for thirty-five years until his retirement in 1996, but his career in Jersey very nearly ended almost as soon as it had begun. One Friday he traipsed into Ken's office to collect his weekly wages as usual, oblivious that anything was wrong. Handing Shep his wage packet, Ken said to him quite casually, 'Here's your wages – and one week's notice.' Ken was sacking him!

'I couldn't believe it. He was dismissing me! Just like that! With no warning or explanation. I wasn't expecting it. I hadn't seen it coming and couldn't think what I'd done wrong. Ken was in conversation with a company rep. at the time and I didn't think it was right that he should sack me in front of a stranger like that. But that's what he did.

I was young and didn't want to make a scene in front of the rep., so all I said was "Thank you" which I admit was a pretty lame thing to say, and scuttled out of his office.'

It turned out that Ken was displeased by the amount of time it took Shep to do his job. Ken was determined that the zoo should look presentable with all the cleaning out done by the time the public was admitted at ten o'clock. This was the most hectic part of the day for the keepers, for they had only two hours from when they started work at eight o'clock to get all the routine chores done. This included raking over the floors in the bird aviaries, scrubbing out and refilling drinking bowls, cleaning the viewing windows, and removing the food dishes from the previous day's feed so that they could be washed and replenished. Ken also insisted that the aviaries were regularly bedecked with freshly cut branches. Shep had trouble keeping to this tight schedule. He took great pride in the zoo's flock of hens, which he used as broodies to incubate the eggs of some of the pheasant and duck species in the collection. It was a time-consuming task, but one he took inordinate care over. 'I find the pheasants rather interesting. Most of them are very attractive birds which appeal to the eye and appeal to me. I have kept all kinds of chickens over the years and they are very similar. Most of them are also easy to breed.'

The problem was, he always attended to his broody hens first thing in the morning, with the result that he was invariably late sprucing up the aviaries and he was often still at it by the time the public was milling around. Ken ran a tight ship and it had not gone unnoticed that on numerous occasions, instead of being able to admire some rare bird in an immaculate aviary, visitors had been treated to the sight of cleaning utensils propped against the front of the aviary as Shep hurried to complete his cleaning tasks. This would never do. 'If you want to know why I'm dismissing you,' said Ken when Shep crept back later for an explanation, 'it's because you're always doing those bloody chickens.'

Nowadays, of course, keepers accused of wasting time would be soundly instructed to buck up their ideas but, back then, infractions of this kind were treated more harshly, and a minor transgression could mean the sack. No right of appeal. No second chance.

'That was just Ken's way,' said Shep. 'He didn't tolerate inefficiency or what he perceived as time-wasting.'

Fortunately for Shep, he had a valuable ally in the form of Peter Glover, one of the other keepers. Slightly older than Shep, Peter shared the Smiths' flat in the manor and was on very good terms with them. He was able to convince Ken to reconsider. On the Friday, Shep was told his employment was terminated; just over a week later, on the Sunday, he found himself suddenly reinstated. He was, however, moved off the bird section and put on the section loosely known as *Outside Mammals*. 'I was a bird-man through and through, when suddenly I found myself working with a load of mammals. It was some while before I managed to get back with the birds again, but fortunately for me I was eventually put back on birds.'

Outside Mammals was generally considered the lowest and least enviable of all the animal sections. As its name suggests, it included all the hardier animals, such as the dingoes, Himalayan bear, tapir, peccaries, wallabies, badgers, and most of the cats, that were housed in outdoor enclosures and paddocks with only the most rudimentary sleeping quarters. During the winter, for the keepers attending to those animals, it could be unpleasant, chilblain-inducing work, as, at best, all they had by way of indoor accommodation was a tiny shed. As the paddocks were quite small, they were soon churned up by the animals and then the keepers had to plod across cloying mud that pulled at their Wellingtons. There were times, with the rain beating down, or the snow piling in drifts, when they looked upon their colleagues, snug in the various animal houses, with envy. The reptile keepers worked in comfort in the Reptile House (maintained at a positively balmy 80°F); the bird keepers could always find work to do in the Tropical Bird House (70°); the keepers on *Small Mammals* had the Mammal House. Those keepers on *Outside Mammals*, on the other hand, just shivered or got soaked or, during the summer, risked sunburn. No cosy animal houses for them.

Peter Glover was, in effect, Ken's unofficial lieutenant and something of an unknown quantity. The fact that he lived with the Smiths, ate at their table, conversed at great length with them after work, meant everyone had to be very careful what they said in his presence. 'Pete was a great guy,' John Hartley told me; 'everybody liked him, but there must have been occasions during the general banter over the evening meal when he inadvertently let slip something he should've kept to himself. I'm not saying he deliberately set out to get any of us into trouble with the boss, but it is easy to see how things could have found their way back to Ken.' John is probably right. In that situation it was almost unavoidable that, off his guard in the relaxed atmosphere after work, occasionally Peter would, without thinking, say to Ken something along the lines of 'so-and-so did this today' or 'such-and-such happened in the zoo today.'

Nothing escaped Ken's punctilious eye. Shep recalls that one day Ken brought to the tapir keeper's attention some litter in the form of a discarded bit of paper that was lying in the paddock. 'But I checked the paddock this morning, Mr Smith,' the keeper protested. 'Well, I suggest you get in there and remove it NOW,' ordered Ken, 'and when you do, have a close look at it.' Mystified, the keeper picked up the bit of paper. Written on it, in Ken's own handwriting, was a date already three days old. The implication was all too clear to the suitably abashed tapir keeper. Ken must have seen the piece of litter several days ago and inscribed the date on it and replaced it where he had found it. There could be no argument, no protestation of innocence. The keeper had been found out.

Ken lived life fast. To his staff he appeared to be always on the go, always in a hurry. It seemed to them that he looked upon time as the enemy; there were never enough hours in the day to accomplish everything that he had to do. 'Excuse me, Mr Smith,' they would begin tentatively. 'Yes, yes, what is it?' he would snap impatiently for there were many things he had to do, but he was not unapproachable and there were times when he would suddenly round up the staff and take them for a quick drink at a local pub or even occasionally for a light meal. Unlike Gerald Durrell, whose drinking was already starting to worry his friends, Ken was not a boozer but he did enjoy an occasional half pint of pale ale. 'I always found him a most interesting and pleasant person to talk to,' wrote Jeremy Mallinson many years later, 'and was able to glean much from his great experience.' Ken relished these rare moments of relaxation when he could escape from the zoo and all its problems. He did smoke, as did most people in those days, but, according to Trudy, not heavily and quit the habit after his children were born.

Ken possessed an excellent personal library of animal books, and when Jeremy expressed an interest in looking through the tomes, Ken graciously granted him unlimited access, perhaps remembering that Herbert Whitley had done the same for him at Paignton Zoo. Jeremy had a thirst for knowledge; completely off his own back, he started a primitive animal records system (Jersey Zoo's first). It was not an official database but one created for his own personal use to further his knowledge of the animal kingdom and in particular the animals kept at Jersey. Ken moaned, 'He's forever asking me bloody questions about all the animals. I mean every conceivable facet about every bird, beast and reptile in the place. And he writes everything down like a bleeding detective.' But one senses that Ken was secretly rather pleased that Jeremy was so enthusiastic about his job and keen to expand his knowledge.

Ken was a pretty snappy dresser – in contrast to Trudy, whose signature work attire was a duffel coat. Believing in the popular aphorism that 'clothes maketh the man', Ken was always impeccably dressed, and was hardly ever observed without a jacket and tie even when he took Caroline to the beach. In fact, this was not so unusual in those days, and to men of his generation it was almost unthinkable to be seen in public without a tie. Many years later, George Jacobs ('Big George'), one of the keepers at the zoo in those early days, remarked on his former boss's sartorial elegance in his book *Memoirs of a Coarse Zoo Keeper*:

In a flush of affluence he had bought a magnificent suit, a masterpiece of the tailor's art which he would insist on ruining by wearing a thick, ugly belt – not a belt really, more a leather cummerbund.

Ken was a good animal man whom we all respected though we did not much appreciate his new-found finery which caused him to pussyfoot on heel and tiptoe through the animal dung with his trouser turn-ups hitched delicately above his ankles for fear of staining. But he cut a marvellous figure chatting up the dolly-bird visitors.

It so happened that an opossum died and those lads in favour of a bit of devilment, which was everybody, took it down to a tall tree and arranged it in a lifelike pose among the uppermost branches.

Then, a little later, somebody told Ken that the opossum had gone missing and Ken, being a keen and conscientious keeper and manager, organised a search. By carefully engineering the situation, he was gently led in the direction of the tree where eagle-eyed Ken spotted the missing animal.

'Net the tree,' he ordered and dutifully we spread in a circle the catching nets. But nobody was willing to climb the tree. 'You are the expert, you ought to show us how,' suggested some cunning character appealing to his vanity – well, any man with a suit like that must be vain.

So up the tree went Ken. And it was a particularly twiggy, prickly, well-foliaged tree which required a lot of squirming under branches and sliding round the trunk. Soon dark sap stains began to appear on Ken's suit and there were ominous sounds of tearing.

'Oh, tough luck, Ken,' said a sympathetic voice from below.

With Opening Day scheduled for Easter 1959, the animals begin to arrive at Jersey Zoo. This photo was taken on the day Ken and Trudy landed in Jersey and shows KS holding a Spot-nosed guenon while an Amazon parrot perches on Trudy's shoulder and a young keeper has a firm grip on a Vervet monkey. The man standing next to Ken is the zoo's catering manager, Mr Huckstable. © *Jersey Evening Post*.

The venture begins. It is believed this photo was taken on the day of Jersey Zoo's official opening, 26 March 1959. Ken helped launch Jersey Zoo and was its de facto first director. The long two-storey building on the left is the Mammal House. The walled garden is behind the wall to the right and the manor forecourt is through the archway. © *Jersey Evening Post*.

The Monkey House, Jersey Zoo, March 1959. All the early animal houses were conversions of existing buildings. Notice the absence of a safety barrier, not a mandatory requirement back then. © *Jersey Evening Post*.

A young drill, seen from the other side of the wire, Jersey Zoo, circa 1959. © *R.W. Dingle*

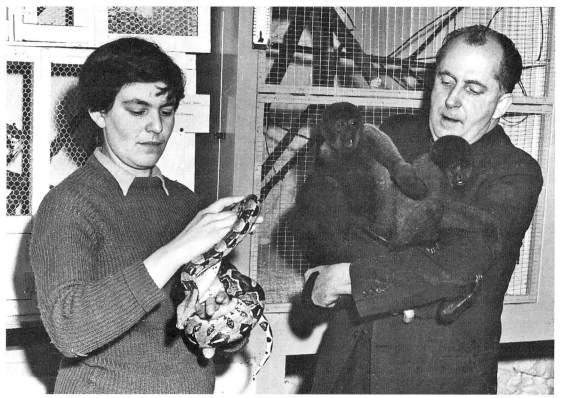

KS struggles to restrain two Woolly monkeys while Trudy cradles a Common boa, Jersey Zoo, March 1959. © *Jersey Evening Post*.

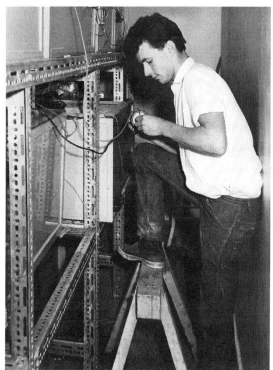

Left: Lee Thomas set up Jersey Zoo's first Reptile House. Lee worked for Ken at Paignton Zoo, Jersey Zoo and Exmouth Zoo, and also undertook an animal-collecting expedition to British Guiana, bringing back more animals for Jersey Zoo. Right: KS in an unguarded moment in his office at Jersey Zoo, 1959.

Left: Ken was very proud of the fact that it was he, not the zoo's founder, Gerald Durrell, who discovered Jeremy Mallinson and others of his calibre to work at Jersey Zoo. Without dedicated people like Jeremy on board, Jersey Zoo would probably have folded early on. Right: Ken and Trudy with daughter Caroline in front of the manor house at Jersey Zoo. Ken loved parenthood and was immensely proud of all his children.

The dingoes at Jersey Zoo. KS had less than four months to stock Jersey Zoo before it opened its gates to the public and had to rely on whatever animals were available at the time. As a result, not all the animals conformed to Gerald Durrell's vision of establishing a breeding centre for endangered species. The dingoes were one of many kinds of animal on show in the early days in no imminent danger of extinction. The young girl is Caroline, Ken and Trudy's first child who was born shortly before they moved to Jersey. © *Rosemary Gilliat*.

Left: Mother and Son. Gertrude visiting Ken in Jersey, early 1960s. Ken was renowned for his smart appearance at all times and usually wore a jacket and tie even when relaxing on the beach. The girl is his daughter Caroline and the boy is his young nephew, Brian. Right: KS surprised by the camera while checking stock in Jersey Zoo's souvenir shop. Only a very small shop, it stocked mostly decorative ceramics from the Jersey Potteries, books on the fauna and flora of the Channel Islands and, of course, Gerald Durrell's books.

In the early days of Jersey Zoo, Gerald Durrell did not spend as much time with his animals as his fans and loyal readers of his books fondly imagined. Here, N'Pongo instinctively reaches out for the more familiar figure of Caroline, a regular playmate.
© *Rosemary Gilliat.*

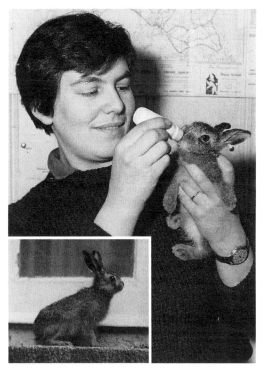

Left: Trudy with one of the leverets (baby hares) born in southern England and hand-reared in Jersey. Inset: One of the released hares. Because they had been hand-reared, some grew extremely tame and stayed in and around the manor house even after they were independent. Right: To make the embryonic Jersey Zoo as visitor-friendly as possible, Ken had no objections to visitors bringing in their dogs, even going so far as to encourage the practice with this sign. The fantasy writer, T.H. White, was so taken aback by such a relaxed attitude when he visited Jersey Zoo that he asked Ken to pose for a photo holding the sign. Visitors were also allowed to feed many of the animals, unthinkable policy today.

In the early days, Jersey Zoo had a varied collection of both Old and New World monkeys. A Sclater's guenon from Africa, circa 1961. This species is thought to be the most endangered kind of guenon.
© W. Suschitzky.

The only way to move a recalcitrant porcupine – with a broom, a shovel and a best-selling author. The porcupine is Delilah, familiar to readers of Gerald Durrell's book Menagerie Manor. © *Estate of Gerald Durrell*.

KS sorting through Jersey Zoo's fruit order with Gerald Durrell, November 1961. In fact Gerald Durrell rarely involved himself with such matters, preferring to leave the more mundane aspects of zoo business to Ken.

The closest of friends: Caroline and the young gorilla N'Pongo, Jersey Zoo.

'Shall I go and get your jeans?' another asked helpfully.

'Too bloody late now,' Ken's voice grunted from aloft.

Then came a strained, tortured gasp: 'The…flaming…thing…won't…budge…'

Next came the forerunner of what has become one of the most famous lines spoken in the Monty Python television series, but instead of a parrot it was an opossum. 'This opossum's dead…grunt…grunt…but I can't move the thing…' He couldn't move it because it was nailed to the tree by two six-inch nails.

The rest of the incident is shrouded in mystery and ignorance; none of us ever knew what happened because by the time Ken had climbed down there wasn't a soul in sight.

It is an amusing story – save for that bit about the dead opossum being nailed to the branch, which, if true, showed an astonishing lack of reverence and sensitivity on the part of the keepers – but who came up with the idea for the prank? It has the hallmark of Shep Mallet – known for his penchant for playing practical jokes – stamped all over it. It sounds like just the sort of high jinks he would perpetrate. There is, however, one thing about it that doesn't ring true. It is hard to believe the keepers would play a practical joke of this nature on their supervisor. Ken was, after all, their *boss*. He took a dim view of animal-keepers larking about. On the occasions when he lost his temper, he could be an intimidating figure. As the zoo's Superintendent, his position demanded total respect. Indeed, the place could not have functioned effectively without it. George Jacobs does in fact mention that everyone on the staff respected Ken a great deal – a funny way to show it then. Ken did not hesitate to castigate someone if he thought they deserved it. Would he really have allowed himself to be humiliated in this way? It is almost inconceivable the young keepers would have *dared* to humiliate their boss like that.

Determined to get to the bottom of it, I asked Trudy if she recalled the incident. Yes, she did; however, she remembered it very differently.

'It didn't happen like that at all. For one thing, Ken was too old by then to be clambering about in trees.'

I was surprised by her remark as he was only about fifty at the time, surely not too senescent for climbing trees.

She went on to explain that it hadn't been her husband who had been so cruelly tricked into scaling the tree, but one of the zoo's newest recruits, young John Hartley. Her version does make more sense. Hartley was fresh out of school and still wet behind the ears. Being naïve and willing to do whatever was asked of him without question, he was ripe material for a practical joke. It was a kind of initiation – the equivalent of that hoary prank of a painter sending a new apprentice to the wholesaler's to buy a tin of tartan paint. It is easy to imagine him being the innocent brunt of his colleagues' jokes. Of course the one person who could tell me exactly what happened was John Hartley himself, retired now after forty-three years at the zoo, the only place he ever worked.

'Yes, it was me!' he admitted. He explained that the prank originated, as so many often did, with Shep Mallet (so I was right then), and the dead opossum certainly was *not* nailed to the wood, as George Jacobs told it, but carefully draped over a fork in the branches in a realistic way. It seems that George Jacobs had a vivid imagination because, when he came to relate the tale in his memoirs, he had gilded the lily with a liberal helping of poetic licence; either that or he hadn't been witness to the incident and, like Chinese Whispers, the details changed over time as it was told and retold from person to person, or perhaps the intervening years had caused his memory to block some details and substitute others. John Hartley told me what really happened:

> The opossum lived in a cage on stilts just outside the public toilets and close to the Himalayan bear cage behind which was a huge forty-foot-tall chestnut tree. The opossum died and was found in the early evening by Shep and Peter Glover. At the time I was in the staff cottage just across the yard. They placed the opossum on a slender branch near the top of the tree which was leafless at the time. They then left the cage door open and called me to help in the search for the escapee! After a bit, I spotted it and immediately climbed onto the top of the bear cage and proceeded to climb the tree. Just as I got close and realised it was a hoax, Ken and Trudy came walking down the back drive and saw me. Needless to say, Shep and Pete disappeared very quickly and left me to my fate. At first Ken was not amused but then guessed what had happened and let the matter drop.

Like Trudy, John Hartley was perplexed that George Jacobs's account of the incident should differ so markedly from the reality. 'I don't understand why George should choose to distort the facts like that,' Hartley said to me. 'Maybe he thought, from the point of view of telling a good yarn, it made for a more dramatic story to have the zoo's middle-aged, smartly dressed, manager tricked into climbing the tree, rather than the naïve teenager in normal work fatigues.'

As with all biographies where the subject is no longer around to verify details, disentangling facts from half-fiction is never easy, but the part about Ken being well turned-out at all times was remembered accurately enough by George Jacobs. Ken's nephew, Brian Smith, concurs: 'I met Ken only a few times – as was also the case with my other uncles, Gil and Frank – but whenever I saw him he always seemed to be wearing a tie.' Two or three years after Jersey Zoo first opened, Brian, then only a young boy, holidayed on the island with his grandmother Gertrude, who, in spite of being over eighty, was still remarkably spry and good-humoured. Remembering that childhood holiday of so long ago, Brian told me:

> I can't recall much about the zoo or about Ken. Most days he was probably too busy. Mostly I remember the flight from Herne airport, and of the stewardess walking down the aisle of the aircraft with a card indicating altitude, speed, estimated time of arrival, and so on. Gertrude made extremely embarrassing gesticulations – which I pretended not to see, leading to the stewardess giving

me the card as a souvenir. On our arrival in Jersey, Ken collected us from the airport. I well remember the narrow lanes and the tall hedges and the – to me – huge size and opulence of Gerald Durrell's house, in which we stayed. G.D. was not there. I remember Gertrude and I spending time on the zoo gate. She took the entry fees and I was given the job of selling sweets to the visitors. One woman bought a few pence worth of sweets and tendered half-a-crown. I will never forget the feeling of panic and my stumbling 'Do you have anything smaller?' which prompted her to find the exact amount. But a lot of the time I was left to myself, and remember sitting, as if I owned the place, on top of the lion's cage, chatting to visitors.

Another guest of the Smiths was Robert (Bob) Golding. Not long after leaving school, Bob had accompanied Gerald and Jacquie to the Cameroons in 1957 as their assistant. He first met Ken and Trudy at Paignton Zoo at about the same time when he was introduced to them by Gerald Durrell, and they had gelled immediately, he told me.

A few years later I stayed with them in the manor house in Jersey for a couple of days when Gerald Durrell was away on one of his expeditions. They were a charming and entertaining couple, but I got the feeling that Ken was a bit of a loner who just got on with his job – and his life – without apparently feeling the need for self promotion. He had no ego. That's probably why he is not well remembered now. He was very matter-of-fact and didn't care what people thought of him. In fact, he was a very able and intelligent zoo man, and happiest when he was with animals, even though as the zoo's manager he had to spend a lot of time in the office, he liked to supervise the work to make sure it was done to his satisfaction. I remember he had just bought a gramophone recording of Acker Bilk's *Stranger on the Shore* and kept playing it over and over again, and remarking on what a beautiful piece of music it was. 'Bloody marvellous,' he'd say in a reverential tone. In fact, that seemed to be his favourite expression. If something or someone pleased him greatly, it – or they – were 'bloody marvellous'. Not having a TV set, music was very important to him as a means of relaxation. He had quite a big record collection and loved to discover places with a jukebox. I found him to be a very pleasant, amiable host with a keen sense of humour. He and Trudy were always laughing and joking when I knew them. I also remember his eyes used to blink very rapidly, which probably led some people to believe he was nervous, which I don't think he was, but I suspect he was quite an *intense* man.

Mike Armstrong, in his diary, agreed that Ken was 'a very pleasant man' – but added the qualifying rider 'when not worried by the job.'

When not worried by the job. Overawed by the stress of the job, Ken had a short fuse and inevitably there were many occasions when his genial persona evaporated, to be replaced by an altogether more intemperate and steelier side to his character, as John Hartley found out one hot summer's day when manning the Aquarium paydesk, entrance

6d a head. The Aquarium was at the back of the manor house and the entrance was up a flight of three or four steps. The paydesk, set up at the bottom of the steps, was no more than a simple table (or possibly, according to one person I spoke to, a desk within a sort of sentry-box) piled high with sweets, Mars Bars, Kit Kats, and guide books. John's attention was elsewhere and failed to notice the sun was beating down on the chocolate bars. Tidying up the table, he was alarmed to discover that the entire stock was ruined. At that moment, Ken, on one of his regular spot checks to see that everything was functioning properly, appeared round the corner. He took in the scene at a glance. 'To say he was livid is an understatement,' John told me. 'He was mad as hell, absolutely apoplectic. But he had every right to be; I *had* just cost the zoo a lot of money.'

Hartley was not the only one to feel the full force of Ken's displeasure. Most of the keepers ignited his ire at one time or another. 'It was Smith,' wrote Douglas Botting, 'who made it a habit once or twice a day to tick someone off or dress someone down *pour encourager les autres.*' (Literally: 'to encourage the others', from Voltaire's *Candide*.) Gerald Durrell was always pleased to leave the reprimanding of staff to his Superintendent, finding this a very odious task. Ken was not renowned for his patience and he did not tolerate laziness or incompetence in his workforce. He would have made a good drill sergeant. There was no place on the payroll for shirkers. As someone who worked hard himself, he expected nothing less from others. He demanded obsequiousness in his underlings and he didn't hesitate to scold members of staff for stepping out of line, and his mood could turn in a moment; one minute he would be cheerful and placid, but if something ruffled him he could, and often did, explode. And his frequent tirades were volcanic and frightening to behold, the object of his wrath visibly wilting with the intensity of the blast, like a pot plant standing unprotected in front of an open furnace. It was left to the placatory Trudy to soothe the chastened party by telling him or her not to take it too personally or get too upset. The keepers – except, of course, the poor unfortunate wretch whose turn it was to receive a verbal roasting – found his periodic rants paradoxically comic: 'Ken's off on one again' or 'Ken's lost it!' they would say.

He reserved these explosive outbursts for his workers. 'When I knew him,' remembered Brian Smith, 'he always seemed to be friendly, despite the intense pressure he must have been under at Jersey. I never saw him angry.'

After the zoo opened its gates at ten o'clock, and the visitors started pouring in, it was not always possible for Ken to give someone a dressing-down at the time the offence was committed or first noticed. Instead he would summon the miscreant to his office. 'Ken would like to see you in his office' were words that the keepers dreaded hearing. And if they arrived outside the office to be greeted frostily with the perfunctory instruction 'Come in and shut the door', they knew they were really in for it. But Ken did not harbour resentment, nor keep score of anyone's peccadilloes. He was never vindictive. His outbursts were apoplectic but short-lived. He might give someone a severe dressing-down in the morning, but come the afternoon it was usually all but forgotten. All he asked was that his keepers were conscientious and did their job to the best of their ability. He was not one to bear grudges.

Keepers were discouraged from using their initiative. 'You're not paid to think, you're paid to do what you're told' was his leitmotif, repeated often. Jeremy Mallinson incurred his displeasure one day by using a level of initiative above and beyond the call of duty. The dingoes had just produced a litter of pups, and Mallinson, having previously studied kennel craft on a three-month course in Surrey with the ultimate aim of establishing his own kennels in Jersey (plans which were subsequently thwarted by financial problems and planning restrictions), knew enough of the subject to realise that the parents needed maximum privacy, so he innocently hung a tarpaulin over the front of the cage to shield them from the public gaze. Ken was not at all happy about this. Not only did it look unsightly, but, more importantly, visitors were prevented from seeing the animals they had paid to see and this would never do. Incensed, he stormed back into his office and let his secretary know – in no uncertain terms – exactly what he thought of the young keeper's initiative. 'He can't go around covering the animals up like that,' he stormed, 'or there will be nothing left for people to see!' He must have had a change of heart, however, because he grudgingly permitted Mallinson to keep the tarpaulin over part of the cage front, so the dingoes still had some privacy.

In his diary, Mike Armstrong noted that Ken was 'a good organiser and administrator but allows little personal love towards his animals' and formed the impression that it was just a business to him. Other people, however, attest that Ken always had a very good rapport with the animals in his care. Years later Clinton Keeling visited him at Exmouth Zoo and recalled of that visit that Ken displayed real affection towards his animals, going in with them, talking to them and playing with them.

Ken was an animal-man through and through, but he had seen enough of nature red in tooth and claw not to be sentimental about them. He was well aware that Mother Nature, for all her undoubted splendour, was essentially amoral and he was cynical of those zoos, mostly privately owned, that anthropomorphised their animals to a nauseating degree – what he called 'zoozy-woozy stuff'. Bowed down by the problems of keeping Jersey Zoo afloat, it is not surprising that Ken was inclined to adopt an uncharacteristically detached, business-like attitude that might be construed by some people as hard-nosed. His desire to present the zoo as a paying concern, one where the visitors got their money's worth and went away contented, created a conflict of interests. On the one hand, he instinctively wanted to do his best for the animals, but on the other he knew he could ill-afford to disappoint the paying public, particularly at such a crucial stage in the zoo's development when it was still trying to establish itself, and inevitably there were occasions when the demands of the public were given priority over the animals' desire for privacy. One thing he was adamant about was that as the visitors had parted with their hard-earned cash to see the animals, animals they must see. The last thing he wanted was for anyone to feel cheated. For this reason he detested empty cages – or even cages that were apparently empty because the occupant was out of sight. Animals had to be visible (and preferably active rather than just a gently snoring bundle of fur in a corner of the cage); so the Polecat ferrets, to give one example, were routinely shut out of their indoor quarters during the day in order that the public could see them. When Ken found he had an empty cage, perhaps because the previous occupant had died, he would search for something to fill it as a matter of some urgency and he was not averse to splitting up a pair of animals to move one of them into the vacant cage, so that there could be *something* in there for people to look at.

This was not Gerald Durrell's way. In his view, the public should be placed third in order of priority (after the animals and the people employed to look after the animals). For the moment he was just grateful to have Ken on board, but their different perspectives and his disapproval of certain aspects of Ken's management style were undoubtedly contributory factors that eventually drove a wedge between the two men. Ken knew that one ignored the demands of the customer at one's peril. His father had taught him that the customer was king. He, of course, had been talking about the grocery business, but the principles were the same and, as far as Ken could see, what was true for grocers was equally valid for managers of zoological parks. Both relied for survival on keeping the public on board, and faithful. It was always going to be difficult navigating a course between the needs of the public and the needs of the animals.

Something else Ken did that is hard to condone now, but was considered perfectly acceptable at the time, was to split up a pair of Woolly monkeys in order that one, a very tame specimen, could be loaned to a hotel for the summer season. This happened for two years in succession, with the monkey being returned to the zoo in the autumn, whereupon it would be reunited with its companion. The story goes like this: There was a hotel a short distance from the zoo that had a little pets' corner attached to it as an additional attraction for guests. One of the residents of this pets' corner was a very cantankerous monkey, with a reputation for tearing across its cage, teeth bared, and grabbing at hotel guests whilst shrieking at the top of its voice. Most of all, it detested children, probably stemming from the fact that it had been teased by them, but its belligerence and misanthropic nature made it a rather unfortunate choice for a pets' corner. The more agitated it became, the more the children delighted in annoying it to provoke an even more aggressive reaction until it literally shook with rage. The hotel's management appealed to Ken for help, and an agreement was struck whereby the psychotic primate was deposited at Jersey Zoo, and in return Ken lent the hotel his tame female Woolly monkey as a seasonal replacement. This was not an unreasonable solution, he felt, because the two Woolly monkeys, although they lived together at the zoo, were not especially close to each other, but to Gerald Durrell it was further evidence that Ken was taking the zoo down a path that he did not want it to go, and he began to wonder whether his Superintendent was just too firmly entrenched in the old concept of a zoo as being little more than somewhere you went to gawp at animals 'and get sick on ice cream.' But having granted his old friend autonomy over the zoo, Durrell felt powerless to intervene. In any case, the zoo was popular with holidaymakers, more and more people were visiting it, and everything seemed to be functioning quite well. With Ken's hand firmly on the tiller, Durrell had no desire to rock the boat now, but the earlier camaraderie that had existed between the two men was on the wane and would never be recaptured.

*

Jersey Zoo may have had a long way to go before it could be seen as a haven for endangered species, but one emergent animal collection that *was* attempting to show a way forward for zoos was John Aspinall's private menagerie at Howletts near Canterbury, still many years away from its public opening. In 1961 Ken was privileged to visit this remarkable establishment. Aspinall had had a run of bad luck. There had been several animal escapes at Howletts, which had done nothing to endear him to local residents. So far most of the escapees had been relatively innocuous, but Aspinall's neighbours were getting jittery that the next animal to go AWOL might be a tiger or a bear. The problem as Aspinall saw it was that he did not have any experienced animal-keepers. He contacted Ken and asked him if he could spare one of his keepers to work at Howletts. He was not seeking keepers with degrees and other paper qualifications – which was just as well because the infant Jersey Zoo didn't have any university graduates – but simply someone with experience of wild animals, especially gorillas. He specified that he was looking for someone who was hard-working, dedicated and, most importantly, intuitive. Hitherto, Ken knew little about either Howletts or John Aspinall (hardly anybody at that time did). He had heard tales of Aspinall's eccentricity, that he employed unorthodox methods, but, beyond these rumours, Aspinall remained an enigma to the zoo community. Ken wasn't sure he could spare anyone but, in any case, before acceding to Aspinall's request, Ken asked to see Howletts for himself, and he and Trudy were duly invited to spend a couple of days there, sleeping in the guestroom in Howletts mansion itself. 'The most memorable thing was waking up in the morning to see gorillas gambolling about freely on the lawn in front of the house,' recalled Trudy. 'It was – in a word – magic. There is no other way to describe it. Eventually, when Aspinall started admitting the public, he was forced to cage the gorillas permanently, and I think he found that hard.'

For Ken, the visit proved to be a real eye-opener. He discovered that Aspinall, enthusiastic amateur though he was, was anything but the dilettante he was generally perceived to be by the Zoological Society of London and other such august and conservative bodies – and there was no doubting his passion. Aspinall kept a pair of tigers in a very big enclosure and a pair of Himalayan bears (ex-Palmer's of Camden Town) in a huge moated compound. He also had a pair of chimpanzees, several Woolly monkeys and capuchins and an Indian Ratel (Honey badger), but it was the unique colony of no fewer than seven gorillas that occupied Ken's thoughts more than anything else as he left Howletts and returned to Jersey. He was greatly impressed by the health and vigour of the animals and the individual care bestowed upon them. 'In view of the uncertain future of the gorilla as a wild species,' he wrote in the *International Zoo News*,

> I felt that something very definite was being done by Mr. Aspinall in forming this colony, a work which could be of growing importance in years to come when his gorillas reach breeding age, and its value is enhanced by the fact that the project is being conducted entirely on non-commercial lines.
>
> I wished that some of the leading zoos would emulate Mr. Aspinall's example before it is too late. Extinction may easily overtake the gorilla (both Lowland and Mountain species) in the present political turmoil of Africa, and

the building up of gorilla breeding colonies by enlightened zoos could yet save the animals from total extinction. I am certain posterity would thank us for preserving such a noble species.

Enthralled as he was by everything he had seen at Howletts, no great changes were immediately implemented at Jersey Zoo following his visit. Much as he could see the case for leading zoos of the day such as Philadelphia or the Bronx or even perhaps, some way down the line, London, to establish breeding colonies of gorillas, he was less convinced that Jersey Zoo would ever be in a position, or have the financial wherewithal, to do so. John Aspinall's private zoo was independently funded; he didn't depend on gate money to keep it going (indeed, the only visitors were invited guests) whereas Jersey Zoo needed all the visitors it could get. Ken's obsession with giving the public value for money dominated the zoo in its early days. He liked the animals to put on a good show and it annoyed him that some of them apparently hadn't read the terms of their contract. One of the zoo's most prized and beautiful animals was Peter the cheetah, who lived in a paddock in the walled garden. Peter was a very tame animal who liked nothing better than to romp around with junior keeper Jeremy Mallinson. The problem with wild cats of any description is, handsome and graceful though they are, they generally don't make very good zoo exhibits, being, for the most part, the epitome of sloth. Thanks to pioneering wildlife film-makers, Armand and Michaela Denis, Hans and Lotte Haas, and David Attenborough, people were becoming better informed about animals than at any time in the past. Everyone knew that cheetahs could reach speeds of up to seventy miles per hour in pursuit of prey, and Ken felt that a recumbent Peter or – worse – an almost invisible Peter was something of a letdown to people who had paid their admission fee to see the animals. If, on his rounds, Ken noticed that Peter, indifferent to their disappointment and with scant regard for the gate receipts, was resting in the long grass at the back of his enclosure where the public couldn't see him properly, Jeremy Mallinson would be summoned immediately to rouse the animal. He would be involved in some other duty, such as preparing the evening feeds in the animal kitchen, when the order would come through from Ken to 'Get that cheetah moving so people can see it! It's no use having it if it can't be seen!' Jeremy would then be expected to put everything else into abeyance to go to the walled garden and play with the cheetah for a bit, usually a game of football. Although Ken's primary motivation for insisting on this was so that visitors should not feel short-changed, it is worth noting that it was also very good exercise for the cheetah, providing both physical and mental stimulation.

Chapter Thirteen

The Parting of the Ways *(1962)*

BY 1962 KEN HAD BEEN A ZOO SUPERINTENDENT for ten years, initially of the Cliftonville Lido menagerie in Margate, then Paignton Zoo and finally Jersey Zoo. In all three places he had enjoyed a great deal of independence. Officially, Gerald Durrell was Jersey Zoo's director, but to anyone *au fait* with the reality of the situation it seemed like a nominal position because it was Ken who really ran the whole show. Indeed, to all intents and purposes, Ken can be thought of as Jersey Zoo's *de facto* first director, such was his authority there, but the fact remained that he was only managing the zoo for somebody else. It seemed that he was always destined to be a zoo superintendent, never a zoo owner. He had been at Jersey Zoo for some time when he was approached by Dudley Zoo. Its General Manager, Donald Risdon, was resigning to look for a site where he and his wife could set up a dedicated bird zoo (in 1962 they opened a tropical bird garden at Rode in Somerset) and he had recommended Ken as his successor. Risdon had known him for many years. When Ken had returned from his early collecting trips to Africa and South America, Risdon had been on Liverpool quayside with a Dudley Zoo van to see what rare specimens he could purchase. He had tremendous respect for Ken. Now he invited him to take over the post of General Manager at Dudley Zoo. Ken and Trudy flew to the West Midlands to discuss things further with Donald Risdon. They were shown round Dudley Zoo and they liked what they saw. Dudley was a major collection with most of the traditional zoo animals represented. It was a wonderful opportunity, Ken had no doubt of that, but, flattered though he was to be asked to take over the reins at Dudley, he wavered, uncertain whether or not to accept this prestigious position. He was still weighing up the pros and cons when his mind was abruptly made up for him by Gerald Durrell, who reminded him that he was still under contract at Jersey Zoo. Durrell was genuinely very worried that he might lose his Superintendent, and pleaded with Ken not to go, but to see out his contract. 'Jacquie and I are planning to go away on another trip soon,' he said, 'but, if you leave now, the whole expedition will be in jeopardy. You simply *must* stay; I'm relying on you.'

Faced with such a passionate plea, what could he do? With great regret, Ken declined Risdon's offer. Dudley Zoo would have to find somebody else. Once again he had allowed his heart to be governed by an overwhelming sense of loyalty to Gerald Durrell, and for years afterwards he would be haunted by the thought of '*what if…?*'

Did I make the wrong decision? It was a question he never resolved.

'Maybe Ken should've taken that job – who knows?' Trudy said to me. 'I've often wondered how differently things might have turned out had we gone to Dudley, but it's futile to speculate; we didn't go and that's that. Suffice it to say, had we made the move, we probably never would have bought Exmouth Zoo.'

Paignton Zoo (or, more correctly, the Herbert Whitley Trust, the governing body) had grown weary of the little seasonal indoor zoo it ran on the Exmouth seafront. After the shutters went up at the end of each season, the animals were withdrawn to the main collection at Paignton Zoo, but to find all the animals suitable winter accommodation at Paignton, to crate them up and transport them, and then to repeat the whole procedure in reverse the following spring, had always been a tedious, protracted affair, and already the Paignton Zoo authorities were beginning to think that Exmouth Zoo, born at the height of the Suez Crisis, was something of a liability. The final straw was a devastating fire that broke out at Exmouth Zoo in the early hours of 22 May 1961, causing the deaths of many fine specimens and highlighting, in the worst possible way, the deficiencies of the building.

Two police officers, Sergeant Arthur Lemon and Constable J. Kelly, were patrolling the Exmouth seafront just after midnight when, at about half past twelve, they saw flames coming from the building. Entry from the front without breathing apparatus was found to be impossible. The officers alerted the fire service, which arrived with commendable speed, and the fire, believed to have been caused by a defect in the electric wiring, was quickly extinguished, but for many of the animals it was too late. Firemen with smoke helmets entered the building and opened windows, finally enabling the Curator, Miss Margaret Hadwick, to rescue a chimpanzee, but many other animals had perished in the blaze including birds valued at £275, thought to have been overcome by fumes.

In the aftermath of the fire there was a lot of work to do before Exmouth Zoo was ready to re-open. Since this was obviously going to take some time to complete and entail a great deal of expense, the Herbert Whitley Trust was looking to find a purchaser for the zoo to take it off their hands, and since Ken had been the co-originator of Exmouth Zoo when he was superintendent of Paignton Zoo, it was only appropriate that he should be offered first refusal. Although still gainfully employed at Jersey Zoo, he accepted, and so it was that Herbert Whitley Trust, with the approval of the Exmouth Urban District Council, approved the transfer of the operating licence to Ken Smith. On 1 March 1962, Ken bought the Exmouth Summer Zoo, as it was still known, at a very favourable rate (though not the actual building which continued to be leased from Exmouth Council). Now in his fifties, it was a very proud day for Ken and his family. As tiny as the zoo was, it was nonetheless one he could finally call his own after all those years of working in other people's zoos.

Very little work had been done on Exmouth Zoo in the five years since it was first opened and now there was also fire damage to contend with. Ken despatched one of his keepers from Jersey Zoo, young John Hartley, to Exmouth charged with the responsibility for getting the zoo ready to re-admit the public. The reason Hartley was chosen for this task was because it was his hometown and he knew the district well. It helped that he also had family in the area. 'My parents lived about a mile from the zoo and so I stayed with them, which helped Ken keep his costs down,' he told me.

It was quite a major job and John toiled away with pots of paint, rolls of wire, and boxes of nails and screws to get the place presentable for the public. A sales kiosk was quickly knocked up. He couldn't be expected to manage it all on his own, of course, and professional help was sought with some of the more tricky jobs such as rewiring. 'The whole place needed to be spruced up, painted, cages re-wired, that sort of thing, and I couldn't get it all done at once. I think I went over about three times before I finally got the job finished, staying for about two weeks on each occasion.'

With Jersey Zoo being so understaffed (in 1962 the zoo employed only fourteen people), one wonders how Gerald Durrell reacted when he heard that one of his staff had been relieved of his duties in Jersey to work on getting Exmouth Zoo up to scratch.

'I definitely remained on the Jersey payroll and I suppose Ken reimbursed the zoo,' John told me. 'Gerry was away, as he usually was in the summer, and was probably not even aware of my absence.' We are left to speculate how much Gerald Durrell really did know, but it is hard to believe that Ken's preoccupation with Exmouth Zoo did not contribute in some way to the estrangement that was soon to develop between the two men.

Finally Hartley was finished. At this point, Ken and Trudy might have been expected to move to Exmouth to run it, but they didn't, at least not yet. Instead of leaving Jersey Zoo straightaway, they hung on for several more months, even though there was nothing to hold them there now that Ken's original three-year contract had expired. Why? Did Ken think he could run Exmouth Zoo efficiently at such long range by appointing a curator to take care of the day-to-day matters? It was a question I put to John Hartley. What, I asked, was Ken's motivation for remaining in Jersey? 'I'm not sure,' said John. 'He probably stayed on at Jersey Zoo so that he had some income during the early days of his ownership of Exmouth Zoo.' But there is another reason for his unwillingness to leave at that time. Gerald and Jacquie were half a world away on another major expedition and, if he had quit now, there would have been nobody to run the zoo in Jersey, and so out of a sense of loyalty to Gerald Durrell, he elected to remain at his post, at least for the time being, but it meant that instead of managing just one zoo, he was now in charge of two.

Following his acquisition of Exmouth Zoo, Ken had begun in earnest to obtain animals for it, housing them temporarily at Jersey Zoo. It is unknown exactly what animals he acquired, but a clue to the identity of some of them can be found in an article he wrote for the *International Zoo News* towards the tail-end of 1962 in which he gave an overview of recent developments at Jersey Zoo. In this article he divulged, without adding any further detail, that two Galapagos Giant tortoises were 'deposited at [Jersey] Zoo for three months' and that a big Emperor boa was 'another deposited reptile'. In other words, they didn't belong to Jersey Zoo but were domiciled there on a temporary basis. Were these reptiles intended for Ken's Exmouth Zoo? Certainly, Galapagos Giant tortoises *were* among the species kept at Exmouth at around this time. It could, of course, be just coincidence, but it is very likely that these were the same tortoises that had previously spent several months at Jersey Zoo.

Ken had good cause to feel optimistic about the future. Not only did he now have a zoo, albeit a very small one, of his own, but, at the beginning of the year, Trudy had learned that she was pregnant with their second child. Developments at Jersey Zoo were continuing to proceed apace, even though money was still very tight, if not tighter than ever. And there were other things to look forward to. Jeremy Mallinson would soon be returning from southern Africa with a big collection of animals for Jersey Zoo, and Lee Thomas was shortly to bring back a South American contingent from his expedition to British Guiana. But then things started to go very, *very* wrong.

In February, less than a month before Ken bought the Exmouth Zoo, Gerald and Jacquie Durrell had set out on a seven-month tour of New Zealand, Australia and Malaya in the company of a BBC film crew to make a series of television programmes on the wildlife of these three disparate regions. At the end of this expedition, with the Durrells about to leave the Far East for a spot of R&R in East Africa, they received disquieting news from far-off Jersey. All was far from well with the zoo, they were told ominously. They changed their plans, they changed ships, and they sailed for home immediately.

What they found when they returned in that late summer of 1962 shocked them. In the tautologic words of Gerald Durrell, his precious zoo was 'looking shabby and unkempt', and only the most essential jobs were getting done. Worse, this frail vessel was on the rocks. Despite a record season (in that year, 100,000 people walked through the turnstiles) it was struggling to pay the bills. The books were in disarray and, according to Gerald Durrell, his written instructions and plans had been ignored and money 'frittered away'. Moreover, as if this were not enough, staff morale was at a low ebb, with several key staff on the point of abandoning ship altogether.

As apparently terminal as the crisis was, Durrell was not prepared to fold up the tent just yet. It was a defining moment, a watershed. Until now he had usually deferred to his Superintendent to make the decisions; now a more proactive Durrell emerged from the chaos, dosed up on tranquilisers to counteract the stress he was under, ready to lead the call to man the pumps and prevent the ship from foundering. A firm of independent accountants was hastily drafted in to examine, in minute detail, every aspect of the running of the zoo, and the findings of this audit confirmed everyone's worst fears – the zoo was teetering on the chasm of bankruptcy. With the debts mounting up, the bank was fast losing patience, and nobody knew from one day to the next whether that would be the day the bank foreclosed on the enterprise. Durrell laid the blame squarely at the feet of Ken Smith. 'Whose fault was it?' pondered Durrell. 'Well, it wasn't mine; I was thousands of miles away when the trouble blew up. You tell me who's left.' Now Ken went from hero, the man without whom Jersey Zoo would never have happened, to villain. Backpedalling frantically, Durrell would later admit that he had taken the decision to engage a manager in the first place ('a friend of some years standing whom I thought I could entrust with the task') only with the utmost reluctance, and now believed this had been a mistake and vowed that in future he would trust his instinct, not his sentiment.

Somebody who remembers visiting Jersey Zoo at this pivotal point in its history is Jon Downes, founder of the Centre for Fortean Zoology. 'Even at the age of seven I had read many of Durrell's books and I was expecting to see a marvellous zoo. I was disappointed. It was obviously home-made and down at heel. The cages were made out of orange crates and chicken-wire, and the whole place had a dilapidated air about it. I am only too aware of what a difficult job juggling financial matters is, and I sincerely doubt whether Ken Smith should really be blamed for what happened. Gerry, however, did blame him.'

Ken felt hurt and betrayed, and not a little bewildered. He believed he had done the best he could with very limited resources. After all the hard work he had put in, it was like being punched in the solar plexus. As for the accusation of 'frittering' money away, Ken pointed to the fact that the year had seen a continuation of the zoo's building programme. An important area of ground had been developed which gave space for an ostrich paddock, a big flight aviary for vultures and a larger lion enclosure. Improved quarters for badgers and Malayan Sun bears had been built, and the chimpanzees had been moved to more commodious accommodation.

But not all these improvements met with Durrell's approval. In particular, he was dismayed by the new lion edifice that had been erected in his absence. Constructed from heavy metal girders with a perfunctory breezeblock house at one end, it was, in his view, a ghastly looking cage, totally out of keeping with his notion of a zoo park where the animals were displayed amongst grass and trees and bushes in neat but unimposing enclosures built of sympathetic materials – not that there *were* many enclosures like that at that time. Ken argued that as the zoo had precious little money, cages had, from necessity, to be built that were functional rather than aesthetic. The zoo, he said, could ill-afford to spend money that it simply did not have on desirable but unnecessary furbelows. And there was another even more important consideration. Animal escapes were an all too frequent occurrence. The escapees were usually birds, but other animals, too, had absconded from time to time. He was determined there should be no possibility of Leo the lion getting out. It was one thing, he said, to have the dingoes trotting down the main drive, as they had done on more than one occasion, or a group of monkeys sneaking off to reconnoitre the locale, but quite another to have a lion on the loose in the parish, practising its hunting techniques on the good burghers of Jersey, and accordingly he had opted to have Leo's enclosure built from the strongest materials he could afford. The downside was that aesthetically the cage left a lot to be desired. But Durrell was not convinced.

One reason for the zoo's inability to balance the books was the fact that, despite Ken's original intention to proceed slowly and cautiously, the zoo had fallen into the trap of becoming overly ambitious – not in relation to building work (slightly less than one sixth of the total amount of land available had so far been developed) but in terms of the quantity and variety of animals the zoo was attempting to keep. By 1962 the animal collection, according to the International Zoo Year Book, included no fewer than 73 species of mammals (119 specimens), an even more prodigious 143 kinds of birds (249 specimens), and 37 species of reptiles and amphibians (139 specimens) – a total of more than five hundred animals comprising 253 species, to say nothing of all the fish in the aquarium, and all shoehorned into just five compact acres. Today, only about half a dozen zoos in the British Isles have more species.

Ken and Gerald Durrell had had their disagreements before, but these had always been minor affairs, no more than intense but momentary cloudbursts. In the past when her younger brother had behaved petulantly, Margaret Durrell had assured Ken – with the wisdom of one who knows – that it was only a passing phase. 'Don't take it to heart,' she had told Ken on these occasions, a sentiment echoed by their elder brother, the acclaimed novelist and poet Lawrence ('Larry') Durrell, when he had visited Jersey Zoo at Christmas 1960 during a temporary Smith-Durrell falling-out when Gerald was acting in a lordly and intransigent manner towards his companion. Seeing how much Ken was smarting from Durrell's imperiousness, Lawrence took Ken aside and said, 'Look, don't worry, he'll grow out of it. In a day or two it'll all be forgotten and he'll be fine.' And on that occasion Lawrence was right. This latest disagreement, however, looked – and was – terminal. In later years, Ken would always feel, not without good reason, that he never got the credit he deserved for helping to launch Jersey Zoo. It pained him that, after launching the ship and captaining it while it built up steam, he was left behind on the slipway, a lonely tragic figure, his input all but forgotten or just glossed over, but he maintained his dignity and never publicly expressed the resentment he felt on being ostracised. When, back in the tail end of 1958, he had thrown his lot in with Durrell to come to Jersey and take on the task of creating a zoo from scratch, nobody, least of all Gerald Durrell himself, had really believed that an Easter 1959 opening was even possible (which was partly why Durrell was absent in Argentina at the time – that and the fact that, with a publisher's contract to fulfil, he was always in need of material for his books). But he had shown them. He had transformed a few fields, a cow shed, garage, walled garden, and a former cider *pressoir* into a zoological park, no mean achievement on an island that had never had a zoo before, and now he was being hung out to dry. He believed in the worth of what he was doing. He had worked tirelessly for little remuneration, and even less cognisance, to make the venture commercially viable. The result may not have conformed to Gerald Durrell's dream, but it was, nonetheless, a *fait accompli*, and rapidly establishing itself as one of the most popular tourist attractions on the island.

Trudy said that she and Ken had always got on well with both Gerald and Jacquie, but towards the end of 1962 that friendship had paled quite considerably and a rift had developed between them. 'We had four very happy years in Jersey,' she said, 'but then suddenly, for some reason, at the end things turned sour and ill-feeling set in.'

There is no doubting Gerald Durrell was a great man, a visionary, a pioneer, and the conservation movement owes him a great deal of gratitude. 'Along with Sir Peter Scott, he was my hero – still is in fact,' said Tony Blackler, who did volunteer work at Jersey Zoo in the early days. 'He had so much passion. In fact, by coincidence, I'm re-reading *My Family and Other Animals* for about the fiftieth time at the moment.' But beneath the passion and the effervescence, Durrell had his failings, and one of them was his habit of suddenly 'going off' people. Like Ken.

For some time, Durrell had suspected that his Superintendent, being that much older, was just too set in his ways. What the zoo urgently needed, he reckoned, was an infusion of bold new ideas, a less conservative person to push the zoo forward and ultimately to transform it into a breeding station for endangered species. The more Durrell thought about it, the more convinced he became that he had already met just such a person, and, moreover, somebody who was already working for him at Jersey Zoo: Jeremy Mallinson.

Jeremy was young, a green shoot, malleable, willing to embrace new concepts. With Durrell adamant that his zoo 'must cease just being a mere showplace of animals, and start to contribute something towards the conservation of wildlife,' he began to switch his allegiance, and poor Ken Smith, devoted zoo-man as he was, suddenly found himself marginalised as part of the old brigade, his whole *modus operandi* now relegated as old hat. The fact that Ken had been the driving force behind the creation of the zoo was conveniently forgotten.

Another source of friction was Ken's recent acquisition of Exmouth Zoo, with Durrell questioning whether Ken's thinking, increasingly focused, as it was, on his own small zoo, was distracting him to what was happening at Jersey Zoo.

It was always going to be difficult to run a zoo in Exmouth whilst simultaneously managing Jersey Zoo, and one must wonder how Ken seriously believed he could juggle the two. Inevitably something had to give. But it wasn't all bad news. On 25 September, there was some relief for him from the problems besetting him when Trudy gave birth to their second child, another daughter whom they christened Kelsay. She was very nearly born in a dogs' home. Driving Trudy to the hospital when she went into labour, Ken took the wrong turning and drove into the forecourt of the dogs' home situated next door to the hospital.

This wasn't the only narrow escape Kelsay had. During her pregnancy, Trudy had suffered terrible bouts of morning sickness, and her doctor had prescribed a relatively new kind of drug as an antiemetic to combat the problem. That new drug was called thalidomide. Trudy placed the tablets on the windowsill, but, against her doctor's advice, she did not take any of the tablets immediately, saying to herself that she would take them only if her morning sickness did not improve. If she did take any, it was no more than about two or three, which was just as well because it was not long afterwards that thalidomide hit the headlines when it was found to be responsible for causing horrific abnormalities in developing foetuses. By the time the teratogenic properties of the drug had come to light, between 10,000 to 20,000 severely disabled babies had been born in those countries, mainly in Europe and Africa, where thalidomide was licensed for use, giving rise to the infamous term 'Thalidomide Baby'. Kelsay had had a very lucky escape.

Even in the advanced stages of pregnancy, Trudy had insisted on continuing in her role as head of the mammal section, alarming Gerald Durrell's aged mother who would watch, horrified, from her flat in the manor as Trudy struggled manfully across the forecourt with heavy bags of animal feed or bales of hay. Terrified that Trudy might suffer a miscarriage if she didn't ease up a bit, the old lady would throw open a window and yell at her to remember her condition. 'Mrs Durrell was a wonderfully sweet old lady,' reminisced Trudy. 'Everybody loved her. *But she did worry so.*' Trudy had also continued, while heavily pregnant, to play on the front lawn with N'Pongo, much to the disapproval of Gerald Durrell. He knew that N'Pongo would not deliberately harm her, but the young gorilla was exuberant and, even though still only half grown, was extremely powerful. Afraid that the boisterous young ape might accidentally knock her to the ground during one of their more rumbustious games together, possibly resulting in her losing the baby, he warned Trudy in the strongest possible terms against playing with N'Pongo. Trudy finally stood down as Jersey Zoo's Head of Mammals when she gave birth to Kelsay, and Jeremy Mallinson assumed the role.

Meanwhile, the troubles affecting the zoo continued to deepen. It had become obvious to everyone that relations between Ken and Gerald Durrell had become strained to breaking point, and by now they were barely on speaking terms, any communication between them being conducted through a third person or in terse memos. The final parting, when it came, was acrimonious and full of incrimination. Ken's contract was terminated suddenly on 30 November. Many years later, in *The Ark's Anniversary*, Gerald Durrell wrote, without any ambiguity, 'I sacked my manager and took over myself'. It doesn't get much plainer than that, but in truth, even without counting in their purchase of Exmouth Zoo, Ken and Trudy had never had any intention of remaining indefinitely at Jersey Zoo. Coming to the Channel Islands straight from Devon, they found the tiny island claustrophobic, with comparatively little to do and hardly anywhere to go, and they longed to get away. They had put in long hours at the zoo and by the end of each day they were quite exhausted. Ken seems to have had few interests beyond his family and his zoo work. He was not into sport and his work left little time for a social life. Occasionally they had managed to escape to the cinema for a couple of hours, as they had done from time to time when they lived at Paignton Zoo. Sometimes, just for a break, they would drive to the airport (Ken loved to marvel at the 'planes), have a pot of tea in the restaurant there, and drive back. Simple pleasures like that. Sometimes Jeremy Mallinson would take them out for a night at the cabaret, and they enjoyed that, but increasingly they had found themselves enmeshed in zoo affairs and too tired to go out. They had managed to take the occasional short break away from the island, and on one such jaunt before Kelsay was born, Ken showed Caroline (in her pushchair) around his alma mater, Whipsnade Zoo in Bedfordshire, little changed since the days when he had worked there just after the war, and he delighted in pointing out to his young daughter some of the animals he had worked with. But such pleasant distractions were all too rare and fleeting, his work at Jersey Zoo all consuming, life on the island too circumscribed. Ken and especially Trudy hankered for the space and freedom that the mainland offered. So even if relations with the Durrells hadn't turned sour, their days in Jersey were probably numbered anyway.

At this distance, it is easy to spot mistakes that were made and misunderstandings that went uncorrected, allowing petty disagreements to ferment and escalate, but perhaps, leaving aside the matter of the zoo's financial woes, the real explanation for the fracture in their relationship is that Ken Smith and Gerald Durrell had simply grown apart. It was the end of a long partnership that had seen them rear Pere David's deer calves at Whipsnade together, jointly endure the hardships of the African and South American bush, and finally between them launch a zoo that would one day – had anyone but known it at the time – become a world-renowned centre of excellence for the captive breeding of endangered species. They had been through a lot together. At Jersey Zoo, Ken had been contracted for three years; in the end he had served four. Maybe it was time to move on.

Each member of Jersey Zoo's staff received a perfunctory memo to say that Gerald Durrell wished to speak to each of them in turn. What must they have been thinking?

They were aware the zoo was in a poor state financially and that it had been hovering a shade above bankruptcy virtually from the moment it had opened more than three and a half years earlier. They knew also that the situation had worsened over the last few months. Did they imagine that it was all over? That Gerald Durrell, in despair, was throwing in the towel? Why else would he want to see them if not to break the bad news to them that they would shortly be losing their jobs? One by one they were summoned to his office at the top of Les Augres Manor. It was with a heavy heart that the first of them mounted the stairs. Durrell got to the point straightaway. 'Mr Smith is going to be leaving us very soon and I will be taking over the running of the zoo.'

All the staff had been aware of the tension between the two parties, but still it came as a shock when they heard that Ken and Trudy were to leave the zoo. Not long afterwards, Jeremy Mallinson had tea with the Smiths. It pleased Ken enormously that Jeremy had so far been able to remain neutral, but he was also concerned for Jeremy's sake. 'Aren't you afraid you'll be ostracised for fraternising with me?' Ken asked him pensively at one point.

It was a sad end to Ken's time at Jersey and to his long friendship with Gerald Durrell. Jeremy presented Ken and Trudy with a farewell gift he had had commissioned from the Jersey Potteries: an ashtray, inscribed *Jersey Zoo 1958 – 1962*, depicting a caricatured image of Ken clutching the cashbox, a reference to the fact that in the depths of winter it was often Ken who had prowled round the grounds collecting the entrance fees. It was a wonderfully thoughtful memento of their time in Jersey. Ken was genuinely touched. He had one bit of advice for Jeremy: 'Stay at Jersey Zoo.'

'I know you're still undecided what you want to do with the rest of your life or what sort of career path you want to follow, but I implore you to stay at the zoo come what may, and not even think of leaving to try your luck elsewhere. I know things are tough at the moment, but stick at it, stay the course. It may not seem like it now, but at Jersey Zoo your whole future is mapped out for you.'

Stay the course. Prophetic advice indeed; it was probably the wisest counsel Jeremy would ever hear from anyone.

In a sad parting of the ways, Ken and Trudy left the island in January 1963 and returned to England. They never saw Gerald or Jacquie again. When, in 1967, Gerald Durrell established a Scientific Advisory Committee to provide Jersey Zoo with a panel of expert consultants, Ken was not asked to join. (Their mutual friend, John Yealland, on the other hand, *was* invited and, with typical grace, accepted and served on the committee until his death in 1983.)

After Ken's departure, Jersey Zoo was still to do occasional business with him. In June 1974, Jersey Zoo sold him six African Speckled pigeons, and in November 1975 a pair of Red-necked francolins and three Himalayan Monal pheasants. But such transactions were strictly business. The faithful Ken Smith, to whom Gerald Durrell owed so much, was now *persona non grata* as far as Jersey Zoo's honorary director was concerned. Durrell's 1973 book about his student keeper days at Whipsnade Zoo, *Beasts in my Belfry*, contains not a single reference to Ken, even though that was where the pair first met. When, in 1984, the Jersey Wildlife Preservation Trust produced a souvenir publication celebrating the first quarter of a century of the Jersey Zoo, Ken is mentioned just once, fleetingly, even though without him to set the whole thing in motion it may never have got off the ground at all. Even more significantly, he is completely absent from the one book in which you would expect to find him, Gerald Durrell's *Menagerie Manor*, published in 1964. In this, one of the most popular books he ever wrote, Durrell took a light-hearted look at the first four years of the Jersey Zoo from 1959 to 1963 – the very years in which Ken was at the helm, and yet he doesn't appear anywhere in the whole book. It is as if he has been airbrushed from the story. Several staff members – Jeremy Mallinson, John Hartley, Shep Mallet – crop up repeatedly, and even the maintenance man puts in an appearance, but of Ken Smith there is no sign.

Ken's reaction when he found out he had been totally excluded from the book is not recorded but he could not have been happy about it after everything he had done for the fledgling zoo. In the book it is always Gerald Durrell himself or junior members of his staff who have all the adventures. It is Durrell, accompanied by a posse of keepers, who goes in pursuit of a gallivanting tapir, and Durrell who treats an ailing gibbon and lances an abscess on a chimpanzee. So where was Ken? What's going on here? In fact, as I discovered, at least one anecdote in the book *did* involve Ken Smith, though the reader would never know it because Durrell, in an act of pique, chose to ascribe the story to someone else. In *Menagerie Manor*, Durrell describes his elation when the zoo bred from its pair of Ring-tailed coatis for the first time. A coati (pronounced 'Ko-ar-tee') is an animal similar to the raccoon. Often they are incorrectly called coatimundis but this name should really be applied only to solitary adult males. As the four babies grow and start to explore their surroundings, they discover they can squeeze through the wire-mesh of their cage. At first this is not a problem because whenever their mother notices they have strayed too far away, she calls to them. Hearing her alarm cry, they rush back to her side. As they get older, however, their confidence increases and they begin to venture further away from the security of their cage. One day they are startled by the sudden appearance down the main drive of the zoo van and in their panic they become confused and run in the opposite direction, *away* from their cage and familiar surroundings. In *Menagerie Manor* the van is driven by Jeremy Mallinson, who brings it screeching to a halt. The book tells how Jeremy, concerned for the baby coatis' welfare and thinking they would not be able to find their way back to their cage unaided, jumps out of the van and immediately gives chase. Eventually, in an effort to escape their pursuer, the baby coatis dive into the ladies' lavatories, which, as luck would have it, are unoccupied. Making sure there is no-one around, Jeremy dashes in to retrieve them. The muffled squeaks from inside one of the cubicles betray their whereabouts. It is clear the runaways have squeezed under the door. Cursing, he finds to his annoyance that the only way to get them out was to put a coin in the slot to open the door. That, at least, is the way Durrell relates it in *Menagerie Manor*. It is a comic, almost farcical, tale worthy of the Marx Brothers, and Durrell tells it beautifully. The truth, however, is very different. Trudy told me it wasn't Jeremy – who wasn't even on the scene at the time – but her husband who had been driving the van and was forced to give chase. I later put this to Jeremy and he confirmed that it was indeed Ken – not he – who had startled the escapees. In this case it is hard to come to any other conclusion than that he tinkered with the true facts of the story to avoid having to mention his former partner.

Chapter Fourteen

Multum in parvo: Much in a Small Space *(1963)*

KEN, TRUDY AND THEIR TWO YOUNG DAUGHTERS, Caroline and Kelsay, together with a few animals of their own that they had been keeping at Jersey Zoo, arrived back in England in freezing weather in January 1963. It was Gerald Durrell's sister, Margaret, who rallied to their aid. It was she who met them on their return and she who arranged transport for their animals. She collected the animals from the docks in a hired van and delivered them to her home in St. Alban's Avenue, Bournemouth, where they were installed in temporary accommodation until they could be deposited at Paignton Zoo for safekeeping. A rather embarrassed Margaret found herself in a very awkward position. On the one hand, she was Durrell's sister and had always been one of his staunchest supporters, but on the other hand she valued her friendship with the Smiths and felt they had been treated very badly by her brother.

Providing the animals with sufficient warmth was quite a problem for Britain was in the icy grip of the coldest winter for two hundred years. For three months the country – and even the sea – froze. The snow started to fall on Boxing Day night and the thaw didn't begin to set in until Easter. The ice on the Thames was so thick that cars were able to drive across. All over the country, people were marooned in their houses, cut off by giant snowdrifts, and in London more than two hundred buses broke down, the diesel frozen solid in their tanks. The cold was so intense that farm animals literally froze to death in the fields. Wild animals were in dire straits. With rivers and lakes frozen for weeks on end, piscivorous birds like herons starved to death. It is estimated that across the country only four thousand herons survived the winter, to say nothing of all the other wildlife.

Some of the animals Ken and Trudy brought back with them were ones that Ken had originally purchased for Jersey Zoo with his own money and were therefore his property. Some he had bought expressly for Exmouth Zoo. Others were surplus to Jersey Zoo's requirements. In this latter category was a pair of Brothers Island Rock geckos collected by Gerald Durrell on his recent expedition to New Zealand. The two men may have fallen out, but this did not prevent Durrell from making a gift of the Rock geckos. He was anxious to find a new home for them because space in Jersey Zoo's Reptile House was strictly limited, and the geckos (like most lizards) were fiercely territorial. Jersey Zoo retained some, but Durrell was doubtless grateful when Ken accepted the others.

Other animals almost certainly included a Howler monkey. Ken, as I mentioned earlier, was passionate about Howler monkeys. In July 1962, Lee Thomas had returned from an animal-collecting expedition to British Guiana to procure specimens for Jersey

Zoo, and among the animals he had brought back was a Red Howler monkey. (Ken's old associate, Bob Veerasawmy, now based in London, also organised a collecting trip to British Guiana that year to obtain animals for the London Zoo, so it is reasonable to suppose this was a joint expedition, with the animals being split between the two zoos.) This animal obviously did not remain at Jersey Zoo for long, because in an article Ken wrote for the International Zoo Year Book in June 1963 he stated that 'at the time of writing…it is still thriving at Exmouth Zoo.' Oddly enough, Trudy had no recollection of this animal when I asked her about it, so it was probably not at Exmouth Zoo for very long either. A Rice grackle, also part of the collection brought back from British Guiana by Lee Thomas, was another creature that now appears at Exmouth Zoo. (Grackles are blackbirds from North and South America that look as if they've been slightly stretched.) Nobody can tell me exactly what other animals Ken brought back with him when he left Jersey, but Shep Mallet thinks they possibly included Spot-nosed and Rhesus monkeys – species which were certainly kept at Jersey Zoo at that time – and a Jersey Zoo-bred Barbary macaque (later kept at Poole Park Zoo, the zoo that Ken launched the following year).

The animals were deposited temporarily at Paignton Zoo while final preparations were made to receive them at Exmouth, with Ken and Trudy zipping between Exmouth and Paignton as the work proceeded. They enjoyed being back at Paignton Zoo and renewing their acquaintance with staff and animals alike. Caroline, now four years old and more than a little precocious, could not contain her excitement and ran round and round the zoo, pointing out one animal after another. '*We've* got one of those, *and* one of those, *and* that!' she announced in a loud ringing tone to anybody within earshot. The startled visitors, of course, had no idea what she meant.

At first, the Smiths rented a private flat at 15 Valley Road, Exmouth, not far from their own small zoo, provided for them by a friend of theirs, Marie le Fevre, a wealthy long-term supporter of Paignton Zoo who owned property all over the place. An Exmouth resident herself, Mrs le Fevre had known the Smiths since the days when they had lived in Paignton. Today she is commemorated in the name of Paignton Zoo's latest gorilla and orang-utan complex, the Marie le Fevre Great Ape Conservation Centre.

*

Exmouth Zoo, at the time Ken took it over in 1962, was still a wholly indoor attraction, although he hoped it would be possible to enlarge it in the near future. Limitations of space meant he was restricted as to what animals he could keep, but this was not necessarily a handicap because he aimed to specialise in keeping some of the more delicate species. The Exmouth Urban District Council, the zoo's landlord, was responsible for the upkeep of the exterior of the building (an agreement the council would later renege upon) and Ken and Trudy were responsible for the interior. Only 32,000 people chose to visit the zoo in 1962. This was a rather disappointing figure, especially in light of the fact that few zoos were so eminently placed to tempt the casual passerby who, only five minutes earlier, may not have been thinking about going to a zoo. It was in a perfect catchment area, not much more than a hundred yards from the seafront and adjacent to a coach park (which ironically was to play a major part in the zoo's eventual closure), and with a railway station only half a mile from the zoo. There was a downside. Being situated in a South Coast resort town was not necessarily a good thing. More than a few zoo proprietors have found that a seaside location can be a poisoned chalice. When the weather is warm, the crowds are disinclined to venture away from the beach, and on cold or wet days people are reluctant to trudge round a wind-lashed zoo anyway. As a result, the seaside-resort zoo loses out both ways. Come the winter and its fortunes can plummet even lower. However, Exmouth Zoo's strategic seafront position, coupled with the fact that it was an indoor attraction, conferred an advantage, as did – initially at least – the proximity of that coach park where, throughout the holiday season, coaches constantly disgorged parties of day-trippers hungry for entertainment. Exmouth Zoo was about as close to the sea as it was possible to be without having the waves lap at the foundations but, as almost everything was indoors, it didn't matter what the weather was doing. On the contrary, visitors to Exmouth were grateful to have somewhere to go when it was not warm enough for the beach, and even if the day started off warm and sunny, if there was a sudden and unforeseen cloud-burst they would rapidly vacate the beach in a mass exodus and head for the nearest place that promised shelter – the zoo; and the small size of the place meant it was a perfect way to while away the time until the sun broke through again. Children loved it. In the early 1990s there was a TV situation comedy called *Hope It Rains*, set in a seaside resort not dissimilar from Exmouth, in which the owner of a run-down waxworks museum daily wished for rain because he knew this would send people scurrying into his exhibition. It was a hankering the Smiths understood all too well.

The zoo was just one of a range of attractions vying for custom, but there was no rivalry between them. Everybody just got on with each other. To give just one example: next door to the zoo was a model railway; Ken and Trudy's daughters enjoyed free admission, and, in a reciprocal arrangement, the children of the couple who ran the model railway had unlimited free entry to the zoo.

Exmouth Zoo was popular with holidaymakers and local residents alike. Nonetheless, Ken and Trudy faced an ongoing struggle to make ends meet, particularly in the autumn and winter when the holidaymakers deserted *en masse*, the sky was leaden and the waves were breaking over the sea-walls. Money, or rather the lack of it, became a major issue, with the Smiths living a hand-to-mouth existence. It was Jersey all over again – worse, because this time there was no best-selling author as the bait to lure in the visitors.

'At Exmouth, money was tight, *very* tight,' explained Trudy. 'Whenever we did have some cash in the kitty – which wasn't very often – Ken would prefer to buy a hornbill or other exotic creature with it rather than spend it on a utility bill. It was a tough time for all of us, and the girls had to accept they couldn't have everything they wanted. That must have been hard for them when they saw their friends getting all the latest toys. Foreign holidays were out of the question, although we did take the occasional short break in the U.K. But they accepted it uncomplainingly because they had something that none of their friends had – a zoo!'

By a stroke of good fortune, Exmouth Zoo was blessed with a sympathetic bank manager, a creature rarer even than those Bald-headed rock-crows that Ken had once collected in Sierra Leone. This man, unlike so many of his breed, was patient and understanding. He appreciated that zoos were unlike any other business. Each winter, as Ken and Trudy dipped further into the red, he would reassure them that Easter was on the horizon and, with the advent of the new season, their fortunes were bound to revive, whereas a lesser mortal would have told Ken to accept it wasn't profitable and to pull down the shutters for good.

As at Jersey Zoo, Ken did not want to impose too many rigid restrictions which he felt could be off-putting. Dogs were allowed in if kept under proper control, and feeding of certain animals was permitted with peanuts on sale at the entrance kiosk. Lee Thomas was the first Curator, an appointment that meant he had now worked for Ken in no fewer than three zoos: Paignton, Jersey, and now, to complete the hat-trick, Exmouth. In time he would go on to work at Poole Park Children's Zoo, Welsh Mountain Zoo and Colchester Zoo, but is now dead, having taken to drinking heavily. Most of the time, Exmouth Zoo relied for its staff on young people who could survive on the low wages, and on volunteers. As they got older, Ken and Trudy's daughters also helped out after school, at weekends and in the school holidays. Another person who worked there for a while was an enthusiastic boy by the name of Peter Merrett, whose family lived locally. Eventually he went on to assume the head-keeper's position at Guernsey Zoo, helping to transform this hitherto aimless, shambolic menagerie (embarrassingly close to Jersey's) into a respectable animal collection. His chief interest was the Edentates (sloths, anteaters and armadillos) and in 1983 published a book on the subject.

Somehow a great deal had been packed into a small space. In 1963, according to the International Zoo Year Book, Exmouth Zoo had no fewer than 110 animals representing sixty-four species – a lot for a converted golf clubhouse and a veranda. The collection comprised 27 species of mammals (an increase of eleven from the previous year), 24 kinds of birds (up by five), and 13 species of herptile (the collective term for reptiles and amphibians). There were three staff. Admission charges were 1s 6d for adults and 1s for children. Now open all year round, 1963 saw precisely 38,223 paying visitors tour the collection. Among the rarer or more unusual animals that could be seen there in 1963 were the Galapagos Giant tortoises (in a brand new enclosure built that year) and a trio of gelada (sometimes misleadingly called the Gelada baboon). The first guide book, written by Ken himself, was published at around the same time, a slim pocket-sized brochure illustrated with colour photos of the most important and popular animals in the collection. It is commendable that Exmouth Zoo should produce a guide book because by no means all zoos did, particularly small privately-owned ones on tight budgets.

It is easy to criticise Exmouth Zoo for not embracing conservation or scientific research, but it had a very important part to play by introducing children to the wonders of the natural world. It is impossible to quantify how many people had their interest in nature, that initial spark, kindled when they were young by seeing that disparate collection of animals whilst on a family holiday to Exmouth.

Mike Curzon, one-time Curator at the Tropical Bird Gardens, Rode, visited the zoo on numerous occasions. Whilst impressed by Ken's knowledge and expertise, he was disparaging about the size of the enclosures. 'Most of the animals were in relatively small cages. Ken explained that a lot of animals feel more secure in smaller cages, and I think essentially that's true. There was a strong, musty aroma of hay, urine and warm animal bodies, but that was only to be expected of an indoor zoo with inadequate ventilation and where a number of the small mammals marked their territory with urine.' This was true enough. Galagos, for example, routinely pee on their hands and wipe them on branches to advertise their presence. Nowadays, of course, the building would be fitted with extractor fans to deal with the problem, but back then visitors weren't so easily offended by natural odours.

Mike recalled that the collection was always very strong on primates. 'On most of my visits, there were about a dozen kinds of monkeys on show. Once, I remember seeing some kind of guenon labelled as a "Coppertail monkey" – though I don't know of any species by that name today.' (Possibly a Red-tailed monkey.) 'There was an impressive collection of small mammals, including some that were new to me, and I was very surprised by how many different kinds of birds were kept. There was also a decent reptile collection. I never saw any fish, though.'

Likewise, Trudy cannot recall any fish ever having been kept there – although fish were certainly exhibited at Exmouth Zoo in the pre-Smith days when it was still owned by Paignton Zoo. 'Neither Ken nor I were very fish-orientated,' she explained. 'Not only were we limited for space, but there was a perfectly good public aquarium on the Esplanade. We were good friends with the owner and it just seemed sensible to everybody that he should concentrate on aquatic animals and we should concentrate on terrestrial ones.'

A tame raven named Grip, belonging to a Mr James Baldey, was a guest at the zoo, and surprised visitors by uttering a cheerful 'Hello!' or 'Hello darling!' at odd moments. Sometimes he would inquire 'How are you?' or, as the mood took him, invite startled visitors to 'Come and have a bath'. Grip was given complete liberty at times, but, though he often flew quite a distance away, he always returned to the zoo. Among the reptiles at one point was a young Nile crocodile presented by Bob Golding. Bob was now in charge of the University of Ibadan Zoological Garden in Nigeria. Returning to the U.K. on leave each summer between 1963 and 1979, he often took the opportunity to bring back from that country a small collection of animals for U.K. zoos. He visited Ken and Trudy at Exmouth Zoo several times and presented the baby crocodile on one of these occasions. Ken was always grateful for donations of animals from the public. Two young Crab-eating macaques were a gift from Marie le Fevre, a kinkajou was brought back from South America by a sailor, and two buzzard chicks were brought in when the tree their nest was in fell down.

As a child, Brian Smith had a holiday in Exmouth with his grandmother Gertrude, during which few days he spent a great deal of his time at the zoo. 'I remember Trudy and Caroline being there, but don't remember Ken being around,' he told me. 'I enjoyed helping out at the zoo, and I was amazed at the amount of work that went on behind the scenes, and at the crates of fruit. One of my jobs involved picking live mealworms out of a huge tub of sawdust-like material to feed to the reptiles.'

Brian was also asked to lend his assistance to deal with an escaped badger. He said, 'I think it was confined temporarily in a room in a bungalow, presumably part of the office or storage area for the zoo. Somehow the badger found a weak point in the floorboards and got into the cavity beneath the floor.' Brian was given the job of sticking his head through the hole in the floor and shining a torch into the inky blackness while one of the keepers crawled around on his hands and knees trying to recapture the escapee. Normally shy and retiring, a badger can be quite a formidable animal when threatened. Crawling around on one's belly in the dark confined space beneath the floor, with no possibility of a hasty retreat, with a terrified, cornered and enraged badger, is a perilous undertaking, and the keeper was lucky to emerge unscathed. The keeper may have suffered no ill effects as a result of his escapade, but Brian was not so fortunate. The next day he had an incredibly painful, stiff neck caused by the cold draught that had blown through the hole in the floor, and he could hardly move his head. He was put to work massaging olive oil into the shells of the tortoises, including a couple of Galapagos Giant tortoises, having been assured by everyone that heat was good for a stiff neck, and the tortoise pen was about the warmest area in the zoo. 'I can still remember, to this day, children making faces at me through the glass,' he told me.

Wonderful creatures as badgers, buzzards, Galapagos tortoises, ravens and crocodiles are, Exmouth Zoo's forte was quirky animals. At Jersey, Ken's *idée fixe* had been the acquisition of those animals which he knew would appeal to the public, but at Exmouth he felt less constrained in this direction and more able to indulge his passion for the idiosyncratic – animals which were not necessarily endangered in the wild but which *were* very rare in captivity, and he obtained some real gems.

Particular favourites for Ken were Prickles the Brazilian Tree porcupine and Kinki the kinkajou. Gradually the zoo developed a reputation for exhibiting the kinds of animals not normally associated with small seaside zoos – recherché species like Raccoon dog, Radiated tortoise, Gila monster, Cotton-topped tamarin, acouchis, Titi monkey, and many others which were decided rarities in zoos.

Titi monkeys are among the least known of all the primates – delightful monkeys, elfin-like in appearance and in some ways rather like a fluffy version of a Squirrel monkey. Titi monkeys had been on Ken's wish-list for years ever since he had seen one in a small zoo in Northamptonshire. The zoo owner had little idea of the animal's identity or rarity. Ken gave him the facts, and then tried to acquire the titi in exchange for other animals, but without success. One might venture to suggest his mistake had been apprising the owner of the animal's true worth before trying to appropriate it. The sight of this beautiful monkey had impressed him, and he remembered the red glow and lustre of its coat over the years. So when, in 1963, a dealer listed a pair of Red Titi monkeys for sale, Ken lost no time in purchasing them for Exmouth Zoo. They came with a tame douroucouli, being sold as a trio of cage-mates. Unfortunately one of the titis died within a few days of arrival, but the other one (simply named 'Red') and its douroucouli companion thrived. It was believed to be the only Red Titi monkey in

Europe. Red was reasonably tame and friendly, if a little retiring at times. He would come to the front of the cage when the door was open and accept mealworms from Trudy's fingers, but always remaining fairly circumspect. Most of the time the little monkey was silent but, if alarmed, communicated his unease by yelping very loudly – a high-pitched and stirring cry. The volume of his voice seemed quite extraordinary for such a small animal and took Ken by surprise the first time he heard it, even though he knew from natural history books what to expect. The first time was when Red caught a glimpse of two newly arrived tayras, which are a Titi monkey's natural enemy in the wild state, and the second occasion was when two black visitors passed his cage. Obviously, somewhere deep in the recesses of his mind, he knew that in his native homeland titis were hunted; he wasn't to know that the visitors came from Nyasaland (Malawi), not South America.

A tayra (pronounced 'Tie-rah') is a South American member of the weasel family rarely seen in big mainstream zoos, much less small privately-owned collections. At Exmouth Zoo, they were housed in a simple hutch-type cage fronted by ordinary chicken-wire. There was no stand-off barrier to prevent inquisitive visitors from poking their fingers through, just a small warning label declaring 'WE MAY BITE YOU!' An identical sign appeared on all the enclosures containing animals that could bite, scratch or peck, even the snake cages, although their occupants were safely behind glass.

At one time, Exmouth Zoo possessed the only pair of olingos (a little-known member of the raccoon family) in Europe, but the way they were displayed did not show them to their best advantage.

'The olingo,' wrote Jeff Handley in *Tembo*, the magazine of the National Zoological Society,

> has rarely been seen at British zoos; at the end of the last century London Zoo had a specimen, and as far as I can ascertain only one British zoo at present is exhibiting them. This is Exmouth Zoo, Devon, where Mr Kenneth Smith has three olingos. Being nocturnal all I saw of them during my visit was a ball of fur in the corner of their cage.

The editor of *Tembo* was equally harsh, adding as a footnote, 'Anyone who has visited Exmouth Zoo might query if the olingos were exhibited to their full potential in the quarters provided.' And this was the paradox with Exmouth Zoo – an extremely unusual collection of animals, with most exhibited in very unnoteworthy enclosures.

'Ken had a connoisseur's eye for the unusual,' said Mike Curzon. 'He always had nice – and surprising – things at Exmouth, but of course he was really pandering to himself, as all good zoo directors do, because I don't suppose the majority of the visitors – which, after all, comprised mostly bored holidaymakers looking for somewhere to go on a wet afternoon – were all that interested in the fact that he had, for example, a Wanderoo monkey, which was a very rare species even then and seen in only a handful of zoos. Sadly, to the majority of visitors, a monkey was a monkey, and that was that. I remember on one visit I made in about 1963 or '64, I noticed he had a pair of Grey Peacock pheasants in juvenile plumage. Stunningly beautiful birds in a subtle sort of way. Now, Peacock pheasants were really something special back then, but I almost didn't notice them. They were in a low, gloomy cage underneath another cage, and all I could see of them at first was a couple of silhouettes moving around. As soon as I realised what they were, I had to have them for the Tropical Bird Gardens at Rode. Fortunately Ken agreed to let me have them. Ken was very short of money that winter, as he was most winters, his zoo being utterly dependent on the holiday trade, so he rang me up one day and said, 'You know, Mike, business is poor at the moment and Easter is still such a long way off, so I'd appreciate it if you would settle up for those birds you had.' Those pheasants did very well for us. We bred seven chicks in 1965 and even more the year after. He also possessed a solitary male Malabar Pied hornbill, which we bought as a potential mate for a single female that we had at Rode. Unfortunately his bird – whom we christened Mr Smith – took a dislike to our female and there was no romance between them. He was a super bird, but very imprinted on humans, so naturally when he met another hornbill he didn't know how to behave.'

Robert Bradshaw agrees that the presentation of the animals left something to be desired, but that the collection itself was outstanding. In particular, he recalls seeing a 'grey, short-legged, small fox-like animal with a dark tail' which he believes could have been a geriatric Small-eared dog, an unusual canid from the tropical forests of South America seldom seen in captivity. Even rarer was the White-throated guenon from Nigeria and Benin. Ken had at least one individual of this very rare monkey species at Exmouth Zoo and there is a photograph of him with it. So endangered was this species that, not many years after that photo was taken, the White-throated guenon was declared extinct – or so it was thought – having been hunted out of existence for its fur, and for a while it looked as if Ken's specimen had been among the last of its kind. Fortunately reports of its extinction proved off beam when the species was rediscovered in 1988.

The late Geoffrey Schomberg, Secretary of the Federation of Zoological Gardens of Great Britain and Ireland and a man who really knew his stuff, had this to say on Exmouth Zoo:

> There is very little space, but the animals here really do receive expert care, since Mr Smith is a very experienced zoo man…The quality of the collection marks this as more than just another beachside zoo, and if the weather is not nice enough to go on the beach – or even if it is – you should not miss visiting it.

There it was again – reference to the weather. While other U.K. zoos counted on the sky being a perpetual shade of blue, Ken wistfully hoped for rain.

Chapter Fifteen

As Good As It Gets *(1963–1967)*

THERE IS ONLY ONE THING NICER than owning a zoo, and that is owning more than one zoo. Not content with his acquisition of Exmouth Zoo, Ken spent the next few years building up what amounted to a mini empire of zoos in that southwest corner of England, subsidiaries of the Mother Ship, as it were, at Exmouth. By about 1967 he owned no fewer than three other zoos in addition to the one at Exmouth – at Poole in Dorset, Shaldon in Devon, and Newquay in Cornwall. Tiny as each one was, it was still a considerable achievement.

As soon as he and Trudy had returned from Jersey, he had entered into negotiations with Poole Town Council to establish a small zoo in the borough. When the council agreed in principle to assist him, he could not have been more jubilant. By opening a zoo in Poole, he had done what Gerald Durrell had failed to do, because before Jersey had been in the frame as a possible location for a zoo, Durrell had spent months battling petty bureaucracy as he laboured to establish his own zoo in the popular Dorset resort, but all *his* efforts had been thwarted. Ken's new zoo covered about two acres in Poole Park in the heart of the town, so was considerably bigger and offered more potential than the one at Exmouth. It was fortunate that, as mentioned before, Ken's brother Ronald ran the building and decorating firm of John Jagger (Parkstone) Ltd, a local company with an office and yard at Lilliput. To him fell the job of building the zoo. Brian Smith recalls his father getting the contract. 'I'm pretty sure my father made no profit out of this – more likely a loss,' he said. 'I can remember being present during the construction stage while Ken and my father discussed cage sizes and design and so on. After the place had opened to the public, I got in free a couple of times.'

It was not the first time exotic animals had been exhibited in the park. Shortly before the First World War a bird enclosure was built there and, according to local historian Geoffrey Budworth, this aviary was still standing in 1963 when it was incorporated into Ken Smith's new zoo. It was demolished, along with all the other enclosures and buildings, when the zoo closed in 1994.

Poole Park Children's Zoo, to give its full title, opened on Saturday, 1 June 1963. For many years it was a seasonal attraction, open from Easter to November. Under later owners it would be open all year round. 'It was always very nice and open with paddocks,' said Trudy. 'At first we called it a children's zoo to appease the council.' (Ken learned early on that calling each of his zoos a 'children's zoo' made it easier to obtain planning permission, as it would take a flint-hearted councillor to veto a proposed amenity for children.)

The zoo was an immediate success – rather more successful, in fact, than its parent collection at Exmouth. According to the International Zoo Year Book, the attendance figure for 1963 was 110,000. This seems almost unbelievably high, given that Poole Zoo did not open until half way through the year and closed again for the off-season. Even now, many years after its closure, it is still remembered with affection by many long-term residents of the borough. James Straight, currently writing a book on Poole Zoo, said, 'For me, Poole Park Zoo evokes memories of many happy hours spent there on Sundays from a young age up until my teenage years, studying the behaviour of many of the inmates.'

With Ken and Trudy living about eighty-five miles away in Exmouth (by now they had moved from the flat in Valley Road and had settled in at number 30 Valley Road, and would soon move to Raleigh Road), it made sense to appoint a manager to run the zoo, and the man offered the job was none other than Ken's younger brother, Frank. Frank had already worked very closely with Ken to set the whole thing up and, more importantly, he lived not far away. In fact, the zoo was very much a collaborative family effort. One brother (Ronald) had built it, another (Frank) was in day-to-day charge of it, and Frank's son, Paul, also worked there at one time.

The emphasis at Poole Zoo was on monkeys and birds, but there were plenty of other animals besides, and even a Himalayan bear by the name of Chico, presented by Mrs Katherine Tottenham who was soon to open a short-lived wildlife park in North Devon. Reptiles were maintained hardly at all due to the lack of suitable facilities for them, but there were usually a few tortoises and pythons. On show in that first year were about fifteen species of mammals, fifty-two species of birds, two kinds of reptile, and even one kind of amphibian. In order that it should live up to the name of 'children's zoo', several very familiar animals, carefully chosen for their appeal to younger visitors, were included, including Mary and Mabel the Nubian goats, Greek tortoises, a small group of Humboldt penguins, budgerigars, Vietnamese Pot-bellied pigs, tame rats, lambs, rabbits and guinea-pigs. 'Some children get more delight from recognising their pet favourites in the zoo,' he once wrote, 'than in coming face to face with many of the rarer or stranger animals.' Many of the creatures – those which could be trusted not to bite or peck their young admirers – could be petted by the children, and the zoo did very well from the sale of bags of monkey nuts and other titbits to feed to the animals. But there was also much for those with a more serious interest in wildlife to admire. As at Exmouth, primates were a speciality. There were Spider monkeys, capuchins, macaques, mangabeys, guenons, gelada, a drill, and a chimpanzee, but the cream of the primate collection was arguably the Mongoose lemurs. In those days, comparatively few zoos kept lemurs (unlike the situation today when most zoos have at least one or two species) and Mongoose lemurs were one of the rarer kinds, kept by only a few establishments.

Other animals of note included such unusual and interesting things as tayra, Woolly-necked stork, Cape Barren goose (once the fourth rarest species of goose in the world), Papuan hornbill (thought to be the only one in the country), and some prolific White-nosed coatis. The Calgary Zoological Society presented a Red-tailed hawk, a Swainson's buzzard, and six Great Horned owls. Most of the animals came from Exmouth Zoo and would be returned there at the end of the season. The choice of animals clearly found favour with Geoffrey Schomberg, who wrote, '...this is a limited collection of high quality, with some interesting species not usually seen in the usual run of small seaside zoos, which are few and far between along this part of the south coast.'

So what did the zoo look like? It was surrounded by aesthetically pleasing wicker fencing. Most of the cages were arranged around the perimeter, as was quite logical, with a number of larger pens in the middle. The enclosures were fairly basic, being mostly wooden-framed, welded-mesh or chicken-wire structures typical of the period, simply furnished with branches, shelves, tyres and so on, depending on species. Rudimentary as many of the enclosures were, in 1971 the zoo's caging was formally approved by the Federation of Zoological Gardens of Great Britain and Ireland. The public pathways were gravel. Next to the pay-box was a glass window looking into the pythons' cage. Also in this area were marmosets and tamarins, housed in simple parrot-style cages and available to buy, a reminder that, for much of his career, Ken had been an animal-dealer. The marmosets were on sale for £5 each, the cage an extra £2. In the centre of the zoo was a petting area and, nearby, a concrete cage with green-painted bars for larger, stronger animals. Initially this cage was the domain of Cleo, a white-faced chimpanzee (much less commonly seen than the black-faced kind), ex-London Zoo, who showed great dexterity with a hammer or spanner – although it's not recorded how anyone found this out – but over the years the cage displayed a succession of other animals. A young cassowary had the run of the grounds. It stalked imperiously around the place, generally making a nuisance of itself and getting in everyone's way. Like a feathered bandit, it would descend on unsuspecting visitors it suspected of carrying food, but, as it got older, it became increasingly hostile until the point arrived when it was no longer safe to allow it to consort with the visitors. Brian Smith told me, 'I remember Ken saying it had to be "retired" when it started getting aggressive.' An experienced and knowledgeable animal-man as Ken surely must have known it couldn't be trusted to be around people indefinitely. An enraged adult cassowary is one of nature's most alarming sights and one of the few birds capable of killing a human. Moreover, this particular one had grown up with no fear of humans, making it potentially even more dangerous.

For a short while, Poole Zoo also played host to several kinds of big cats, including a lion, a tiger and both normal and melanistic leopards. These did not belong to Ken, but were the property of – and placed on deposit by – a flamboyant lion-trainer, Nick Nyoka. This was not his real name ('Nyoka' is Swahili for 'Master of Snakes') but it is quite understandable he would want to adopt a nom de guerre. For somebody who earned his living as a lion-trainer and alligator-wrestler, his birth name of Adrian Darley did not have quite the same ring to it. Nyoka led a fairly peripatetic existence in the 1960s and early 1970s, and Poole was only one of several zoos where he found himself at one time or another. In his book, *Where the Zebu Grazed*, Clinton Keeling vividly wrote that Nyoka 'hopped in and out of the smaller zoological gardens like a character in a French farce', and I cannot better that description. Ken had first encountered him in Jersey where Nyoka, a magnificent figure of a man resplendent in jungle attire, was doing a summer season wowing holidaymakers with his feats of derring-do involving some of his animals. I use the term 'encountered' advisedly because, in his white trousers, jungle boots, leopard skin headband and snakeskin tie, Nyoka cut quite an impression. In return for offering him accommodation for his big cats at Poole, Ken was getting animals that were guaranteed to draw in the public, but the arrival of big cats in sedate Poole Park was not without its problems. The lion was swiftly moved on because its habit of roaring in the middle of the night was disturbing – and unnerving – local residents. Eventually Nyoka moved his animals to Sandown Zoo on the Isle of Wight. In time, he would go on to run a zoo at Knaresborough in Yorkshire.

Jim Clubb visited Poole Zoo regularly as a child and remembers it as being a very clean zoo. 'I went there about ten times in all,' he said. 'As far as I could tell, the animals were always very well looked after and never seemed in anything other than perfect condition. Poole Zoo was one of the best of the small seaside collections that were then beginning to proliferate around the country. The two Chipperfield zoos at Plymouth and Southampton were superior, but they had bigger animals like elephants and giraffes. For its size, Poole Zoo had a very good general collection, including some extremely unusual species. I preferred Poole Zoo to its parent at Exmouth.'

*

The little zoo near Teignmouth (the 'Teign' is pronounced 'Tin') was, along with the small children's zoo at Newquay, the least significant of the four collections belonging to Ken Smith. Originally called Teignmouth Children's Zoo, he founded it in 1964. Even more than his zoos at Exmouth and Poole, it was designed expressly with children in mind. Tony Soper, the popular natural history broadcaster and co-founder of the BBC's Natural History Unit, was invited along to perform the opening ceremony. By agreeing to open the new zoo, he was returning a favour because a few years earlier, while staying in Jersey, he had asked Ken, who at that time was still managing Jersey Zoo, to take care of his dog, a Welsh collie called Blodwyn, during a trip that Soper was planning to make to the Galapagos Islands. Neither Ken nor Trudy were really 'doggy' people. Trudy in particular preferred cats to dogs, and they usually had a few cats, usually Siamese or Abyssinian, slinking round the place. Nonetheless, they agreed to Soper's request. I contacted Tony Soper, but most unfortunately, although he could vaguely remember Ken and Trudy and recalled they looked after his dog for a short period when he went abroad on a wildlife filming expedition, he was unable to add anything. There was, he admitted apologetically, 'too much on the mental hard disk and nothing has been properly filed'.

The original name of the zoo was misleading. Strictly speaking, there has never been a zoo in Teignmouth. The zoo was (indeed is, because it survives – considerably altered – to this day) located in the tiny, picturesque fishing village of Shaldon, on the opposite bank of the Teign River, just above an old smugglers' tunnel leading up from Ness Cove (from the hill on which the zoo stands, one gets a lovely view of Teignmouth across the river). Why Ken chose to name it after Teignmouth is unclear; perhaps he thought Teignmouth was more well-known than Shaldon. (Much later, after he and Trudy had relinquished ownership of the zoo, new proprietors renamed it, more appropriately, Shaldon Children's Zoo. Today, it's simply Shaldon Zoo.)

Teignmouth Children's Zoo was tiny, no more than an acre in extent leased from the local corporation. As with Poole Zoo, it was open only during the summer months. At the end of each season, the animals were removed to Exmouth. Rather conveniently, a large municipal car park was adjacent to the zoo. There was a parking charge but the zoo received none of this money, which went to the council. In those days, the zoo comprised little more than a large rectangular shed filled with cages. The small amount of land behind this building was largely undeveloped. In style it was very reminiscent of Exmouth Zoo, but without the variety of animals. With a few exceptions, the animals were of a more predicable type, the emphasis being on species which could be handled safely by children, such as rabbits, guinea-pigs and tortoises, but in addition there were monkeys, parrots, ravens and toucans. Almost all the animals were indoors but there were also about five smallish outside pens. The two biggest cages – near the pay-desk just inside the entrance – usually displayed coatis in one and a Green monkey in the other. The idea behind the zoo was to encourage children to take an interest in animals by allowing close contact wherever possible in the hope that they would want to visit other more varied collections, as well as instilling in them – Ken hoped – a lifelong interest in animals. Drusillas, another small zoo, has a very similar ethos today. The zoo was home to Minnie, a Banded mongoose, who adored having her back scratched by her admiring public through the wire-mesh of her cage (would never be permitted today); Gladys, a Pied hornbill, who liked nothing better than having her throat gently massaged; and Tuki, a tame Toco toucan. There was also a malicious Great hornbill whose mission in life appeared to be to sneak up on his keeper while she was servicing his aviary and whack her on the head with a scything sweep of his bill. He eventually departed for Poole, not because of his misanthropic misdeeds, but so that he could be given a more spacious aviary.

Ken's practical involvement with Teignmouth Children's Zoo was minimal. He visited regularly throughout the season, taking with him bales of hay and straw and other essential provisions, although the older he got the less he relished this task, and occasionally he made the journey to transfer an animal from Exmouth Zoo or back again, but, on the whole, he preferred to leave the running of the zoo to the people who were there all the time (a staff member lived on site in a tiny bedroom behind the animal cages, now converted into an office). His visits were as likely as not hindered by the decrepitude of the zoo van. Ken's ploy had always been to spend as little as possible (no more than a hundred pounds or so) on an old van but with a full year's MOT on it – and then run it until it basically fell apart, or until it failed its MOT, whereupon he would simply buy another very cheap vehicle. The driveway leading down to the zoo was on an extremely steep slope. Driving down was easy; driving back up was an endurance test of his patience. There was no question of parking at the top of the slope because invariably the van was crammed full of things that needed to be unloaded, leaving him with little choice but to drive down, wondering, as he did so, if this would finally be the day when he would be forced to abandon it at the bottom. Once unloaded, he was faced with the problem of coaxing the antiquated and irascible van back up the slope to the road. Putting it into the lowest gear, he would start the painfully slow ascent. The protesting van would cough, groan and lurch as it crawled forward, but, if it was feeling particularly vituperative, it would suddenly give a shudder and die, as if exhausted by the effort of it all.

Three zoos in three years; not bad going by anybody's standards, but there was still one more to come. Newquay Children's Zoo (not to be confused with the present, unrelated, Newquay Zoo, which has been going since 1969) has now been almost completely forgotten. Information about it is almost nonexistent and even the librarian in the Newquay Reference Library was surprised to learn there had once been another animal collection in the resort. Occupying an area close to the boating lake in Trenance Park (coincidentally, the existing Newquay Zoo is also in Trenance Park), ten minutes' walk from the town centre, this tiny, almost entirely indoor, menagerie had been established about ten years earlier by Charles Trevisick, a once popular zoologist, broadcaster and lecturer who owned a small zoo at Comyn Hill near Ilfracombe. In the 1950s, Trevisick, a former dairy farmer who believed that both juvenile delinquency and the circulation of horror comics (of which he heartedly disapproved) could be combated by stimulating an interest in natural history among children, was asked by the Newquay Urban District Council to create a children's zoo in the popular holiday resort. At first, councillors were full of enthusiasm and supportive, and Trevisick worked closely with the town clerk and others to plan the new amenity. Such was its initial success that he was subsequently approached by the councils of other seaside resorts to set up similar children's zoos in their own towns (others were at Bude and Looe in Cornwall, Lynmouth in Devon, and Minehead in Somerset).

Trevisick was a contemporary of Ken Smith. They were sculptured from the same clay, had a similar outlook, shared many of the same views. They had been friends for many years, and so when Trevisick let it be known that he was growing weary of the Newquay Children's Zoo and wished to bow out, Ken was an obvious choice to take over, which he did in about 1966 or 1967. This makes it unique among the four zoos owned by Ken Smith by being the only one not conceived by him (even Exmouth Zoo, you will remember, had originally been his idea when he was Superintendent at Paignton).

Ken's latest acquisition consisted of little more than a single, long, barnlike, building with a door at each end. The main thrust of the collection seems to have been tropical birds, small mammals and children's pets. There were about three low-fenced pens down the middle of the building for rabbits, guinea-pigs and occasionally lambs and goat kids. Along the length of the building on one side (or possibly both sides) were cages containing squirrels, civets, genets, mongooses, coatis, galagos, and marmosets. Outside was a small pay-desk and some aviaries. Andrew Stevens remembers being taken there as a young child during a family holiday to the West Country in the late summer of 1966 around the time that Ken took over. In a letter to me, he wrote:

> I am afraid what I can tell you about the children's zoo in Newquay is insignificant; mind you, it was an insignificant place. There wasn't a lot to see there. My only memory of the zoo is standing behind a barrier in a building looking at a row of cages that I think might have been at a raised level – on something that to my young eyes at least resembled a long table. I can vaguely

recall a tawny-ish animal that might possibly have been a Lar gibbon. After a short while surveying what few animals there were, my mother said, 'Let's go and see the rest of the zoo,' and we made towards the exit at the left of the building. Then someone said, 'You know, I think this is all there is!' and I was really disappointed.

Another visitor around this time was Mike Curzon, who remembers a Hyacinthine macaw on a stand by the entrance to welcome visitors. This spectacular cobalt-blue bird, the biggest of all parrots, was an unusual sight back then. Before the 1970s, the species was very rare in aviculture and often prohibitively expensive to buy.

Perhaps because the idea for the children's zoo at Newquay had not originated with him, Ken could never engender the same level of interest in it as with his other collections, and usually he was content for the manager he had appointed to run it, Peter Lowe, to look after things there. The location, so far from Exmouth, didn't help matters, and Ken didn't keep the zoo for long. With the benefit of hindsight, adding the Newquay menagerie to his portfolio of seaside zoos was a less than shrewd move, but he had been friends with Trevisick for too long to turn it down. In some ways, it was something of an albatross around his neck – although he would never admit it. He was aware that much of the caging was inadequate, but this was hardly his fault as he had inherited the cages from Trevisick and he hadn't had time to implement any changes. He introduced a few different animals and, as was his custom by now, some of them were of the unexpected kind, and no doubt, had he held onto the zoo for longer, he would have improved the exhibits, but he was hamstrung by several factors, of which distance was just one. To drive from Exmouth to Newquay was a round trip of almost a hundred-and-ninety miles. There was also the problem of council apathy. Having sanctioned the zoo ten years earlier in a frenzy of enthusiasm, Newquay Urban District Council had lost interest in its offspring. This is a perennial problem with council-run places. Individual councillors come and go, and often their successors do not share the same fervour.

The site was leased from the council, which helped itself to an unreasonably high percentage of the profits, a recurring theme with all the Smith-owned zoos. In *Zoos, Bird Gardens & Animal Collections of Great Britain & Eire*, first published in 1969, it states that the Newquay Children's Zoo was open throughout the year and displayed a 'representative' collection of small and medium-sized animals. However, the few people who can remember it at all claim it was a strictly seasonal collection, and it does seem extremely unlikely it stayed open once the holidaymakers had departed. 'As far as I remember, it closed for the off-season,' said Trudy, 'whereupon the animals were withdrawn to Exmouth Zoo until the following year.'

*

It is probably fair to say that the years from about the mid 1960s until his health began to deteriorate in the Seventies were among the happiest Ken had known in a rich and fulfilling life. In both his professional and his private life, everything was going well and he was more content than he had been for a long while. As well as having no fewer than four zoos of their own, Ken and Trudy were now the proud parents of three daughters – for on 31 July 1966, the day after England won the football World Cup, Caroline and Kelsay were joined by a baby sister, Kathleen Lynn, forever after known to everyone as Kate, born at home at 15 Raleigh Road, Exmouth. So while the rest of the population rocked in a way it had rarely rocked before, the Smiths had a private but very special celebration of their own. Like her two sisters, Kate was raised surrounded by animals – the perfect upbringing.

Ken loved parenthood and was a devoted father to his three girls, and he was often to be seen with baby Kate in his arms, with the other two not far away.

'He was a wonderfully loving father,' said Kelsay, 'kind and generous, but soft as butter. He'd do anything for us. He was very indulgent. We were cosseted. He would let us get away with anything. Some kids are afraid to stay out late for fear of getting yelled at by their parents, but *we* didn't *want* to stay out late because we knew that Dad would be very worried about us and, even as children, we didn't want to do anything that would cause him distress. He was so laidback with us – always laughing and joking.'

Both Caroline and Kelsay were privately educated and attended a convent school up to the age of about twelve. Every day Ken would polish their outdoor and indoor shoes himself. Nothing was too much trouble. On freezing winter mornings, when the girls were young, he would offer to refill their hot-water bottles for them to save them having to get out of bed to do it for themselves. 'Come on,' he would say, 'give me those cold hot-water bottles.'

It was left to Trudy to provide a measure of firmness. '*What* are you doing?' she would ask as he boiled the kettle.

'It's too cold for the girls to get up.'

It was Ken who always used to pick his daughters up from school. He had instructed them to wait for him by a wall about four hundred yards from the school gates. By picking them up there instead of outside the school entrance, he avoided driving through the worst of the traffic. So every day, after school, the girls would sit on this wall while they waited for him to arrive.

Usually he was late.

'Often he just forgot about us,' said Kelsay. 'There would be some minor disaster at the zoo and he would be so preoccupied with sorting it out that he would lose track of the time, and all the while we would be sitting on the wall and wondering with rising anxiety what had happened to Dad. Twenty minutes would pass, then half an hour, and we would be getting more and more agitated. Eventually, of course, he'd turn up and he'd be ever so contrite, but by then we'd be having histrionics. So he termed it the Wailing Wall, you know, like the one in Jerusalem. I still call it the Wailing Wall to this day.'

He loved singing at the wheel, and the dafter the lyric the more he enjoyed giving his own lusty rendition of it, the girls joining in. Often, as they bowled along, he was disposed to warble this typically English piece of whimsical falderal:

'*OK Toots, you're wearing Russian boots,*
I told you con-fi-den-tially, OK Toots...'

Having been raised in a household full of animals, it is no surprise that all three of his daughters were comfortable about handling anything from a kinkajou to a python, with none of the hang-ups and phobias that affect children whose lives are devoid of regular animal contact. The house became an overspill for the zoo. There was always some animal requiring special attention. At various times there were galagos and snakes and chimpanzees all vying for houseroom. 'The girls were wonderful and always supported us with the animals, and there used to be all types in the house,' said Trudy. Guests were never certain what to expect, whether it would be kinkajous swinging from the curtains or half-grown pumas monopolising the sofa. And always there was some furred or feathered creature in a cardboard box somewhere. When Ken and Trudy's first grandchild was born in the 1970s, everyone joked that it was a wonder *she* wasn't placed in a cardboard box, since this was the usual receptacle for any helpless, newborn creature.

Ken and Trudy, pushing Kate in her pram, would sometimes slip away to the small café along the road from the zoo, if they had time, for lunch or a late breakfast. It wasn't far to walk, and if the weather was fine they would leave Kate asleep in her pram outside the café while they popped inside. Nowadays, one would never dream of leaving a baby outside in the street, but in those far-off halcyon days almost every parent did it, secure in the knowledge that the baby and pram would still be there when they re-emerged. Ken would usually order poached egg on toast for two shillings, washed down with lashings of tea. He enjoyed these brief moments of respite from the zoo. It was a chance to unwind over a pot of tea, to chat, confidant they were not going to be disturbed, and dissect the news stories of the day while simultaneously dissecting the eggs on toast. Occasionally they became so engrossed in conversation that they forgot that baby Kate was outside. More than once they arrived back at the zoo to be greeted by the shrill ringing of the telephone. It was the manageress of the café. 'I think you've left the zoo baby here.'

On busier days when there was less time, Ken would get something to eat from a kiosk opposite the zoo run by somebody called Nev, who did a line in Cornish pasties. They were not, it has to be said, the finest examples of patisserie one could buy, but they were quite nourishing if somewhat cold. When microwave ovens appeared on the scene, they failed to improve Nev's pasties and, despite their time spent in the oven, they were still served half-frozen.

Ken and Trudy regularly visited schools, playgroups, fetes, Scout organisations and women's institutes with a selection of animals. They also introduced some of their animals to a wider audience on TV in programmes including *Blue Peter* and *Animal Magic*. In particular, they became good friends with the genial host of *Animal Magic*, the avuncular Johnny Morris, and frequently received invitations to appear on the programme, which was filmed in Bristol. A dressing-room was always put at their disposal where the animals could be kept in their travelling boxes until needed for filming, but Ken preferred to have the cages stacked in a corner of the studio, from where he could get to the animals quickly and without undue fuss. Sometimes Ken would appear on the programme, sometimes Trudy, but, as they grew up, the girls also appeared on the show. Never very comfortable about being live on camera himself, Ken was very impressed by how relaxed, how confident, each of his daughters seemed in front of the cameras, even as youngsters. They showed off the animals and spoke a little about them without a hint of nerves like seasoned presenters. Morris, a quietly-spoken, gentle man, liked them all but he adored Kate because she was the youngest. To Ken's great relief, increasingly he found he was able to leave it to one or other of his daughters to go on the programme in his stead, and soon the girls were appearing quite regularly, not all together but usually in rotation.

The popularity of TV programmes like *Animal Magic* was just one manifestation of the popularity of zoos in general. The 1960s witnessed an unprecedented proliferation of animal collections all over the country. By the end of the decade one new zoo (and by zoo I mean any collection of wild animals including bird gardens and aquaria) was said to open every six weeks in Britain. The decade saw the birth of the first so-called wildlife park, and the rebranding of zoos had begun. To many people, the word 'zoo' was stubbornly synonymous with concrete and bars, whereas the name 'wildlife park' conjured up an altogether more sylvan scene of unobtrusive enclosures set amongst trees and wide undulating lawns. The owner of one of these new wildlife parks – at Cricket St. Thomas in Somerset – got in touch with Ken. Had he much experience of elephants?

'What do you want to know?' Ken asked.

'Well, as you may know, here we're very fortunate that a tributary of the River Axe cuts straight through the middle of our wildlife park. In the nineteenth century it was dammed with weirs to create a series of lakes and waterfalls. We believe the view down the valley is without parallel in any other animal park in the country.'

'So what's the problem?'

'We think it would enhance the area still further to have elephants down by the river. Tell me – if we did put elephants there, d'you think they'd wander away?'

In 1968 a wildlife park opened at Sparkwell, near Plymouth, not much more than forty miles from Exmouth Zoo, founded by a former racing car driver, the idiosyncratic Ellis Bowen Daw, but it had a completely different range of goods on show, for whereas Exmouth Zoo exhibited animals from all over the world, the Dartmoor Wildlife Park was one of the new generation of collections endeavouring to specialise in just one group of animals, in this case mainly British and European mammals and birds. The Smiths got to know Ellis Daw quite well. He visited Exmouth Zoo occasionally and they let him have their lone caracara hawk, as Ellis too owned a single specimen and they thought it would be nicer to pair them up.

In 1966 a completely new concept in animal presentation was unleashed on the Great British Public when the first safari park outside Africa was opened at Longleat. For the first time in this country, in a reversal of protocol, lions roamed in comparative freedom while the visitors were in cages (their cars). Ken and Trudy visited The Lions of Longleat, as it was then called, not long after it was first opened. Unlike Gerald Durrell, who was outspoken in his contempt for safari parks, believing them to be too commercialised and lacking a serious scientific purpose, Ken thought they were, in essence, a good thing. One consequence he perhaps didn't foresee was that, having viewed animals wandering about in a fifty acre field, people would be more critical of conventional zoos where the animals were on view in much smaller spaces.

Chapter Sixteen

Ringo, Sue and Henry Too *(1967–1969)*

EVERY ZOO NEEDS ITS 'STARS', a fact of life that Ken had long recognised, and without a doubt the most popular animals at Exmouth Zoo were Ringo and Susie, the chimpanzees. Ringo in particular was a very clever ape (it doesn't automatically follow that all apes are clever). He had arrived as a baby from Charles Trevisick. When they were young, both chimpanzees were often taken to play on the beach where they would assist Ken and Trudy's daughters in building sandcastles, but Ringo, as he got older, became quite a bad-tempered, unpredictable animal, as is not unusual with adult male chimpanzees, and his visits to the beach had to stop. 'Ringo could be a stroppy old devil when he put his mind to it,' said Trudy, with feeling. Even though, by now, Ringo was quite a big, powerful and potentially very dangerous ape, this did not stop Ken continuing to enter the cage as he had always done. 'That was typical of Ken. He would casually pick up venomous snakes or go in with adult chimps. He never used to think of the danger.'

Ken would often sit in the cage with Ringo, talking to him softly. Sometimes he would pass him a comb, and Ringo, having seen enough visitors with combs to know what they were for, would use it for the purpose for which it was intended by combing Ken's hair. The sight of a chimpanzee, a look of concentration on its face, combing a middle-aged man's hair, and the man murmuring, 'Now, now, Ringo…*ouch*…don't tug, do it gently,' caused many a visitor to do a double-take. Whenever Ken had any routine work to do in Ringo's cage, he would always reassure the ape of his benign intentions by giving him a running commentary in a calm, measured tone. 'I'm just going to wipe down your shelf…that's it…nothing to get excited about…I'm just going to replace this worn-out rope, Ringo.' The inter-species relationship between them had to be seen to be believed – if then.

Opposite Ringo's cage were three bird flight cages with glass fronts. The glass got dirty very quickly and needed regular cleaning. Ken would rub at the glass with a damp newspaper, which was very effective for removing most of the smears, bird droppings and fruit residue, occasionally pausing to pick at a particularly stubborn piece of dirt with his fingernail. Ringo would sit in his cage, studying him intently, entranced by this performance. Rub and pick. Rub and pick. Then somebody had the idea of giving the ape a wet cloth to see what he would do. To everyone's amazement he copied Ken's actions exactly. First Ringo would wipe the wall, then he would stop and pick at a real or even imaginary bit of encrusted dirt, then wipe some more.

The chimpanzees were regularly given, in addition to their normal zoo diet, hot baked potatoes to eat and – especially in winter – warm Ribena to drink. They also developed a penchant for chocolates and, worse, cigarettes. The chocolates they acquired quite legitimately from Ken, the cigarettes they obtained illicitly.

It was Ken's job to refill the chocolate-dispensing machines. One of these vending machines stood next to the chimpanzee cage. As Ken moved from one machine to the next, he was usually trailed by his daughters hoping to cadge some of the chocolates, like gulls following a plough. Arriving at the vending machine by the chimpanzees, he would adopt an invariable routine. First he would load a chocolate into the machine.

'One for the machine…'

Next he would place a chocolate in Caroline, Kelsay or Kate's eagerly outstretched hand.

'One for you…'

And finally he would give a chocolate to the chimp.

'…and this one for Ringo.'

Then he would repeat the whole procedure until the vending machine was full.

More worrying was Ringo's predilection for cigarettes. Nicotine is as addictive to chimpanzees as it is to humans, and just as harmful. The zoo was popular with Marines on shore-leave, but their behaviour was less than exemplary. Laughing uproariously at Ringo and Susie's all-too-human actions, they would unthinkingly, and stupidly, offer the apes lighted cigarettes. Ringo would carefully take the cigarette in his pursed lips and, mirroring the actions of the humans he had studied doing exactly the same thing, would puff away on it like a wizened old man, much to the Marines' ribald amazement. Ringo instinctively seemed to know that one end of the cigarette was red-hot and he was very careful not to touch this end. He was extremely careful, too, not to lay the cigarette down on the sawdust- and straw-covered floor where it might cause a fire.

Ken had encountered this irresponsible behaviour in humans before. At Jersey Zoo, he had been horrified to find N'Pongo the young gorilla being offered lighted cigarettes by moronic visitors on the very first day that she was put on show to the public. He was apt to lose his temper with such people – but who can blame him? Ken, of course, was passionate about primates of all kinds. Two of the zoos he owned – Exmouth and Poole – had very good primate collections, but there were usually a few species on display at his Teignmouth Children's Zoo and Newquay Children's Zoo as well. Ever since he had visited British Guiana for the first time in 1950, he had been fascinated by the more delicate New World species in particular, convinced that eventually the problems of keeping such 'difficult' monkeys as howlers and sakis would be surmounted. It distressed him that these monkeys usually did not survive very long in captivity, for reasons which were then not fully understood. He strongly suspected that where the majority of zoos were going wrong was not giving their New World monkeys enough personal care and attention. He must have looked on with considerable interest at what the Murrayton Monkey Sanctuary (opened in 1964) near Looe in Cornwall was doing with Woolly monkeys, another South American primate that mainstream zoos were struggling even to keep alive for long, and the success that place was having. Where the Monkey Sanctuary differed from traditional zoos was that it had been founded by an enthusiast (Leonard Williams) for the sole purpose of keeping just a single species, and the selfless staff dedicated themselves tirelessly to devising new ways to entertain the monkeys. This reinforced Ken's long-held belief that pampering was the key (an over-simplification as diet and exposure to natural sunlight are very important, too). He felt strongly that what Leonard Williams had demonstrated to be fundamental for Woolly monkeys was equally applicable to sakis and other New World monkeys, and he was confident that if he ever managed to obtain Saki monkeys for Exmouth Zoo, they would exceed the British longevity record previously set by Paignton Zoo.

He did not hold out much hope that he would be able to add Saki monkeys to the collection because at that time – the late Sixties – no British zoo possessed sakis, so difficult were they to maintain. Then, out of the blue, he received a short note from a young animal-importer female friend of his by the name of Christina Wood, informing him that she had just landed a pair of wild-caught White-faced Saki monkeys in a major consignment of animals from Guyana (as British Guiana was now calling itself following independence). Would he be interested in buying them? Would he?!! Christina had sent a similar letter to Paignton Zoo, so there was no time to be lost. Ken and Trudy telephoned her immediately. They were so excited that they kept interrupting each other as they pleaded with her to let them buy the sakis.

It later turned out that Paignton Zoo had also wanted the monkeys, but was much slower in responding and consequently lost out to the Smiths. Paignton Zoo would just have to be patient until Christina could import some more.

Having been promised the monkeys, Ken anxiously awaited their arrival in Exmouth. There was, however, a delay. Having fallen deeply in love with them, Christina was unwilling to dispatch them immediately because she wanted the job of acclimatising them herself. The Smiths were unhappy about this because, by her own admission, Christina, a former journalist, was a relative novice whereas Ken had considerable experience in acclimatising newly imported animals and, not unnaturally, he believed the monkeys stood the best chance with him. As the weeks passed, he grew more and more impatient. He telephoned her every week, and each time she assured him that he would not have much longer to wait, but with every passing week her excuses for the delay became increasingly contrived. Her promises began to have a very hollow-sounding ring to them. He was always polite enough to her on the telephone and gave every indication of receiving each transparently lame excuse with equanimity, so much so that she probably never realised how much he was incensed by her procrastination, but the moment he got off the 'phone, he let his impatience and frustration show.

'Wretched, wretched woman!' he moaned bitterly to Trudy. 'Mark my words, she'll lose them! She'll lose them, I tell you!'

But, to his surprise, she didn't lose them, and when it became clear that the monkeys – which she had named 'The Old Man and his Missus' – were progressing well, Ken gradually relaxed. Everyone agreed that the reason they were thriving was because of the amount of time Christina spent with them, for as she explained:

A keeper doesn't have the time, and seldom the inclination to spend hours with just one pen of animals, talking to them, hand-feeding them, watching them closely for any sign of discomfort or fretting. I was able to do all this: I had the time and a surfeit of inclination. For hours each day I was closeted with the Old

Man and his Missus, feeding them titbits, playing with them, improving their small but comfortable cage. The relationship between us was so close that if one of them suffered so much as a twinge of indigestion I knew about it immediately.

Six weeks after the Saki monkeys had arrived in England, Christina felt they were ready for the onward journey to Exmouth. Ken and Trudy were delighted with them and continued to indulge them, with Trudy feeding them by hand such treats as chocolate cake and Smarties.

*

At one time, primate collections were blighted by a mysterious, chronic, malady for which there was no apparent remedy, known as cage-paralysis. The condition developed very slowly. One day the animal would be observed to have a slight stiffness in its hips. Within a few days it would be shuffling, rather than walking, around the cage, and increasingly it would show a disinclination to move around at all. Eventually both hind limbs would seem to become fused at the joints from the waist down and the animal would be forced to move, when it had to, in a sort of rabbit-hopping motion. The paralysis did not stop there, but would creep inexorably up the body until the stage was reached whereby an observer could be forgiven for thinking the animal had broken its neck, at which point the owner would have no option but to have it humanely destroyed.

Few zoos in those days were lucky enough to avoid cases of cage-paralysis in their primates completely. The cause was unclear, but there was a suspicion that it might be due to a vitamin or mineral deficiency of some kind. Some success had been reported in zoos which had tried daily injections of vitamins, but one can't just haul a full-grown monkey or ape out of its cage to administer regular injections.

To Ken's distress, Ringo fell victim to this creeping cage-paralysis. Before long, he was completely paralysed from the waist down, unable to move except by pulling himself along with his arms. For Ken, who had had the ape for about seven years, it was heartbreaking to see this pathetic creature slumped listless and unmoving for hour upon hour in one corner of the cage. He was advised by a primatologist to have Ringo destroyed to save further suffering. It is always hard to know when the moment has arrived to end an animal's life but when that animal is an anthropoid ape, the decision must seem akin to murder – or execution. Ringo was his friend. It was a horrible decision and one that he wished he didn't have to make, but he was ultimately responsible for Ringo's welfare and he had seen enough cases of cage-paralysis in other primates to know the eventual outcome. Still he couldn't bring himself to pick up the telephone and summon the vet to perform the deed. So he continued to make Ringo as comfortable as possible, whilst hoping for a miracle.

A few weeks earlier, two monkeys, both affected by the disease to some degree, had arrived at his Teignmouth Children's Zoo. One, an adult Celebes Crested Black macaque, was in the very early stages of the disease, the only clue that it was smitten by this terrible condition being a slight stiffness in the legs; the other, an adult male Pig-tailed macaque, was at a much more advanced stage, its legs already locked.

With Ken being based at Exmouth Zoo, his *modus operandi* was to appoint managers to run the other zoos, answerable to him and expected to consult with him before any decisions were made. Impressed by Christina Wood's expertise in dealing with the Saki monkeys, he had recently hired her to run Teignmouth Children's Zoo. The macaques had been in her charge for about a month when suddenly she had a brainwave. She began to wonder whether the solution might be as close as the local chemist's. In her animal-importer days, she had found Abidec, a pale yellow multi-vitamin solution with a very sweet smell and taste, to have certain prophylactic properties, and wondered if adding a few drops to the macaques' food might effect an improvement in their condition. It must be safe, she reasoned, because it was often recommended for human babies. First of all, she had to get permission from Ken to start dosing the monkeys.

'If Abidec in a normal dose *prevents* cage-paralysis – which I think I've proved with my own animals – then surely there's a theoretical chance that massive doses of Abidec would *cure* it?' she said.

Ken's initial response was one of scepticism. 'Christina, you don't seriously think that a simple thing like a vitamin additive would really cure bone malformation, and joints and muscles which have gone totally out of use?'

'No – but it *might*. It's worth a shot anyway. Do I have your permission to try?'

'Yes, of course, but I think you're pinning too much faith on a miracle cure.'

The way she administered it was to cut a hard-boiled egg in half and drip the viscous liquid onto the yolk, and directly hand each monkey one half of the egg. For the first few days, she put only the smallest drop of the pungent solution onto the monkeys' food to accustom them to the taste. Then she raised the quantity to the normal recommended daily dose for an adult human. Two weeks later, when there was still no sign of improvement in either animal, she doubled the dosage, then upped it still further to two-and-a-half times the normal adult human dose rate. A month after commencing treatment, she reported excitedly to Ken that the Celebes macaque had lost all stiffness in its legs and, although the improvement in the Pig-tailed macaque's condition was less profound (which was only to be expected as the disease had been at a more advanced stage), even that monkey was slightly more mobile.

Ken was full of praise for her noble efforts. 'That's excellent,' he enthused. 'Never say die, eh? Do you think the Pig-tailed macaque will yet make a full recovery?'

'Yes, Mr Smith, I believe he will.'

And she was right. Within two weeks, the Pig-tailed macaque could move its hind limbs independently of each other and after three months of treatment he was completely cured.

Once it became obvious that the two macaques were on the road to recovery, Christina tried to persuade Ken to start dosing Ringo with the Abidec, but Ken felt that, for all its wondrous properties, it wouldn't prove efficacious in Ringo's case. Ringo, he told her, was *in extremis* and, realistically, euthanasia was the only option left. But a stubborn voice in his head kept saying 'What if Christina is right? Do I not owe it to

Ringo to explore every avenue, no matter how apparently hopeless? And what have I got to lose anyway?'

So Ken gave Ringo a massive daily dose of Abidec – treble the amount usually recommended for an adult human – but, as a indication of how ill the chimpanzee was, it took five or six weeks before he showed any signs of improvement, and four months before he was completely cured. Eventually, however, he was his old energetic self once more with no hint that this was the same creature that had once been so close to death.

Christina left Teignmouth Children's Zoo after just two seasons to resume her work as an animal-importer. Having been bitten by the travel bug, she also longed to get back to the tropics. Ken mischievously nicknamed one of her two daughters, 'Bonobo', because the child's small stature reminded him irresistibly of a bonobo ape (a close cousin of the chimpanzee, sometimes misleadingly known as the Pygmy chimpanzee). Her ultimate ambition was to establish an island sanctuary in somewhere like Guyana or Suriname, release a load of animals onto it, and erect a lodge where people could come on holiday to observe the animals in a semi-free state in their natural habitat. It was a lovely, romantic dream, but sadly one that was to remain unfulfilled, for Christina died tragically young. She was cremated and her ashes were scattered on Dartmoor.

*

Exmouth Zoo was unusual among small privately-owned seaside-resort collections in exhibiting venomous snakes including rattlesnakes, adder (Common viper), Puff adder, and Gaboon viper. (This last species is noted for being the heaviest viper species and for having the longest fangs (up to two inches) and the highest venom yield of any venomous snake.) Generally, proprietors of such collections tend to shy away from keeping venomous creatures because of the risk of accidents, but few of these other collections were run by somebody as experienced as Ken Smith, who knew what he was doing. Also on display at Exmouth Zoo were Mexican Beaded lizards and Gila monsters, which have long been considered to be the only two venomous species of lizard in the world (this has recently been challenged by new research which claims some other lizards can produce toxins, notably the monitors). Both Gila monsters (pronounced 'Heela') and Beaded lizards are laggard, non-aggressive creatures that bite only in self-defence. The bite, although excruciatingly painful, is normally not fatal to human beings due to the relatively small amount of toxin delivered into the wound. Ken was very proud of the pair of Gila monsters. They were long-term residents of the zoo, having been there since about 1962. On warm days in midsummer he would take them for a walk by planting them on the sandy beach near the zoo where they could take full advantage of the sun's rays. Trudy would watch her husband in horror as he casually picked up one of the portly and potentially dangerous lizards by its fat tail so that it dangled in midair.

'Oh Ken, you mustn't,' she would implore him, with visions of one of the Gila monsters biting some innocent holidaymaker, as he set off in the direction of the crowded beach with the two reptiles.

Ken would airily shrug off her concerns. 'But they love it. Don't worry, I'll keep an eye on them. I won't let them bite anyone.'

Gila monsters may be capable of inflicting a nasty bite, but generally they are inoffensive, squat, sluggish lizards, not easily provoked. Ken understood this. He would stand guard over the lizards and if one of them started to crawl in the direction of someone's legs, he would gently prod it with his walking stick and usually this was sufficient to stop its waddling advance. Then, using the stick, he would gently steer it in another direction. Today, the thought of venomous lizards being exercised on a public beach would cause health and safety officials to have a syncopic fit; but fortunately for Ken, back then, people were not strangulated by red tape as they are now, and he could get away with this sort of thing.

Ken had worked with enough animals not to get complacent, but even he made an occasional miscalculation and pushed his luck too far. Usually any bites or scratches he sustained were fairly minor, but occasionally they were more serious. One of the worst incidents occurred late at night when he was alone in the zoo and unguardedly entered the cage belonging to the coatis and was attacked simultaneously by the two occupants. One animal wrapped itself round his leg and sank its teeth into his thigh muscle, while the other clung to his arm and mauled his shoulder. Both of them inflicted terrible injuries, and it was only with some effort that he was able to tear the enraged animals off him and escape from the cage. I asked Judy Banford (who, as Judith Bond, was Exmouth Zoo's Curator for nearly ten years) what she thought Ken had done wrong to provoke the coatis into launching such a savage attack.

'He didn't necessarily do anything wrong,' she said. 'Those coatis were unpredictable at the best of times and didn't need an excuse to turn on someone. They were a breeding pair and quite untrustworthy. Ken probably just entered the cage at the wrong time. Perhaps the female was in season or maybe she had just had a litter of babies.'

But why had he been alone in the zoo late at night?

That was so characteristic of Ken. He thought nothing of going down to the zoo at odd hours, checking everything was OK, and he always went round last thing at night to give the monkeys a drink of Ribena. All the monkeys adored Ken, and, in their own way, they all responded to him. The zoo was his joy, his passion. He was fascinated by all animals. Of course the zoo was not ideal by today's standards. The cages were quite small. But any money as he did have, which was never much, he would spend on the animals, often forgoing things himself.

I was on very friendly terms with the whole family, and on the rare occasions when he and Trudy were able to go out for the evening, I would be asked if I minded looking after the girls for a few hours. Of course I didn't mind at all. Once, when I had toothache and in urgent need of an analgesic, Ken, a firm believer in home remedies, gave me a slug of brandy and said, 'Here, try this! That'll help the pain!'

Ken and Trudy had always been an inseparable team, but the older he got, the more uxorious he became. He was thoroughly dependent on her. Judy told me, 'Every now and then throughout the day he would call out to her and she would drop whatever she was doing and hurry over to see what he wanted and to lend some assistance.' So frequently did he call her name that one of the talking birds (Judy can't remember what sort) learnt to imitate his voice. At regular intervals, the bird would pipe up, 'Trudy!...Trudy!...Trudy!' Hearing her husband's voice, Trudy would call out, 'What do you what?' to which Ken would answer, 'It wasn't me, it was that bloody bird again!'

One of Ken's favourite characters at Exmouth Zoo was a superb Papuan hornbill called Henry, who was inclined to be savage and untrustworthy towards everybody – everybody, that is, except for Ken. Henry would sit on a branch just above his head and, if it felt that Ken wasn't paying it enough attention, would gently tap him on the head with its massive beak as a less than subtle reminder to produce another grape. The remarkable thing was, it was the gentlest of taps. Even though Henry was perfectly capable of delivering a powerful hammer drill of a clout with its bill that could have inflicted a severe injury had it wanted to, it didn't – not with Ken anyway. The bird would perch on his shoulder, nibble his ear, run its beak delicately through his hair, and accept grapes from him with no evidence of the malice it displayed towards other people. They would even mutually feed each other. Ken would hold a grape between his lips and Henry would gently take it from him. Even more remarkably, the hornbill would reciprocate by offering *him* a grape in the same manner.

It is a well known fact that when the female hornbill is ready to lay her eggs, she chooses an existing cavity, usually in a tree, for her nest site. Using mud, droppings and fruit pulp, she walls herself in, sometimes assisted by the male, leaving only a narrow aperture through which her beak can protrude to receive food brought by her mate. Thus entombed, she lays and incubates her eggs, and moults, only breaking out again when the young are almost ready to fledge. Ken's daughters frequently used to joke that, had it been able to, Henry would have delighted in sealing Ken into a hollow in a tree as if *he* were a female hornbill, and passing him freshly killed lizards and other irresistible provender through the slit.

It was obvious to everyone that Henry was as fond of Ken as he was of Henry, but whilst the hornbill showed *him* absolute trust and affection, with everyone else it was an entirely different matter.

Nobody but Ken dared enter Henry's aviary.

Chapter Seventeen

Winding Down *(1969–1974)*

OVER THE YEARS, KEN HAD WRITTEN a number of short, concise, non-technical articles for various zoological periodicals including *The Avicultural Magazine*, *Animals*, *International Zoo News*, and *Zoo Life*. The articles were never more than a few pages in length and often much shorter. But now that outflow of articles abruptly and inexplicably ceases. After 1964, I have found only one more article written by Ken. Quite by chance I came across an actual typescript of this article amongst a load of papers from the Estate of Clinton Keeling. It was probably written around 1968 – though it might have been earlier. It is possible that Ken wrote later articles than this, but, if he did, I have not found them. Given the title *The Agile Angwantibo*, it is a two-page essay on cheap paper, carefully typed in red ink with generous margins, wide indents and double line-spacing. On the title page is handwritten, in blue pen, 'Copy' and the number of words (610), which clearly suggests the original was despatched to some journal editor with a view to publication. If the article *was* published, I have yet to find the edition of the magazine in which it appeared. The only clue to when it was written is a line he had added, also in pen, at the bottom of the title page: 'Sent to Lee 4/6/68'.

Who was Lee? This might have been Lee Thomas. He and Ken had always enjoyed a good working relationship, and the subject matter would certainly have appealed to him. Or perhaps the recipient was Lee Crandall, the well respected General Curator Emeritus of the New York Zoological Park, whom Ken almost certainly knew. Did Ken send Crandall a copy of the article, hoping he would offer constructive criticism on the text?

After that article, I know of no others he wrote. Why suddenly stop now?

He had long given up going abroad to see animals in their natural habitat. Ken Smith may have had animals in the blood, but not, it seems, foreign travel. His last animal-collecting expedition had been way back in 1956. After that trip he does not seem to have gone abroad again. It does seem strange that Ken, who had been so mesmerised by everything he had seen the first time he had set foot in a tropical rainforest, was able to resist the allure of the tropics for the last twenty-three years of his life. (Foreign travel had never held any allure for Trudy ever since she had suffered seasickness as a child.) I have already examined some possible explanations as to why he should have given up so suddenly, but it is quite likely that an impoverished bank account and lack of time were also major factors. Gerald Durrell, on the other hand, would continue to organise collecting trips almost to the end of his life, bringing back animals for his Jersey Zoo, but *his* agenda was different. Unlike Ken, Durrell *needed* to keep on going abroad on filming and collecting trips to provide himself with material to write about in his best-selling books, which was how he earned his living. In any case, from 1968 onwards, these were not the large-scale indiscriminate expeditions he had previously organised, but officially sanctioned rescue missions for a few select endangered species. One advantage Durrell had by this stage was a fairly large staff. He was able to leave his zoo for considerable periods of time, safe in the knowledge that it would be run efficiently *in absentia* by a board of management and a well structured chain of command, something Ken was unable to do. It was much more difficult for Ken and Trudy to get away, even for short periods. Very importantly, Gerald Durrell was childless whereas Ken had a young family to think about, and he was not prepared to leave Trudy and the children at home while he spent up to six months away on a collecting trip, even if they had been able to finance one. By the time the children were older and it might have been possible, Ken's health had let him down.

Although Ken's own globetrotting days were behind him, he derived a lot of pleasure from hearing about the overseas trips of friends and colleagues. When he learnt that Judith (Judy), his Curator, was planning to visit India and Pakistan during the winter of 1972–73 to observe the wildlife of that region, he was immediately interested and asked her if she would try, whilst out there, to obtain some animals for Exmouth Zoo. 'Nothing too big, you understand, just whatever you can find in the local markets,' he said. In particular, he told her, he was keen to get hold of some Indian and Pakistani bird species. She agreed immediately and set about investigating what import arrangements needed to be made. Ken looked forward to receiving some beautiful birds from the Orient, but he was to be doomed to disappointment for since he had last ventured into the tropics, the legislation had mushroomed and she was unable to obtain all the necessary paperwork. After weeks of getting nowhere, she finally had to admit defeat. 'Well, thanks for trying,' said Ken. 'Let me know how much you're out of pocket and I'll see you're reimbursed.' But Judith would not hear of receiving any payment for her trouble, and so, to salve his conscience, he presented her with some Indian jays, which he managed to obtain for her as a token of his appreciation. The exact identity of these birds is unclear but it is likely they were the species known today as the Indian roller, but formerly called the Blue Jay (not to be confused with the American blue jays, that still go by that label). Famed for the aerobatic displays of the male during the breeding season, the roller is emblematic of the Indian subcontinent, so much so that it has been chosen as the state bird of four Indian states.

By the early 1970s there were signs that things were getting too much for Ken, and his health began to deteriorate. He suffered the first of a series of strokes that were to plague him for the rest of his life. He had been collecting some birds for Teignmouth Children's Zoo when the first – relatively mild – attack occurred as he drove back to Exmouth. Frightening though the experience was, he somehow managed to complete the journey. Judith was dismayed as he climbed unsteadily out of the car. 'I suddenly don't feel well,' he said. His mouth was lopsided and his speech was slurred. It was obvious something dreadful had happened to him while he was out, and everything pointed to it having been a stroke. The family gathered round. Caroline asked, 'Are you all right now, Dad?'

'Fine,' he replied, indistinctly, shrugging off his ailing condition. He didn't want his family to worry.

He made the tough decision to sell the zoos at Poole and Teignmouth (Shaldon), both as going concerns, in order to concentrate all his energies on the parent collection at Exmouth. As for his Newquay Children's Zoo, that had already closed down. Newquay Urban District Council had woken up to the fact that what the resort needed as an attraction for tourists was a 'proper' zoo with lions, bears, leopards, sealions, deer, penguins, flamingos, and other such perennially popular animals. The opening of the new municipal Newquay Zoological Gardens in May 1969 (in Trenance Park, only a stone's throw from the children's zoo) sounded the death knell for Ken's attraction. The location was unfortunate. With the opening of the new, larger, and more ambitious zoo, the council (the Smiths' landlord) saw little sense in having two animal collections practically next-door to each other in Trenance Park, and gave the Smiths notice to quit by the end of the season. For four months the two collections operated concurrently, but in September 1969 the Newquay Children's Zoo closed for the final time. Its manager, Peter Lowe, transferred to Newquay Zoo to take his place as its first Curator. His appointment was greeted by rumblings of displeasure from staff at Exmouth Zoo, loyal to Ken, who regarded Peter Lowe's decision as nothing short of defection.

The closure of the Newquay Children's Zoo was followed not long afterwards by Ken relinquishing his interest in both the Teignmouth Children's Zoo and Poole Park Children's Zoo. Nobody was really surprised when Ken sold the Teignmouth Children's Zoo, but a few eyebrows were raised in surprise when he announced his intention to sell off the zoo at Poole. According to the International Zoo Year Book, Poole Zoo passed first to one B.S.A. Lunnon in about 1970 (from the same source, we find the insuppressible Lee Thomas cropping up again, this time as Curator of Poole Zoo). However, Lunnon (whoever he or she was) didn't hold the reins for long because in 1972 the zoo changed hands again. Ken's decision to disburden himself of Poole Zoo was one that some of his zoological colleagues found hard to fathom. 'I could never understand why Ken got rid of the zoo in Poole,' said Mike Curzon. 'I think in his situation, looking to downsize, *I* would've retained Poole Zoo, and off-loaded the one at Exmouth, but, for whatever reason, he chose not to do that.' This would not have been a bad idea. Poole Zoo was considerably larger in area; it was also the more popular, attracting about three times as many visitors every year as Exmouth Zoo. And there was an additional consideration: the future of Exmouth Zoo itself was far from secure, there being the small matter of the lease which was due to expire in 1977. The powers-that-be might be persuaded to renew the lease, but on the other hand they might not, in which case Exmouth Zoo would be forced to close.

So why did he and Trudy not keep Poole Zoo and vacate Exmouth Zoo instead? It seems there is no single answer but a combination of factors. Poole Council was becoming increasingly obstructive (whilst still content to help itself to a third of Poole Zoo's takings), introducing a litany of rules and regulations. Councillors didn't want any noisy or 'smelly' animals there that might disturb the serenity of the park, and they certainly didn't want any big or potentially dangerous animals that would pose a threat if they escaped. Think of the negative publicity to the town! Ken was even prevented, by an arbitrary decree from Poole Town Hall, from opening his zoo on Monday and Wednesday evenings. It got to the point that Ken and Trudy began to feel they could not operate the zoo in the way they wanted because of petty-minded bureaucrats who had no conception of the amount of hard work and worry that went into running a zoo.

The council's hardened attitude was not the only reason Ken had become disillusioned. Being situated in the middle of a public park with no one living on site, Poole Zoo had often suffered damage from vandals *(Homo terribilis)* after the staff had gone home, a problem which had been getting worse lately. Exmouth Zoo, on the other hand, was largely immune from such loutish behaviour. But undoubtedly a major reason the Smiths didn't retain ownership of Poole Zoo and renounce Exmouth Zoo instead was because it would have been too much hassle. They lived very close to their zoo at Exmouth, and even when they moved to a council house at 19 Midway, Littleham, they were still only two miles from Exmouth. To sell Exmouth Zoo and keep Poole Zoo on, they would have had to uproot and move to Dorset, and for the girls it would have meant changing schools, with the attendant inevitable upset and disruption to their education that this would have caused. In any case, it was Exmouth Zoo, not Poole Zoo, which had always held a warm place in Ken and Trudy's affections. Exmouth had been the first zoo he had truly been able to call his own and, irrespective of its limitations, it had always been his favourite. Perhaps *this* was the main reason he didn't keep Poole Zoo on.

Having committed himself to Exmouth Zoo, Ken was determined to make improvements. In 1972, in spite of his own failing health, he and Trudy excitedly drew up plans to expand the zoo into the grassy area at the rear of the building. Here they had about half an acre at their disposal, but it was enough to create some outside aviaries and other exterior pens at last, increasing the scope of the collection. Exmouth Urban District Council gave the zoo a small grant of five hundred pounds to assist in fencing the plot of land, while a legacy from the estate of one Alvin Bransgrove of Auckland, New Zealand, paid for the construction of a range of seven largish aviaries for various hawks, parrots, pheasants and curassows.

The early 1970s brought deep sadness as well. On 3 March 1973, Gertrude died of heart failure in a Bournemouth nursing home at the grand old age of ninety-three. She had seen much, lived through two world wars, the 1918 influenza pandemic and the Great Depression of the 1930s, raised five children and had her heart broken by the untimely death of her only daughter, but now it was time to go. Her youngest son, Frank, was the informant. For the last thirty years of her life she had lived in Parkstone, for most of that time at 21 Dunford Road. Ken had used to visit his mother quite regularly when he had lived in Paignton and he had resumed these visits when he moved to Exmouth. Only during the four years that he was in Jersey was he unable to see her as often as he would have liked.

'My grandmother lived in a house in Upper Parkstone, and very often I used to go there after school,' recalled Brian Smith. 'She lived on her own and had space where I was allowed to indulge my hobbies of chemistry and radio. It was at her house that I watched the first moon landing in 1969, viewing the amazing BBC pictures several seconds after the shortwave radio commentary. I also happened to be there a few times when Ken visited his mother. He never stayed long; he always seemed to be in a rush.'

Gertrude's death marked the beginning of Ken's long, slow decline. He had always enjoyed a warm relationship with his mother, as evidenced by the fact that, although her death was hardly unexpected in view of her extreme old age, he was visibly distraught at her passing. Trudy summed up everyone's feelings. 'She was a lovely old lady who always made us feel very welcome.'

*

In 1974 the new extension to Exmouth Zoo was ready to be opened to the public. Notes made by Robert Bradshaw during a visit a few years later reveal this outside area held a disparate, but extremely interesting, mixture of creatures – buzzards, kestrels, Barn and Tawny owls, peafowl, a pair of turacos, a Crested curassow, a pair of guans, a White-nosed coati ('very distinctive looking animal, dark coat, variable shades'), a nice trio of pumas, a Patas monkey, a Crab-eating macaque, a big male Barbary macaque, and a group of Nigerian Pygmy goats. Exmouth Zoo was also one of comparatively few zoos in those days to give its tamarins access to an outside enclosure (so accustomed are we to seeing marmosets and tamarins outside in zoos that we forget that at one time they were generally regarded as too delicate to be housed in anything other than permanently heated buildings).

Also found in this new area (when not gripped by a sense of wanderlust) was a pair of Crested screamers, big ground-dwelling birds affiliated to the waterfowl, with bodies about the size of a large goose but with longer legs. At first, the screamers were not feather-clipped, as Ken believed this would spoil their appearance. Most of the time they were content to stay in their pen, but occasionally a desire to rove would overcome them and they would take to the wing, flapping over the pay-desk to touch down, a trifle inelegantly, on The Maer, a large expanse of grass outside the zoo, or, if they misjudged their landing, in the middle of the coach park or sometimes even further afield. Ken would then get an urgent call from a concerned member of the public to say that two 'weird-looking ducks' had been spotted in the town and were they anything to do with the zoo? Returning them to the zoo was never a problem. They were obliging birds and all Ken or Trudy had to do was to get behind them and slowly walk them back home. But their airborne antics were an inconvenience, and Ken was worried that sooner or later they would get knocked down by a car or a coach, and eventually he conceded to clip their feathers to prevent their periodic escapes.

By now the zoo was attracting 33,000 visitors a year. It deserved more. By comparison, Exmouth Aquarium was receiving over 38,000. The zoo claimed to be the first in Britain to breed and rear the kinkajou. If true, it would have been one in the eye for the bigger establishments with their superior accommodation and scientifically-devised diets, and Ken really did believe he had succeeded where all the other zoos had failed, but unfortunately he was mistaken. The earliest record I can find for Exmouth Zoo breeding the species is 1973, whereas Belle Vue Zoo was breeding kinkajous as long ago as 1960, with Chester Zoo following suit in 1963. In the Sixties, Belle Vue was breeding the species annually. It is surprising that Ken, knowledgeable and well-read as he was, should have been unaware of the achievement of these other zoos.

The kinkajou babies were hand-reared and very appealing. Other breeding successes at Exmouth Zoo included the coatis (these were the less commonly seen Costa Rican form) which bred to several generations, the galagos, Slender lorises, and the pumas.

A small portico in front of the building had been divided into compartments for the larger animals such as the pumas. The breeding pair, Apollo and Amigo, produced litters consistently well over several years, but the first time they did so was unexpected. One day a visitor went up to Caroline and asked, 'How old are the pumas?'

'About six or seven years,' she replied.

'No, no, no,' the visitor snapped impatiently, 'I mean the small ones, you know, the babies.'

Caroline was mystified. 'Babies?'

She relayed this surprising development to her parents, and when Trudy investigated she was surprised to find several newborn cubs in the cage. They had obviously not fed, so she stuffed them up her jumper and took them back to the house to rear them by hand. At first they required bottle-feeding every three hours both day and night, but the Smiths' tireless efforts were rewarded because they grew up into fine, strong animals – strong being the operative word, as Caroline explained:

> If a half-grown puma decides to stretch itself out on the settee, and you want to sit down to watch telly, but the animal refuses to budge, well, there's not a lot you can do about it. I mean, who would argue with a puma? They won the argument every time. It was fun to see the expression of disbelief, not unmixed with fear, on people's faces whenever we had guests round. As they were ushered into the sitting-room, they were confronted with the sight of a big cat draping itself across the furniture, but eventually we had to send the cubs to another zoo.

Ken appreciated true friendship and he could be very generous. One recipient of his kindness was his good friend, Charles Trevisick. Among the attractions at Trevisick's small zoo at Comyn Hill was a breeding pair of pumas. The pair's first litter consisted of two fine healthy cubs. As much as the female appeared to be an exemplary mother and the cubs seemed to be flourishing, Trevisick was concerned that they were not putting on weight quickly enough, and he decided to supplement the natural milk they were getting from their mother with regular bottle-feeds. In reality, as Trevisick himself admitted, this was done more as an excuse to cuddle the cubs than from any real anxiety Trevisick felt that they were not developing properly. Fortunately his female puma was trusting of human beings and did not seem unduly upset when, twice every day, she was enticed away from her offspring. Not surprisingly, after watching the cubs sucking greedily at the teat, all the children who visited the zoo wanted to feed or stroke them too, but the age when they could be safely handled by strangers had past, and, much as he would have liked, Trevisick didn't dare take the risk in case a child got scratched or bitten.

Then Ken happened to ring him on another matter, and Trevisick explained his predicament. 'The cubs are so appealing that everyone wants to pet them, but I know it

Ken saw one of his most important roles as being to infuse people, especially young people, with an interest for the natural world. © *Tiverton Gazette*.

'Your Dad used to work here.' KS takes time off from running Jersey Zoo for a short break in England, possibly staying in London, during which he took the opportunity to return to Whipsnade Zoo, this time as a visitor, with Caroline, early 1960s.

Left: The creature on the left is a kinkajou. Kinkajous bred very successfully at Ken's Exmouth Zoo. The zoo claimed to be the first in the U.K. to breed the species. This, however, turned out to be untrue. The monkey on Ken's other arm has been identified as a White-throated guenon, a great rarity from Nigeria and Benin. © *Western Times*. Right: This young cassowary originally had the run of Ken's Poole Park Zoo. Typical of cassowaries, it became very unfriendly and untrustworthy towards visitors as it matured. © *Western Times*.

Left: Trudy and fox cubs. Right: Trudy with baby White-nosed coatis, a species seen in captivity much less frequently than the commoner Ring-tailed coati. Ken had a reputation for exhibiting animals at his Exmouth Zoo that were not normally seen in British zoos at that time. © *Chris Ware*.

The perfect upbringing. Having been surrounded by a wide variety of animals from birth, Ken and Trudy's daughters developed none of the inhibitions and phobias that beset children raised in households where animal contact is minimal or non-existent. Here, Kelsay confidently handles a Carpet python. © *Western Times.*

Kate feeding a baby kinkajou.

Left: Kelsay and kinkajou. © *Robert Chapman*. Right: The back of this photograph is annotated 'Ringo & Kate'. However, Trudy told me that Ringo the chimpanzee was too boisterous and unpredictable to be allowed onto a public beach and it is more likely the chimp pictured is Susie, Ringo's more sedate companion. Exmouth Zoo can be clearly seen in the background. © *Freddie Collins*.

Kelsay and Kate play Snakes and Ladders, with real snakes. © *John D. Drysdale.*

Kate with a Blomberg's toad, Exmouth Zoo.
Blomberg's toad is the world's *longest*
species of toad (and not, as some books
erroneously state, the *largest*: that distinction
belongs to the Cane toad). © *John D. Drysdale.*

Holding a sprig of mistletoe, Kelsay plants a festive kiss on the nose of a tame muntjac called Bambi (what else!) at Exmouth Zoo in one of the last photos taken before the zoo closed its doors for the final time.

A frail, uncharacteristically unjacketed, Ken Smith (but still wearing a tie) deals with a powerful anaconda at Exmouth Zoo, 1970s. © *Edward Lucas*.

What was once Exmouth Zoo is now an amusement arcade. In the foreground is the coach park that was a major reason for the zoo's demise.

> **Zoological Society of London**
> **LEMUR ISLAND**
> Dedicated to the memory of
> Gerald Durrell
> Author
> Founder of Jersey Wildlife Preservation Trust
> Student Keeper Whipsnade Wild Animal Park 1945/46
> Opened by
> Dr Lee Durrell
> 12th May 1998

The Gerald Durrell Memorial Plaque on the Lemur House at ZSL Whipsnade Zoo. Ken was employed at Whipsnade Zoo at the same time as Gerald Durrell but, unlike Durrell, no commemorative inscription or other memorial exists to him there or at any of the other zoos where he had worked.

A remarkable bond between bird and man. This photo, perhaps more than any other, illustrates the affection Ken had for all creatures. Henry, a Papuan hornbill, behaved very affectionately towards Ken but could be savage and untrustworthy towards anybody else. © *Les Owen.*

wouldn't be safe. Even with someone they know, they make quite a show of aggression with unsheathed claws and bared teeth when they are first picked up, though they soon relax when they see the bottle.'

'You're probably right,' said Ken; 'I wouldn't chance it. A puma cub, even one a few weeks old, can do some damage.' He paused as if in contemplation. 'Hmm, I tell you what, it's a long time since we met – how about getting together for a chat?'

'That's a good idea. Where?'

'I suggest Crediton. It's about equidistance from Ilfracombe and Exmouth, and we could meet in the teashop there.'

When they met up a few days later, Ken listened sympathetically while Trevisick talked at greater length about the puma cubs and how all the children were clamouring to hold them and their acute disappointment on being told they could not.

'Perhaps,' said Ken, sliding his hand into his pocket, 'I might be able to help.'

Allowing himself a wry grin, he slowly and carefully pulled his hand out of his pocket and opened his fingers. Sitting in the palm was a tiny three-week-old puma cub. It was so young that its eyes had only just begun to open, but at that moment they were just narrow slits.

'He's yours – if you'd like him. His name is Puddy. Ordinarily I wouldn't have taken him from his mother at such an early age, but there were four in the litter and she couldn't cope. But you'll need to bottle-feed him for some time yet, at two-hourly intervals to begin with, day and night. When he gets a bit older, you should be able to exercise him round your zoo on a lead, and I confidently predict that, having been raised in the house, he will take to being handled by your younger visitors with equanimity, at least until he gets too heavy to pick up.'

Trevisick was overwhelmed by Ken's magnanimity. As Ken forecast, Puddy became the star attraction at Ilfracombe Zoo, with some children badgering their parents into taking them to the zoo almost every day during the school holidays to see him. Such was the level of 'Puddymania' (there is no other word for it), eventually Trevisick had to restrict the cub's personal appearances, imposing set times for Puddy to met his adoring public and charging a nominal fee (donated to charity) for children to have their photo taken holding him in their arms.

*

The 1970s were a difficult time for many businesses, with industrial strife, frequent power blackouts and galloping inflation. Suddenly utility services like electricity and water soared, as did rent and rates, animal feed, veterinary services, and all the other bills. All businesses were affected, but those that depended on a healthy tourism industry, like Exmouth Zoo, even more so. Animals continued to arrive – by now the collection comprised about 260 specimens of more than 120 species – but Ken was reaching an age when most men would be thinking of retirement and increasingly the effort of running the zoo was proving too much of a strain for him. Caroline, Kelsay and Kate helped out in the evenings after school, as they had always done, but still it was a struggle. In the fourteenth edition of the International Zoo Year Book (relating to the year 1972), for the first time Trudy was named as Exmouth Zoo's Assistant Director, a sign that Ken was having to rely on her more and more. A regular feature of the Year Book, this extensive but incomplete list of the world's zoos and aquaria depended on the co-operation of zoo directors and curators to complete the questionnaire sent every year from the Year Book office based at the Zoological Society of London. This was the last time the questionnaire would be filled in by Ken – or anyone else from Exmouth Zoo, for that matter. From then onwards, two ominous words appeared after Exmouth Zoo's entry in the International Zoo Year Book: *No reply*. It was as if Ken could no longer be bothered to fill in the questionnaire. By the eighteenth edition (for 1976), Exmouth Zoo's entry, still with the words *No Reply* appended to it, had been reduced to less than two-and-a-half lines. In the 1978 listing it had disappeared altogether.

There were indications that Ken was growing weary of life's struggle, a situation only exacerbated by his mother's death. He had, as far as anyone can tell, long given up writing articles for zoological magazines. His failure now to provide data for the Year Book was a further sign that he was slowing down, although he did work on a long-overdue new edition of the zoo's guide book. And things were set to get a lot worse. His zoo, which had provided recreation for countless holidaymakers and residents alike, was increasingly being seen by some of the more insular councillors as a nuisance, a relic of a bygone era when small seaside collections were all the vogue. They ignored the fact that by featuring regularly on television the zoo was a source of publicity for the town, bringing people to Exmouth who otherwise might never have come to the resort, but this, apparently, counted for nothing. The council increased the rent to a level that Ken could barely afford, whilst forgetting about its obligation to maintain the building's exterior, which continued to deteriorate. The council, which had once welcomed a zoo in Exmouth, was becoming increasingly antagonistic. The fact that the zoo occupied prime land right on the seafront made the site, in the eyes of some councillors, an attractive proposition for redevelopment.

But if the zoo were to be swept away, what could replace it? Unbeknownst to Ken and Trudy, a few nebulous ideas had already been discussed, and discarded. Then someone on the council suggested enlarging the coach park adjacent to the zoo.

'Regrettably this does mean the zoo will have to go.'

A ripple of interest circulated round the council chamber.

Chapter Eighteen

'We Feel Like Shuttlecocks' *(1975–1979)*

As 1975 GOT UNDERWAY, Exmouth Zoo had on display over 260 mammals, birds, reptiles and amphibians of no fewer than 126 species, looked after by three employees. Ken and Trudy would usually go home at about five o'clock for a meal, leaving their three daughters to look after the zoo. They would return later in the evening, and it was not unusual for work to finish as late as half past seven to eight o'clock, or occasionally even later. The animals ranged in size from the pumas, chimpanzees and a tame muntjac called Bambi at one end of the scale to lizards, frogs and a young Blue tit at the other. The Blue tit was not long out of the nest and was brought in by a woman into whose washing on the line the bird had flown. Tentative Tom, as he was known, hadn't hurt himself – or not much, anyway – by his collision with the lady's smalls but, having had such an unnerving experience at such a young age on what probably had been his maiden flight, he flatly refused to fly away in case of further mishap, hence his name. Tentative Tom was a charming, if slightly imbecilic, character. Flies had to be caught for him, and chicken eggs had to be hard-boiled and chopped for him. The 'Tom' part of his name was after 'tomtit', an alternative name for the Blue tit, and if Tom eventually turned out to be a female, Ken and Trudy had an answer for that: they could always say it was short for Tomasina or – or something.

Another animal character who stamped his personality on everyone he met was little Gitahtavit, a Nigerian Pygmy goat kid. When Gitahtavit was born in 1975, his mother looked at him with unaccountable distaste and would have nothing further to do with him. So Ken and Trudy took him home and hand-reared him. But the little kid, like any high-spirited young child, soon made his presence felt by getting into mischief. Soon he was into everything, chewing whatever he found to see if it was edible (and, to a goat, almost anything is edible), tripping people up, and generally getting in everyone's way, causing Ken or Trudy to cry in an exasperated tone of voice, 'Get aht of it.' Being so frequently admonished in this fashion, he soon came to believe this was how he was known and, instead of fleeing the scene of carnage as instructed, he came on all the more in response to – as he thought – his name being called. Admitting defeat, Ken – working on the principle that if you can't beat 'em, join 'em – agreed that henceforth the little goat kid should be known as 'Gitahtavit'.

At around this time, Exmouth Zoo published a new edition of its guide book, some twelve years after the first. It was to be its last guide book. A slim, precious publication, at only nine pages (including the inside back cover), it was just over half the length of its predecessor. A fetching picture of nine-year-old Kate with a tame kinkajou, identified only as 'Baby kinkajou and child', graced the front cover. Mindful that (back then) a woeful number of animal collections were run by inexperienced and clueless dilettantes whose unprofessional activities threatened to drag all zoos into disrepute, Ken was quick to establish, right from the introduction, his own bona fides to be in charge of a zoo. The guide book made it clear that he had plenty of experience of handling animals, both in the wild and in zoos. As a perfunctory reference to a 'zoological collecting' expedition he had once been on to Aden and North-east Africa showed, he had absorbed some of Gerald Durrell's flair for exaggeration and poetic licence. Ken's early sally to this part of the world cannot be counted as an animal-collecting expedition in the strict sense of the term because he was in the RAF at the time, and merely captured some of the smaller desert creatures he had encountered during his leisure time. By the mid 1970s, a tide of anti-zoo feeling was rising in Britain, which most zoos, complacently, were very slow to counter. In an effort to quell detractors, he took this opportunity to put the case for zoos.

'Zoos,' he wrote,

serve many important functions, although in the past they have sometimes been the object of criticism. Nowadays they are regarded as places of entertainment and relaxation for the visiting public; as each year goes by life gets more artificial and complex, so that wandering around a zoo or wild life park comes as a relief from the industrialism or urban way of living to which we have become accustomed. The zoo acts as a kind of oasis or refuge from the strains of modern life for visitors.

Entertainment arouses interest, and interest leads to a desire for knowledge, to education, so that these dual purposes of a zoo become intertwined. From education a more advanced form of learning is developed, often resulting in scientific studies, so that zoos can become centres for research.

But a new approach to zoo work has developed, dovetailing into these functions. The new approach or attitude is concerned, often actively, with conservation and with maintaining and breeding species of fauna which are being threatened with extinction in their natural habitats.

With the advancement of civilisation in places which were once remote areas of the world, and the growth of human populations in all continents, wild life has had to pay the price for man's progress. Vast areas of virgin forest, of marshland and other natural terrain, have been destroyed or transformed by mankind. Animal, bird and fish [*sic*] populations have often been wiped out or fragmented in the process and in consequence zoos, wild life parks and similar organisations have become increasingly important in the fields of preservation and conservation. They are able to help by building up reserve populations of animals to those still existing in the dwindling wildernesses.

Zoos have often become places of refuge for rare animals, sanctuaries for creatures sorely pressed in their native or natural homes. The management and control of zoos has altered and improved in recent times, and much money and effort is expended towards the provision of larger enclosures, paddocks and aviaries. Zoo denizens benefit also from better diets, more accurate control of temperature and humidity conditions, also from the wealth of knowledge now circulated and made available among the zoos all over the world.

It is surprising that Ken should have made the fundamental error of referring to 'animals, birds and fish' when, as a zoologist, he knew perfectly well that birds and fish were animals, too. What he meant, of course, was '*mammals*, birds and fish'. His lapse is even more extraordinary in view of the fact that he – correctly – made a distinction between 'preservation' and 'conservation', because the two terms, contrary to popular belief, are not synonymous.

Ken believed that if zoos didn't exist, somebody would have to invent them. His argument that zoos were an essential component of human society, and likely to become even more important in the future, was a timely piece of rhetoric, but while this was fine for larger zoos with big budgets, the reality was that Exmouth Zoo was in no position to indulge in scientific research *or* to initiate breeding programmes for endangered species with a view to saving them from extinction. There was never enough money to go round, even for the essential things. Paying the staff wages was a constant problem, which was why the zoo had always had to rely to some extent on school-leavers or teenagers helping out at weekends and after school. The zoologist Clinton Keeling, who had once had his own small zoo in Derbyshire and knew from personal experience just what was involved, was scathing about what he saw as a flawed practice:

> I think the only thing [at Exmouth Zoo] of which I could not really approve – although I cannot really complain about it as I have been forced to do the same myself – was the utilisation of offspring and teenage 'volunteers' as staff, which in my opinion is rarely really satisfactory, as employing the former often leads to domestic trouble and as a rule the latter are worse than useless: the trouble is, of course, it is usually done of necessity for economic reasons.

Over the years Exmouth Zoo had had its share of no-hopers: what are known in the zoo world as 'bunny-huggers' – mostly young people, still at school or fresh from it, who believe that all the job involves is close physical contact with the animals, but are unprepared for, even shocked by, the hard graft of mucking out or the unglamorous task of preparing gory meat for the carnivores. It was not always possible, at the interview stage, to discern who would make a good animal-keeper, hard-working and conscientious, and who would not; but sometimes a young person did appear who displayed all the admirable qualities that the Smiths were looking for. Nigel Wilkinson, who is now the managing director of a website design company based in Exmouth, had a weekend job at the zoo from 1976 (when he was just thirteen years old) until he left school in 1979.

1976 is memorable for being the year of the Great Drought, when, for weeks on end, the sun beat down relentlessly from a clear blue sky and daytime temperatures in some parts of the country regularly topped 90°F (32.2°C). It was the hottest summer Britain had experienced since records began. Heaths and woodlands burned. Rivers became little more than trickles and some ran dry completely, as did many reservoirs. £500 million worth of crops failed and, as a consequence, food prices rose by 12 per cent – which hit Exmouth Zoo hard. Although the majority of the animals were tropical species, many of them felt the heat acutely. So severe was the drought that the crowd at Lord's Cricket Ground cheered when a few drops of rain stopped play for a quarter of an hour in mid-June. Parts of southwest England went forty-five days in July and August without any rain at all and public standpipes were in use in Devon and other parts of the country as water supplies dwindled. It wasn't just the lack of water or the escalating food prices that were having a detrimental effect on the zoo's fortunes. The only thing most holidaymakers to the resort wanted to do was to laze on the beach like comatose seals. In extreme conditions like these, zoos near the coast could not be expected to do record business, but Exmouth's, with most of the exhibits indoors, was in a worse predicament. When the downpour that the nation had been praying for finally did arrive, perhaps predictably it chose the August bank holiday.

Nigel Wilkinson relished the close contact with many of the animals that his weekend job at the zoo afforded him. 'Exmouth Zoo was a fantastic little place – I loved it, but without doubt the small size of the cages contributed to its eventual demise,' he told me.

> The zoo exhibited some extremely unusual animals that I had never seen or, in some cases, even heard of before, such as kinkajous and the smaller marmosets. Ken and Trudy specialised in quirky little animals like that. There were familiar animals too, but it was the rarer ones I found most interesting. I had visited the zoos at London and Paignton but even big, historic zoos like those didn't have some of the animals that the Smiths possessed at Exmouth. I was paid 20p an hour, which was not much for a Saturday job even then – most of my mates were grumbling about being paid as little as £1 an hour in *their* part-time jobs – but I didn't mind because I was doing something I enjoyed, and Ken was a fantastic guy, very dedicated to what he was doing. Some people who are good with animals don't get on well with other people. Ken wasn't like that at all: he was a people-person, too.
>
> It was wonderful to work with so many marvellous animals. I would hold hands through the bars with Ringo the chimp, which I thought was a tremendous privilege. But one of my favourite animals was the Barbary macaque. As a treat I used to feed it melon pips and custard tarts.
>
> I remember they had a breeding pair of kinkajous, which I was warned could be quite vicious and on no account was I to go in with them. Even Ken, who had a way with most animals, couldn't handle them. But we also had a young hand-reared kinkajou and that was a delight. It did have one slightly unpleasant habit, though, which was to climb up my back and sit on my head while I stood at the sink washing the animal food pots. I didn't mind that but sooner or later the end of its tail would drop into the cold shitty water and then it would wrap the clammy wet tail around my neck.

But not all the animals were as friendly towards Nigel as the baby kinkajou or the Barbary macaque. One of the hornbills, well disposed towards everybody else, took an instant dislike to him for some unknown reason and, without any provocation, attacked him when he entered the aviary, and Ken had to intervene to get the bird off him before it could inflict serious injury. Funnily enough, however, one of the fiercest creatures Nigel confronted was also one of the unlikeliest, as he explained to me:

> As I've said, the zoo had some very rare and unusual creatures, and yet paradoxically some of the most popular animals were rabbits, guinea-pigs and goats, that sort of thing. I don't know if this bothered Ken after he had gone to so much trouble to obtain animals that set his zoo apart from most other seaside menageries. I suppose it must have done. Anyway, a new rabbit had just arrived. Ken warned me it was aggressive, but I thought he was pulling my leg. 'Oh yeah,' I thought, 'very funny. It's a rabbit; what can it possibly do to me?' Well, I soon found out the first time I tried to clean it out. It clawed me down both my arms. Really nasty. It was like something straight out of that film, *Monty Python and the Holy Grail*, you know, the scene with the killer rabbit! By that stage I had been in with pumas, coatis, mongooses, Silver foxes – but it was the rabbit that got me!

One of the pumas was regularly exercised along the beach on a lead to the incredulity, not unmixed with consternation, of some of the other users of the beach. It was a hand-reared animal, and quite tame. Nigel regrets that he was never invited to walk the puma.

> I always hoped Ken would ask me,' he said, 'but he never did. Perhaps he thought I wasn't strong enough to control it. But I would have loved to have been given that job because it would have been so *cool*. I was a normal teenage boy, remember, and to be seen with a puma on a lead would have been a sure-fire way to impress all the nubile bikini-clad girls on the beach. So much more impressive than a Dalmatian or a collie, a puma has a "wow!" factor that a dog on a lead just doesn't have.'

*

The last decade of Ken Smith's life was a very difficult one for him. By now he was not a well man. Photographs taken around this time show him looking frail and tired. The death of his mother, though hardly unexpected, and the severance of his roots this brought about, was a hefty hammer blow. But now, as if he didn't have enough to contend with, storm clouds were coalescing over Exmouth Zoo: dark, forbidding, nimbostratus clouds, ominous and intense, that would soon threaten the very existence of the zoo. There was mounting and often unfair criticism of the little zoo he had helped launch back in 1956, and of which he had been the owner and director since 1962. Increasingly, Exmouth Zoo represented the old-style menagerie, the animals in small or relatively small cages. Back in the 1960s this had been seen as quite acceptable and the norm in most zoos, but by the mid-Seventies the pendulum of public opinion was swinging against keeping animals in this way. Gerald Durrell always maintained that many animals do surprisingly well in smallish enclosures, a view supported by Clinton Keeling (possibly the only thing on which the two men did agree) – but Durrell and Keeling were in the minority. The general public, accustomed to regularly seeing spectacular images on television of animals in their natural habitat, was becoming more critical. Suddenly cages which were once looked on as acceptable were now considered anachronistic. Many zoos were able to adapt by building bigger and bigger enclosures, placating all but the most hardened detractors, but Exmouth Zoo was unable to do this. Like an arthropod encased in a rigid exoskeleton, there was no room for expansion. Perhaps the best course of action, had anybody suggested it, would have been to redefine the place's whole ethos, phase out the bigger animals such as the pumas, chimpanzees and monkeys, and concentrate on smaller fry – reptiles, amphibians, fish and invertebrates, rodents, tree-shrews, and some of the nocturnal prosimians and small carnivores. After all, indoor zoos have not gone away – they are with us still – but these days they tend to adopt a rainforest theme (good examples are Tropical World in Leeds and The Living Rainforest in Berkshire) and specialise in showing some of the smaller denizens of the tropics. Perhaps the big mistake Exmouth Zoo made was to remain a general collection without a unifying theme. Although the animals were well looked after, the cages were in a poor state of repair and really needed to be replaced.

Mike Curzon told me, 'I was surprised by how rundown the zoo looked, but the animals themselves appeared to be in fine fettle – and that's the true barometer. Whenever I visited, Ken and Trudy were always there, but on most of my visits I don't recall seeing any staff. I know they did employ staff, but never very many – they couldn't afford to – and that may have been the problem. So much to do and just never enough hours in the day. Of course their daughters used to help out whenever they could. In fact, the whole family was devoted to the animals.'

It didn't help when the old Exmouth Urban District Council was absorbed into East Devon Council. This *uber*-council immediately increased the zoo's rent and rates quite substantially and reneged on its obligation to maintain the outside of the building (in fact very little had been spent on repairs and maintenance in all the years the zoo had been open, with the result that the building was now in a poor condition). Ken, visibly buckling under the strain, began to suspect that the council, whilst it was content to extract a king's ransom in rent and rates from him, no longer really *wanted* a zoo there.

He wasn't wrong. After bandying about a half-baked idea to turn the site into some sort of adventure playground, the council drew up plans to remove the zoo in order to extend the coach park (at a projected cost to the council of up to £12,000). The irony was not lost on the Smiths. The council was proposing to sweep away one of Exmouth's all-weather attractions to replace it with a larger coach park to accommodate all the day-trippers and holiday-makers lured to the coastal resort precisely *because* of those same attractions. By preferring coaches to coatis and curassows, the council showed itself to be indifferent to the wishes of the majority of voters for the zoo enjoyed a lot of support from Exmouth residents who, unlike the intransigent, faceless, bureaucrats calling the shots, recognised the town would be the poorer if it lost its zoo. Fortunately the Smiths had a vociferous ally in the form of the *Exmouth Journal*. 'Wasteful and unnecessary' was how the *Journal* described the plan. The zoo's lease was due to expire on 30 September 1977, and the omens were that East Devon Council's Amenities Committee would not be renewing it (in the event it was extended several times while the argument dragged on). Although Ken and Trudy were willing to negotiate further with the council, they got the strong impression that the council had made up its mind already and would not be swayed whatever arguments were presented in favour of keeping the zoo open. It was unfortunate that the leader of the council, Mr Ted Pinney, who lived not in Exmouth but in Sidmouth, had emerged as one of the zoo's most outspoken opponents. He had paid a fleeting visit to the zoo in an unofficial capacity, without the knowledge of the Smiths, prior to a meeting of the Amenities Committee in January 1978. Conveniently forgetting that it was the council's responsibility to maintain the building, at this meeting he gratuitously described Exmouth Zoo as 'a dreadful place. The whole place reeked of piddle and I was astonished that anything publicly owned could be in that state. I really don't think it is suitable for a zoo. It is not a zoo. It is quite unsuitable.'

In flagrant contravention of normal council etiquette, Mr Pinney expressed his contemptuous remarks in open committee during the discussion of another subject. This was a serious error of judgement on his part. Since the discussion of leases was supposed to be confidential and should not have been mentioned in open session, his comments were embarrassing to the council, which was forced to eat humble pie by writing to the Smiths, apologising for this unacceptable breach of protocol.

The battle lines were drawn. Leading the charge for the Smiths was the *Exmouth Journal*, riled not only by the fact that Ted Pinney was attempting to undermine Ken's impeccable credentials, but also because he had the presumption to interfere in Exmouth affairs. As the zoo was situated *in* Exmouth, the final decision on the future of the zoo should, the *Journal* declared, be left to the people *of* Exmouth. It is obvious from the tone of the editorial that the paper had no time for bumbledom in general and Mr Pinney in particular, whom it wasted no opportunity to lambaste, as the following extract shows:

> Having regard to the esteem in which Mr. Smith is held in the realms of zoology throughout the world, it could be said with some justification that Mr. Smith's eminence in his sphere is far greater than that of Mr. Pinney's in his, and it is unfortunate that Mr. Smith, unlike Mr. Pinney, has no official platform from which to refute Mr. Pinney's allegations…It is true that the building is not ideal for a zoo, but if there is to be any blame for that, it must rest with the local authority for allowing it to be used as such before the Smiths acquired the lease.

The castigation of the zoo was not confined to Ted Pinney. His views were shared by a Mr William Faulkner who, unlike the articulate but outspoken Mr Pinney, *was* an Exmouth resident. Whilst coming down firmly in the Pinney camp, William Faulkner did concede, however, that the 'health people' who had visited the zoo from time to time could find nothing wrong with it, 'although complaints have been made over the last five years'. He was, however, vague as to the nature of these complaints or who had received them. In fact, in over five years, just two complaints about the zoo had been lodged with the Information Bureau in Exmouth, and one of *those* concerned the price of admission.

Trudy told a lively meeting that the zoo attracted about 30,000 visitors a year and, far from being the bad advertisement for Exmouth that Mr Faulkner claimed, was a vital amenity and the source of a good deal of national publicity for the town. 'Furthermore,' she said, 'if its unique collection of animals is broken up, it can never be replaced.'

The Secretary of the Exmouth Ratepayers' Association, Mrs Maureen Chandler, agreed. 'The sea front needs amenities and I feel we should keep the zoo,' she said. 'It is a pity it has been allowed to get into this state over the years, but it would be a great mistake to pull it down.'

A former chairman of the old Exmouth Urban District Council came, unsolicited, to the support of Ken and Trudy. Mr Ernest Stewart, with a lifetime of service to the country and in public office behind him, waded into the debate by reminding East Devon Council of its obligations and why Exmouth Zoo, despite its rundown state, was important and worth fighting for. He told the *Exmouth Journal*:

> The council is supposed to maintain the building under the terms of the lease given by the old Exmouth Urban Council. If there are any faults in the building, it is the council's responsibility.
>
> The Smiths, to my knowledge, co-operated in every way with the Exmouth Urban Council, and I believe with East Devon Council.
>
> They brought something new to Exmouth. They have preserved rare animals and have looked after and cared for casualties, both birds and animals [*mammals*]. Exmouth Zoo is worth preserving, despite what Mr. Pinney may say.

But Mr Stewart's impassioned plea fell on deaf ears. At a meeting of the Amenities Committee in April, East Devon Council formally served Exmouth Zoo with a notice to quit when its lease ran out in the autumn. Ken and Trudy were dismayed by the decision, but not surprised.

In a statement following the announcement Trudy said, 'Apart from our personal feelings on the matter, the zoo is one of Exmouth's attractions, and its closure would be a great loss to the town. The number of visitors to the area is expected to increase, yet this reduces amenities for them once they get here.'

Ken added, 'We are engaging solicitors to see what can be done to keep the zoo open. I agree that the present premises are not ideal in many ways, but we have someone who is prepared to join us and finance improvements. We are prepared to go into all this with the council, but from the high-handed way they have dealt with us so far, I get the impression that they don't want us to do anything. They just want us to get out and then knock the place down.' In fact, although the lease was due to expire at the end of September, the council was duty-bound to give the Smiths six months' notice, which would take the zoo into the third week of October. 'Since the possibility of closure first arose, we have had many offers for our animals, but we want to keep the animals together, and to keep the zoo in Exmouth. We will go to any reasonable lengths with the council, and we are hoping that some agreement can be reached within the next six months.'

The Smiths' hopes were raised when the proprietor of the nearby Sandy Bay Holiday Park, John Lee, generously offered to re-site the zoo on two-and-a-half-acres of ground on the periphery of his holiday park, but this proposal – this lifeline – was rejected in May by the myopic Devon County Council Development Control Sub-committee (by eight votes to seven), which directed East Devon Council to refuse planning permission despite almost everybody else being in favour of the application: the general public, Exmouth Town Committee, and East Devon Council (including – rather surprisingly in view of his earlier antipathy towards the zoo – its chairman Ted Pinney). Everyone, that is, except the out-of-touch county councillors in their ivory tower. The reason the deputy chief planning officer of Devon County Council gave for refusing planning permission was that it was contrary to the Coastal Preservation Area Policy which stated that only essential development was permitted in such an area (a tenuous argument because that part of the coast had already been substantially affected by holiday developments anyway, so one more thing probably wouldn't have made much impact). There was general incredulity at the county council's decision, one person commenting, 'This is absolutely ridiculous. This is a holiday park, and this is exactly where you would expect to find this sort of thing.' But Devon County Council was unwavering, arguing that to relocate the zoo to Sandy Bay was unthinkable and would set a dangerous precedent. When it was pointed out to the council that a new traction engine and countryside museum had been built there only a few years earlier (so one could hardly talk about the zoo setting a precedent as one had already been set), the Planning Officer (the appropriately named Mr Turpin), clutching at straws, came up with another excuse to justify the decision to turn the application down. He told the sub-committee that technically the application was invalid anyway because it had not been advertised by the applicant himself (ignoring the fact that it *had* received extensive publicity in the local press, albeit not in the official advertising columns). John Turpin visited the zoo in connection with its proposed removal, but commented afterwards that he couldn't think why they wanted to move it as it was ideally situated for holiday-makers, with a car park and the beach right opposite.

The proposed relocation of the zoo was between the new museum and some farm buildings, very close to the holiday park and relatively well screened by the museum building, and even the Inspector considered that the general area of the site was appropriate, but still his report failed to convince county councillors. Three times the Development Control Subcommittee of Devon County Council discussed the application to move the zoo from its seafront site to Sandy Bay, and three times it reaffirmed its decision to direct East Devon Council to refuse permission. The ratepayers – the people to whom the puffed-up councillors owed their position – were allowed no say in the matter. A deflated and bitter John Lee, baffled and frustrated in equal measure by Devon County Council's zealous adherence to the rule book, spoke for many when he said, 'Now we have people from way out of the area telling us what we can and cannot do. I think that local people should have had their say, but it seems their views were disregarded.' He announced, with regret, that he would not be appealing against the decision.

In an interview with the *Exmouth Journal*, Trudy said, 'We are very sad and disappointed. The zoo continues to be very popular and many local people have told us that it would be tragic if it has to go.'

It was a sentiment shared by Exmouth county councillor Peter Thorpe. 'The project was supported by Exmouth's three county councillors and all the district councillors, and I was distressed that what would have been a first-class attraction for Exmouth as a holiday centre is now to be lost,' he said. 'We are not likely to see any development of similar quality from public funds. On principle the committee is justified in its decision as the site is in a coastal preservation area but common sense should have said that this was a perfect place for the zoo.'

So why was the county council so resistant to the idea of moving the zoo to Sandy Bay? A credible theory was put forward by none other than Ted Pinney that a longstanding rankle over the museum could have been the reason for the intransigence of Devon's Development Control Subcommittee. A few years earlier, the County Planning Committee had refused to allow the building of the traction engine museum at Sandy Bay, but, to its humiliation, this decision was overturned on appeal by the Secretary of State for the Environment. It had had to concede defeat over the museum, and it had been a bitter pill to swallow. So now, in what can only be described as an act of pique, the county council was less willing to give its approval to *any* new developments. If Ted Pinney's analysis of the position was right, it was all really rather childish. He was annoyed that East Devon Council's carefully thought out and reasoned arguments in favour of the move should be so bluntly rejected by county councillors, and angry too that the proposed move to Sandy Bay could not be discussed at a full session of the county council. He declared that should John Lee change his mind and decide to challenge the decision, his appeal would receive the full support of the district council. Suddenly, in the eyes of the local press, Ted Pinney went from being the villain of the piece to being the zoo's champion.

Meanwhile, as the matter of the zoo was bounced from one council to the next, Ken and Trudy were left feeling increasingly marginalised. Sometimes they felt as if they were the last people to know what was happening.

'We feel like shuttlecocks, being tossed from one to the other,' complained Trudy bitterly, adding that she and Ken had only learned of the subcommittee's decision from the local newspaper.

We had no idea what was happening. What a pity they are going to spend something like £10,000 to knock the old zoo buildings down – haven't the buildings been roughly valued at about £40,000? – to lay out a day-trippers' coach park. Perhaps it wouldn't cost quite £10,000 to make this building suitable for our zoo.

It would cost about £3,000 to lower the roof to retain the necessary heat in the building, and to remove the old veranda from the front to improve the appearance. We would carry out work inside, such as providing new caging, improve the kitchen, and concrete parts of the floor where it was necessary.

They were under no delusions that a great deal of work was required to bring the zoo up to an acceptable standard but, with the zoo's future hanging in doubt, Ken saw little point in making improvements or doing anything but the most rudimentary repairs since it was looking increasingly likely that the council would tear the building down anyway. Although most of the defects were of a cosmetic nature, it would still take a lot of money to put things right, money that the Smiths just did not have. The building required a whole new floor with a proper drainage system. It needed better ventilation. Two windows were broken and an old animal-feed sack had been stuffed into one of the holes as a makeshift measure. The wire-mesh of some of the animal cages had come away from the frames. A gap at the bottom of the cage belonging to a Pig-tailed macaque had had a heavy stone shoved into it instead of being repaired properly. The bolts on some of the other cages were insecure. Electrical wiring was dried and cracked, and plugs were overloaded due to a shortage of sockets. The problem was the building had not been designed for animals. At its heart, it was – and remained – a sports hut that just happened to have been adapted for animals. At first this hadn't mattered too much but, as the building aged and little maintenance work was done on it, shortcomings became more apparent and what had started out as minor deficiencies became magnified.

Ken's failure to upgrade the place was not just down to a lack of money or the realisation that it would all be in vain if, as seemed probable, the zoo was forced to close anyway. His health was failing and he was no longer able to do many of the maintenance jobs that were needed. Throughout the 1970s he suffered a series of strokes, each more debilitating than the last. His poor health meant that increasingly he could not have the hands-on approach with his animals that he had once enjoyed, nor could he supervise the zoo to the same extent. Geoffrey Schomberg, who, in 1970, had given Exmouth Zoo a rhapsodic review in his book *The Penguin Guide to British Zoos*, was under the mistaken belief that Ken had suffered a heart attack. Although Schomberg was wrong about the heart attack, he was convinced that Ken's poor health was the main reason behind Exmouth Zoo's decline. As news filtered back to him from colleagues who had visited the zoo of late that it had a dilapidated air about it (although the animal collection still impressed), he was forced to concede that menageries of this type probably had had their day. 'Ken is a good man, but he's been very ill lately,' he wrote in a letter to an associate who had contacted him expressing concern about the deterioration of the zoo at Exmouth.

Although the little zoo continued to operate, there was a very real sense it was living on borrowed time. Throughout this very difficult period, it continued to enjoy strong local support, however, and pressure was put on East Devon Council to give the zoo more time in the hope that a solution, amiable to all parties, could yet be found, and eventually it did acquiesce and the lease was extended for a further year. Exmouth councillor, Mrs Freda Morgan, summed up the mood when she said, 'Having lost our fight to have the zoo moved to Sandy Bay, we have now got to fight to keep the zoo in

Exmouth – where it is – and we have got to discuss ways and means of doing this.' Then, in an unexpected development, in about February 1979 an anonymous Exmouth businessman suddenly appeared like a genie out of a lamp and announced that he would be willing to spend between £20,000 and £30,000 to renovate the zoo buildings. There was just one proviso: in return for investing so much of his own money he would be seeking a substantial lease period – not unreasonable in the circumstances – and Exmouth Town Committee was urged to press East Devon Council to agree to this. After all the worry and uncertainty the Smiths had endured over the past few years, it was nothing short of miraculous. The *Exmouth Journal* was jubilant at the news and excitedly announced that it now seemed that Exmouth would not lose its seafront amenity after all. Such optimism was sadly misplaced, however, for it turned out to be a false dawn, and unfortunately nothing came of it.

Exmouth seemed to be turning against its animal attractions. In March 1979 time was called on the Exmouth Aquarium (its lease had run out) and it was beginning to look as if it wouldn't be long before the zoo went the same way. Strangely enough, when Anthony Smith's (no relation) seminal book on British Zoos, *Animals On View*, first published in 1977, was reprinted in a revised edition in 1979, there was no hint of the crisis affecting the zoo. Everything appeared to be 'business as usual' and indeed animals continued to arrive (one of the latest new arrivals was a Green Tree python) and the zoo continued to feature on nationwide television (Kate appeared on *Animal Magic* again, this time showing a snake). The local press continued its campaign for Exmouth to keep its zoo, but its yeomanly efforts could only delay the inevitable. This was one battle that David with his slingshot couldn't win. With the Smiths' hopes of relocating to a new site, or of a rescue package from a philanthropic businessman, dashed, it was obvious Exmouth Zoo's days were numbered, and although East Devon Council wavered and granted a stay of execution several times, the writing was on the wall.

In any case, Ken's health was in a tail-spin and by now he presented quite a frail figure who walked with the aid of sticks, his decline doubtless exacerbated by the continuing worry over the zoo. Then came an incident that really brought home to him how far he had gone down. Exmouth Zoo had come to the rescue of a Barbary macaque suffering from severe arthritis. Its fingers were twisted and it had difficulty grasping anything but, as Ken found out, it was still remarkably fleet of foot when it put its mind to it. One day, as he stepped into the cage, the monkey bolted for the open door, bowling him over as if he had been poleaxed. He lay helplessly on his back in the open doorway, unable to move. It was a clear indication to him how far he had sunk.

Distressed as he was by his rapidly deteriorating condition, it pleased him enormously that he had lived long enough to see his first grandchild, Caroline's daughter Emma. Ken tired easily by this stage, and most days he would leave the zoo in the afternoon to go home for a nap, or sometimes, if there was a good cowboy film on, he would watch that. So invariable was his routine that baby Emma soon learned to time her naps to coincide with his, so they both took an invigorating snooze at the same time. Since Ken's three daughters, and even Trudy, all called him 'Dad', Emma emulated them, and, almost from the moment she could talk, addressed him in the same way.

The erstwhile world traveller rarely stepped outside his own familiar orbit now. One place that did still hold an attraction for him was the local airport. Although nothing was allowed to compete with his passion for natural history, he had an interest in aviation, possibly stemming from his days in the RAF and, when he could, he liked to wander round Exeter Airport and watch the planes take off and land. Simple pleasures. Security was not as rigorous as it is today, and he could get right up to the aeroplanes as they squatted on the asphalt. The runway had been specially lengthened in order to accommodate Concorde, a frequent visitor to Exeter. Concorde was one of Ken's favourite aircraft. He loved the shape, the juxtaposition of gracefulness and power, and the bizarre nosecone that probably reminded him of the beak of some bird. 'Bloody marvellous,' he would mutter in awe, gazing up at the aeroplane as if mesmerised, standing so close to it that when it swung round on the runway he could feel the heat from its engines.

But time was catching up with him. In September 1977 an event had taken place at the Natural History Museum in London which, if news of it reached Ken's ears, must have invoked in him more than a pang of nostalgia. A film about the wildlife of the jungles of the former Siam was reverently removed from the airtight canister in which it had been sealed exactly half a century earlier with instructions that it was not to be opened until five decades had rolled by. This was the film *Chang* and afterwards it was deposited with the British Film Institute, where it resides to this day. I have described this film in chapter two, and how interested the young Kenneth Smith had been all those years ago when he learned that this important footage had been presented to the Natural History Museum. We cannot know for certain whether Ken heard that the film had been unsealed at last, but if he did hear about it, did his mind turn back those fifty years to his salad days when, as a sixteen-year-old schoolboy at the Friends' School in 1927, just setting out on life's journey, he had penned this line for the school's Natural History Society: 'A copy of that wonderful film of Siamese jungle life – 'Chang' – has been deposited at the Natural History Museum, where it is to be kept sealed for fifty years.' That was a very long time ago, half a century, and he had done so much – seen so much – in those fifty years while the film had lain undisturbed and half-forgotten in its tin. Was he imbued with an impossible yearning to be that boy again? Fifty years. What a journey he had been on. So many animals, so many experiences. No one could say his life had been an uneventful one. The former electrician and insurance agent had truly lived a 'life less ordinary', but now, almost at journey's end, he was visibly fading as each fresh attack robbed him of a little bit more of his personality. His own father had died of a stroke and, the way things were going, it was looking as if this would be his fate, too. Ken had no choice but to withdraw from the zoo almost completely, as by now he soon became exhausted and even the simplest of tasks defeated him. Towards the end of his life, his speech was slurred and virtually unintelligible. Fortunately his devoted wife Trudy could understand him and was able to act as interpreter. It was a slow, sad decline. I am reminded of a Jim Steinman lyric: 'You start out always fast but the end is always slow.'

For Trudy, shouldering the burden of looking after what was still a big collection, it was a punishing workload. Ken viewed his rapidly declining health and increasing incapacitation with considerable dismay. Frustrated by his inability to do much, there were long periods when he became quite sullen. Some years earlier his old expeditionary partner, Gerald Durrell, had suffered a mental breakdown and at his lowest ebb, according to his first wife Jacquie, had even contemplated suicide. Ken did not break down, and he wasn't the suicidal type, but there were frequent moments when he just seemed to withdraw into himself, although he would usually brighten whenever any of his zoological colleagues paid him a visit. Infrequent though they were, these visits gave him the chance to relive some of the great moments from his past – and what times they were. Merlin's gift. A life filled with animals of every description. However, it was obvious to everyone who saw him that he was on a downward spiral. When Clinton Keeling visited the Smiths at Exmouth Zoo in September 1978, he was distressed to find his friend so badly affected by his latest stroke. He was pleased to note, however, that despite Ken's failing health, the animal collection was still top-notch:

> I saw immediately that here was a well-kept collection looked after by an experienced all-rounder. For the life of me I could not explain how one can tell this as it's nothing you can specifically put your finger on – it just comes with long years of looking after your own animals and noticing those of others. The indoor animals were housed in rather small and snug compartments, and as far as I could see there was not one which would not have passed a stiff veterinary examination. At that time I was beginning to build up what has become quite a reasonable animal slide library, and the Smiths were only too happy to let us take out and photograph a very wide range of subjects – the huge Blomberg's Toad, Gila Monster (fifteen years there and perfectly handleable), the Yellow or Southern Anaconda, various parrots – there were so many tame and steady animals there, and this is yet another sign of a carefully tended and well-loved place.

Ken Smith died on 21 December 1979 in the Royal Devon and Exeter Hospital, Exeter. He had been taken ill quite suddenly and rushed to hospital, but there was little that could be done and he died after only a few days. Death was due to bronchopneumonia and liver failure. He was sixty-eight. On his death certificate, his occupation was recorded as 'Zoo Proprietor (Retired)'. By now his star had waned considerably, and it is a sad fact that his passing went largely unnoticed and unrecorded, even by the zoological journals for which he had once contributed articles. When Gerald Durrell died a little over fifteen years later, the obituaries were long and hagiographic (with headlines like 'Star whose love of animals delighted millions' and 'A covenant with the ark') and the worldwide TV news coverage was exhaustive, and nobody was left in any doubt that a zoological colossus had passed away. In stark contrast, Ken Smith, his one-time right-hand man, slipped quietly away and there were few obituaries. Perhaps that's what this unassuming man – who had never craved publicity – would have wanted.

The most moving and personal tribute was provided by his old friend Charles Trevisick, who wrote:

He was one of the world's experts on wildlife of all kinds, a kindly man never seeking honours which he deserved. Many children and their parents will miss seeing Ken Smith at his little zoo on Exmouth's seafront. I have known him over very many years. He had collected animals and birds with Gerald Durrell from all over the world, and was an expert at acclimatising them in their new homes. He was fearless in picking up venomous snakes, and animals that could give a nasty bite. A humble man, he never sought the bright lights or zoological dinners, but would much rather talk to families who visited his little zoo…Although not a great churchman, he will receive a great welcome from his Creator who had entrusted him with the care of all his creatures. To Trudy, his wife, and the children, we record the passing of a great man.

That last line would have bemused and even faintly embarrassed Ken. He had never believed himself to be a great man. As far as he had been concerned, he was just an ordinary guy, a self-effacing family man lacking all pretensions of grandeur who had enjoyed his work and the close contact it had afforded him with a bewildering variety of animals. Unlike Durrell, he hadn't set out to change the world; but, of course, his life *did* have a lasting impact on the world, as we will see.

A *great man*. It's not a bad epitaph.

Chapter Nineteen

Coda: *Après le reve*

T HE FUNERAL SERVICE was held at Exeter Crematorium and afterwards Ken's ashes were scattered there in the Garden of Remembrance. Exmouth Zoo – the place he and Trudy had strove so hard to make a success of, the embodiment of all their dreams and the culmination of his life's work – did not last much longer. Shortly after Ken died, the zoo suffered another tragedy when a fatal combination of high tides, a violent storm and an excessively turbulent sea caused the outside area to flood, resulting in the loss of a number of animals. For Trudy and her family, it was one more calamity. The outside area was prone to flooding anyway, but never before on this scale. 'I really do believe that the final straw was a flood which put the zoo three feet under water,' recalled Nigel Wilkinson.

Coming, as it did, at the same time as the local authority was pressing to regain the lease of the land that the zoo occupied, was doubly tragic. It was the end, really. It happened around Christmas time. I don't *think* it was actually on Christmas Day itself, but it was some time around then that I got a frantic telephone call. Trudy and the girls were beside themselves. Could I get down to the zoo immediately as there had been a disaster? What I found when I got there was heartbreaking. In places the water was waist-high. Some of the animals had perished in their flooded pens, though the goats had managed to scramble to safety. Several of the smaller and less nimble animals had not been so fortunate. Others we rescued in the nick of time. There were two gangly, long-legged birds – I honestly can't remember what kind they were – which were locked inside their shed each night. I opened the door, fearing the worst, and the water was up to their chins. Another couple of inches and they would have been completely submerged. They were very lucky.

Back in 1961, shortly before Ken took over the operating lease from Paignton Zoo, there had been a devastating fire at the zoo, and now, at the end, it was overwhelmed by flood water. Fire and flood. Ken's tenure of the zoo had ended as it had begun – with tragedy. Among the casualties were two of his favourite birds. The exact identity of these birds has been forgotten with the passage of time, but Trudy has a vague recollection they were possibly Ken's beloved pair of Crested screamers. If the screamers did perish in the disaster, it would be quite surprising because screamers, being related to the geese, are able swimmers – but not impossible. Whatever kind of birds they were, Ken had been very fond of them, his daughters remarking that 'Dad loved them so much he took them with him.'

Trudy soldiered on with the zoo for another season but, even if the council hadn't pulled the plug when it did, her heart was no longer in it now that Ken was gone, and that erstwhile sports hut on Exmouth seafront, which had been home to so many exotic creatures from all over the world, closed its doors for the final time as a zoo in October 1980. I say 'as a zoo' advisedly because it was soon to reopen in a completely different guise. The closure of Exmouth Zoo was not only reported by the local and regional press, but the *Daily Mirror* also got wind of the story and, in typically sensationalist journalese, announced that the closure was 'due to council orders regarding cramped living conditions for the animals. An extension was planned but denied by the council, so over 200 zoo animals had to be re-homed or put down.'

This was journalistic story-telling at its worst. For one thing, the zoo was not closed on council orders (in fact the council had put off closure a couple of times) but because the lease had expired. Pure and simple. That bit about animals having to be destroyed was also misleading. Whenever a zoo announces it is to close down, the newspapers are invariably full of horror stories of animals condemned to death, making the failing zoo sound like the Killing Fields. When, in 1992, the London Zoo signalled its intention to close at the end of the tourist season after 164 years (it received an eleventh-hour reprieve) one newspaper, that should have known better, printed a story under the arresting heading 'London Zoo slaughter by Christmas', in which it reported that some of London Zoo's best-loved animals, including chimpanzees, tigers and giraffes, were unlikely to find new homes and there would be no alternative but to destroy them, and that the lives of many others would be put at risk by what it described as 'arduous journeys to other zoos'. The truth is somewhat different. Fortunately, most people – and that certainly includes zoo personnel – realise that zoo animals are not commodities to be discarded at will. Whenever a zoo *is* forced to close for economic or other reasons, determined efforts are always made to find homes for all the animals, and rarely are more than about two or three of the larger mammals destroyed and only then as a last resort (almost always very old or infirm animals that are almost impossible to place anywhere else), and it is a decision that is always taken with regret.

According to Trudy, no animals were destroyed when Exmouth Zoo closed down. It helped that closure had been on the cards for some time, as it meant there had been sufficient time to find suitable buyers for the animals. In the event, Paignton Zoo took most of the animals (which rather neatly brought the whole thing full circle because of course it was Paignton Zoo that had been responsible for launching Exmouth Zoo in the first place). The price Trudy received for the animals was a rather less than munificent two thousand pounds. Among the animals destined for Paignton Zoo were the pumas, Slender lorises, Gila monsters and Beaded lizards. Henry, the pathologically aggressive Papuan hornbill, was also sent to live at Paignton Zoo, where unfortunately he died not long afterwards.

But not everything ended up at Paignton. It was entirely appropriate that some animals, including the ravens, went to the zoo at Shaldon. Ringo the chimpanzee, on his own now following the death of his companion Susie, went to Newquay Zoo. Some while later, Exmouth Zoo's former Curator, Judith Bond, visited him in his new abode at Newquay to see how he was settling in. At that time, Newquay Zoo used to close during the winter months (these days it is open all year round), and as she was intending to visit off-season, she contacted the zoo in advance to ask if it would be all right for her to call in. Despite not having seen her for some time, Ringo recognised his former keeper immediately; he reached through the bars of his cage, and they held hands like two friends reunited, which indeed is what they were.

Trudy presented a Senegal parrot (by the name of Youki) to Ken's old friend, Clinton Keeling. He was genuinely touched by this kind gesture. It was nice, he later remarked, to have an animal that had once belonged to Ken Smith. Two months before Exmouth Zoo closed, he made the last of all his visits there. He found an atmosphere of despondency hanging over the place like a cloud. He recalled of this occasion:

> Mrs Smith made me most welcome and took me round the now depleted collection. This was well into its closing era, and quite a number of animals had gone to new homes. Behind the scenes was a young Hedgehog which she gave me, together with several beautiful Arabian Spiny Mice of which she had a truly flourishing colony – which is good going as this is not the easiest of species to keep if more than just a few are housed together. There was almost an air of despair there, though, and in a way I was not sorry to leave.

Truth be told, Trudy was relieved that Ken had been spared the ordeal of seeing it all end. In a final twist of irony, the planned extension to the coach park (one of the main reasons given for the council's decision not to renew the zoo's lease) never went ahead. Once the zoo was gone, the proposal was quietly dropped, and the building was not demolished after all but stands to this day, reborn as an amusement arcade. Where once there were monkeys and mongooses, parrots and porcupines, all vying for attention, today there are banks of slot machines, and the shrill piercing cries of the macaws and the birdlike squeaks of the marmosets have been replaced by mechanical noises and the cascade of coins.

The early Eighties saw the end of one era of zoo-keeping and the beginning of another. The traditional menagerie had had its day. From then on, buzz words like 'conservation' and 'captive breeding' were to be the driving forces behind most zoos as they prepared to cross the threshold into a new century.

As for the other zoos formerly owned by Ken and Trudy Smith, they had contrasting fortunes. Newquay Children's Zoo had closed down a full decade earlier, of course, and today hardly anybody, even people domiciled in the North Cornish resort for many years, can remember it.

Poole Park Zoo, after changing hands several times, finally closed down in February 1994 after thirty-one years. The reasons are manifold, but, as with both Exmouth and Newquay Children's Zoo, some of the blame for its demise must rest with the local council that imposed restrictions on opening hours and even what kinds of animals could be kept there, as well as helping itself to a large proportion of the gate-money. Criticised for the small size of many of the enclosures, the zoo was picketed in the eighties and early nineties by an increasingly militant anti-zoo fraternity. Activists started off with petitions and a simple leaflet and poster campaign and ended up spraying graffiti on the zoo walls and, it was alleged, throwing paint stripper over two zoo vehicles. It is easy to knock Poole Council for not supporting the zoo more, and certainly several councillors were unsympathetic and sometimes openly antagonistic towards the zoo, but the council resisted the call to close it for a very long time, renewing the zoo's operating licence on several occasions. Eventually Poole Zoo closed when the last leaseholder defaulted on his rent.

Ironically it was tiny, insignificant, unassuming Teignmouth Children's Zoo that ultimately confounded everybody by proving to have the most staying power. Ken had relinquished it in the early to mid-Seventies. With the energetic and knowledgeable Smith gone from the scene, the place bumped along aimlessly, becoming shabbier and shabbier and unloved by almost everyone – unloved by the general public, unloved by the local council, and unloved by the RSPCA. At some point the name was changed (goodbye Teignmouth Children's Zoo, hello Shaldon Children's Zoo, which at least was geographically correct) but it was not enough to arrest the decline. Successive owners failed to reverse the degeneration until, towards the end of 1979, with permanent closure looming, the site changed hands yet again. Ken lived just long enough to see it fall into the possession of two former London Zoo keepers, brimming with ideas on ways to reform the place, Stewart Muir and Mike Moore. Although it had had several owners in quick succession before Stewart and Mike came on the scene, they were very keen to meet Ken and Trudy, as the originators of the zoo. 'Unfortunately I did not meet Ken in person,' Stewart said to me. 'I went over to meet Trudy at Exmouth for the first time during that winter, at which time Ken was seriously ill in hospital and died shortly afterwards. It was a particularly difficult time for Trudy, as you can imagine. Her daughters were all quite young at the time and maintaining the zoo at Exmouth was obviously a struggle.'

Recognising Shaldon Zoo's potential as more than just a simple children's zoo, Stewart and Mike pleaded with the council for a stay of execution of one year to see if they could bring about the place's redemption. This they succeeded in doing, breathing new life into it, reinvigorating it. It dropped the 'Children's' from its name, and in 1985, with its new identity as the Shaldon Wildlife Trust firmly established, it was granted charitable status. Shaldon Zoo is with us still, the only survivor of Ken's quadruplet of small children's zoos, and going from strength to strength – ambitious, forward-thinking, punching above its weight, never content to rest on its laurels, even supporting projects to assist animals in the wild, as all zoos should. It is an excellent example of what can be achieved with even the smallest area with a little imaginative flair, the right choice of animals, and the support of the local community. At a mere two acres (including an extension into the surrounding woodland, opened in 2010, which at a single stroke doubled the size of the zoo), it is one of the smallest zoos in the U.K., but smallness is seen as being almost a virtue here, not something to the zoo's detriment. Never has the expression 'Small is Beautiful' seemed more apt. Among the community of zoos, it is highly regarded and keeps a number of rare and endangered species, most of which have bred. Recognising its limitations of space, there are no big animals, but an interesting assortment of small to medium-sized mammals together with a smaller number of birds, reptiles, amphibians and invertebrates. Were he around today, Ken would not recognise the place, so much has it changed, but you feel sure he would not be displeased at how it has turned out. It has assumed an importance he could never have imagined. In his day, almost all the animals were housed indoors, whereas today most of the animals have access to well-designed and surprisingly roomy outside enclosures. Primates are a particular interest (this would have delighted Ken) and the Shaldon Wildlife Trust is recognised as one of the top zoos in the U.K. for the conservation of endangered primates. In 2011, after an absence of several years, Saki monkeys took up residence at the zoo in a brand new enclosure. It would have pleased Ken enormously to know that his old Teignmouth Zoo was doing so well with White-faced Saki monkeys, a favourite species of his that had caused him so much trouble over the years.

Shaldon Zoo, then, is Ken's real legacy, his most important and enduring accomplishment, even though he didn't live to witness its glorious flowering. Although a very different place from the modest children's zoo it was in his day, the unalterable fact remains that it owes its existence to Ken Smith (one can arguably say the same for the former Jersey Zoo, which benefitted from his organisational prowess during its most crucial period), but what of the other zoos where Ken worked at one time or another? I have described already what happened to Oxford Zoo in chapter three. The Margate Aquarium and Mini Zoo, which he managed for a very short time in the Fifties, is also long-gone, its passing unlamented, and today it is completely forgotten by almost everybody. Both the Belle Vue Zoo Park and Calderpark Zoo have also gone, the former in 1977, the latter in 2003. Unlike the menagerie at Margate, the demise of these two zoological institutions, particularly Belle Vue, was widely mourned by zoo enthusiasts. Paignton Zoo has overcome financial problems of its own and is currently enjoying record attendances. New exhibits and buildings are sprouting up all the time and hardly anything now remains of the old zoo that Ken knew. After many years in the doldrums during which time it remained largely unchanged, Whipsnade Zoo (or, more correctly these days, ZSL Whipsnade Zoo) is also evolving rapidly, with new developments the order of the day.

As hinted earlier, it may not be hyperbole to suggest that, without Ken Smith to set the wheels in motion, possibly there might have been no Jersey Zoo – and consequently no Jersey Trust. Ken had the practical expertise to turn Gerald Durrell's idea for a zoo into a *fait accompli*, something which Durrell, for all his farsightedness and idealism, lacked. We will never know whether Gerald Durrell would have achieved his lifetime ambition had he not been able to call on his old pal. In 1963, not long after Ken left the island, Durrell formed the Jersey Wildlife Preservation Trust to take over the zoo. Thirty-six years later on 26 March 1999 (the fortieth anniversary – to the day – of the official opening of Jersey Zoo) the Trust was renamed the Durrell Wildlife Conservation Trust, a time for celebration and to look to the future, but also a time to take stock and reflect on what had brought it to this point. The name 'Jersey Zoological Park', which it had borne since its inception, was quietly dropped. Today the word 'zoo', with its negative connotations, is anathema to the Durrell organisation. Such a word is no longer in accordance with the image the Trust wishes to convey. From now on, the headquarters of the Trust were to be known as 'Durrell Wildlife' or, even more simply, as just 'Durrell'. But if not a zoo, what is it? It's a wildlife park, I was told.

When Gerald Durrell died in 1995, it lost not only its founder but also its figurehead and a primary source of publicity. The years since then have been difficult ones for the Trust. It has seen a significant decline in both its membership and attendance figures; it has had to sell off some of its assets and there have been staff redundancies, but despite all this it has maintained its position as the island's top visitor attraction. While some of this downturn can be directly attributed to Durrell's passing, the main reason is that fewer people are choosing the Channel Islands as a holiday destination. Since 1992 the number of holidaymakers to Jersey has shrunk by almost forty per cent as a result of the faltering economy combined with the relative inexpensiveness of package flights to mainland Europe. Whilst the remote island location may have appealed to Gerald Durrell's romanticism (in one of his books he called himself a 'confirmed islomaniac') it is, perhaps, its biggest problem, as the wildlife park is dependent on an unreliable holiday trade. Ken, of course, had captained the vessel through another period of financial instability, but back in the early Sixties things were much more straightforward; now it is a world-wide organisation with commitments in many countries. Originally there were only about ten employees; now there are a hundred. To try to reverse the downward trend, it has brought in many more species, particularly ones guaranteed to appeal to the visiting public, and it is a more diverse and interesting collection as a result, even if not all the animals it has added to its inventory in recent years have been endangered species. By bringing back such ubiquitous animals as Ring-tailed coatis, Lar gibbons and Pekin robins – all present in Ken Smith's day but eventually phased out as being too commonplace for a zoo that was beginning to concentrate on endangered species – it has, in a sense, gone full circle.

*

In some ways, Ken was born too soon. He was born into a world where comparatively little was understood about even quite familiar animal species. He learnt his trade at the coalface, so to speak, not in the classroom or the laboratory, and inevitably he made mistakes. If he didn't know what a particular animal fed on, he would experiment by tempting it with a range of likely foodstuffs and hoped it would respond by choosing something. However, there were no guarantees. Sometimes an animal fed, sometimes it didn't, but always he was learning. Ken would be amazed by all the advancements in animal husbandry since he bade farewell to this earth. Problems which, only a few years ago, seemed insurmountable, are now circumvented with ease. The terrible creeping cage-paralysis that, for a long time, plagued captive primates, and which nearly claimed the life of Ringo, is now a thing of the past. The most likely cause is generally thought to have been a phosphorus deficiency or a vitamin D3 deficiency resulting in the animal being unable to assimilate phosphorus where it *was* present in the diet. In particular, it seems to have been the scourge of New World primates, although Old World species too were not infrequently affected. In retrospect, the reason for this geographic imbalance now seems obvious, though it was not realised at the time. New World monkeys were generally regarded as being less hardy than their African and Asiatic counterparts and as a result were often confined in zoos to heated indoor cages without access to the outside. Denied natural sunlight (an important source of vitamin D), it is little wonder they were more prone to this complaint. Nowadays, most zoos allow their monkeys (New World as well as Old World) access to outdoor enclosures. This, combined with a greater understanding of the dietary requirements of captive primates and the advent of nutritionally balanced foods means that keepers and zoo-owners will never again have the trauma of watching helplessly, as Ken did, as their cherished charges become slowly paralysed.

Slowly but surely, animals regarded as being almost impossible, if not actually impossible, to keep in captivity are giving up their secrets. It would have given Ken tremendous satisfaction to know that the problems of keeping Howler monkeys and White-faced Saki monkeys have been overcome and both are now exhibited often in zoos. Ingrained notions die hard, however, and as recently as 2009 one book on primates was adamant that Saki monkeys 'rarely survive for very long away from their natural forest homes and are almost never seen in zoos'. This may be true for some saki species, but the White-faced (or Guyanan) Saki monkey is firmly established in captivity and moves are afoot to establish the rarer Red-backed Bearded saki in U.K. zoos. Black-&-White Colobus monkeys, like howlers and sakis, were once considered almost impossible to keep alive in captivity for any length of time, but are now regularly seen in zoos.

Other nuts are proving a lot harder to crack, however, and in some cases progress has been made hardly at all since the days when Ken Smith confronted them. Some of the animal species he encountered on his collecting expeditions to Africa and South America still defy attempts to establish them in captivity, despite all the advances in zoological knowledge. The difficulties of keeping the various forms of Red Colobus monkey have still not been solved and, at time of writing, there is probably none held in any zoo. The diminutive Silky anteater is notoriously hard to keep now as it was back in the 1950s. The Three-toed sloth is frequently cited as being impossible to keep in captivity. There *are* some zoos keeping them, but with only limited success. (Two-toed sloths, on the other hand, have always been much less demanding.) But the problems of keeping these animals will be solved one day. There can be little doubt of that.

The once world-famous Palmer's, the Regent Pet Stores, where Ken obtained so many rare and unusual animals, is still to be found in Camden Town, but today it occupies a building on the opposite side of the road from the original site at 35-37 Parkway. It is also a much smaller shop and there is one other major difference, for whereas once it was possible to buy almost any animal from Palmer's, as a sign of the times these days no animals, not even goldfish or white mice, are sold there. It is strictly animal feeds, treats, beds, brushes, and pet cages only. Walk across the road and up the street a little way and you come to the original premises, now a specialist tearoom where you can imbibe tea from a cup the size of a soup bowl. Outwardly little has changed. Stand on the pavement outside and look upwards and you can still clearly see, imprinted above the windows in big bold lettering, the immortal words MONKEYS and PARROTS and NATURALISTS, words that once enticed zoo-people from far and wide to cross the portals of this hallowed place. It is pleasing these words have been retained –

and long may they remain – even though you can't help feeling they must cause a certain amount of confusion for customers of the tearoom.

*

Exmouth Zoo may have gone, but Trudy continued to keep a variety of animals at her home – tortoises, chinchillas, Spiny and Zebra mice and African Dwarf dormice, and, of course, her beloved Siamese cats. She maintained her contacts within the zoo world and occasionally she would be offered other animals. The temptation to accept was sometimes acute. More often than not it was her practical-minded youngest daughter, Kate, who provided the voice of reason by dissuading her mother from taking on too much responsibility. Eventually she stopped keeping snakes and lizards altogether, thereby saving herself the rather onerous chore of feeding dead mice to the snakes and live insects to the lizards. In 1997, in a letter to a friend, she wrote: 'I keep planning to cut down and I have, quite a bit. Don't keep reptiles anymore as the feeding is always a problem, and Kate (we share the house) isn't very keen!'

I asked Trudy whether she missed the zoos. To my surprise, she assured me she didn't.

Not really.

'They were good times,' she said, 'but it was hard work. We were exhausted by the end of the day, and of course it meant we had almost no time for a social life. Looking back you only ever remember the good bits, like the birth of an animal or the arrival of a eagerly anticipated species, or the look of wonderment on the faces of the visitors when they see some strange creature for the first time. You forget those times when you stayed up all night trying to coerce a sick animal to feed, or the constant worry about how you were going to pay the next bill. They were great days and I wouldn't have missed them for the world, but it was all a long time ago, and things move on.'

In the preface I bemoaned the fact that modern zoo directors often have little or no practical experience of animal husbandry. Naturally there are exceptions. But perhaps, in some dark Orwellian future, with ever more restrictive regulations and ballooning red tape (to the satisfaction of civil servants who get off on this kind of thing), the only zoos that will stand a chance of succeeding in this Kafkaesque world will be those run by people who have the patience and the business acumen to deal with all this. Maybe the day of the naturalist zoo director, as exemplified by the likes of Ken Smith, Gerald Durrell, Clinton Keeling and Charles Trevisick is over. I hope not.

Over a hundred years ago Mark Twain exhorted people to live life to the full: 'Twenty years from now you will be more disappointed by the things you did not do than by the ones you did do. So throw off the bowlines. Sail away from the safe harbour. Catch the trade winds in your sails. Explore. Dream. Discover.'

Those words could have been Ken Smith's personal mantra.

Explore. Dream. Discover.

He did all that, and more.

Postscript

The Zoo ranks high as recreation because, like all good recreations, it calls forth our intellectual curiosity and our physical sympathy.

From *Zoo* by Louis Macneice (1938)

SATURDAY 26 JUNE 2010 was an auspicious occasion for the Shaldon Wildlife Trust, for on that day the little zoo that Ken Smith had founded forty-six years earlier celebrated the official opening of the new £150,000 extension to the zoo grounds that took visitors deeper into the woods to meet lemurs, monkeys, meerkats and other animals. Trudy was invited to attend. 'We were delighted that Trudy Smith came to celebrate with us,' said Tracey Moore, the zoo's director. Visitors, Shaldon Wildlife Trust members, local councillors and invited guests saw the unveiling of impressive new signage at the zoo entrance and witnessed the burial of a time capsule which included a scroll from Shaldon Primary School predicting what the world might look like in another twenty-five years.

Trudy was under the impression that she had been invited along because of her friendship with Tracey. What happened next came as a complete surprise to her. Stewart Muir, who along with Mike Moore had saved Shaldon Zoo from closure in 1979 and was now the Shaldon Wildlife Trust's honorary director, stepped up to the microphone to address the assembled crowd. He made a heartfelt speech and then suddenly Trudy heard her name mentioned.

'I am very pleased to see Trudy Smith is here because if it were not for her late husband, Ken, we would not be here today. Without Ken and Trudy there would be no Shaldon Zoo, for it was they who launched it way back in the early Sixties. On behalf of the Shaldon Wildlife Trust and everyone here, I should like to say well done and thank you.'

Ken Smith had been recognised at last.

THE END

Ken Smith's Genealogy

Ken's Parents
Herbert Smith 1872–1933
Gertrude Emmeline Smith (*née* Jolly) 1879–1973

Ken's Paternal Grandparents
Thackwell Smith 1834–1905
Marianna Smith (*née* Gillett) 1835–1906

Ken's Maternal Grandparents
John Frank Jolly 1846–1924
Mary Elizabeth Jolly (*née* Stock) 1851–1937
(often known by her second name)

Thackwell and Marianna had eleven children: Thackwell Gillett 1862–1928; Hannah Eliza 1863–1951; Anne Caroline *b.* 1864; Marian *b.* 1865; Theodore 1867–1869; George Scuse 1869–1869; Kate 1870–1906; Herbert 1872–1933 (*Ken's father*); Frank Scuse *b.* 1874; Sophia 1875–?1954; Arthur John *b.* 1877

John and Mary had eight children: Ada Maude *b.* 1872; Henrietta *b.* 1873; John William *b.* 1875; Frederick James c.1878–1961; Gertrude 1879–1973 (*Ken's mother*); Norah *b.* 1881; Nellie (a.k.a. Emily) Ellen *b.* 1883 and her twin brother Montague *b.* 1883 *d.* 1883

Ken's Siblings

Ronald Thackwell Smith 1910–1990, a builder. He and Ken were very close and, in an act of fraternal affection, Ronald gave his son Peter the middle name 'Kenneth'. Like Ken, Ronald was hard-working but endured years of never quite having enough money.

Herbert Gillett Smith ('Gil') 1915–1998, a music teacher.

Violet Kathleen Smith 1918–1951, often known as Kathleen Violet, died tragically young from leukaemia.

Frank Eric Smith 1919–2009, a businessman. Frank operated a furniture business in the Charminster Road in Bournemouth that is still going strong. In business, he was the most successful of Herbert and Gertrude's five children.

Appendix II

IN NOVEMBER 1927, the sixteen-year-old Ken Smith, then a scholar at the Friends' School, Saffron Walden, and an active member of that school's Senior Natural History Society, was chosen to write an essay outlining some of the archaeological and natural history events of the day using newspapers as his primary source. This essay, which I discovered in the archives of the Essex Record Office, is, as far as I know, his earliest surviving piece of writing. (There were earlier articles, also written for the Senior Natural History Society, but these do not appear to have been preserved.) It is reproduced here in full. Ken's account presents a fascinating contemporary record of long-forgotten events. My own comments are in parenthesis.

Current Events Report
November 10 – Nov. 24 1927

The 'Illustrated London News' for November 12th contains four pages illustrating important discoveries at Beisan made by the Pennsylvania University Museum Expedition to Palestine. New light is thrown on the Canaanites by the discoveries; the relics are over three thousand years old, and one of the most interesting is a portrait of the builder of Dagon's temple – mentioned in the Old Testament. The excavations also led to the discovery of two Canaanite temples.

Another page of the same newspaper gives four photographs of discoveries made at Sakkara – on the edge of the Libyan desert – by Mr. Cecil Firth who has been excavating for the Egyptian Department of Antiquities. The results of the excavations include the discovery of the first stone buildings found in Egypt, a unique statue of King Zoser of the Third Dynasty, and his temple precincts around the famous Step Pyramid.

The 'I.L.N.' for November 19th gives a page of photographs of some newly discovered Persian sculptures calculated to be about five thousand years old. On one rock a German archaeologist has discovered a carving of two seated gods, and on a doorpost at Pasargadae was discovered a carving of a four-winged angel.

'The Sphere' of November 19th shows a photograph of some members of the International Archaeological Commission who are searching at Glozel for remains of the Neolithic or Palaeolithic period. [From 1924 to 1930 over 3,000 artefacts were discovered at Glozel, a hamlet in central France, including clay tablets, sculptures and vases, some of which were inscribed with symbols or letters.]

On the same page is a picture taken on board the 'Discovery', Captain Scott's famous vessel which has just returned from a research cruise in Antarctic waters and is now open to public exhibition in West India Dock.

Three pages of the 'Sphere' of November 12th are devoted to pictures of life in the swamplands of northern Australia which have just been traversed by Francis Birtles the explorer. This is one of the most desolate regions in the World, and the fauna of these parts has not yet been properly classified. For instance, instead of having proper scientific names the fish are called by such names as 'Big eye' and 'Cheeky fellah'. The whole country is infested with deep bogs and shallow streams in which the natives hunt fish and crocodiles. The natives' methods of capturing fish are very primitive, for they stand on tree trunks overhanging the river and stand motionless – then when a fish passes beneath it is cleverly speared. [By the middle of 1927 Francis Edwin Birtles (1881-1941) had completed more than seventy transcontinental crossings of Australia. In that same year, this Australian adventurer was very much the man of the moment when he became the first man to drive a car from England to Australia.]

W.P. Pycraft, in one of his interesting articles in the 'I.L.N.', writes about midges and describes in full their life history.

The 'Sphere' of November 19th gives a splendid full page photo of a huge male gorilla shot in the Belgian Congo by two English big-game hunters for Lord Rothschild's private museum at Tring. The great ape put up a running fight for three hours before it was slain by the English hunters and their pygmy guides. The dead gorilla has a barrel 62" in circumference and a biceps measurement of 18". The natives and pygmies of the Congo relish the flesh of the gorilla.

The 'Illustrated London News' of November 19th contains two photographs with notes on an elephant hunt in Mysore. The herd of wild elephants is driven into a stockaded [sic] *enclosure by natives with fire and noise. Then the wild elephants are led away one by one by native mahouts mounted on trained elephants.*

A copy of that wonderful film of Siamese jungle life – 'Chang' – has been deposited at the Natural History Museum, where it is to be kept sealed for fifty years. 'Chang' is the native name for elephant, and the film – which is one of the most remarkable ever taken – deals with a family's struggle for existence against the beasts of the jungle.

The daily newspapers have shown photographs of an African elephant [a stuffed one] *being moved into the Natural History Museum. In April the specimen was sent to the Rowland Ward Studios to be remounted, and when it was returned the other day half of the main entrance had to be removed to give it passage.*

In 'John O' London's Weekly' of November 12th, Professor J. Arthur Thomson discusses in an article entitled 'Single Blessedness' whether animals have a sexual morality. Here he contrasts a polygamous creature like the pheasant with strictly monogamous creatures such as gorillas, chimpanzees and rhinos. [Two of these animals are very odd examples, as both gorillas and chimpanzees are polygamous, not monogamous. One wonders how the learned Professor could make such a fundamental mistake in his original article, or why Ken repeated the assertion without questioning the veracity of it.]

'The Children's Newspaper' informs us than an international conference has just met in London intent on discovering ways and means of limiting the pitiless slaughter of migrating birds such as the wild duck and curlew.

In the same paper we read that steps are being taken to reduce the numbers of pigeons and starlings in London. The birds make St. Paul's Cathedral and other buildings unsightly, and traps and wide nets are being put in places where the birds have been accustomed to come for food.

L.G. Mainland of the 'Daily Mail' announces the arrival at the 'Zoo' of a pair of koalas or Australian tree-bears, the first of their species to reach the Gardens for nearly forty years. The creatures, which are only about twelve inches long, feed on eucalyptus leaves, and the Zoological Society is making great efforts to ensure a regular supply of these leaves. A photograph of the koalas appears on the back page of the same newspaper. [Unhappily the two koalas, which arrived at the London Zoo on November 10, survived at the zoo for little more than a month. One died on 13 December, followed by the other two days later.]

London is pleased to welcome back the albino or pink elephant from America. It arrived yesterday (Nov. 24th) but was greyish black in colour, having been painted with glycerine and charcoal to keep out the cold and to make it less noticeable in the streets – by the New York camouflage experts. The albino elephant will be washed at the 'Zoo' where it is stopping only for a short time, prior to an ocean voyage to the land of its birth – Burma. [Named Pawah (Pa Wa), this Asian elephant was wild-caught in Burma as a yearling in 1919 by a Dr. Saw D. Po Min. Even today, the capture of a white elephant in modern-day Myanmar (Burma) is hailed as an auspicious omen. In 1926, realising he could make a lot of money from his property, the mercenary doctor loaned Pawah to the Ringling Brothers and Barnum & Bailey Circus in the United States. En route, the elephant spent a few months at the London Zoo. Once in America, it proved to be a big draw for the circus, with one fascinated observer writing in a letter, 'One of the most interesting sights I ever saw was the albino elephant Pa Wa with RBBB in 1927, this was on the lake front in Chicago. Standing before this exhibit I could hear the chumps around me wondering why they had one of the elephants "scrubbed up".'

On the return journey to Burma, Pawah once again had a brief stopover in London in a small house especially constructed for it. Its young keeper, San Dwe, was retained by the London Zoo on a permanent basis in the Elephant House. In 1928, San Dwe brutally murdered a fellow elephant keeper, for reasons which are still unclear. Tragically, Pawah died in the same year at just ten years old.]

Appendix III

IN 1956 KEN SMITH led an expedition to British Guiana (Guyana) and returned to England with arguably the biggest collection of animals ever to be brought back to the U.K. from that country, most of them destined for Paignton Zoo. The consignment included the following animals. (The symbol '∞' indicates that several individuals of an undisclosed number were brought back.)

Mammals

1	Two-toed sloth
1	Northern tamandua
1	Giant anteater
1	Red-handed tamarin
2	Red Howler monkeys
2	White-faced Saki monkeys
2	Squirrel monkeys
∞	Capuchin monkeys
1	Margay
1	Ocelot
1	Kinkajou
3	Crab-eating raccoons
2	Savannah rats (see Note 1)
1	Red Marsh rat
2	Long-tailed Tree rats
7	Agoutis
2	Acouchis
2	Spotted pacas

Birds

4	Tinamou (2 species)
1	Tiger bittern
2	Black-crowned herons (see Note 2)
10	Cattle egrets
10	Little Blue herons
8	Tricolored herons
3	Black-crowned Night herons
7	Red-billed Whistling ducks
1	Harpy eagle
1	Everglades kite
10	South American Black vultures
3	Red-necked Turkey vultures
1	Grant's guan (see Note 3)
1	White-crested guan
1	Crested curassow
4	Grey-winged trumpeters
8	Venezuelan Wood rails
1	Surinam jacana
18	Grey-fronted doves
7	Ruddy Ground doves
2	Scarlet macaws
5	Green-winged macaws
4	Blue & Yellow macaws
2	Red-bellied macaws
1	Hahn's macaw
1	Mealy parrot
8	Yellow-headed parrot (see Note 4)
12	Orange-winged parakeets
1	Golden-winged parakeet
20	Blue-winged parrotlets
12	Brown-throated conures
2	Brazilian Barn owls
1	Spectacled owl
2	Sulphur-breasted toucans
4	Mount Roraima aracaris
5	Kiskadee flycatchers
∞	Glossy grassquits
1	Greater saltator

3	Bishop tanagers		*Reptiles*
3	Palm tanagers		
3	Maroon tanagers	18	Brazilian tortoises
3	Lesser Rufous-headed tanagers	20	Great teguexins
8	Violet tanagers	18	Green anacondas
1	Magpie tanager	8	Common boas
3	Rice grackles	3	Garden Tree boas
1	Swainson's grackle	1	Cooke's Golden Tree boa
1	Cayenne Red-breasted marshbird	4	Pileated Water snakes (see Note 5)
2	Yellow-headed marshbirds	4	Indigo snakes
14	Glossy cowbirds	∞	Merren's Water snakes
8	Yellow-crowned troupials	1	Canaina Rat snake
		1	Two-lined Pit viper

NOTES

1.   Possibly the Savannah Arboreal Rice rat.
2.   It is tempting to think the Black-crowned heron must be the Black-crowned Night heron, except that Ken Smith lists this latter species separately.
3.   I can find no species of guan known as a Grant's guan. It is possible it is known today by another name.
4.   The Yellow-headed or Singing parrot comes not from South America but from the Bismarck Archipelago (east of New Guinea) and the Solomon Islands, an apparent anomaly that could be explained if Ken Smith was presented with them by the Georgetown Zoo.
5.   The identity of this species is a mystery. Pileated Water snake could be an archaic name. The word 'pileated', meaning 'crested', is usually applied to birds. It is hard to imagine a crested snake.

This list was compiled from a letter written by Ken to Marvin Jones in 1956 and appears to be incomplete. Several species known to have been collected by Ken on this expedition are inexplicably absent. There is, for example, no mention of the Electric eel he brought back, even though it lived at Paignton Zoo for many years. Another specimen missing from the list is the Cayenne owl (although it appears in the 1957 Paignton Zoo guide book) and there are a number of other unaccountable omissions.

Not all the animals ended up at Paignton Zoo. Some went to the London Zoo. According to London Zoo's Occurrences Book for 1956, they included the following:

2	Savannah rats	2	unidentified egrets
1	Red Marsh rat	2	Tricolored herons
∞	Long-tailed Tree rats*	2	South American Black vultures

2	Venezuelan Wood rails	4	Green anacondas
2	Sulphury flycatchers	1	Cooke's Tree boa
1	Magpie tanager*	1	Two-lined Pit viper

* Not mentioned in Occurrences Book.

All were received in exchange for other animals except for two of the anacondas, which were placed by Paignton Zoo at London Zoo on deposit.

Bibliography

BOOKS REFERRING TO KENNETH SMITH
Ken Smith appears in several books, albeit in almost all cases only fleetingly.

Baker, Jack, *Chimps, Champs & Elephants*, SJH Publications Ltd., Paignton, 1988
Botting, Douglas, *Gerald Durrell: The Authorised Biography*, HarperCollins, London, 1999
Durrell, Gerald, *The Bafut Beagles*, Rupert Hart-Davies, London, 1954
—— *Three Singles to Adventure*, Rupert Hart-Davies, London, 1954
Jacobs, George (as told to Franklyn Wood), *Memoirs of a Coarse Zoo Keeper*, Frederick Muller Ltd., London, 1982
Keeling, C.H., *Where the Crane Danced*, Clam Publications, Shalford, 1985
—— *Where the Macaw Preened*, Clam Publications, Shalford, 1993
—— *Where the Penguin Plunged*, Clam Publications, Shalford, 1995
—— *Where the Leopard Lazed*, Clam Publications, Shalford, 1999
Mallinson, Jeremy, *The Touch of Durrell: A Passion for Animals*, Book Guild Publishing, Brighton, 2009
Pendar, Lucy, *Whipsnade Wild Animal Park 'My Africa'* , The Book Castle, Dunstable, Beds., 1991
Schomberg, Geoffrey, *British Zoos*, Allan Wingate Ltd., London, 1957
—— *The Penguin Guide to British Zoos*, Penguin Books, Harmondsworth, Middlesex, 1970
Trevisick, Charles, *My Home is a Zoo*, Stanley Paul & Co. Ltd., London, 1976
Wood, Christina, *The Magic Sakis*, Thomas Nelson & Sons Ltd., London, 1972

OTHER BOOKS
The following books are referred to in the text. Kenneth Smith does not appear in any of them, although in three (marked here with an asterisk) he is obliquely – and briefly – alluded to, but not named.

Bennett, Clive & Barnaby, David, *The Reptiles of Belle Vue 1950–1977*, Zoological Society of Greater Manchester, 1989
Bergamar, Kate, *Zoos, Bird Gardens & Animal Collections in Great Britain & Eire*, first edition, Shire Publications, Tring, Herts., 1969
Bisson, Mike (ed.), *The First Twenty Five Years: The Jersey Zoo*, Jersey Evening Post, 1984
Budworth, Geoffrey, *Poole Park: The People's Park*, The History Press Ltd., Stroud, Glos., 2008
Clarke, Dorothy E., *Tangled Tapes: Fred Deely, A Gentleman of Deddington*, 1994
Durrell, Gerald, *Island Zoo*, Collins, London, 1961
Durrell, Gerald, *Menagerie Manor*, Rupert Hart-Davies, London, 1964

Durrell, Gerald, *Beasts in My Belfry*, William Collins Sons & Co. Ltd., 1973

Durrell, Gerald, *The Stationary Ark*, William Collins Sons & Co. Ltd., London, 1976 *

Durrell, Gerald, *The Ark's Anniversary*, William Collins Sons & Co. Ltd., London, 1990 *

Durrell, Jacquie, *Beasts in My Bed*, Collins, London, 1967 *

Iles, Gerald, *At Home in the Zoo*, W.H. Allen & Co. Ltd., London, 1960

Keeling, C.H., *Where the Zebu Grazed*, Clam Publications, Shalford, 1989

Kohler, Charles, *Unwillingly to School*, Kohler & Coombes, Dorking, 1985

Pearson, John, *The Gamblers*, Century, 2005

Merrett, P.K., *Edentates: Project for city and guilds animal management course*, Zoological Trust of Guernsey, 1983

Smith, Anthony, *Animals On View*, revised edition, Granada Publishing Ltd, St. Albans, Herts.,1979

Taylor, Audrey M., *Gilletts: Bankers at Banbury and Oxford*, Clarendon Press on behalf of Gillett Brothers Discount Co. Ltd., London, 1964

Yealland, J.J., *Cage Birds in Colour*, first English edition: H.F. & G. Witherby Ltd., London, 1958

ARTICLES REFERRING TO, OR WRITTEN BY, KENNETH SMITH

Anonymous, *Hairy Frogs for the Zoo*, The Times, Aug. 26, 1949

Anonymous, *New Insects at the Zoo*, The Times, Sep. 14, 1949

Anonymous, *Two Additions to the Population at Exmouth Zoo*, Exmouth Journal, July 12, 1975

Anonymous, *Bicton College 'Investigates' Zoo Idea*, Exmouth Journal, Nov. 20, 2009

Cansdale, G.S., *Recent Additions to the Zoo*, Zoo Life, Bulletin of the Zoological Society of London, vol. 5, no. 4, Winter 1950, pp. 116–117

— *Recent Arrivals at the London Zoo*, Zoo Life, Bulletin of the Zoological Society of London, vol. 6, no. 3, Autumn 1951, pp. 86–88

Handley, Jeff, *The Olingo*, 'Tembo', The Official Organ of the National Zoological Society, no. 16, Summer 1975, pp. 8–9

Irven, Paul M., *The History of Poole Park Zoo*, The Bartlett Society Journal, no. 18, 2007, pp. 33–47

Jones, Marvin L., *A Visit to 20 European Zoos*, International Zoo News, vol. 3, no. 1, Jan. 1956, pp. 6–8

Osmont, Isobel, *A Zoo to the Manor Born*, Temps passé, Mar. 1999

Smith, Kenneth, *Elephants*, unpubl. article for Natural History Society, Friends' School, Saffron Walden, Dec. 1926

— *Rare Zoo Inmates*, unpubl. article for Natural History Society, Friends' School, Saffron Walden, June 1927

— *Some Zoo Youngsters and Views on Evolution*, unpubl. article for Natural History Society, Saffron Walden, Oct. 1927

— *Notes on the Fauna of British Guiana*, ORYX, vol. 1, no. 5, Apr. 1952, pp. 247–249

— *The Bird Collection at the Paignton Zoological Gardens*, The Avicultural Magazine, vol. 60, no. 1, Jan/Feb. 1954, pp. 19–22
— *Reflections on Storks*, The Avicultural Magazine, vol. 61, no. 4, July/Aug. 1955, pp. 202–203
— *Herbert Whitley Obituary*, The Avicultural Magazine, vol. 61, no. 6, Nov/Dec. 1955
— *Expedition to Guiana*, International Zoo News, vol. 3, no. 2, March 1956, p.30
— *Red Howling Monkey*, Zoo Life, vol. 12, no. 2, Summer 1957, pp. 37–40
— *A Unique Colony of Gorillas*, International Zoo News, vol. 8, no. 5, Oct–Dec. 1961, p.143
— *Jersey Zoological Park in 1962*, International Zoo News, vol. 10, no. 1, Jan/Feb. 1963, pp. 6–7
— *Birds in the Jersey Zoological Park*, The Avicultural Magazine, vol. 69, no. 2, Mar/Apr. 1963, pp. 86–87
— *Notes on the Nutrition of Primates*, International Zoo Yearbook, vol. IV, 1963, pp. 130–131
— *The Red Titi Monkey*, Animals Magazine, vol. 5, no. 11, 22 Dec. 1964, pp. 318–319
— *The Agile Angwantibo* (written ca. 1968)
Theobald, Connie, *Rare B.G. Birds and Animals to Adorn British Zoos*, Georgetown Sunday Chronicle, April 22, 1956, p.14
Tofts, Russell, *Jersey Zoo: The First Four Years: March 1959–July 1963*, The Bartlett Society Journal, no. 15 part 2, 2004, pp. 5–20

I have deposited copies of many of the articles above in the archive of the Bartlett Society.

For chapter 18, about the protracted battle to save Exmouth Zoo from closure, I am indebted to Eve Bollen of the Exmouth Library for running to earth numerous articles from the *Exmouth Journal* (a.k.a. *Exmouth and East Devon Journal*) dating from the 1970s. These were:

'Exmouth Should Advise on Exmouth Zoo's Future', March 5, 1977
'Exmouth Zoo Given Notice to Quit', April 23, 1977
'Yes–No Conflict Over Zoo Plan', November 5, 1977
'New Zoo Site Hope "Caged"', December 3, 1977
'Zoo: The Sad Saga Continues', January 23, 1978
'Zoo: Exmouth Anger Against "By-the-Book" County Committee', June 10, 1978
'Zoo: The Reason for County Stubbornness', June 17, 1978
'Businessman Steps in to Save Exmouth Zoo', March 3, 1979

OTHER

Anonymous, *Zoo Asks Troops for Lizards*, Sunday Dispatch, Feb. 11, 1945
Anonymous, *Birds Valued at £275 Die in Fire*, The Times, May 23, 1961

Smith, Kenneth, *Another Eagle*, Letter to the Editor, The Times, Jan. 1, 1946, p.5

— *Monte Bello Islands*, Letter to the Editor, The Times, Jul. 31, 1952, p.7

— *Oil Pollution*, Letter to the Editor, The Times, Feb. 4, 1954, p.7

— *Hunter in the Sky*, Letter to the Editor, The Times, Jul. 5, 1955, p.11

— *Chameleons at the Zoo*, Letter to the Editor, The Times, Oct. 23, 1959, p.15

Smith, Trudy, *No Surprise at MP's Response*, Letter to the Editor, Exmouth Journal, Dec. 24, 2009

Also very useful to me were the guide book to the Paignton Zoological and Botanical Gardens (11th edition, June 1957), the first Jersey Zoo guide book (1959), two guides to Exmouth Zoo (ca. 1963 and ca. 1975) and an early guide to Poole Park Children's Zoo (ca. 1965).

Index

The Smiths

The Jollys
(sometimes spelt with an 'e')

Thomas Smith

m.

Mary

Thomas Smith
b. c. 1760
'Hatter' of Reading

m.
[c.1786]

Hannah Thackwell (of Worcester)
c. 1765 - 1817
d. Witney

Samuel Smith
1790 - 1840
b. Witney
Baconcurer & Cheesemonger of Witney

m.
[1827]
Chipping Norton

Hannah Tyler
1803 - 1867
b. Newington
*d. Witney
Grocer & Draper of Witney*

John Jolly
c. 1825 - 1904
d. Woodbridge, Suffolk

m.
[1844]

Sophia Agnes Harvey

Thackwell Smith
1834 - 1905
b. Witney
bur. Charlbury
Grocer

m.
[1860]
Brailes, Warks

Marianna Gillett
1835 - 1906
bur. Charlbury

John Frank Jolly
1846 - 1924
b. Framlingham, Suffolk
bur. Deddington
Tailor

m.
[1872]
Bedford

Mary Elizabeth Stock
1851 - 1937
b. Bedford
bur. Deddington

Herbert Smith
1872 - 1933
b. Charlbury
d. Colchester
Grocer

m.
[1908]
Deddington

Gertrude Emmeline Jolly
1879 - 1973
b. Faringdon
d. Bournemouth

Ronald Thackwell
1910 - 1990

Kenneth John
1911 - 1979

Herbert Gillett ('Gil')
1915 - 1998

Violet Kathleen
1918 - 1951
(Kathleen Violet in Marriage Index)

Frank Eric
1919 - 2009

*N.B. This is a simplified family tree.
Only Ken's parents, grandparents, siblings
and direct ancestors are shown here.
Uncles, aunts and other relatives are omitted*

The Gillett Connection

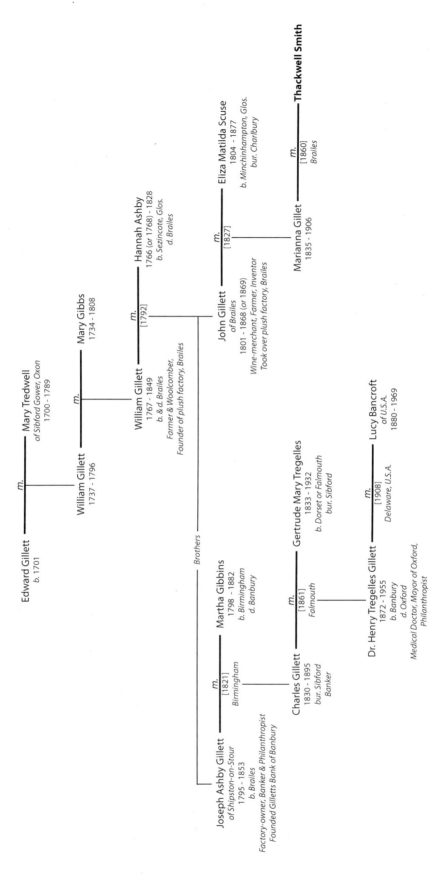

Edward Gillett
b. 1701

m.

Mary Tredwell
of Sibford Gower, Oxon
1700 - 1789

William Gillett
1737 - 1796

m.

Mary Gibbs
1734 - 1808

William Gillett
1767 - 1849
b. & d. Brailes
Farmer & Woolcomber,
Founder of plush factory, Brailes

m.
[1792]

Hannah Ashby
1766 (or 1768) - 1828
b. Sezincote, Glos.
d. Brailes

Brothers

John Gillett
of Brailes
1801 - 1868 (or 1869)
Wine-merchant, Farmer, Inventor
Took over plush factory, Brailes

m.
[1827]

Eliza Matilda Scuse
1804 - 1877
b. Minchinhampton, Glos.
bur. Charlbury

Marianna Gillet
1835 - 1906

m.
[1860]
Brailes

Thackwell Smith

Joseph Ashby Gillett
of Shipston-on-Stour
1795 - 1853
b. Brailes
Factory-owner, Banker & Philanthropist
Founded Gilletts Bank of Banbury

m.
[1821]
Birmingham

Martha Gibbins
1798 - 1882
b. Birmingham
d. Banbury

Charles Gillett
1830 - 1895
bur. Sibford
Banker

m.
[1861]
Falmouth

Gertrude Mary Tregelles
1833 - 1932
b. Dorset or Falmouth
bur. Sibford

Dr. Henry Tregelles Gillett
1872 - 1955
b. Banbury
d. Oxford
Medical Doctor, Mayor of Oxford,
Philanthropist

m.
[1908]
Delaware, U.S.A.

Lucy Bancroft
of U.S.A.
1880 - 1969